Touring Spain & Portugal

Also available:

© The Caravan Club Limited 2016
Published by The Caravan Club Limited
East Grinstead House, East Grinstead
West Sussex RH19 1UA

General Enquiries: 01342 326944
Travel Service Reservations: 01342 316101
Red Pennant Overseas Holiday Insurance:
01342 336633
Website: www.caravanclub.co.uk
Email: enquiries@caravanclub.co.uk

Editor: Kate Walters
Email: kate.walters@caravanclub.co.uk

Printed by Stephens & George Ltd
Merthyr Tydfil

ISBN 978-0-9932781-2-9

Cover: Douro river, Porto ©StevanZZ

Wish you
were here?

FREE Venture Abroad brochure

Venture Abroad

TAKE YOUR ADVENTURE ABROAD

Join today to book your overseas holiday
Visit www.caravanclub.co.uk/overseas
or call us on 01342 488717

- Over 250 Club-inspected campsites in 16 countries
- Family friendly and peaceful sites
- The best ferry rates, guaranteed
- Insurance designed for caravanners and motorhomers

THE
CARAVAN
CLUB

Welcome
to Touring Spain & Portugal 2016

The fantastic thing about touring in your own 'home-from-home', whether that be a caravan, motorhome, trailer tent or tent, is that you really do have the freedom to make your holiday exactly what you want it to be.

You can pitch up in one place for a long stay, discover everything the area has to offer, find hidden gems and get to know the locals. Or you can move around to explore a wider area, covering countryside, towns and the coast in one trip. If you turn up to a site and it isn't your cup of tea you can simply move on; you can extend your stay if you find your own personal paradise.

Touring Spain and Portugal is designed to be the ultimate aide to enjoying the freedom that touring offers. This guide, like sister titles *Touring France* and *Touring Europe*, lists hundreds of sites, including helpful comments from previous visitors, and offers basic information on a vast number of touring-related subjects. You will be able to find the information you need without an internet connection – sometimes an elusive thing if you're pitched in the middle of nowhere!

So as you start another year of touring adventures I would like to thank you for continuing to buy and contribute to these unique guides. If you can, please spare five minutes to fill in one of the forms at the back of this book or visit www.caravanclub.co.uk/europereport to let us know what you think about the sites you've stayed on this year. The more site reports we receive, the more people we can help to enjoy the freedom of independent touring in Europe. Happy touring!

Kate Walters

Kate Walters, Editor

Contents

Continental Campsites

Site Listings

How to use this guide

The information contained within *Touring Spain & Portugal* is presented in the following categories:

The Handbook

This includes general information about touring in Europe, such as legal requirements, advice and regulations. The Handbook chapters are at the front of the guide and are separated as follows:

Planning Your Trip	Information you'll need before you travel including information on the documents and insurance you'll need, advice on money, customs regulations and planning your channel crossings.
Motoring Advice	Advice on motoring overseas, essential equipment and roads in Europe including mountain passes and tunnels.
During Your Stay	Information for while you're away including telephone, internet and TV advice, medical information and advice on staying safe.
Continental Campsites	Advice on choosing your site and the differences you might find overseas.

Country Introduction

Following on from the Handbook chapters you will find the Country Introductions containing information, regulations and advice specific to each country. You should read the Country Introduction in conjunction with the Handbook chapters before you set off on your holiday.

Campsite Entries

After the Country Introduction you will find the campsite entries listed alphabetically under their nearest town or village. Where several campsites are shown in and around the same town they will be listed in clockwise order from the north.

To find a campsite all you need to do is look for the town or village of where you would like to stay, or use the maps at the back of each site section to find a town where sites are listed. Where there are no sites listed in a relatively large or popular town you may find a cross reference, directing you to the closest town which does have sites.

In order to provide you with the details of as many sites as possible in *Touring Spain & Portugal* we use abbreviations in the site entries.

For a full and detailed list of these abbreviations please see the following pages of this section.

We have also included some of the most regularly used abbreviations, as well as an explanation of a campsite entry, on the fold-out on the back cover.

Campsite Fees

Campsite entries show high season fees per night for an outfit plus two adults, as at the year of the last report. Prices given may not include electricity or showers, unless indicated. Outside of the main holiday season many sites offer discounts on the prices shown and some sites may also offer a reduction for longer stays.

Campsite fees may vary to the prices stated in the site entries, especially if the site has not been reported on for a few years. You are advised to always check fees when booking, or at least before pitching, as those shown in site entries should be used as a guide only.

Site Maps

Each town and village listed alphabetically in the site entry pages has a map grid reference number, e.g. 3B4. The map grid reference number is shown on each site entry. The maps can be found at the end of each country's site entry pages. The reference number will show you where each town or village is located, and the site entry will tell you how far the site is from that town. Place names are shown on the maps in two colours:

Red where we list a site which is open all year (or for at least eleven months of the year)

Black where we only list seasonal sites which close in winter.

These maps are intended for general campsite location purposes only; a detailed road map or atlas is essential for route planning and touring.

Town names in capital letters (**RED**, **BLACK** or in *ITALICS*) correspond with towns listed on the Distance Chart.

The scale used for the map means that it is not possible to pinpoint every town or village where a campsite exists, so some sites in small villages may be listed under a nearby larger town instead.

Satellite Navigation

Most campsite entries now show a GPS (sat nav) reference. There are several different formats of writing co-ordinates, and in this guide we use decimal degrees, for example 48.85661 (latitude north) and 2.35222 (longitude east).

Minus readings, shown as -1.23456, indicate that the longitude is west of the Greenwich meridian. This will apply to sites in western France, most of Spain and all of Portugal - the rest of Europe is east of the Greenwich meridian.

Manufacturers of Sat Navs all use different formats of co-ordinates so you may need to convert the co-ordinates before using them with your device. There are plenty of online conversion tools which enable you to do this quickly and easily - just type 'co-ordinate converter' into your search engine.

Please be aware if you are using a sat nav device some routes may take you on roads that are narrow and/or are not suitable for caravans or large outfits.

The GPS co-ordinates given in this guide are provided by members and checked wherever possible, however we cannot guarantee their accuracy due to the rural nature of most of the sites. The Caravan Club cannot accept responsibility for any inaccuracies, errors or omissions or for their effects.

Site Report Forms

With the exception of campsites in The Club's Overseas Site Booking Service (SBS) network, The Caravan Club does not inspect sites listed in this guide. Virtually all of the sites listed in *Touring Spain & Portugal* are from site reports submitted by users of these guides. You can tell us about great sites you have found or update the details of sites already within the books.

We rely on you, the users of this guide, to tell us about campsites you have visited

Sites which are not reported on for five years are deleted from the guide, so even if you visit a site and find nothing different from the site listing we'd appreciate a update to tell us as much.

You will find site report forms towards the back of this guide which we hope you will complete and return to us by freepost (please post when you are back in the UK). Use the abbreviated site report form if you are reporting no changes, or only minor changes, to a site entry. The full report form should be used for new sites or sites which have changed a lot since the last report.

You can complete both the full and abbreviated versions of the site report forms by visiting www.caravanclub.co.uk/europereport.

Please submit reports as soon as possible. Information received by **mid August 2016** will be used wherever possible in the next edition of *Touring Spain & Portugal*. Reports received after that date are still very welcome and will appear in the following edition. The editor is unable to respond individually to site reports submitted due to the large quantity that we receive.

Tips for Completing Site Reports

- If possible fill in a site report form while at the campsite. Once back at home it can be difficult to remember details of individual sites, especially if you visited several during your trip.
- When giving directions to a site, remember to include the direction of travel, e.g. 'from north on D137, turn left onto D794 signposted Combourg' or 'on N83 from Poligny turn right at petrol station in village'. Wherever possible give road numbers, junction numbers and/or kilometre post numbers, where you exit from motorways or main roads. It is also helpful to mention useful landmarks such as bridges, roundabouts, traffic lights or prominent buildings.

We very much appreciate the time and trouble you take submitting reports on campsites that you have visited; without your valuable contributions it would be impossible to update this guide.

Acknowledgements

The Caravan Club's thanks go to the AIT/FIA Information Centre (OTA), the Alliance Internationale de Tourisme (AIT), the Fédération International de Camping et de Caravaning (FICC) and to the national clubs and tourist offices of those countries who have assisted with this publication.

Every effort is made to ensure that information contained in this publication is accurate and that the details given in good faith in the site report forms are accurately reproduced or summarised. The Caravan Club Ltd has not checked these details by inspection or other investigation and cannot accept responsibility for the accuracy of these reports as provided by members and non-members, or for errors, omissions or their effects. In addition The Caravan Club Ltd cannot be held accountable for the quality, safety or operation of the sites concerned, or for the fact that conditions, facilities, management or prices may have changed since the last recorded visit. Any recommendations, additional comments or opinions have been contributed by caravanners and people staying on the site and are not generally those of The Caravan Club.

The inclusion of advertisements or other inserted material does not imply any form of approval or recognition, nor can The Caravan Club Ltd undertake any responsibility for checking the accuracy of advertising material.

Explanation of a Campsite Entry

The town under which the campsite is listed, as shown on the relevant Sites Location Map at the end of each country's site entry pages

Distance and direction of the site from the centre of the town the site is listed under in kilometres (or metres), together with site's aspect

Site Location Map grid reference

Indicates that the site is open all year

Campsite name

Telephone and fax numbers including national code where applicable

Description of the campsite and its facilities

Contact email and website address

Directions to the campsite

⊞ BLANES 3C3 (1km S Coastal) 41.65933, 2.77000 Camping Blanes, Avda Vila de Madrid 33, 17300 Blanes (Gerona) [972-33 15 91; fax 972-33 70 63; info@campingblanes.com;www.campingblanes.com] Fr N on AP7/E15 exit junc 9 onto NII dir Barcelona & foll sp Blanes. Fr S to end of C32, then NII dir Blanes. On app Blanes, foll camping sps & Playa S'Abanell - all campsites are sp at rndabts; all sites along same rd. Site adj Hotel Blau-Mar. Lge, mkd pitch, shd; wc; chem disp; mv service pnt, shwrs inc; shop; el pnts (5A) inc; gas; lndtte; supmkt; snacks high ssn; bar; playgrnd; pool; solarium; dir access to sand beach; watersports; cycle hire; games rm; wifi; entmnt; dogs; phone; bus; poss cr; Eng spkn; quiet; ccard acc; red low ssn. "Excel site, espec low ssn; helpful owner; easy walk to town cent; trains to Barcelona & Gerona." ◆
€ 36.95   2011*

Unspecified facilities for disabled guests. If followed by 'ltd' this indicates that the facilities are limited.

The year in which the site was last reported on by a visitor

NOJA 1A4 (700m N Coastal) 43.49011, -3.53636 Camping Playa Joyel, Playa del Ris, 39180 Noja (Cantabria) [942-63 00 81; fax 942-63 12 94; playajoyel@telefonica.net; www.playajoyel.com] Fr Santander or Bilbao foll sp A8/E70 (toll-free). Approx 15km E of Solares exit m'way junc 185 at Beranga onto CA147 N twd Noja & coast. On o'skirts of Noja turn L sp Playa del Ris, (sm brown sp) foll rd approx 1.5km to rndabt, site sp to L, 500m fr rndabt. Fr Santander take S10 for approx 8km, then join A8/E70. V lge, mkd pitch, pt sl, pt shd; wc; chem disp; mv service pnt; baby facs; shwrs inc; el pnts (6A) inc; gas; lndtte (inc dryer); supmkt; tradsmn; rest; snacks; bar; BBQ (gas/charcoal); playgrnd; pool; paddling pool; jacuzzi; direct access to sand beach adj; windsurfing; sailing; tennis; hairdresser; car wash; cash dispenser; wifi; entmnt; games/TV rm; 15% statics; no dogs; no c'vans/m'vans over 8m high ssn; phone; recep 0800-2200; poss v cr w/end & high ssn; Eng spkn; adv bkg; ccard acc; quiet at night; red low ssn; snr citizens; CCI. "Well-organised site on sheltered bay; v busy high ssn; pleasant staff; gd, clean facs; superb pool & beach; some narr site rds with kerbs; midnight silence enforced; Wed mkt outside site; highly rec." ◆
15 Apr-1 Oct. € 47.40 SBS - E05   2011*

Campsite address

Charge per night in high season for car, caravan + 2 adults as at year of last report

Opening dates

GPS co-ordinates – latitude and longitude in decimal degrees. Minus figures indicate that the site is west of the Greenwich meridian

Comments and opinions of caravanners who have visited the site (within inverted commas)

The site accepts Camping Cheques see the **Continental Campsites** chapter for details

Booking reference for a site the Club's Overseas Travel Service work with, i.e. bookable via The Club.

Site Description Abbreviations

Each site entry assumes the following unless stated otherwise:

Level ground, open grass pitches, drinking water on site, clean wc unless otherwise stated (own sanitation required if wc not listed), site is suitable for any length of stay within the dates shown.

aspect
urban – within a city or town, or on its outskirts
rural – within or on edge of a village or in open countryside
coastal – within one kilometre of the coast

size of site
sm – max 50 pitches
med – 51 to 150 pitches
lge – 151 to 500 pitches
v lge – 501+ pitches

pitches
hdg pitch – hedged pitches
mkd pitch – marked or numbered pitches
hdstg – some hard standing or gravel

levels
sl – sloping site
pt sl – sloping in parts
terr – terraced site

shade
shd – plenty of shade
pt shd – part shaded
unshd – no shade

Site Facilities

adv bkg
Advance booking accepted;
adv bkg rec – advance booking recommended

baby facs
Nursing room/bathroom for babies/children

beach
Beach for swimming nearby;
1km – distance to beach
sand beach – sandy beach
shgl beach – shingle beach

bus/metro/tram
Public transport within an easy walk of the site

chem disp
Dedicated chemical toilet disposal facilities;
chem disp (wc) – no dedicated point; disposal via wc only

CKE/CCI
Camping Key Europe and/or Camping Card International accepted

CL-type
Very small, privately-owned, informal and usually basic, farm or country site similar to those in the Caravan Club's network of Certificated Locations

dogs
Dogs allowed on site with appropriate certification (a daily fee may be quoted and conditions may apply)

el pnts
Mains electric hook-ups available for a fee;
inc – cost included in site fee quoted
10A – amperage provided
conn fee – one-off charge for connection to metered electricity supply
rev pol – reversed polarity may be present
(see *Electricity and Gas* in the section *DURING YOUR STAY*)

Eng spkn
English spoken by campsite reception staff

entmnt
Entertainment facilities or organised entertainment for adults and/or children

fam bthrm
Bathroom for use by families with small children

gas
Supplies of bottled gas available on site or nearby

internet
Internet point for use by visitors to site;
wifi – wireless local area network available

lndtte
Washing machine(s) with or without tumble dryers, sometimes other equipment available, eg ironing boards;
lndtte (inc dryer) – washing machine(s) and tumble dryer(s)
lndry rm – laundry room with only basic clothes-washing facilities

Mairie
Town hall (France); will usually make municipal campsite reservations

mv service pnt
Special low level waste discharge point for motor caravans; fresh water tap and rinse facilities should also be available

NH

Suitable as a night halt

noisy

Noisy site with reasons given;
quiet – peaceful, tranquil site

open 1 Apr-15 Oct

Where no specific dates are given, opening
dates are assumed to be inclusive, ie Apr-Oct –
beginning April to end October
(NB: opening dates may vary from those shown;
check before travelling, particularly when
travelling out of the main holiday season)

phone

Public payphone on or adjacent to site

playgrnd

Children's playground

pool

Swimming pool (may be open high season only);
htd – heated pool
covrd – indoor pool or one with retractable
cover

poss cr

During high season site may be crowded or
overcrowded and pitches cramped

red CCI/CCS

Reduction in fees on production of a Camping
Card International or Camping Card Scandinavia

rest

Restaurant;
bar – bar
BBQ – barbecues allowed (may be restricted to a
separate, designated area)
cooking facs – communal kitchen area
snacks – snack bar, cafeteria or takeaway

SBS

Site Booking Service (pitch reservation can be
made through the Caravan Club's Travel Service)

serviced pitch

Electric hook-ups and mains water inlet and grey
water waste outlet to pitch;
all – to all pitches
50% – percentage of pitches

shop(s)

Shop on site;
adj – shops next to site
500m – nearest shops
supmkt – supermarket
hypmkt – hypermarket
tradsmn – tradesmen call at the site, eg baker

shwrs

Hot showers available for a fee;
inc – cost included in site fee quoted

ssn

Season;
high ssn – peak holiday season
low ssn – out of peak season

50% statics

Percentage of static caravans/mobile homes/
chalets/fixed tents/cabins or long term seasonal
pitches on site, including those run by tour
operators

sw

Swimming nearby;
1km – nearest swimming
lake – in lake
rv – in river

TV

TV available for viewing by visitors (often in
the bar);
TV rm – separate TV room (often also a games
room)
cab/sat – cable or satellite connections to pitches

wc

Clean flushing toilets on site;
(cont) – continental type with floor-level hole
htd – sanitary block centrally heated in winter
own san – use of own sanitation facilities
recommended

Other Abbreviations

AIT	Alliance Internationale de Tourisme
a'bahn	Autobahn
a'pista	Autopista
a'route	Autoroute
a'strada	Autostrada
adj	Adjacent, nearby
alt	Alternative
app	Approach, on approaching
arr	Arrival, arriving
avail	Available
Ave	Avenue
bdge	Bridge
bef	Before
bet	Between
Blvd	Boulevard
C	Century, eg 16thC
c'van	Caravan
CC	Caravan Club
ccard acc	Credit and/or debit cards accepted (check with site for specific details)
CChq acc	Camping Cheques accepted

cent	Centre or central
clsd	Closed
conn	Connection
cont	Continue or continental (wc)
conv	Convenient
covrd	Covered
dep	Departure
diff	Difficult, with difficulty
dir	Direction
dist	Distance
dual c'way	Dual carriageway
E	East
ent	Entrance/entry to
espec	Especially
ess	Essential
excel	Excellent
facs	Facilities
FIA	Fédération Internationale de l'Automobile
FICC	Fédération Internationale de Camping & de Caravaning
FFCC	Fédération Française de Camping et de Caravaning
FKK/FNF	Naturist federation, ie naturist site
foll	Follow
fr	From
g'ge	Garage
gd	Good
grnd(s)	Ground(s)
hr(s)	Hour(s)
immac	Immaculate
immed	Immediate(ly)
inc	Included/inclusive
indus est	Industrial estate
INF	Naturist federation, ie naturist site
int'l	International
irreg	Irregular
junc	Junction
km	Kilometre
L	Left
LH	Left-hand
LS	Low season
ltd	Limited
mkd	Marked
mkt	Market
mob	Mobile (phone)
m'van	Motor caravan
m'way	Motorway
N	North
narr	Narrow
nr, nrby	Near, nearby
opp	Opposite
o'fits	Outfits

o'look(ing)	Overlook(ing)
o'night	Overnight
o'skts	Outskirts
PO	Post office
poss	Possible, possibly
pt	Part
R	Right
rd	Road or street
rec	Recommend/ed
recep	Reception
red	Reduced, reduction (for)
reg	Regular
req	Required
RH	Right-hand
rlwy	Railway line
rm	Room
rndabt	Roundabout
rte	Route
RV	Recreational vehicle, ie large motor caravan
rv/rvside	River/riverside
S	South
san facs	Sanitary facilities ie wc, showers, etc
snr citizens	Senior citizens
sep	Separate
sh	Short
sp	Sign post, signposted
sq	Square
ssn	Season
stn	Station
strt	Straight, straight ahead
sw	Swimming
thro	Through
TO	Tourist Office
tour ops	Tour operators
traff lts	Traffic lights
twd	Toward(s)
unrel	Unreliable
vg	Very good
vill	Village
W	West
w/end	Weekend
x-ing	Crossing
x-rds	Cross roads

Symbols Used

◆   Unspecified facilities for disabled guests check before arrival

⊞   Open all year

*   Last year site report received (see Campsite Entries in Introduction)

Documents

Camping Card Schemes

Camping Key Europe (CKE) is a useful companion for touring in Europe. Not only does it serve as a valid ID at campsites, meaning that you don't have to leave your passport with the site reception, it also entitles you to discounts at over 2200 sites.

CKE also offers third-party liability insurance for families including up to three children, which provides cover for loss or damage that occurs while on site. Full details of the levels of cover are provided with the card. For more information on the scheme and all its benefits visit www.campingkey.com.

You can purchase the CKE from The Club by calling 01342 336633, or it is provided free for Red Pennant Overseas Holiday Insurance customers taking out the 'Motoring' level of cover.

An alternative scheme is Camping Card International (CCI) - to find out more visit www.campingcardinternational.com.

If you are using a CKE or CCI card as a method of ID at a site, make sure that you collect your card when checking out. Also check that you have been given your own card instead of someone else's.

Driving Licence

A full (not provisional), valid driving licence should be carried at all times when driving abroad. You must produce it when asked to do so by the police and other authorities, or you may be liable for an immediate fine and confiscation of your vehicle(s).

If your driving licence is due to expire while you are away it can normally be renewed up to three months before the expiry date - contact the DVLA if you need to renew more than three months ahead.

All European Union countries recognise the pink EU-format driving licence introduced in the UK in 1990, subject to the minimum age requirements (normally 18 years for a vehicle with a maximum weight of 3,500 kg carrying no more than eight people). However, there are exceptions in some European Countries and the Country Introductions contain specific details.

Old-style green UK paper licences or Northern Irish licences issued before 1991 should be updated to a photocard licence before travelling as they may not be recognised by local authorities.

Selected post offices and DVLA local offices offer a premium checking service for photocard applications but the service is not available for online applications.

MOT Certificate

Carry your vehicle's MOT certificate (if applicable) when driving on the Continent. You may need to show it to the authorities if your vehicle is involved in an accident, or in the event of random vehicle checks. If your MOT certificate is due to expire while you are away you should have the vehicle tested before you leave home.

Passport

Many countries require you to carry your passport at all times. Enter next-of-kin details in the back of your passport and keep a separate photocopy or record of your passport details. It's also a good idea to leave a photocopy of it with a relative or friend at home.

The following information applies to British passport holders only. For information on passports issued by other countries you should contact the local embassy.

Applying for a Passport
Each person travelling out of the UK (including babies) must hold a valid passport - it is no longer possible to include children on a parent's passport. A standard British passport is valid for 10 years, or five years for children under 16.

All newly issued UK passports are now biometric, also known as e-passports, which contain a microchip with information which can be used to authenticate the holder's identity.

Full information and application forms are available from main post offices or from the Identity & Passport Service's website, www.gov.uk where you can complete an online application. Allow at least six weeks for first-time passport applications, for which you may need to attend an interview at your nearest Identity and Passport Service (IPS) regional office. Allow three weeks for a renewal application or replacement of a lost, stolen or damaged passport.

Post offices offer a 'Check & Send' service for passport applications which can prevent delays due to errors on your application form. To find your nearest 'Check & Send' post office call 0345 611 2970 or see www.postoffice.co.uk.

Passport Validity

Passport Validity
Most countries in the EU only require your passport to be valid for the duration of your stay. However, in case your return home is delayed it is a good idea make sure you have six month's validity remaining. Any time left on a passport (up to a maximum of nine months) will be added to the validity of your new passport on renewal.

Schengen Agreement
The Schengen Agreement allows people and vehicles to pass freely without border checks from country to country within the Schengen area (a total of 26 countries). Where there are no longer any border checks you should still not attempt to cross land borders without a full, valid passport. It is likely that random identity checks will continue to be made for the foreseeable future in areas surrounding land borders.

The United Kingdom and Republic of Ireland do not fully participate in the Schengen Agreement.

Pet Travel Scheme (PETS)

The Pet Travel Scheme (PETS) allows owners of dogs, cats and ferrets from qualifying European countries to bring their pets into the UK (up to a limit of five per person) without quarantine. The animal must have an EU pet passport, be microchipped and be vaccinated against rabies. Dogs must also have been treated for tapeworm. It also allows pets to travel from the UK to other EU qualifying countries. Some countries may not allow entry to certain breeds of dogs and may have rules relating to muzzling and transporting dogs in cars – check the Country Introductions for any specific details or see www.caravanclub.co.uk/pets for more details.

Pets resident anywhere in the British Isles (excluding the Republic of Ireland) are able to travel freely within the British Isles and are not subject to PETS rules. For details of how to obtain a Pet Passport visit www.defra.gov.uk of call 0370 241 1710.

Returning to the UK
On your return to the UK with your pet you will need to visit a vet between 24 and 120 hours prior to your return journey in order for your pet to be treated for tapeworm. The vet will need to sign your pet passport - ensure that they put the correct date against their signature or you may not fall within the correct time range for travel. Ask your campsite to recommend a local vet.

Travelling with Children

Some countries require evidence of parental responsibility for people travelling alone with children, especially those who have a different surname to them (including single parents, grandchildren etc.). The authorities may want to see a birth certificate, a letter of consent from the child's parent (or other parent if you are travelling alone with your own child) and some evidence as to your responsibility for the child.

For further information on exactly what will be required at immigration contact the Embassy or Consulate of the countries you intend to visit.

Vehicle Tax

While driving abroad you still need to have current UK vehicle tax. If your vehicle's tax is due to expire while you are abroad you may apply to re-license the vehicle at a post office, by post, or in person at a DVLA local office, up to two months in advance.

Since October 2014 the DVLA have no longer issued paper tax discs - EU Authorities are aware of this change.

Vehicle Registration Certificate

You must always carry your Vehicle Registration Certificate (V5C) when taking your vehicle abroad. If yours has been lost, stolen or destroyed you should apply to a DVLA local office on form V62. Call DVLA Customer Enquiries on 0300 790 6802 for more information.

Caravan – Proof of Ownership (CRIS)

In Britain and Ireland, unlike most other European countries, caravans are not formally registered in the same way as cars. This may not be fully understood by police and other authorities on the Continent. You are strongly advised, therefore, to carry a copy of your Caravan Registration Identification Scheme (CRIS) document.

Hired or Borrowed Vehicles

If using a borrowed vehicle you must obtain a letter of authority to use the vehicle from the registered owner. You should also carry the Vehicle Registration Certificate (V5C).

In the case of hired or leased vehicles, including company cars, when the user does not normally possess the V5C, ask the company which owns the vehicle to supply a Vehicle On Hire Certificate, form VE103, which is the only legal substitute for a V5C. The BVRLA, the trade body for the vehicle rental and leasing sector, provide advice on hired or leased vehicles - see www.bvrla.co.uk or call them on 01494 434747 for more information.

If you are caught driving a hired vehicle abroad without this certificate you may be fined and/or the vehicle impounded.

Visas

British citizens holding a full UK passport do not require a visa for entry into any EU countries, although you may require a permit for stays of more than three months. Contact the relevant country's UK embassy before you travel for information.

British subjects, British overseas citizens, British dependent territories citizens and citizens of other countries may need visas that are not required by British citizens. Again check with the authorities of the country you are due to visit at their UK embassy or consulate. Citizens of other countries should apply to their own embassy, consulate or High Commission.

Insurance

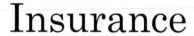

Car, Motorhome and Caravan Insurance

It is important to make sure your outfit is covered whilst you are travelling abroad. Your car or motorhome insurance should cover you for driving in the EU or associated countries, but you should check what you are covered for before you travel. If you are travelling outside the EU or associated countries you'll need to inform your insurer and may have to pay an additional premium.

Make sure your caravan insurance includes travel outside of the UK, speak to your provider to check this. You may need to notify them of your dates of travel and may be charged an extra premium dependent on your current levels of cover.

The Caravan Club's Car, Caravan and Motorhome Insurance schemes extend to provide policy cover for travel within the EU free of charge, provided the total period of foreign travel in any one year does not exceed 270 days for Car and Motorhome Insurance and 182 for Caravan Insurance. It may be possible to extend this period, although a charge may apply.

Should you be delayed beyond these limits notify your broker or insurer immediately in order to maintain your cover until you can return to the UK.

If your outfit is damaged during ferry travel (including while loading or unloading) it must be reported to the carrier at the time of the incident. Most insurance policies will cover short sea crossings (up to 65 hours) but check with your insurer before travelling.

Visit www.caravanclub.co.uk/insurance or call 01342 336610 for full details of The Caravan Club's Caravan Insurance or for Car or Motorhome Insurance call 0345 504 0334.

European Accident Statement
Your car or motorhome insurer may provide you with a European Accident Statement form (EAS), or you may be given one if you are involved in an accident abroad. The EAS is a standard form, available in different languages, which gives all parties involved in an accident the opportunity to agree on the facts. Signing the form doesn't mean that you are accepting liability, just that you agree with what has been stated on the form. Only sign an EAS if you are completely sure that you understand what has been written and always make sure that you take a copy of the completed EAS.

Vehicles Left Behind Abroad
If you are involved in an accident or breakdown abroad which prevents you taking your vehicle home, you must ensure that your normal insurance will cover your vehicle if left overseas while you return home. Also check if you're covered for the cost of recovering it to your home address.

In this event you should remove all items of baggage and personal belongings from your vehicles before leaving them unattended. If this isn't possible you should check with your insurer if extended cover can be provided. In all circumstances, you must remove any valuables and items liable for customs duty, including wine, beer, spirits and cigarettes.

Legal Costs Abroad

If an accident abroad leads to you being taken to court you may find yourself liable for legal costs – even if you are not found to be at fault. Most UK vehicle insurance policies include cover for legal costs or have the option to add cover for a small additional cost – check if you are covered before you travel.

Holiday Travel Insurance

A standard motor insurance policy won't cover you for all eventualities, for example vehicle breakdown, medical expenses or accommodation so it's important to also take out adequate travel insurance. Make sure that the travel insurance you take out is suitable for a caravan or motorhome holiday.

Remember to check exemptions and exclusions, especially those relating to pre-existing medical conditions or the use of alcohol. Be sure to declare any pre-existing medical conditions to your insurer.

The Caravan Club's Red Pennant Overseas Holiday Insurance is designed specifically for touring holidays and can cover both motoring and personal use. Depending on the level of cover chosen the policy will cover you for vehicle recovery and repair, holiday continuation, medical expenses and accommodation.

Visit www.caravanclub.co.uk/redpennant for full details or call us on 01342 336633.

Holiday Insurance for Pets

Taking your pet with you? Make sure they're covered too. Some holiday insurance policies, including The Club's Red Pennant, can be extended to cover pet expenses relating to an incident normally covered under the policy – such as pet repatriation in the event that your vehicle is written off.

However in order to provide cover for pet injury or illness you will need a separate pet insurance policy which covers your pet while out of the UK. For details of The Club's Pet Insurance scheme visit www.caravanclub.co.uk/petins or call 0345 504 0336.

Home Insurance

Your home insurer may require advance notification if you are leaving your home unoccupied for 30 days or more. There may be specific requirements, such as turning off mains services (except electricity), draining water down and having somebody check your home periodically. Read your policy documents or speak to your provider.

The Caravan Club's Home Insurance policy provides full cover for up to 90 days when you are away from home (for instance when touring) and requires only common sense precautions for longer periods of unoccupancy. See www.caravanclub.co.uk/homeins or call 0345 504 0335 for details.

Personal Belongings

The majority of travellers are able to cover their valuables such as jewellery, watches, cameras, laptops, and bikes under a home insurance policy. This includes The Caravan Club's Home Insurance scheme.

Specialist gadget insurance is now commonly available and can provide valuable benefits if you are taking smart phones, tablets, laptops or other gadgets on holiday with you. The Club offers a Gadget Insurance policy - visit www.caravanclub.co.uk/gadget or call 01342 779413 to find out more

Customs Regulations

Caravans and Vehicles

You can temporarily import a caravan, trailer tent or vehicle from one EU country to another without any Customs formalities. Vehicles and caravans may be temporarily imported into non-EU countries generally for a maximum of six months in any twelve month period, provided they are not hired, sold or otherwise disposed of in that country.

If you intend to stay longer than six months, dispose of a vehicle while in another country or leave your vehicle there in storage you should seek advice well before your departure from the UK.

Borrowed vehicles
If you are borrowing a vehicle from a friend or relative, or loaning yours to someone, you should be aware of the following:

- The total time the vehicle spends abroad must not exceed the limit for temporary importation (generally six months).
- The owner of the caravan must provide the other person with a letter of authority.
- The owner cannot accept a hire fee or reward.
- The number plate on the caravan must match the number plate on the tow car.

- Both drivers' insurers must be informed if a caravan is being towed and any additional premium must be paid.

Currency

You must declare cash of €10,000 (or equivalent in other currencies) or more when travelling between the UK and a non-EU country. The term 'cash' includes cheques, travellers' cheques, bankers' drafts, notes and coins. You don't need to declare cash when travelling within the EU.

For further information contact HMRC Excise & Customs Helpline on 0300 200 3700.

Customs Allowances

Travelling within the European Union
If you are travelling to the UK from within the EU you can bring an unlimited amount of most goods without being liable for any duty or tax, but certain rules apply. The goods must be for your own personal use, which can include use as a gift (if the person you are gifting the goods to reimburses you this is not classed as a gift), and you must have paid duty and tax in the country where you purchased the

goods. If a customs official suspects that any goods are not for your own personal use they can question you, make further checks and ultimately seize both the goods and the vehicle used to transport them. Although no limits are in place, customs officials are less likely to question you regarding your goods if they are under the following limits:

- 800 cigarettes
- 400 cigarillos
- 200 cigars
- 1kg tobacco
- 10 litres of spirits
- 20 litres of fortified wine (e.g. port or sherry)
- 90 litres of wine
- 110 litres of beer

The same rules and recommended limits apply for travel between other EU countries.

Travelling outside the EU
There are set limits to the amount of goods you bring back into the UK from countries outside of the EU. All goods must be for your own personal use. Each person aged 17 and over is entitled to the following allowance:

- 200 cigarettes, or 100 cigarillos, or 50 cigars, or 250g tobacco

- 1 litre of spirits or strong liqueurs over 22% volume, or 2 litres of fortified wine, sparkling wine or any other alcoholic drink that's less than 22% volume
- 4 litres of still wine
- 16 litres of beer
- £390 worth of all other goods including perfume, gifts and souvenirs without having to pay tax and/or duty
- For further information contact HMRC National Advice Service on 0300 200 3700.

Medicines

There is no limit to the amount of medicines you can take abroad if they are obtained without prescription (i.e. over the counter medicines). Medicines prescribed by your doctor may contain controlled drugs (e.g. morphine), for which you will need a licence if you're leaving the UK for 3 months or more. Visit www.gov.uk/travelling-controlled-drugs or call 020 7035 0771 for a list of controlled drugs and to apply for a licence.

You don't need a licence if you carry less than 3 months' supply or your medication doesn't contain controlled drugs, but you should carry a letter from your doctor stating your name, a list of your prescribed drugs and dosages for each drug. You may have to show this letter when going through customs.

Personal Possessions

Visitors to countries within the EU are free to carry reasonable quantities of any personal possessions such as jewellery, cameras, and electrical equipment required for the duration of their stay. It is sensible to carry sales receipts for new items in case you need to prove that tax has already been paid.

Prohibited and Restricted Goods
Regardless of where you are travelling from the importation of some goods into the UK is restricted or banned, mainly to protect health and the environment. These include:

- Endangered animals or plants including live animals, birds and plants, ivory, skins, coral, hides, shells and goods made from them such as jewellery, shoes, bags and belts.
- Controlled, unlicensed or dangerous drugs.
- Counterfeit or pirated goods such as watches, CDs and clothes; goods bearing a false indication of their place of manufacture or in breach of UK copyright.
- Offensive weapons such as firearms, flick knives, knuckledusters, push daggers, self-defence sprays and stun guns.

- Pornographic material depicting extreme violence or featuring children

This list is not exhaustive; if in doubt contact HMRC on 0300 200 3700 (+44 2920 501 261 from outside the UK) or go through the red Customs channel and ask a Customs officer when returning to the UK.

Plants and Food

Travellers from within the EU may bring into the UK any fruit, vegetable or plant products without restriction as long as they are grown in the EU, are free from pests or disease and are for your own consumption. For food products Andorra, the Channel Islands, the Isle of Man, San Marino and Switzerland are treated as part of the EU.

From most countries outside the EU you are not allowed to bring into the UK any meat or dairy products. Other animal products may be severely restricted or banned and it is important that you declare any such products on entering the UK.

For up to date information contact the Department for Environment, Food and Rural Affairs (Defra) on 0345 33 55 77 or +44 20 7238 6951 from outside the UK. You can also visit www.defra.gov.uk to find out more.

Money

Being able to safely access your money while you're away is a necessity for you to enjoy your break. It isn't a good idea to rely on one method of payment, so always have a backup plan. A mixture of a small amount of cash plus one or two electronic means of payment are a good idea.

Traveller's cheques have become less popular in recent years as fewer banks and hotels are willing or able to cash them. There are alternative options which offer the same level of security but are easier to use, such as prepaid credit cards.

Local Currency

It is a good idea to take enough foreign currency for your journey and immediate needs on arrival, don't forget you may need change for tolls or parking on your journey. Currency exchange facilities will be available at ports and on ferries but rates offered may not be as good as you would find elsewhere. The Post Office, banks, exchange offices and travel agents offer foreign exchange. All should stock Euros but

during peak holiday times or if you need a large amount it may be sensible to pre-order your currency. You should also pre-order any less common currencies. Shop around and compare commission and exchange rates, together with minimum charges.

Banks and money exchanges in central and eastern Europe won't usually accept Scottish and Northern Irish bank notes and may be reluctant to change any sterling which has been written on or is creased or worn.

Foreign Currency Bank Accounts

Frequent travellers or those who spend long periods abroad may find a Euro bank account useful. Most such accounts impose no currency conversion charges for debit or credit card use and allow fee-free cash withdrawals at ATMs. Some banks may also allow you to spread your account across different currencies, depending on your circumstances. Speak to your bank about the services they offer.

Prepaid Travel Cards

Prepaid travel money cards are issued by various providers including the Post Office, Travelex, Lloyds Bank and American Express.

They are increasingly popular as the PIN protected travel money card offers the security of Traveller's Cheques, with the convenience of paying by card. You load the card with the amount you need before leaving home, and then use cash machines to make withdrawals or use the card to pay for goods and services as you would a credit or debit card. You can top the card up over the telephone or online while you are abroad. However there can be issues with using them with some automated payment systems, such as pay-at-pump petrol stations and toll booths, so you should always have an alternative payment method available.

These cards can be cheaper to use than credit or debit cards for both cash withdrawals and purchases as there are usually no loading or transaction fees to pay. In addition, because they are separate from your bank account, if the card is lost or stolen you bank account will still be secure.

Credit and Debit Cards

Credit and debit cards offer a convenient way of spending abroad. For the use of cards abroad most banks impose a foreign currency conversion charge of up to 3% per transaction. If you use your card to withdraw cash there will be a further commission charge of up to 3% and you will be charged interest (possibly at a higher rate than normal) as soon as you withdraw the money.

There are credit cards available which are specifically designed for spending overseas and will give you the best available rates. However they often have high interest rates so are only economical if you're able to pay them off in full each month.

If you have several cards, take at least two in case you encounter problems. Credit and debit 'Chip and PIN' cards issued by UK banks may not be universally accepted abroad so check that your card will be accepted if using it in restaurants or other situations where you pay after you have received goods or services

Contact your credit or debit card issuer before you leave home to let them know that you will be travelling abroad. In the battle against card fraud, card issuers frequently query transactions which they regard as unusual or suspicious, causing your card to be declined or temporarily stopped. You should always carry your card issuer's helpline number with you so that you can contact them if this happens. You will also need this number should you need to report the loss or theft of your card.

Dynamic Currency Conversion

When you pay with a credit or debit card, retailers may offer you the choice of currency for payment, e.g. a euro amount will be converted into sterling and then charged to your card account. This is known as a 'Dynamic Currency Conversion' but the exchange rate used is likely to be worse than the rate offered by your card issuer, so will work out more expensive than paying in the local currency.

Emergency Cash

If an emergency or theft means that you need cash in a hurry, then friends or relatives at home can send you emergency cash via money transfer services.

The Post Office, MoneyGram and Western Union all offer services which allows the transfer of money to over 233,000 money transfer agents around the world. Transfers take approximately ten minutes and charges are levied on a sliding scale.

Ferries & the Channel Tunnel

Booking Your Ferry

If travelling at peak times, such as Easter or school holidays, make reservations as early as possible. Each ferry will have limited room for caravans and large vehicles so spaces can fill up quickly, especially on cheaper crossings. If you need any special assistance or arrangements request this at the time of booking.

When booking any ferry crossing, make sure you give the correct measurements for your outfit including bikes, roof boxes or anything which may add to the length or height of your vehicle - if you underestimate your vehicle's size you may be turned away at boarding.

The Caravan Club is an agent for most major ferry companies operating services. Call The Club's Travel Service on 01342 316 101 or see www.caravanclub.co.uk/ferries to book.

The table at the end of this section shows current ferry routes from the UK to the Continent and Ireland. Some ferry routes may not be operational all year, and during peak holiday periods the transportation of caravans or motorhomes may be restricted. For the most up-to-date information on ferry routes and prices visit www.caravanclub.co.uk/ferries or speak to The Club's Travel Services team.

On the Ferry

Arrive at the port with plenty of time before your boarding time. Motorhomes and car/caravan outfits will usually either be the first or last vehicles boarded onto the ferry. Almost all ferries are now 'drive on – drive off' so you won't be required to do any complicated manoeuvres. You may be required to show ferry staff that your gas is switched off before boarding the ferry.

Be careful using the ferry access ramps, as they are often very steep which can mean there is a risk of grounding the tow bar or caravan hitch. Drive slowly and, if your ground clearance is low, consider whether removing your jockey wheel and any stabilising devices would help.

Vehicles are often parked close together on ferries, meaning that if you have towing extension mirrors they could get knocked or damaged by people trying to get past your vehicle. If you leave them attached during the ferry crossing then make sure you check their position on returning to your vehicle.

Channel Tunnel

The Channel Tunnel operator, Eurotunnel, accepts cars, caravans and motorhomes (except those running on LPG) on their service between Folkestone and Calais. You can just turn up and see if there is availability on the day, however prices increase as it gets closer to the departure time so if you know your plans in advance it is best to book as early as possible.

On the Journey

You will be asked to open your roof vents prior to travel and you will also need to apply the caravan brake once you have parked your vehicle on the train. You will not be able to use your caravan until arrival.

Pets

It is possible to transport your pet on a number of ferry routes to the Continent and Ireland, as well as on Eurotunnel services from Folkestone to Calais. Advance booking is essential as restrictions apply to the number of animals allowed on any one crossing. Make sure you understand the carrier's terms and conditions for transporting pets.

Once on board pets are normally required to remain in their owner's vehicle or in kennels on the car deck and you won't be able to access your vehicle to check on your pet while the ferry is at sea. On longer crossings you should make arrangements at the on-board information desk for permission to visit your pet in order to check its well-being. You should always make sure that ferry staff know your vehicle has a pet on board.

Information and advice on the welfare of animals before and during a journey is available on the website of the Department for Environment, Food and Rural Affairs (Defra), www.defra.gov.uk.

Gas

UK based ferry companies usually allow up to three gas cylinders per caravan, including the cylinder currently in use, however some may restrict this to a maximum of two cylinders. Some operators may ask you to hand over your gas cylinders to a member of the crew so that they can be safely stored during the crossing. Check that you know the rules of your ferry operator before you travel.

Cylinder valves should be fully closed and covered with a cap, if provided, and should remain closed during the crossing. Cylinders should be fixed securely in or on the caravan in the position specified by the manufacturer.

Gas cylinders must be declared at check-in and the crew may ask to inspect each cylinder for leakage before travel.

The carriage of spare petrol cans, whether full or empty, is not permitted on ferries or through the Channel Tunnel.

LPG vehicles

Vehicles fully or partially powered by LPG can't be carried through the Channel Tunnel. Gas for domestic use (e.g. heating, lighting or cooking) can be carried, but the maximum limit is 47kg for a single bottle or 50kg in multiple bottles. Tanks must be switched off before boarding and must be less than 80% full; you will be asked to demonstrate this before you travel.

Most ferry companies will accept LPG-powered vehicles but you must let them know at the time of booking. During the crossing the tank must be no more than 75% full and it must be turned off. In the case of vehicles converted to use LPG, some ferry companies also require a certificate showing that the conversion has been carried out by a professional - before you book speak to the ferry company to see what their requirements are.

Caravan Club Sites Near Ports

If you've got a long drive to the ferry port, or want to catch an early ferry then an overnight stop near to the port gives you a relaxing start to your holiday. The following table lists Caravan Club sites which are close to ports.

Caravan Club Members can book online at www.caravanclub.co.uk or call 01342 327490. Non-members can book by calling the sites directly on the telephone numbers below when the sites are open.

Please note that Commons Wood, Daleacres, Fairlight Wood, Hunter's Moon, Mildenhall, Old Hartley and Rookesbury Park are open to Caravan Club members only. Non-members are welcome at all other sites listed below.

Port	Nearest Club Site	Tel No.
Cairnryan, Stranraer	New England Bay	01776 860275
Dover, Folkestone, Channel Tunnel	Bearsted	01622 730018
	Black Horse Farm*	01303 892665
	Daleacres	01303 267679
	Fairlight Wood	01424 812333
Fishguard, Pembroke	Freshwater East	01646 672341
Harwich	Cambridge Cherry Hinton*	01223 244088
	Commons Wood*	01707 260786
	Mildenhall	01638 713089
Holyhead	Penrhos	01248 852617
Hull	York Beechwood Grange	01904 424637
	York Rowntree Park	01904 658997
Newcastle upon Tyne	Old Hartley	0191 237 0256
Newhaven	Brighton*	01273 626546
Plymouth	Plymouth Sound	01752 862325
Poole	Hunter's Moon*	01929 556605
Portsmouth	Rookesbury Park	01329 834085
Rosslare	River Valley	00353 (0)404 41647
Weymouth	Crossways	01305 852032

* Site open all year

Ferry routes and Operators

Route	Operator	Approximate Crossing Time	Maximum Frequency
Belgium			
Hull – Zeebrugge	P & O Ferries	12½ hrs	1 daily
France			
Dover – Calais	P & O Ferries	1½ hrs	22 daily
Dover – Calais	DFDS Seaways	1½ hrs	10 daily
Dover – Dunkerque	DFDS Seaways	2 hrs	12 daily
Folkestone – Calais	Eurotunnel	35 mins	3 per hour
Newhaven – Dieppe	DFDS Ferries	4 hrs	2 daily
Plymouth – Roscoff	Brittany Ferries	6 hrs	2 daily
Poole – Cherbourg	Brittany Ferries	4½ hrs	1 daily
Poole – St Malo (via Channel Islands)	Condor Ferries	5 hrs	1 daily (May to Sep)
Portsmouth – Caen	Brittany Ferries	6 / 7 hrs	3 daily (maximum)
Portsmouth – Cherbourg	Brittany Ferries	3 hrs	2 daily (maximum)
Portsmouth – Cherbourg	Condor Ferries	5½ hrs	1 weekly (May to Sep)
Portsmouth – Le Havre	Brittany Ferries	3¼ / 8 hrs	1 daily (minimum)
Portsmouth – St Malo	Brittany Ferries	9 hrs	1 daily
Ireland – Northern			
Cairnryan/Troon – Larne	P & O Irish Sea	1 / 2 hrs	11 daily
Liverpool (Birkenhead) – Belfast	Stena Line	8 hrs	2 daily
Cairnryan – Belfast	Stena Line	2 / 3 hrs	7 daily
Ireland – Republic			
Cork – Roscoff†	Brittany Ferries	14 hrs	1 per week
Fishguard – Rosslare	Stena Line	2 / 3½ hrs	3 daily
Holyhead – Dublin	Irish Ferries	1¾ / 3¼ hrs	4 daily
Holyhead – Dublin	Stena Line	3¼ hrs	4 daily
Liverpool – Dublin	P & O Irish Sea	8 hrs	2 daily
Pembroke – Rosslare	Irish Ferries	4 hrs	2 daily
Rosslare – Cherbourg*	Irish Ferries	19½ hrs	3 per week
Rosslare – Cherbourg	Stena Line	19 hrs	3 per week
Rosslare – Roscoff†	Irish Ferries	19½ hrs	4 per week
Netherlands			
Harwich – Hook of Holland	Stena Line	6½ hrs	2 daily
Hull – Rotterdam	P & O Ferries	10¼ hrs	1 daily
Newcastle – Ijmuiden (Amsterdam)	DFDS Seaways	15½ hrs	1 daily
Spain			
Portsmouth – Bilbao	Brittany Ferries	24 / 32 hrs	1 - 3 per week
Portsmouth or Plymouth – Santander	Brittany Ferries	20 / 32 hrs	4 per week

Not bookable through the Club's Travel Service.
Note: Services and routes correct at time of publication but subject to change.

Motoring Advice

Preparing for Your Journey

The first priority in preparing your outfit for your journey should be to make sure it has a full service. Make sure that you have a fully equipped spares kit, and a spare wheel and tyre for your caravan – it is easier to get hold of them from your local dealer than to have to spend time searching for spares where you don't know the local area.

Club members should carry their UK Sites Directory & Handbook with them, as it contains a section of technical advice which may be useful when travelling. The Club also has a free advice service covering a wide range of technical topics – download free information leaflets at www.caravanclub.co.uk/advice or contact the team by calling 01342 336611 or emailing technical@caravanclub.co.uk.

For advice on issues specific to countries other than the UK, Club members can contact the Travel Service Information Officer, email: travelserviceinfo@caravanclub.co.uk or call 01342 336766.

Weight Limits

From both a legal and a safety point of view, it is essential not to exceed vehicle weight limits. It is advisable to carry documentation confirming your vehicle's maximum permitted laden weight - if your Vehicle Registration Certificate (V5C) does not state this, you will need to produce alternative certification, e.g. from a weighbridge.

If you are pulled over by the police and don't have certification you will be taken to a weighbridge. If your vehicle(s) are then found to be overweight you will be liable to a fine and may have to discard items to lower the weight before you can continue on your journey.

Some Final Checks

Before you start any journey make sure you complete the following checks:

- All car and caravan or motorhome lights are working and sets of spare bulbs are packed
- The coupling is correctly seated on the towball and the breakaway cable is attached
- Windows, vents, hatches and doors are shut

- On-board water systems are drained
- Mirrors are adjusted for maximum visibility
- Corner steadies are fully wound up and the brace is handy for your arrival on site
- Any fires or flames are extinguished and the gas cylinder tap is turned off. Fire extinguishers are fully charged and close at hand
- The over-run brake is working correctly
- The jockey wheel is raised and secured, the handbrake is released.

Driving in Europe

Driving abroad for the first time can be a daunting prospect, especially when towing a caravan. Here are a few tips to make the transition easier:

- Remember that Sat Navs may take you on unsuitable roads, so have a map or atlas to hand to help you find an alternative route.
- It can be tempting to try and get to your destination as quickly as possible but we recommend travelling a maximum of 250 miles a day when towing.

- Share the driving if possible, and on long journeys plan an overnight stop.
- Remember that if you need to overtake or pull out around an obstruction you will not be able to see clearly from the driver's seat. If possible, always have a responsible adult in the passenger seat who can advise you when it is clear to pull out. If that is not possible then stay well back to get a better view and pull out slowly.
- If traffic builds up behind you, pull over safely and let it pass.
- Driving on the right should become second nature after a while, but pay particular attention when turning left, after leaving a rest area, petrol station or site or after a one-way system.
- Stop at least every two hours to stretch your legs and take a break.

Fuel

Grades of petrol sold on the Continent are comparable to those sold in the UK; 95 octane is frequently known as 'Essence' and 98 octane as 'Super'. Diesel may be called 'Gasoil' and is widely available across Europe.

E10 petrol (containing 10% Ethanol) can be found in certain countries in Europe. Most modern cars are E10 compatible, but those which aren't could be damaged by filling up with E10. Check your vehicle handbook or visit www.acea.be and search for 'E10' to find the publication 'Vehicle compatibility with new fuel standards'.

Members of The Caravan Club can check current average fuel prices by country at www.caravanclub.co.uk/overseasadvice.

Away from major roads and towns it is a good idea not to let your fuel tank run too low as you may have difficulty finding a petrol station, especially at night or on Sundays. Petrol stations offering a 24-hour service may involve an automated process, in some cases only accepting credit cards issued in the country you are in.

Automotive Liquefied Petroleum Gas (LPG)

The increasing popularity of dual-fuelled vehicles means that the availability of LPG – also known as 'autogas' or GPL – has become an important issue for more drivers.

There are different tank-filling openings in use in different countries. Currently there is no common European filling system, and you might find a variety of systems. Most Continental motorway services will have adaptors but these should be used with care – see www.autogas.ltd.uk for more information.

Low Emission Zones

Many cities in countries around Europe have introduced 'Low Emission Zones' (LEZ's) in order to regulate vehicle pollution levels. Some schemes require you to buy a windscreen

sticker, pay a fee or register your vehicle before entering the zone. You may also need to provide proof that your vehicle's emissions meet the required standard. Before you travel visit www.lowemissionzones.eu for maps and details of LEZ's across Europe. Also see the Country Introductions later in this guide for country specific information.

Motorhomes Towing Cars

A motorhome towing a small A-frame or towing dolly is illegal in most European countries. Motorhome users towing a small car should transport it on a braked trailer so that all four of the car's wheels are off the ground.

Priority and Roundabouts

When driving on the Continent it can be difficult to work out which vehicles have priority in different situations. Watch out for road signs which indicate priority and read the Country Introductions later in this guide for country specific information.

Take care at intersections – you should never rely on being given right of way, even if you have priority; especially in small towns and villages where local traffic may take right of way. Always give way to public service and military vehicles and to buses and trams.

In some countries in Europe priority at roundabouts is given to vehicles entering the roundabout (i.e. on the right) unless the road signs say otherwise.

Public Transport

In general in built-up areas be prepared to stop to allow a bus to pull out from a bus stop when the driver is signalling his intention to do so.

Take particular care when school buses have stopped and passengers are getting on and off.

Overtaking trams in motion is normally only allowed on the right, unless on a one way street where you can overtake on the left if there is not enough space on the right. Do not overtake a tram near a tram stop. These may be in the centre of the road. When a tram or bus stops to allow passengers on and off, you should stop to allow them to cross to the pavement. Give way to trams which are turning across your carriageway. Don't park or stop across tram lines; trams cannot steer round obstructions!

Pedestrian Crossings

Stopping to allow pedestrians to cross at zebra crossings is not always common practice on the Continent as it is in the UK. Pedestrians expect to wait until the road is clear before crossing, while motorists behind may be taken by surprise by your stopping. The result may be a rear-end shunt or vehicles overtaking you at the crossing and putting pedestrians at risk.

Traffic Lights

Traffic lights may not be as easily visible as they are in the UK, for instance they may be smaller or suspended across the road with a smaller set on a post at the roadside. You may find that lights change directly from red to green, bypassing amber completely. Flashing amber lights generally indicate that you may proceed with caution if it is safe to do so but you must give way to pedestrians and other vehicles.

A green filter light should be treated with caution as you may still have to give way to pedestrians who have a green light to cross the road. If a light turns red as approached, continental drivers will often speed up to get through the light instead of stopping. Be aware that if you brake sharply because a traffic light has turned red as you approached, the driver behind might not be expecting it.

Motoring Equipment

Essential Equipment

The equipment that you legally have to carry differs by country. For a full list see the Essential Equipment table at the end of this chapter, or see the Country Introductions of this book for country specific information. Please note equipment requirements and regulations can change frequently. To keep up to date with the latest equipment information please visit www.caravanclub.co.uk/overseasadvice.

Fire Extinguisher

As a safety precaution, an approved fire extinguisher should be carried in all vehicles. This is a legal requirement in several countries in Europe.

Glasses

In some countries it is a legal requirement for residents to carry a spare pair of glasses if they are needed for driving, and it is recommended that visitors also comply. Elsewhere, if you do not have a spare pair, you may find it helpful to carry a copy of your prescription.

Lights

When driving on the Continent headlights need to be adjusted to deflect to the right if they are likely to dazzle other road users. You can do this by applying beam deflectors, or some newer vehicles have a built-in adjustment system. Some modern high-density discharge (HID), xenon or halogen-type lights, may need to be taken to a dealer to make the necessary adjustment. Remember also to adjust headlights according to the load being carried and to compensate for the weight of the caravan on the back of your car. Even if you do not intend to drive at night, it is important to ensure that your headlights are correctly adjusted as you may need to use them in heavy rain, fog or in tunnels. If using tape or a pre-cut adhesive mask remember to remove it on your return home.

Dipped headlights should be used in poor weather conditions and in a tunnel even if it is well lit. You may find police waiting at the end of a tunnel to check vehicles. In some countries the use of dipped headlights is compulsory at all times and in others they must be used in built-up areas, on motorways or at certain times of the year.

Headlight-Flashing

On the Continent headlight-flashing is used as a warning of approach or as an overtaking signal at night, and not, as is commonly the case in the UK, an indication that you are giving way. Be more cautious with both flashing your headlights and when another driver flashes you.

Hazard Warning Lights

Hazard warning lights should not be used in place of a warning triangle, but they may be used in addition to it.

Nationality Plate (GB/IRL)

A nationality plate must be fixed to the rear of both your car or motorhome and caravan. Checks are made and a fine may be imposed for failure to display a nationality plate correctly. If your number plates have the Euro-Symbol on them there is no requirement to display an additional GB sticker within the EU and Switzerland. If your number plate doesn't have the EU symbol or you are planning to travel outside of the EU you will need a GB sticker.

GB is the only national identification code allowed for cars registered in the UK. Registration plates displaying the GB Euro-Symbol must comply with the appropriate British Standard.

Reflective Jackets/Waistcoats

If you break down outside of a built-up area it is normally a legal requirement that anyone leaving the vehicle must be wearing a reflective jacket or waistcoat. Make sure that your jacket is accessible from inside the car as you will need to put it on before exiting the vehicle. Carry one for each passenger as well as the driver.

Route Planning

It is always a good idea to carry a road atlas or map of the countries you plan to visit, even if you have Satellite Navigation. You can find information on UK roads from Keep Moving – www.keepmoving.co.uk or call 09003 401100. Websites offering a European route mapping service include www.google.co.uk/maps, www.mappy.com or www.viamichelin.com.

Satellite Navigation/GPS

Continental postcodes don't cover just one street or part of a street in the same way as UK postcodes. A French five-digit postcode, for example, can cover a very large area.

GPS co-ordinates and full addresses are given for site entries in this guide wherever possible, so that you can programme your device as accurately as possible.

It is important to remember that sat nav devices don't usually allow for towing or driving a large motorhome and may try to send you down unsuitable roads. Always use your common sense, and if a road looks unsuitable find an alternative route.

Use your sat nav in conjunction with the directions given in the site entries, which have been provided by members who have actually visited. Please note that the directions given in site entries have not been checked by The Caravan Club.

In nearly all European countries it is illegal to use car navigation systems which actively search for mobile speed cameras or interfere with police equipment (laser or radar detection). Car navigation systems which give a warning of fixed speed camera locations are legal in most countries with the exception of France, Germany, and Switzerland where this function must be de-activated.

Seat Belts

The wearing of seat belts is compulsory throughout Europe. On-the-spot fines will be incurred for failure to wear them and, in the event of an accident failure to wear a seat belt may reduce any claim for injury. See the country introductions for specific regulations on both seat belts and car seats.

Spares

Caravan Spares

It will generally be much harder to get hold of spare parts for caravans on the continent, especially for UK manufactured caravans. It is advisable to carry any commonly required spares (such as light bulbs) with you.

Take the contact details of your UK dealer or manufacturer with you, as they may be able to assist in getting spares delivered to you.

Car Spares Kits

Some car manufacturers produce spares kits; contact your dealer for details. The choice of spares will depend on the vehicle and how long you are away, but the following is a list of basic items which should cover the most common causes of breakdown:

- Radiator top hose
- Fan belt
- Fuses and bulbs
- Windscreen wiper blade
- Length of 12V electrical cable
- Tools, torch and WD40 or equivalent water repellent/ dispersant spray

Spare Wheel

Your local caravan dealer should be able to supply an appropriate spare wheel. If you have any difficulty in obtaining one, The Caravan Club's Technical Department can provide Club members with a list of suppliers on request.

Tyre legislation across Europe is more or less consistent and, while the Club has no specific knowledge of laws on the Continent regarding the use of space-saver spare wheels, there should be no problems in using such a wheel provided its use is in accordance with the manufacturer's instructions. Space-saver spare wheels are designed for short journeys to get your vehicle to a place where it can be repaired and there will usually be restrictions on the distance and speed at which the vehicle should be driven.

Towbar

The vast majority of cars registered after 1 August 1998 are legally required to have a European Type approved towbar (complying with European Directive 94/20) carrying a plate giving its approval number and various technical details, including the maximum noseweight. Your car dealer or specialist towbar fitter will be able to give further advice.

From 2011 for brand new motorhome designs (launched on or after that date) and 2012 for existing designs (those already being built before 29 April 2011), all new motorhomes will need some form of type approval before they can be registered in the UK and as such can only be fitted with a type approved towbar. This change will not affect older vehicles, which can continue to be fitted with non-approved towing brackets.

Tyres

Tyre condition has a major effect on the safe handling of your outfit. Caravan tyres must be suitable for the highest speed at which you can legally tow, even if you choose to drive slower.

Most countries require a minimum tread depth of 1.6mm but motoring organisations recommend at least 3mm. If you are planning a long journey, consider if they will still be above the legal minimum by the end of your journey.

Tyre Pressure

Tyre pressure should be checked and adjusted when the tyres are cold; checking warm tyres will result in a higher pressure reading. The correct pressures will be found in your car handbook, but unless it states otherwise add an extra 4 - 6 pounds per square inch to the rear tyres of a car when towing to improve handling. Make sure you know what pressure your caravan tyres should be. Some require a pressure much higher than that normally used for cars. Check your caravan handbook for details.

Tyre Sizes

It is worth noting that some sizes of radial tyre to fit the 13" wheels commonly used on older UK caravans are virtually impossible to find in stock at retailers abroad, e.g. 175R13C.

After a Puncture

A lot of new cars now have a liquid sealant puncture repair kit instead of a spare wheel. These sealants should not be used to achieve a permanent repair and in some cases have been known to make repair of the tyre impossible. If you need to use a liquid sealant you should get the tyre repaired or replaced as soon as possible.

Following a caravan tyre puncture, especially on a single-axle caravan, it is advisable to have the opposite side (non-punctured) tyre removed from its wheel and checked inside and out for signs of damage resulting from overloading during the deflation of the punctured tyre.

Winter driving

Winter tyres should be used in severe winter climates and in some countries they are a legal requirement. Winter tyres minimise the hardening effect of low temperatures which can lead to less traction on the road, and to provide extra grip on snow, ice or wet conditions.

Snow chains may be necessary on some roads in winter. They are compulsory in some countries, indicated by a road sign. They are not difficult to fit but it's a good idea to carry sturdy gloves to protect your hands when handling the chains in freezing conditions. Polar Automotive Ltd sells and hires out snow chains, tel 01892 519933 www.snowchains. com, email: polar@snowchains.com.

Warning Triangles

In almost all European countries it is a legal requirement to use a warning triangle in the event of a breakdown or accident.

A warning triangle should be placed on the road approximately 30 metres (100 metres on motorways) behind the broken down vehicle on the same side of the road. Always assemble the triangle before leaving your vehicle and walk with it so that the red, reflective surface is facing oncoming traffic. If a breakdown occurs round a blind corner, place the triangle in advance of the corner. Hazard warning lights may be used in conjunction with the triangle but they do not replace it.

Essential Equipment Table

The table on the following page shows the essential equipment required for each country. The Country Introduction chapters also include details of specific rules for each country. Please note that this information was correct at the time of going to print but is subject to change. For up to date equipment requirements visit www.caravanclub.co.uk/overseasadvice.

Country	Warning Triangle	Spare Bulbs	First Aid Kit	Reflective Jacket	Additional Equipment to be Carried/Used
Andorra	Yes (2)	Yes	Rec	Yes	Dipped headlights in poor daytime visibility. Winter tyres recommended; snow chains when road conditions or signs dictate.
Austria	Yes	Rec	Yes	Yes	Winter tyres from 1 Nov to 15 April.*
Belgium	Yes	Rec	Rec	Yes	Dipped headlights in poor daytime visibility.
Croatia	Yes (2 for vehicle with trailer)	Yes	Yes	Yes	Dipped headlights at all times from last Sunday in Oct - last Sunday in Mar. Spare bulbs compulsory if lights are xenon, neon or LED. Snow chains compulsory in winter in certain regions.*
Czech Rep	Yes	Yes	Yes	Yes	Dipped headlights at all times. Replacement fuses. Winter tyres or snow chains from 1 Nov - 31st March.*
Denmark	Yes	Rec	Rec	Rec	Dipped headlights at all times. On motorways use hazard warning lights when queues or danger ahead.
Finland	Yes	Rec	Rec	Yes	Dipped headlights at all times. Winter tyres Dec - Feb.*
France	Yes	Rec	Rec	Yes	Dipped headlights recommended at all times. Legal requirement to carry a breathalyser, but no penalty for non-compliance.
Germany	Rec	Rec	Rec	Rec	Dipped headlights recommended at all times. Winter tyres to be used in winter weather conditions.*
Greece	Yes	Rec	Yes	Rec	Fire extinguisher compulsory. Dipped headlights in towns at night and in poor daytime visibility.
Hungary	Yes	Rec	Yes	Yes	Dipped headlights at all times outside built-up areas and in built-up areas at night. Snow chains compulsory on some roads in winter conditions.*
Italy	Yes	Rec	Rec	Yes	Dipped headlights at all times outside built-up areas and in poor visibility. Snow chains from 15 Oct - 15 April.*
Luxembourg	Yes	Rec	Rec	Yes	Dipped headlights at night and in daytime in bad weather.
Netherlands	Yes	Rec	Rec	Rec	Dipped headlights at night and in bad weather and recommended during the day.
Norway	Yes	Rec	Rec	Rec	Dipped headlights at all times. Winter tyres compulsory when snow or ice on the roads.*
Poland	Yes	Rec	Rec	Rec	Dipped headlights at all times. Fire extinguisher compulsory.
Portugal	Yes	Rec	Rec	Rec	Dipped headlights in poor daytime visibility, in tunnels and in lanes where traffic flow is reversible.
Slovakia	Yes	Rec	Yes	Yes	Dipped headlights at all times. Winter tyres compulsory when compact snow or ice on the road.*
Slovenia	Yes (2 for vehicle with trailer)	Yes	Rec	Yes	Dipped headlights at all times. Hazard warning lights when reversing. Use winter tyres or carry snow chains 15 Nov - 15 Mar.
Spain	Yes (2 Rec)	Rec	Rec	Yes	Dipped headlights at night, in tunnels and on 'special' roads (roadworks).
Sweden	Yes	Rec	Rec	Rec	Dipped headlights at all times. Winter tyres 1 Dec to 31 March.
Switzerland (inc Liechtenstein)	Yes	Rec	Rec	Rec	Dipped headlights recommended at all times, compulsory in tunnels. Snow chains where indicated by signs.

NOTES:
1) All countries: seat belts (if fitted) must be worn by all passengers.
2) Rec: not compulsory for foreign-registered vehicles, but strongly recommended
3) Headlamp converters, spare bulbs, fire extinguisher, first aid kit and reflective waistcoat are strongly recommended for all countries.
4) In some countries drivers who wear prescription glasses must carry a spare pair.
5) Please check information for any country before you travel. This information is to be used as a guide only and it is your responsibility to make sure you have the correct equipment.

* For more information and regulations on winter driving please see the Country Introductions.

Route Planning

ATLANTIC OCEAN

N
W E
S

Motorways
Major roads
Main roads
Ferry routes
⊕ Major airports

Bay
of
Biscay

UNITED KINGDOM
Cardiff
Bristol
Plymouth Weymouth Peole Portsmouth
Newhaven
English Channel
Guernsey
Jersey
Roscoff
Brest
Cherbourg-Octeville
Le Havre
Caen
St Malo
Rennes
Nantes
La Rochelle
Poitier
Limoges
Bordeaux

Ferrol
Santiago de Compostela
Vigo
Ourense
Braga
Porto
Aveiro
Viseu
Gijón
Oviedo
León
Santander
Bilbao
Vitoria-Gasteiz
Irun
Pamplona
Logroño
Valladolid
Salamanca
Zaragoza
Lleida Manresa
Sabadel
ANDORRA
Reus

PORTUGAL
Coimbra
Leiria
SPAIN
MADRID
Alcalá de Henares
Talavera de la Reina
Toledo
LISBOA
Setúbal
Évora
Badajoz
Sagunto
Torrent Valencia Palma de Mallo
Puertollano
Albacete
Alcoy-Alcoi
Elda
Elche-Elx
Murcia
Linares
Eivissa Eivissa (Ibiza)
Faro
Sevilla
Córdoba
Granada
Lorca
Cartagena
El Puerto de Santa María
Jerez de la Frontera
Cádiz
Marbella
Malaga
Almeria
Algeciras GIBRALTAR
Tánger (Tangier)
Ceuta (Spain)

© Collins Bartholomew Ltd 2015

Mountain Passes & Tunnels

Advice for Drivers

Mountain Passes

Mountain passes can create difficult driving conditions, especially when towing or driving a large vehicle. You should only use them if you have a good power to weight ratio and in good driving conditions. If in any doubt as to your outfit's suitability or the weather then stick to motorway routes across mountain ranges if possible.

The tables on the following pages show which passes are not suitable for caravans, and those where caravans are not permitted. Motorhomes aren't usually included in these restrictions, but relatively low powered or very large vehicles should find an alternative route. Road signs at the foot of a pass may restrict access or offer advice, especially for heavy vehicles. Warning notices are usually posted at the foot of a pass if it is closed, or if chains or winter tyres must be used.

Caravanners are particularly sensitive to gradients and traffic/road conditions on passes. The maximum gradient is usually on the inside of bends but exercise caution if it is necessary to pull out. Always engage a lower gear before taking a hairpin bend and give priority to vehicles ascending. On mountain roads it is not the gradient which puts strain on your car but the duration of the climb and the loss of power at high altitudes: approximately 10% at 915 metres (3,000 feet) and even more as you get higher. To minimise the risk of the engine overheating, take high passes in the cool part of the day, don't climb any faster than necessary and keep the engine pulling steadily. To prevent a radiator boiling, pull off the road safely, turn the heater and blower full on and switch off air conditioning. Keep an eye on water and oil levels. Never put cold water into a boiling radiator or it may crack. Check that the radiator is not obstructed by debris sucked up during the journey.

A long descent may result in overheating brakes; select the correct gear for the gradient and avoid excessive use of brakes. Even if you are using engine braking to control speed, caravan brakes may activate due to the overrun mechanism, which may cause them to overheat.

Travelling at altitude can cause a pressure build up in tanks and water pipes. You can prevent this by slightly opening the blade valve of your portable toilet and opening a tap a fraction.

Tunnels

Long tunnels are a much more commonly seen feature in Europe than in the UK, especially in mountainous regions. Tolls are usually charged for the use of major tunnels.

Dipped headlights are usually required by law even in well-lit tunnels, so switch them on before you enter. Snow chains, if used, must be removed before entering a tunnel in lay-bys provided for this purpose.

'No overtaking' signs must be strictly observed. Never cross central single or double lines. If overtaking is permitted in twin-tube tunnels, bear in mind that it is very easy to underestimate distances and speed once inside. In order to minimise the effects of exhaust fumes close all car windows and set the ventilator to circulate air, or operate the air conditioning system coupled with the recycled air option.

If you break down, try to reach the next lay-by and call for help from an emergency phone. If you cannot reach a lay-by, place your warning triangle at least 100 metres behind your vehicle. Modern tunnels have video surveillance systems to ensure prompt assistance in an emergency. Some tunnels can extend for miles and a high number of breakdowns are due to running out of fuel so make sure you have enough before entering the tunnel.

Mountain Pass Information

The dates of opening and closing given in the following tables are approximate. Before attempting late afternoon or early morning journeys across borders, check their opening times as some borders close at night.

Gradients listed are the maximum which may be encountered on the pass and may be steeper at the inside of curves, particularly on older roads.

Gravel surfaces (such as dirt and stone chips) vary considerably; they can be dusty when dry and slippery when wet. Where known to exist, this type of surface has been noted.

In fine weather winter tyres or snow chains will only be required on very high passes, or for short periods in early or late summer. In winter conditions you will need to use them at altitudes exceeding 600 metres (approximately 2,000 feet).

Converting Gradients

20% = 1 in 5	11% = 1 in 9
16% = 1 in 6	10% = 1 in 8
14% = 1 in 7	8% = 1 in 12
12% = 1 in 8	6% = 1 in 16

Tables and maps

Much of the information contained in the following tables was originally supplied by The Automobile Association and other motoring and tourist organisations. The Caravan Club haven't checked this information and cannot accept responsibility for the accuracy or for errors or omissions to these tables.

The mountain passes, rail and road tunnels listed in the tables are shown on the following maps. Numbers and letters against each pass or tunnel in the tables correspond with the numbers and letters on the maps.

Abbreviations

MHV	Maximum height of vehicle
MLV	Maximum length of vehicle
MWV	Maximum width of vehicle
MWR	Minimum width of road
OC	Occasionally closed between dates
UC	Usually closed between dates
UO	Usually open between dates, although a fall of snow may obstruct the road for 24-48 hours.

CLUB INSURANCE

Protect your adventure

Why choose Club insurance?

- Club know-how ensures great cover
- Created with your touring needs in mind
- Superb value for money
- Friendly call handlers
- The aftercare you expect from The Club

I'm delighted with the service, the premium is very competitive and the online quote system was so easy Sara Reynolds, member, Cheshire

Get a quote today
www.caravanclub.co.uk/insure or call

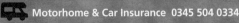

Caravan Insurance	01342 336610	
Overseas Holiday Insurance	01342 336633	
Gadget Insurance	01342 489163	
Key Cover	01342 489162	

Lines are open Mon-Fri 8.45am-5.30pm

Motorhome & Car Insurance 0345 504 0334
Home Insurance 0345 504 0335
Pet Insurance 0345 504 0336

Lines are open Mon-Fri 8.30am-7.00pm & Sat 9.00am-1.00pm & Sun 10.00am-4.00pm. Service provided by Devitt Insurance Services Ltd.

Mayday UK Breakdown & Recovery 0800 731 0112

Mon-Fri 8.00am-8.00pm, Sat 9.00am-5.00pm & Sun 10.00am-4.00pm. Service provided by GreenFlag.

THE CARAVAN CLUB

Calls may be recorded. Motorhome and car insurance new business is not available for drivers aged over 80.

Major Mountain Passes – Pyrenees and Northern Spain

Before using any of these passes, **PLEASE READ CAREFULLY THE ADVICE AT THE BEGINNING OF THIS CHAPTER**

	Pass Height In Metres (Feet)	From To	Max Gradient	Conditions and Comments
①	**Aubisque** (France) 1710 (5610)	Eaux Bonnes Argelès-Gazost	10%	UC mid Oct–Jun. MWR 3.5m (11'6") Very winding; continuous on D918 but easy ascent; descent including Col-d'Aubisque 1709m (5607 feet) and Col-du-Soulor 1450m (4757 feet); 8km (5 miles) of very narrow, rough, unguarded road with steep drop. **Not recommended for caravans**.
②	**Bonaigua** (Spain) 2072 (6797)	Viella (Vielha) Esterri-d'Aneu	8.5%	UC Nov–Apr. MWR 4.3m (14'1") Twisting, narrow road (C28) with many hairpins and some precipitous drops. **Not recommended for caravans**. Alternative route to Lerida (Lleida) through Viella (Vielha) Tunnel is open all year. See *Pyrenean Road Tunnels* in this section.
③	**Cabrejas** (Spain) 1167 (3829)	Tarancon Cuenca	14%	UO. On N400/A40. Sometimes blocked by snow for 24 hours. MWR 5m (16')
④	**Col-d'Haltza and Col-de-Burdincurrutcheta** (France) 782 (2565) and 1135 (3724)	St Jean-Pied-de-Port Larrau	11%	UO. A narrow road (D18/D19) leading to Iraty skiing area. Narrow with some tight hairpin bends; rarely has central white line and stretches are unguarded. Not for the faint-hearted. **Not recommended for caravans.**
⑤	**Envalira** (France – Andorra) 2407 (7897)	Pas-de-la-Casa Andorra	12.5%	OC Nov–Apr. MWR 6m (19'8") Good road (N22/CG2) with wide bends on ascent and descent; fine views. MHV 3.5m (11'6") on N approach near l'Hospitalet. Early start rec in summer to avoid border delays. Envalira Tunnel (toll) reduces congestion and avoids highest part of pass. See *Pyrenean Road Tunnels* in this section.
⑥	**Escudo** (Spain) 1011 (3317)	Santander Burgos	17%	UO. MWR probably 5m (16'5") Asphalt surface but many bends and steep gradients. **Not recommended in winter**. On N632; A67/N611 easier route.
⑦	**Guadarrama** (Spain) 1511 (4957)	Guadarrama San Rafael	14%	UO. MWR 6m (19'8") On NVI to the NW of Madrid but may be avoided by using AP6 motorway from Villalba to San Rafael or Villacastin (toll).
⑧	**Ibañeta (Roncevalles)** (France – Spain) 1057 (3468)	St Jean-Pied-de-Port Pamplona	10%	UO. MWR 4m (13'1") Slow and winding, scenic route on N135.
⑨	**Manzanal** (Spain) 1221 (4005)	Madrid La Coruña	7%	UO. Sometimes blocked by snow for 24 hours. On A6.
⑩	**Navacerrada** (Spain) 1860 (6102)	Madrid Segovia	17%	OC Nov–Mar. On M601/CL601. Sharp hairpins. Possible but **not recommended for caravans**.

Before using any of these passes, PLEASE READ CAREFULLY THE ADVICE AT THE BEGINNING OF THIS CHAPTER

Pass Height In Metres (Feet)	From To	Max Gradient	Conditions and Comments
(11) Orduna (Spain) 900 (2953)	Bilbao / Burgos	15%	UO. On A625/BU56; sometimes blocked by snow for 24 hours. Avoid by using AP68 motorway.
● (12) Pajares (Spain) 1270 (4167)	Oviedo / Léon	16%	UO. On N630; sometimes blocked by snow for 24 hours. **Not recommended for caravans.** Avoid by using AP66 motorway.
(13) Paramo-de-Masa (Spain) 1050 (3445)	Santander / Burgos	8%	UO. On N623; sometimes blocked by snow for 24 hours.
● (14) Peyresourde (France) 1563 (5128)	Arreau / Bagnères-de-Luchon	10%	UO. MWR 4m (13'1") D618 somewhat narrow with several hairpin bends, though not difficult. **Not recommended for caravans.**
(15) Picos-de-Europa: Puerto-de-San Glorio, Puerto-de-Pontón, Puerto-de-Pandetrave (Spain), 1609 (5279)	Unquera / Riaño	12%	UO. MWR probably 4m (13'1") Desfiladero de la Hermida on N621 good condition. Puerto-de-San-Glorio steep with many hairpin bends. For confident drivers only.
	Riaño / Cangas-de-Onís		Puerto-de-Ponton on N625, height 1280 metres (4200 feet). Best approach fr S as from N is very long uphill pull with many tight turns.
	Portilla-de-la-Reina / Santa Marina-de-Valdeón		Puerto-de-Pandetrave, height 1562 metres (5124 feet) on LE245 not rec when towing as main street of Santa Marina steep & narrow.
(16) Piqueras (Spain) 1710 (5610)	Logroño / Soria	7%	UO. On N111; sometimes blocked by snow for 24 hours.
(17) Port (France) 1249 (4098)	Tarascon-sur-Ariège / Massat	10%	OC Nov-Mar. MWR 4m (13'1") A fairly easy, scenic road (D618), but narrow on some bends.
● (18) Portet-d'Aspet (France) 1069 (3507)	Audressein / Fronsac	14%	UO. MWR 3.5m (11'6") Approached from W by the easy Col-des-Ares and Col-de-Buret; well-engineered but narrow road (D618); care needed on hairpin bends. **Not recommended for caravans.**
● (19) Pourtalet (France – Spain) 1792 (5879)	Laruns / Biescas	10%	UC late Oct-early Jun. MWR 3.5m (11'6") A fairly easy, unguarded road, but narrow in places. Easier from Spain (A136), steeper in France (D934). **Not recommended for caravans.**
(20) Puymorens (France) 1915 (6283)	Ax-les-Thermes / Bourg-Madame	10%	OC Nov-Apr. MWR 5.5m (18') MHV 3.5m (11'6") A generally easy, modern tarmac road (N20). Parallel toll road tunnel available. See *Pyrenean Road Tunnels* in this section.

Before using any of these passes, PLEASE READ CAREFULLY THE ADVICE AT THE BEGINNING OF THIS CHAPTER

	Pass Height In Metres (Feet)	From To	Max Gradient	Conditions and Comments
21	**Quillane** (France) 1714 (5623)	Axat Mont-Louis	8.5%	OC Nov-Mar. MWR 5m (16'5") An easy, straightforward ascent and descent on D118.
22	**Somosierra** (Spain) 1444 (4738)	Madrid Burgos	10%	OC Mar-Dec. MWR 7m (23') On A1/E5; may be blocked following snowfalls. Snow-plough swept during winter months but wheel chains compulsory after snowfalls. Well-surfaced dual carriageway, tunnel at summit.
23	**Somport** (France – Spain) 1632 (5354)	Accous Jaca	10%	UO. MWR 3.5m (11'6") A favoured, old-established route; not particularly easy and narrow in places with many unguarded bends on French side (N134); excellent road on Spanish side (N330). Use of road tunnel advised – see *Pyrenean Road Tunnels* in this section. NB Visitors advise re-fuelling no later than Sabiñánigo when travelling south to north.
24	**Toses (Tosas)** (Spain) 1800 (5906)	Puigcerda Ribes-de-Freser	10%	UO MWR 5m (16'5") A fairly straightforward, but continuously winding, two-lane road (N152) with with a good surface but many sharp bends; some unguarded edges. Difficult in winter.
25	**Tourmalet** (France) 2114 (6936)	Ste Marie-de-Campan Luz-St Sauveur	12.5%	UC Oct-mid Jun. MWR 4m (13'1") The highest French Pyrenean route (D918); approaches good, though winding, narrow in places and exacting over summit; sufficiently guarded. Rough surface & uneven edges on west side. **Not recommended for caravans.**
26	**Urquiola** (Spain) 713 (2340)	Durango (Bilbao) Vitoria/Gasteiz	16%	UO. Sometimes closed by snow for 24 hours. On BI623/A623. **Not recommended for caravans.**

Pyrenees & Northern Spain

Map legend:

- Motorway
- Motorway (Proposed)
- Motorway Road Tunnel
- Major/Main Roads
- Minor Mountain Passes (suitability for caravans not checked)
- (3) Major Mountain Passes Suitable for Caravans
- (10) Major Mountain Passes Unsuitable for Caravans
- CC Major Road Tunnels

0 10 20 30 40 50 km

These maps should be used in conjunction with the information in the Mountain Passes and Tunnels tables in this chapter.

- 2000m – +3000m
- 1000m – 2000m
- 100m – 1000m
- 0 – 100m

© Collins Bartholomew Ltd 2015

Keeping in Touch

Telephones and Calling

Most people need to use a telephone at some point while they're away, whether to keep in touch with family and friends back home or call ahead to sites. Even if you don't plan to use a phone while you're away, it is best to make sure you have access to one in case of emergencies.

International Direct Dial Calls

International access codes are given in the relevant Country Introduction - first dial the international access code then the local number. If the area code starts with a zero this should be omitted (except in Italy where the full number should be dialled).

Some countries' telephone numbers do not have area codes (e.g. Denmark, Luxembourg, Norway). In these cases you should dial the international access code and the number in full. The international access code to dial the UK from anywhere in the world is 0044.

Ringing Tones

Ringing tones vary from country to country, so may sound very different to UK tones. Some ringing tones sound similar to error or engaged tones that you would hear on a UK line.

Phone cards

You can buy pre-paid international phone cards which offer much lower rates for international calls than most mobile phone providers. You load the card with your chosen amount (which you can top up at any time) and then dial an access code from any mobile or landline to make your call. See www.planetphonecards.com or www.thephonecardsite.com for more details.

Using Mobile Phones Abroad

Mobile phones have an international calling option called 'roaming' which will automatically search for a local network when you switch your phone on. You should contact your service provider to ask about their roaming charges as these are partly set by the foreign networks you use and fluctuate with exchange rates. Most network providers offer added extras or 'bolt-ons' to your tariff to make the cost of calling to/from abroad cheaper.

Storing telephone numbers in your phone's contact list in international format (i.e. use the prefix of +44 and omit the initial '0') will mean that your contacts will automatically work abroad as well as in the UK.

Global SIM Cards

If you're planning on travelling to more than one country consider buying a global SIM card. This will mean your mobile phone can operate on foreign mobile networks, which will be more cost effective than your service provider's roaming charges. For details of SIM cards available, speak to your service provider or visit www.0044.co.uk or www.globalsimcard.co.uk. You may find it simpler to buy a SIM card or cheap 'pay-as-you-go' phone abroad if you plan to use a mobile phone a lot for local calls, e.g. to book campsites or restaurants. Buying a local SIM or pay-as-you-go mobile may mean that you still have higher call charges for international calls (such as calling the UK). Before buying a different SIM card, check with you provider whether your phone is locked against use on other networks.

Hands-Free

Legislation in Europe forbids the use of mobile or car phones while driving except when using hands-free equipment. If you are involved in an accident whilst driving and, at the same time, you were using a hand-held mobile phone, your insurance company may refuse to honour the claim.

Accessing the Internet

Mobile Internet Costs - Data Roaming

Accessing the internet via your mobile while outside of the UK can be very expensive. It is recommended that you disable your internet access by switching 'data roaming' to off to avoid a large mobile phone bill.

Internet Access

Wi-Fi is available on lots of campsites in Europe, sometimes the cost in included in your pitch fee and other sites charge extra for access. Most larger towns may have internet cafés or libraries where you can access the internet, however lots of fast food restaurants and coffee chains now offer free Wi-Fi for customers and visiting them for a cup of coffee or bite to eat is often the most economical way if you only need access for a short time.

Many people now use their smartphones for internet access or have a dongle – a device which, when connected to your laptop or tablet, allows you to access the internet using a mobile phone network. While these methods are economical in the UK, if you do the same abroad you will be charged data roaming charges which can run into hundreds or thousands of pounds depending on how much data you use. If you plan on using your smartphone or a dongle abroad speak to your service provider before you leave the UK to make sure you understand the costs. There may even be an overseas package that you can add to your plan to make data roaming cheaper.

Making Calls from your Laptop

If you download Skype to your laptop you can make free calls to other Skype users anywhere in the world using a Wi-Fi connection. Rates for calls to non-Skype users (landline or mobile phone) are also very competitively-priced. You will need a computer with a microphone and speakers, and a webcam is handy too. It is also possible to download Skype to an internet-enabled mobile phone to take advantage of the same low-cost calls – see www.skype.com.

Club Together

If you want to chat to other members either at home or while you're away, you can do so on The Club's online community Club Together.

You can ask questions and gather opinions on the forums. Just visit www.caravanclub.co.uk/together.

Radio and Television

Radio

The BBC World Service broadcasts radio programmes 24 hours a day worldwide and you can listen on a number of platforms: online, via satellite or cable, DRM digital radio, internet radio or mobile phone. You can find detailed information and programme schedules at www.bbc.co.uk/worldservice.

Listeners in northern France can currently listen to BBC Radio 5 Live on either 693 or 909 kHz medium wave or BBC Radio 4 on 198 kHz long wave. Whereas analogue television signals were switched off in the UK during 2012, no date has yet been fixed for the switch off of analogue radio signals.

Digital Terrestrial Television

As in the UK, television transmissions in most of Europe have been converted to digital. The UK's high definition transmission technology may be more advanced than any currently implemented or planned in Europe. This means that digital televisions intended for use in the UK might not be able to receive HD terrestrial signals in some countries.

Satellite Television

For English-language TV programmes the only realistic option is satellite, and satellite dishes are a common sight on campsites all over Europe. A satellite dish mounted on the caravan roof or clamped to a pole fixed to the drawbar, or one mounted on a foldable free-standing tripod, will provide good reception and minimal interference. Remember however that obstructions to the south east (such as tall trees or even mountains) or heavy rain, can interrupt the signals.

A specialist dealer will be able to advise you on the best way of mounting your dish. You will also need a satellite receiver and ideally a satellite-finding meter.

The main entertainment channels such as BBC1, ITV1 and Channel 4 can be difficult to pick up in mainland Europe as they are now being transmitted by new narrow-beam satellites. A 60cm dish should pick up these channels in most of France, Belgium and the Netherlands but as you travel further afield, you'll need a progressively larger dish. See the website www.satelliteforcaravans. co.uk (created and operated by a Caravan Club member) for the latest changes and developments, and for information on how to set up your equipment.

Medical Matters

You can find country specific medical advice, including details of any vaccinations you may need from the NHS choices website, www.nhs.uk/healthcare abroad. Your GP surgery should also be able to give you advice on vaccinations and precautions. For general enquiries about medical care abroad you can contact NHS England on 0300 311 22 33 or email england.contactus@nhs.uk.

If you have any pre-existing medical conditions you should check with your GP that you are fit to travel. Ask your doctor for a written summary of any medical problems and a list of medications currently used. This is particularly important for travellers whose medical conditions require them to use controlled drugs or hypodermic syringes, in case customs officers question why you are carrying them.

Always make sure that you have enough of your medication to last the duration of your holiday and some extra in case you are delayed in returning to the UK. Ask your doctor for the generic name of any drugs you use, as brand names may be different abroad. If possible carry a card giving your blood group and details of any allergies or dietary restrictions (translations may be useful for restaurants).

An emergency dental kit is available from High Street chemists which will allow you temporarily to restore a crown, bridge or filling or to dress a broken tooth until you can get to a dentist.

A good website to check before you travel is www.nathnac.org/travel. This website gives general health and safety advice and reports of disease outbreaks, as well as highlighting potential health risks by country.

European Heath Insurance Card (EHIC)

Before leaving home apply for a European Health Insurance Card (EHIC). British residents temporarily visiting another EU country, as well Norway and Switzerland, are entitled to receive state-provided emergency treatment during their stay on the same terms as residents of those countries, but you must have a valid EHIC to claim these services.

To apply for your EHIC visit www.ehic.org.uk, call 0300 330 1350 or pick up an application form from a post office. An EHIC is required by each individual family member - children under 16 must be included in a parent or guardian's application.

The EHIC is free of charge, is valid for up to five years and can be renewed up to six months before its expiry date. Before you travel remember to check that your EHIC is still valid.

Private treatment is generally not covered by your EHIC, and state-provided treatment may not cover everything that you would expect to receive free of charge from the NHS. If charges are made, these cannot be refunded by the British authorities but may be refundable under the terms of your travel insurance policy.

An EHIC is not a substitute for travel insurance and it is strongly recommended that you arrange full travel insurance before leaving home regardless of the cover provided by your EHIC. Some insurance companies require you to have an EHIC and some will waive the policy excess if an EHIC has been used.

If your EHIC is stolen or lost while you are abroad contact 0044 191 2127500 for help. If you experience difficulties in getting your EHIC accepted, telephone the Department for Work & Pensions for assistance on the overseas healthcare team line 0044 (0)191 218 1999 between 8am to 5pm Monday to Friday. Residents of the Republic of Ireland, the Isle of Man and Channel Islands, should check with

their own health authorities about reciprocal arrangements with other countries.

Holiday Travel Insurance

Despite the fact that you have an EHIC you may incur thousands of pounds of medical costs if you fall ill or have an accident. The cost of bringing a person back to the UK, in the event of illness or death, is never covered by the EHIC. You may also find that you end up with a bill for treatment as not all countries offer free healthcare.

Separate additional travel insurance adequate for your destination is essential, such as The Caravan Club's Red Pennant Overseas Holiday Insurance, available to Club members – see www.caravanclub.co.uk/redpennant.

First Aid

A first aid kit containing at least the basic requirements is an essential item, and in some countries it is compulsory to carry one in your vehicle (see the Essential Equipment Table in the chapter Motoring – Equipment). Kits should contain items such as sterile pads, assorted dressings, bandages and plasters, antiseptic wipes or cream, cotton wool, scissors, eye bath and tweezers. Also make sure you carry something for upset stomachs, painkillers and an antihistamine in case of hay fever or mild allergic reactions.

If you're travelling to remote areas then you may find it useful to carry a good first aid manual. The British Red Cross publishes a comprehensive First Aid Manual in conjunction with St John Ambulance and St Andrew's Ambulance Association.

Vaccinations

The Department of Health advises long stay visitors to some eastern European countries to consider vaccination against hepatitis A. Your GP surgery can advise you if this or any other vaccinations are required.

Accidents and Emergencies

If you are involved in or witness a road accident the police may want to question you about it. If possible take photographs or make sketches of the scene, and write a few notes about what happened as it may be more difficult to remember the details at a later date.

The telephone numbers for police, fire brigade and ambulance services are given in each Country Introduction, however in all EU member states the number 112 can be used from landlines or mobile phones to call any of the emergency services.

Sun Protection

Never under-estimate how ill exposure to the sun can make you. If you are not used to the heat it is very easy to fall victim to heat exhaustion or heat stroke. Avoid sitting in the sun between 11am and 3pm and cover your head if sitting or walking in the sun. Use a good quality sun-cream with high sun protection factor (SPF) and re-apply frequently. Make sure you drink plenty of fluids.

Tick-Borne Encephalitis (TBE) and Lyme Disease

Hikers and outdoor sports enthusiasts planning trips to forested, rural areas should be aware of tick-borne encephalitis, which is transmitted

by the bite of an infected tick. If you think you may be at risk, seek medical advice on prevention and immunisation before you leave the UK.

There is no vaccine against Lyme disease, an equally serious tick-borne infection, which, if left untreated, can attack the nervous system and joints.

You can minimise the risk by using an insect repellent containing DEET, wearing long sleeves and long trousers, and checking for ticks after outdoor activity. Avoid unpasteurised dairy products in risk areas. See www.tickalert.org or telephone 01943 468010 for more information.

Water and Food

Water from mains supplies throughout Europe is generally safe, but may be treated with chemicals which make it taste different to tap water in the UK. If in any doubt, always drink bottled water or boil it before drinking. Food poisoning is potential anywhere, and a complete change of diet may upset your stomach as well. In hot conditions avoid any food that hasn't been refrigerated or hot food that has been left to cool. Be sensible about the food that you eat – don't eat unpasteurised or undercooked food and if you aren't sure about the freshness of meat or seafood then it is best avoided.

Returning Home

If you become ill on your return home tell your doctor that you have been abroad and which countries you have visited. Even if you have received medical treatment in another country, always consult your doctor if you have been bitten or scratched by an animal while on holiday.

If you were given any medicines in another country, it may be illegal to bring them back into the UK. If in doubt, declare them at Customs when you return.

Electricity and Gas

Electricity – General Advice

The voltage for mains electricity is 230V across the EU, but varying degrees of 'acceptable tolerance' mean you may find variations in the actual voltage. Most appliances sold in the UK are 220-240V so should work correctly. However, some high-powered equipment, such as microwave ovens, may not function well – check your instruction manual for any specific instructions. Appliances marked with 'CE' have been designed to meet the requirements of relevant European directives.

The table below gives an approximate idea of which appliances can be used based on the amperage which is being supplied (although not all appliances should be used at the same time). You can work it out more accurately by making a note of the wattage of each appliance in your caravan. The wattages given are based on appliances designed for use in caravans and motorhomes. Household kettles, for example, have at least a 2000W element. Each caravan circuit will also have a maximum amp rating which should not be exceeded.

Electrical Connections – EN60309-2 (CEE17)

EN60309-2 (formerly known as CEE17) is the European Standard for all newly fitted connectors. However there is no requirement

Amps	Wattage (Approx)	Fridge	Battery Charger	Air Conditioning	LCD TV	Water Heater	Kettle (750W)	Heater (1kW)
2	400	✓	✓					
4	900	✓	✓		✓	✓		
6	1300	✓	✓	*	✓	✓	✓	
8	1800	✓	✓	✓**	✓	✓	✓	✓**
10	2300	✓	✓	✓**	✓	✓	✓	✓**
16	3600	✓	✓	✓	✓	✓	✓	✓**

*   *Usage possible, depending on wattage of appliance in question*
**   *Not to be used at the same time as other high-wattage equipment*

for sites to replace connectors which were installed before this was standardised so you may still find some sites where your UK 3 pin connector doesn't fit. For this reason it is a good idea to carry a 2-pin adapter. If you are already on site and find your connector doesn't fit, ask campsite staff to borrow or hire an adaptor. You may still encounter a poor electrical supply on site even with an EN60309-2 connection.

Other Connections

French – 2-pin, plus earth socket. Adaptors available from UK caravan accessory shops. German – 2-pin, plus 2 earth strips, found in Norway and Sweden and possibly still Germany. Switzerland - 3-pin, but not the same shape as UK 3-pin. Adapters available to purchase in Switzerland. Most campsites using the Swiss 3-pin will have adaptors available for hire or to borrow.

If the campsite does not have a modern EN60309-2 (CEE17) supply, ask to see the electrical protection for the socket outlet. If there is a device marked with IDn = 30mA, then the risk is minimised.

Hooking Up to the Mains

Connection

Connection should always be made in the following order:

- Check your outfit isolating switch is at 'off'.

- Uncoil the connecting cable from the drum. A coiled cable with current flowing through it may overheat. Take your cable and insert the connector (female end) into your outfit inlet.

- Insert the plug (male end) into the site outlet socket.

- Switch outfit isolating switch to 'on'.

- Use a polarity tester in one of the 13A sockets in the outfit to check all connections are correctly wired. Never leave it in the socket. Some caravans have these devices built in as standard.

It is recommended that the supply is not used if the polarity is incorrect (see Reversed Polarity overleaf).

If you are in any doubt of the safety of the system, if you don't receive electricity once connected or if the supply stops then contact the site staff.

If the fault is found to be with your outfit then call a qualified electrician rather than trying to fix the problem yourself.

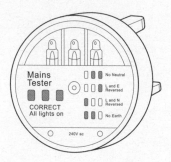

To ensure your safety you should never use an electrical system which you can't confirm to be safe. Use a mains tester such as the one shown above to test the electrical supply. Always check that a proper earth connection exists before using the electrics. Please note that these testers may not pick up all earth faults so if there is any doubt as to the integrity of the earth system do not use the electrical supply.

Disconnection

• Switch your outfit isolating switch to 'off'.

• At the site supply socket withdraw the plug.

• Disconnect the cable from your outfit.

Motorhomes – if leaving your pitch during the day, don't leave your mains cable plugged into the site supply, as this creates a hazard if the exposed live connections in the plug are touched or if the cable is not seen during grass-cutting.

Reversed Polarity

Even if the site connector meets European Standard EN60309-2 (CEE17), British caravanners are still likely to encounter the problem known as reversed polarity. This is where the site supply 'live' line connects to the outfit's 'neutral' and vice versa. You should always check the polarity immediately on connection, using a polarity tester available from caravan accessory shops. If polarity is reversed the caravan mains electricity should not be used. Try using another nearby socket instead. Frequent travellers to the Continent can make up an adaptor themselves, or ask an electrician to make one for you, with the live and neutral wires reversed. Using a reversed polarity socket will probably not affect how an electrical appliance works, however your protection is greatly reduced. For example, a lamp socket may still be live as you touch it while replacing a blown bulb, even if the light switch is turned off.

Shaver Sockets

Most campsites provide shaver sockets with a voltage of 220V or 110V. Using an incorrect voltage may cause the shaver to become

Site Hooking Up Adaptor

ADAPTATEUR DE PRISE AU SITE (SECTEUR)
CAMPINGPLATZ-ANSCHLUSS (NETZ)

EXTENSION LEAD TO CARAVAN
Câble de rallonge à la caravane
Verläengerungskabel zum wohnwagen

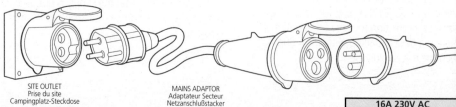

SITE OUTLET
Prise du site
Campingplatz-Steckdose

MAINS ADAPTOR
Adaptateur Secteur
Netzanschlußstacker

16A 230V AC

hot or break. The 2-pin adaptor available in the UK may not fit Continental sockets so it is advisable to buy 2-pin adaptors on the Continent. Many modern shavers will work on a range of voltages which make them suitable for travelling abroad. Check you instruction manual to see if this is the case.

Gas – General Advice

Gas usage can be difficult to predict as so many factors, such as temperature and how often you eat out, can affect the amount you need. As a rough guide allow 0.45kg of gas a day for normal summer usage.

With the exception of Campingaz, LPG cylinders normally available in the UK cannot be exchanged abroad. If possible, take enough gas with you and bring back the empty cylinders. Always check how many you can take with you as ferry and tunnel operators may restrict the number of cylinders you are permitted to carry for safety reasons.

The wide availability of Campingaz across Europe means it is worth considering using it while touring overseas. However, prices can vary from country to country, and maximum cylinder sizes are quite limited (2.75kg of gas in a 907 cylinder), making it less practical for routine use in larger vehicles with several gas appliances. A Campingaz adapter is relatively inexpensive, though, and is widely available in the UK.

If you are touring in cold weather conditions use propane gas instead of butane. Many other brands of gas are available in different countries and, as long as you have the correct regulator, adaptor and hose and the cylinders fit in your gas locker these local brands can also be used.

Gas cylinders are now standardised with a pressure of 30mbar for both butane and propane within the EU. On UK-specification caravans and motorhomes (2004 models and later) a 30mbar regulator suited to both propane and butane use is fitted to the bulkhead of the gas locker. This is connected to the cylinder with a connecting hose (and sometimes an adaptor) to suit different brands or types of gas. Older outfits and some foreign-built ones may use a cylinder-mounted regulator, which may need to be changed to suit different brands or types of gas.

Warnings:

- Refilling gas cylinders intended to be exchanged is against the law in most countries, however you may still find that some sites and dealers will offer to refill cylinders for you. Never take them up on this service as it can be dangerous; the cylinders haven't been designed for user-refilling and it is possible to overfill them with catastrophic consequences.

- Regular servicing of gas appliances is important as a faulty appliance can emit carbon monoxide, which could prove fatal. Check your vehicle or appliance handbook for service recommendations.

- Never use a hob or oven as a space heater.

The Caravan Club publishes a range of technical leaflets for its members including detailed advice on the use of electricity and gas – you can request copies or see www.caravanclub.co.uk/advice-and-training.

Safety and Security

EU countries have good legislation in place to protect your safety wherever possible. However accidents and crime will still occur and taking sensible precautions can help to minimise your risk of being involved.

Beaches, Lakes and Rivers

Check for any warning signs or flags before you swim and ensure that you know what they mean. Check the depth of water before diving and avoid diving or jumping into murky water as submerged objects may not be visible. Familiarise yourself with the location of safety apparatus and/or lifeguards.

Use only the designated areas for swimming, watersports and boating and always use life jackets where appropriate. Watch out for tides, undertows, currents and wind strength and direction before swimming in the sea. This applies in particular when using inflatables, windsurfing equipment, body boards, kayaks or sailing boats. Sudden changes of wave and weather conditions combined with fast tides and currents are particularly dangerous.

Campsite Safety

Once you've settled in, take a walk around the site to familiarise yourself with its layout and locate the nearest safety equipment. Ensure that children know their way around and where your pitch is.

Natural disasters are rare, but always think about what could happen. A combination of heavy rain and a riverside pitch could lead to flash flooding, for example, so make yourself aware of site evacuation procedures.

Be aware of sources of electricity and cabling on and around your pitch – electrical safety might not be up to the same standards as in the UK.

Poison for rodent control is sometimes used on sites or surrounding farmland. Warning notices are not always posted and you are strongly advised to check if staying on a rural site with dogs or children.

Incidents of theft on campsites are rare but when leaving your caravan unattended make sure you lock all doors and shut windows. Conceal valuables from sight and lock up any bicycles.

Children

Watch out for children as you drive around the site and don't exceed walking pace. Children's play areas are generally unsupervised, check which are suitable for your children's ages and abilities. Read and respect the displayed rules. Remember it is your responsibility to supervise your children at all times.

Be aware of any campsite rules concerning ball games or use of play equipment, such as roller blades and skateboards. When your children attend organised activities, arrange when and where to meet afterwards.

Make sure that children are aware of any places where they should not go and never leave children alone inside a caravan.

Fire

Fire prevention is important on sites, as fire can spread quickly between outfits. Never use paraffin or gas heaters inside your caravan. Gas heaters should only be fitted when air is taken from outside the caravan. Don't change your gas cylinder inside the caravan. If you smell gas turn off the cylinder immediately, extinguish all naked flames and seek professional help.

Make sure you know where the fire points and telephones are on site and know the site fire drill. Make sure everyone in your party knows how to call the emergency services.

Where site rules permit the use of barbecues, take the following precautions to prevent fire:

- Never locate a barbecue near trees or hedges.
- Have a bucket of water to hand in case of sparks.
- Only use recommended fire-lighting materials.
- Don't leave a barbecue unattended when lit and dispose of hot ash safely.
- Never take a barbecue into an enclosed area or awning – even when cooling they continue to release carbon monoxide which can lead to fatal poisoning.

Swimming Pools

Familiarize yourself with the pool area before you venture in for a swim, especially if you're travelling with children. Check the pool layout – identify shallow and deep ends and the location of safety equipment. Check the gradient of the pool bottom as pools which shelve off sharply can catch weak or non-swimmers unawares.

Never dive or jump into a pool without knowing the depth – if there is a no diving rule it usually means the pool isn't deep enough for safe diving.

For pools with a supervisor or lifeguard, note any times or dates when the pool is not supervised, e.g. lunch breaks or in low season. Read safety notices and rules posted around the pool.

On the Road

Do not leave valuables on car seats or on view in caravans, even if they are locked. Ensure that items on roof racks or cycle carriers are locked securely.

Beware of a 'snatch' through open car windows at traffic lights, filling stations or in traffic jams. When driving through towns and cities keep your doors locked. Keep handbags, valuables and documents out of sight at all times.

If flagged down by another motorist for whatever reason, take care that your own car is locked and windows closed while you check outside, even if someone is left inside.

Be particularly careful on long, empty stretches of motorway and when you stop for fuel. Even if the people flagging you down appear to be officials (e.g. wearing yellow reflective jackets or dark, 'uniform-type' clothing) lock your vehicle doors immediately. They may appear to be friendly and helpful, but could be opportunistic thieves. Have a mobile phone to hand and, if necessary, be seen to use it.

Road accidents are a significant risk in some countries where traffic laws may be inadequately enforced, roads may be poorly maintained, road signs and lighting inadequate, and driving standards poor. It's a good idea to keep a fully-charged mobile phone with you in your car with the number of your breakdown organisation saved into it.

On your return to the UK there are increasing issues with migrants attempting to stowaway in vehicles, especially if you're travelling from Calais. The UK government have issued the following instructions to prevent people entering the UK illegally:

- Where possible all access to vehicles or storage compartments should be fitted with locks.

- All locks must be engaged when the vehicle is stationary or unattended

- Immediately before boarding your ferry or train check that the locks on your vehicle haven't been compromised.

- If you have any reason to suspect someone may have accessed your outfit speak to border control staff or call the police. Do not board the ferry or train or you may be liable for a fine of up to £2000.

Overnight Stops

Overnight stops should always be at campsites and not at motorway service areas, ferry terminal car parks, petrol station forecourts or isolated 'aires de services' or 'aires de repos' on motorways where robberies and muggings are occasionally reported. If you decide to use these areas for a rest then take appropriate precautions, for example, shutting all windows, securing locks and making a thorough external check of your vehicle(s) before departing. Safeguard your property, e.g. handbags, while out of the caravan and beware of approaches by strangers.

For a safer place to take a break, there is a wide network of 'Stellplätze', 'Aires de Services', 'Aree di Sosta' and 'Áreas de Servicio' in cities, towns and villages across Europe, many specifically for motorhomes with good security and overnight facilities. It is rare that you will be the only vehicle staying on such areas, but avoid any that are isolated, take sensible precautions and trust your instincts. For example, if the area appears run down and there are groups of people hanging around who seem intimidating, then you are probably wise to move on.

Personal Security

Petty crime happens all over the world; however as a tourist you are more vulnerable to it. This shouldn't stop you from exploring new horizons, but there are a few sensible precautions you can take to minimise the risk.

- Leave valuables and jewellery at home. If you do take them, fit a small safe in your caravan or lock them in the boot of your car. Don't leave money or valuables in a car glovebox or on view. Don't leave bags in full view when sitting outside at cafés or restaurants, or leave valuables unattended on the beach.

- When walking be security-conscious. Avoid unlit streets at night, walk away from the kerb edge and carry handbags or shoulder bags on the side away from the kerb. The less of a tourist you appear, the less of a target you are.

- Keep a separate note of your holiday insurance details and emergency telephone numbers.

- Beware of pickpockets in crowded areas, at tourist attractions and in cities, and be cautious of bogus plain-clothes policemen who may ask to see your foreign currency or credit cards and passport. If approached, decline to show your money or to hand over your passport but ask for credentials and offer instead to go to the nearest police station.

- Laws and punishment vary from country to country so make yourself aware of anything which may affect you before you travel. Be especially careful on laws involving alcohol consumption (such as drinking in public areas), and never buy or use illegal drugs abroad.

- Respect customs regulations - smuggling is a serious offence and can carry heavy penalties. Do not carry parcels or luggage through customs for other people and do not cross borders with people you do not know in your vehicle, such as hitchhikers

The Foreign & Commonwealth Office produces a range of material to advise and inform British citizens travelling abroad about issues affecting their safety - www.gov.uk/foreign-travel-advice has country specific guides.

Money Security

We would rarely walk around at home carrying large amounts of cash, but as you may not have the usual access to bank accounts and credit cards you are more likely to do so on holiday. You are also less likely to have the same degree of security when online banking as you would in your own home. The following precautions are sensible to keep your money safe:

- Carry only the minimum amount of cash and don't rely on one person to carry everything. Never carry a wallet in your back pocket. Moneybelts are the most secure way to carry cash and passports.

- Keep a separate note of bank account and credit/debit card numbers. Carry your credit card issuer/bank's 24-hour UK contact number with you.

- Be careful when using cash machines (ATMs) – try to use a machine in an area with high footfall and don't allow yourself to be distracted. Put your cash away before moving away from the cash machine.
- Always guard your PIN number, both at cash machines and when using your card to pay in shops and restaurants. Never let your card out of your sight while paying.
- If using internet banking do not leave the PC or mobile device unattended and make sure you log out fully at the end of the session.

British Consular Services Abroad

British Embassy and Consular staff offer practical advice, assistance and support to British travellers abroad. They can, for example, issue replacement passports, help Britons who have been the victims of crime, contact relatives and friends in the event of an accident, illness or death, provide information about transferring funds and provide details of local lawyers, doctors and interpreters. But there are limits to their powers and a British Consul cannot, for example, give legal advice, intervene in court proceedings, put up bail, pay for legal or medical bills, or for funerals or the repatriation of bodies, or undertake work more properly done by banks, motoring organisations and travel insurers.

If you are charged with a serious offence, insist on the British Consul being informed. You will be contacted as soon as possible by a Consular Officer who can advise on local procedures, provide access to lawyers and insist that you are treated as well as nationals of the country which is holding you. However, they cannot get you released as a matter of course.
British and Irish embassy contact details can be found in the Country Introduction chapters.

Continental Campsites

The quantity and variety of sites across Europe means you're sure to find one that suits your needs – from full facilities and entertainment to quiet rural retreats. If you haven't previously toured outside of the UK you may notice some differences, such as pitches being smaller or closer together. In hot climates hard ground may make putting up awnings difficult.

In the high season all campsite facilities are usually open, however bear in mind that toilet and shower facilities may be busy. Out of season some facilities such as shops and swimming pools may be closed and office opening hours may be reduced. If the site has very low occupancy the sanitary facilities may be reduced to a few unisex toilet and shower cubicles.

Booking a Campsite

To save the hassle of arriving to find a site full it is best to book in advance, especially in high season. If you don't book ahead arrive no later than 4pm (earlier at popular resorts) to secure a pitch, after this time sites fill up quickly. You also need to allow time to find another campsite if your first choice is fully booked.

You can often book directly via a campsite's website using a credit or debit card to pay a deposit if required. Please be aware that some sites regard the deposit as a booking or admin fee and will not deduct the amount from your final bill.

Overseas Travel Service

The Caravan Club's Overseas Travel Service offers members an overseas site booking service to over 250 campsites in Europe. Full details of these sites plus information on Ferry special offers and Red Pennant Overseas Holiday Insurance can be found in the Club's Venture Abroad brochure – call 01342 327410 to request a copy or visit www.caravanclub.co.uk/overseas.

Overseas Site Booking Service sites are marked 'SBS' in the site listings. Many of them can be booked at www.caravanclub.co.uk. The Caravan Club cannot make advance reservations for any other campsites listed in this guide. Only those sites marked SBS have been inspected by Caravan Club staff.

Camping Cheques

The Caravan Club operates a low season scheme in association with Camping Cheques,

offering flexible holidays. The scheme covers approximately 635 sites in 29 countries.

Camping Cheques are supplied as part of a package which includes return ferry fare and a minimum of seven Camping Cheques. Those sites which feature in the Camping Cheques scheme and which are listed in this guide are marked 'CChq' in their site entries. For full details of the Camping Cheque scheme visit www.caravanclub.co.uk/campingcheques.

Caravan Storage Abroad

Storing your caravan on a site in Europe can be a great way to avoid a long tow and to save on ferry and fuel costs. Even sites which don't offer a specific long-term storage facility may be willing to negotiate a price to store your caravan for you.

Before you leave your caravan in storage abroad always check whether your insurance covers this, as many policies don't.

If you aren't covered then look for a specialist policy - Towergate Insurance (tel: 01242 538431 or www.towergateinsurance.co.uk) or Look Insurance (tel: 0333 777 3035 or www.lookinsuranceservices.co.uk) both offer insurance policies for caravans stored abroad.

Facilities and Site Description

All of the site facilities shown in the site listings of this guide have been taken from member reports, as have the comments at the end of each site entry. Please remember that opinions and expectations can differ significantly from one person to the next.

The year of report is shown at the end of each site listing – sites which haven't been reported on for a few years may have had significant changes to their prices, facilities, opening dates and standards. It is always best to check any specific details you need to know before travelling by contacting the site or looking at their website.

Sanitary Facilities

Facilities normally include toilet and shower blocks with shower cubicles, wash basins and razor sockets. In site listings the abbreviation 'wc' indicates that the site has the kind of toilets we are used to in the UK (pedestal style). Some sites have footplate style toilets and, where this is known, you will see the abbreviation 'cont', i.e. continental. European sites do not always provide sink plugs, toilet paper or soap so take them with you.

Waste Disposal

Site entries show (when known) where a campsite has a chemical disposal and/or a motorhome service point, which is assumed to include a waste (grey) water dump station and toilet cassette-emptying point. You may find fewer waste water disposal facilities as on the continent more people use the site sanitary blocks rather than their own facilities.

Chemical disposal points may be fixed at a high level requiring you to lift cassettes in order to empty them. Disposal may simply be down a toilet. Wastemaster-style emptying points are not very common in Europe. Formaldehyde chemical cleaning products are banned in many countries. In Germany the 'Blue Angel' (Blaue Engel) Standard, and in the Netherlands the 'Milieukeur' Standard, indicates that the product has particularly good environmental credentials.

Finding a Campsite

Directions are given for all campsites listed in this guide and most listings also include GPS co-ordinates. Full street addresses are also given where available. The directions have been supplied by member reports and haven't been checked in detail by The Club.

For information about using satellite navigation to find a site see the Motoring Equipment section.

Overnight Stops

Many towns and villages across Europe provide dedicated overnight or short stay areas specifically for motorhomes, usually with security, electricity, water and waste facilities. These are known as 'Aires de Services', 'Stellplatz' or 'Aree di Sosta' and are usually well signposted with a motorhome icon. Facilities and charges for these overnight stopping areas will vary significantly.

Many campsites in popular tourist areas will also have separate overnight areas of hardstanding with facilities often just outside the main campsite area. There are guidebooks available which list just these overnight stops, Vicarious books publish an English guide to the Aires including directions, GPS co-ordinates and photographs. Please contact 0131 208 3333 or visit their website www.vicarious-shop.co.uk.

For security reasons you shouldn't spend the night on petrol station service areas, ferry terminal car parks or isolated 'Aires de Repos' or 'Aires de Services' along motorways.

Municipal Campsites

Municipal sites are found in towns and villages all over Europe, in particular in France. Once very basic, many have been improved in recent years and now offer a wider range of facilities. They can usually be booked in advance through the local town hall or tourism office. When approaching a town you may find that municipal sites are not always named and signposts may simply state 'Camping' or show a tent or caravan symbol. Most municipal sites are clean, well-run and very reasonably priced but security may be basic.

These sites may be used by seasonal workers, market traders and travellers in low season and as a result there may be restrictions or very high charges for some types of outfits (such as twin axles) in order to discourage this. If you may be affected check for any restrictions when you book.

Naturist Campsites

Some naturist sites are included in this guide and are shown with the word 'naturist' after their site name. Those marked 'part naturist' have separate areas for naturists. Visitors to naturist sites aged 16 and over usually require an INF card or Naturist Licence - covered by membership of British Naturism (tel 01604 620361, visit www.british-naturism.org.uk or email headoffice@british-naturism.org.uk) or you can apply for a licence on arrival at any recognised naturist site (a passport-size photograph is required).

Opening Dates and times

Opening dates should always be taken with a pinch of salt - including those given in this guide. Sites may close without notice due to refurbishment work, a lack of visitors or bad weather. Outside the high season it is always best to contact campsites in advance, even if the site advertises itself as open all year.

Most sites will close their gates or barriers overnight – if you are planning to arrive late or are delayed on your journey you should call ahead to make sure you will be able to gain access to the site. There may be a late arrivals area outside of the barriers where you can pitch overnight. Motorhomers should also consider barrier closing times if leaving site in your vehicle for the evening.

Check out time is usually between 10am and 12 noon – speak to the site staff if you need to leave very early to make sure you can check out on departure. Sites may also close for an extended lunch break, so if you're planning to arrive or check out around lunchtime check that the office will be open.

Pets on Campsites

Dogs are welcome on many sites, although you may have to prove that all of their vaccinations are up to date before they are allowed onto the site. Certain breeds of dogs are banned in some countries and other breeds will need to be muzzled and kept on a lead at all times.

A list of breeds with restrictions by country can be found at www.caravanclub.co.uk/pets.

Sites usually charge for dogs and may limit the number allowed per pitch. On arrival make yourself aware of site rules regarding dogs, such as keeping them on a lead, muzzling them or not leaving them unattended in your outfit.

In popular tourist areas local regulations may ban dogs from beaches during the summer. Some dogs may find it difficult to cope with changes in climate. Also watch out for diseases transmitted by ticks, caterpillars, mosquitoes or sandflies - dogs from the UK will have no natural resistance. Consult your vet about preventative treatment before you travel.

Visitors to southern Spain and Portugal, parts of central France and northern Italy should be aware of the danger of Pine Processionary Caterpillars from mid-winter to late spring. Dogs should be kept away from pine trees if possible or fitted with a muzzle that prevents the nose and mouth from touching the ground. This will also protect against poisoned bait sometimes used by farmers and hunters.

In the event that your pet is taken ill abroad a campsite should have information about local vets.

Most European countries require dogs to wear a collar identifying their owners at all times. If your dog goes missing, report the matter to the local police and the local branch of that country's animal welfare organisation.

See the Documents section of this book for more information about the Pet Travel Scheme.

Prices and Payment

Prices per night (for an outfit and two adults) are shown in the site entries. If you stay on site after midday you may be charged for an extra day. Many campsites have a minimum amount for credit card transactions, meaning they can't be used to pay for overnight or short stays. Check which payment methods are accepted when you check in.

Sites with automatic barriers may ask for a deposit for a swipe card or fob to operate it.

Extra charges may apply for the use of facilities such as swimming pools, showers or laundry rooms. You may also be charged extra for dogs, Wi-Fi, tents and extra cars.

A tourist tax, eco tax and/or rubbish tax may be imposed by local authorities in some European countries. VAT may also be added to your campsite fees.

Registering on Arrival

Local authority requirements mean you will usually have to produce an identity document on arrival, which will be retained by the site until you check out. If you don't want to leave your passport with reception then most sites will accept a camping document such as the Camping Key Europe (CKE) or Camping Card International (CCI) - if this is known site entries are marked CKE/CCI.

CKE are available for Caravan Club members to purchase by calling 01342 336633 or are free to members if you take out the 'motoring' level of cover from the Club's Red Pennant Overseas Holiday Insurance.

General Advice

If you've visiting a new site ask to take a look around the site and facilities before booking in. Riverside pitches can be very scenic but keep an eye on the water level; in periods of heavy rain this may rise rapidly.

Speed limits on campsites are usually restricted to 10 km/h (6 mph). You may be asked to park your car in a separate area away from your caravan, particularly in the high season.

The use of the term 'statics' in the campsite reports in this guide may to any long-term accommodation on site, such as seasonal pitches, chalets, cottages, fixed tents and cabins, as well as static caravans.

Complaints

If you want to make a complaint about a site issue, take it up with site staff or owners at the time in order to give them the opportunity to rectify the problem during your stay.

The Caravan Club has no control or influence over day to day campsite operations or administration of the sites listed in this guide. Therefore we aren't able to intervene in any dispute you should have with a campsite, unless the booking has been made through our Site Booking Service - see listings marked 'SBS' for sites we are able to book for you.

Campsite Groups

Across Europe there are many campsite 'groups' or 'chains' with sites in various locations.

You will generally find that group sites will be consistent in their format and the quality and variety of facilities they offer. If you liked one site you can be fairly confident that you will like other sites within the same group.

If you're looking for a full facility site, with swimming pools, play areas, bars and restaurants on site you're likely to find these on sites which are part of a group. You might even find organised excursions and activities such as archery on site.

Portugal
Country Introduction

National Palace of Pena, Sintra

Welcome to Portugal

With around 3000 hours of sunshine a year, 850 kilometres of spectacular beaches and a wonderfully vibrant and varied landscape, Portugal is a visitor's paradise.

The country has been heavily influenced by its nautical tradition and position on the Atlantic. Many local delicacies are fish-based dishes, such as grilled sardines and salt cod, while some of Portugal's most splendid architecture date from when it was a global maritime empire.

Country highlights

Ceramic tiles, or azelujos, are a common element of Portuguese designs. Often depicting aspects of Portuguese culture and history, these tiles are both beautiful and functional, and are a significant part of Portugal's heritage.

Portugal is the birthplace of port, and the Douro region is one of the oldest protected wine regions in the world. Taking its name from the city of Porto, this smooth, fortified wine is exclusively produced in the Duoro Valley of Northern Portugal.

Major towns and cities

- Lisbon – Portugal's capital is known for its museums and café culture.
- Porto – an extravagant city filled with beautiful and colourful sights.
- Braga – an ancient city with filled with churches and Roman ruins.
- Faro – the prefect base to explore the Algarve.

Attractions

- Jerónimos Monastery – this UNESCO heritage site is a masterpiece and houses two museums.
- Guimarães Castle – this medieval castle is known as the Cradle of Portugal.
- National Palace of Pena – a striking palace filled with wonderful works of art.
- Lisbon Oceanarium – enjoy stunning and educational living ocean exhibits in one of Portugal's most popular tourist attractions

Find out more

www.visitportugal.com

Tel: (0)1 21 11 40 200 Portuguese Tourism

Country Information

Population (approx): 10.8 million

Capital: Lisbon (population approx 545,245)

Area: 92,951 sq km (inc Azores and Madeira)

Bordered by: Spain

Terrain: Rolling plains in south; mountainous and forested north of River Tagus

Climate: Temperate climate with no extremes of temperature; wet winters in the north influenced by the Gulf Stream; elsewhere Mediterranean with hot, dry summers and short, mild winters

Coastline: 1,794km

Highest Point (mainland Portugal): Monte Torre 1,993m

Language: Portuguese

Local Time: GMT or BST, i.e. the same as the UK all year

Currency: Euros divided into 100 cents; £1 = €1.42, €1 = £0.71 (September 2015)

Emergency numbers: Police 112; Fire brigade 112; Ambulance 112

Public Holidays 2016: Jan 1; Feb 9; Mar 25, 27; Apr 25; May 1, Jun 10 (National Day); Aug 15; Dec 8, 25.

Due to austerity measures imposed by the Portuguese government, four Public Holidays have been suspended for 5 years from 2013. These dates are: Corpus Christi (60 days after Easter), Oct 5, Nov 1 (All Saints Day) and Dec 1 (Independence Day).

Other holidays and saints' days are celebrated according to region. School summer holidays run from the end of June to the end of August.

Camping and Caravanning

There are numer campsites in Portugal, and many of these are situated along the coast. Sites are rated from 1 to 4 stars.

There are 22 privately owned campsites in the Orbitur chain. Caravanners can join the Orbitur Camping Club for discounts of at lease 15% at these sites. The joining fee is €21, with a 50% discount for senior citizens. You can buy membership at Orbitur sites or www.orbitur.com.

Casual/wild camping is not permitted.

Motorhomes

A number of local authorities now provide dedicated short stay areas for motorhomes called 'Áreas de Serviçio'. It is rare that yours will be the only motorhome staying on such areas, but take sensible precautions and avoid any that are isolated.

Cycling

In Lisbon there are cycle lanes in Campo Grande gardens, also from Torre de Belém to Cais do Sodré (7km) along the River Tagus, and between Cascais and Guincho. Elsewhere in the country there are few cycle lanes.

Transportation of Bicycles

Legislation stipulates that the exterior dimensions of a vehicle should not be exceeded and, in practice, this means that only caravans or motorhomes are allowed to carry bicycles/motorbikes at the rear of the vehicle. Bicycles may not extend beyond the width of the vehicle or more than 45cms from the back. However, bicycles may be transported on the roof of cars provided that an overall height of 4 metres is not exceeded. Cars carrying bicycles/motorbikes on the back may be subject to a fine.

If you are planning to travel from Spain to Portugal please note that slightly different regulations apply and these are set out in the Spain Country Introduction.

Electricity and Gas

Usually current on campsites varies between 6 and 15 amps. Plugs have two round pins. CEE connections are commonplace.

The full range of Campingaz cylinders is available.

Entry Formalities

Holders of British and Irish passports may visit Portugal for up to three months without a visa. For stays of over three months you will need to apply for a Registration Certificate from the nearest office of Servico de Estrangeiros e Fronteiras (immigration authority) or go to www.sef.pt.

Medical Services

For treatment of minor conditions go to a pharmacy (farmacia). Staff are generally well trained and are qualified to dispense drugs, which may only be available on prescription in Britain. In large towns there is usually at least one pharmacy whose staff speak English, and all have information posted on the door indicating the nearest pharmacy open at night.

All municipalities have a health centre. State emergency health care and hospital treatment is free on production of a European Health Insurance Card (EHIC). You will have to pay for items such as X-rays, laboratory tests and prescribed medicines as well as dental treatment. Refunds can be claimed from local offices of the Administracão Regional de Saúde (regional health service).

For serious illness you can obtain the name of an English speaking doctor from the local police station or tourist office or from a British or American consulate.

Normal precautions should be taken to avoid mosquito bites, including the use of insect repellents, especially at night.

Opening Hours

Banks – Mon-Fri 8.30am-3pm; some banks in city centres are open until 6pm.

Museums – Tue-Sun 10am-5pm/6pm; closed Mon and may close 12.30pm-2pm.

Post Offices – Mon-Fri 9am-6pm; may close for an hour at lunch.

Shops – Mon-Fri 9am-1pm & 3pm-7pm, Sat 9am-1pm; large supermarkets open Mon-Sun 9am/9.30am-10pm/11pm.

Safety and Security

The crime rate is low but pickpocketing, bag snatching and thefts from cars can occur in major tourist areas. Be vigilant on public transport, at crowded tourist sites and in public parks where it is wise to go in pairs. Keep car windows closed and doors locked while driving in urban areas at night. There has been an increase in reported cases of items stolen from vehicles in car parks.

Thieves distract drivers by asking for directions, for example, or other information. Be cautious and alert if you are approached in this way in a car park.

Take care of your belongings at all times. Do not leave your bag on the chair beside you, under the table or hanging on your chair while you eat in a restaurant or café.

Death by drowning occurs every year on Portuguese beaches. Warning flags should be taken very seriously. A red flag indicates danger and you should not enter the water when it is flying. If a yellow flag is flying you may paddle at the water's edge, but you may not swim. A green flag indicates that it is safe to swim, and a chequered flag means that the lifeguard is temporarily absent.

Do not swim from beaches which are not manned by lifeguards. The police are entitled to fine bathers who disobey warning flags.

During long, hot, dry periods forest fires can occur, especially in northern and central parts of the country. Take care when visiting or driving through woodland areas: ensure that cigarettes are extinguished properly, do not light barbecues, and do not leave empty bottles behind.

Portugal shares with the rest of Europe an underlying threat from terrorism. Attacks could be indiscriminate and against civilian targets in public places including tourist sites.

British Embassy
RUA DE SÃO BERNARDO 33,
1249-082 LISBOA
Tel: 21 392 4000
www.ukinportugal.fco.gov.uk

There is also a British Consulate in Portimão.

Irish Embassy
VENIDA DA LIBERDADE No 200, 4th FLOOR
1250-147 LISBON
Tel: 213 308 200
www.embassyofireland.pt

Documents

Driving Licence
All valid UK driving licences should be accepted in Portugal but holders of an older all green style licence are advised to update it to a photocard

licence before travelling in order to avoid any local difficulties. Alternatively carry an International Driving Permit, available from the AA, the RAC or selected Post Offices.

Passport
You must carry proof of identity which includes a photograph and signature, e.g. a passport or photocard licence, at all times.

Vehicle(s)
When driving you must carry your vehicle registration certificate (V5C), proof of insurance and MOT certificate (if applicable). There are heavy on the spot fines for those who fail to do so.

Money

The major credit cards are widely accepted and there are cash machines (Multibanco) throughout the country. A tax of €0.50 may be added to credit card transactions, especially at petrol stations. Carry your credit card issuers'/banks' 24 hour UK contact numbers in case of loss or theft.

Motoring in Portugal

Many Portuguese drive erratically and vigilance is advised. By comparison with the UK, the accident rate is high. Particular blackspots are the N125 along the south coast, especially in the busy holiday season, and the coast road between Lisbon and Cascais. In rural areas you may encounter horse drawn carts and flocks of sheep or goats. Otherwise there are no special difficulties in driving except in Lisbon and Porto, which are unlimited 'free-for-alls'.

Accident Procedures

The police must be called in the case of injury or significant material damage.

Alcohol

The maximum permitted level of alcohol is 50 milligrams in 100 millilitres of blood, i.e. lower than permitted in the UK (80 milligrams). For newly qualified drivers (those with under 3 year's experience), the legal limit is 20 milligrams per 100 millilitres of blood. It is advisable to adopt the 'no drink-driving' rule at all times.

Breakdown Service

The Automovel Club de Portugal (ACP) operates a 24 hour breakdown service covering all roads in mainland Portugal. Its vehicles are coloured red and white. Emergency telephones are located at 2km intervals on main roads and motorways. To contact the ACP breakdown service call +351 219 429113 from a mobile or 707 509510 from a landline.

The breakdown service comprises on the spot repairs taking up to a maximum of 45 minutes and, if necessary, the towing of vehicles. The charges for breakdown assistance and towing vary according to distance, time of day and day of the week, plus motorway tolls if applicable. Payment by credit card is accepted.

Alternatively, on motorways breakdown vehicles belonging to the motorway companies (their emergency numbers are displayed on boards along the motorways) and police patrols (GNR/ Brigada de Trânsito) can assist motorists.

Essential Equipment

Reflective Jackets/Waistcoats
If your vehicle is immobilised on the carriageway you should wear a reflective jacket or waistcoat when getting out of your vehicle. This is a legal requirement for residents of Portugal and is recommended for visitors. Passengers who leave a vehicle, for example, to assist with a repair, should also wear one. Keep the jackets within easy reach inside your vehicle, not in the boot.

Warning Triangles
Use a warning triangle if, for any reason, a stationary vehicle is not visible for at least 100 metres. In addition, hazard warning lights must be used if a vehicle is causing an obstruction or danger to other road users.

Child Restraint System
Children under 12 years of age and less than 1.35m in height are not allowed to travel in the front passenger seat. They must be seated in a child restraint system adapted to their size and weight in the rear of the vehicle, unless the vehicle only has two seats, or if the vehicle is not fitted with seat belts.

Children under the age of 3 years old can be seated in the front passenger seat as long as they are in a suitable rear facing child restraint system and the airbag has been deactivated.

Fuel

Credit cards are accepted at most filling stations but a small extra charge may be added and a tax of €0.50 is added to credit card transactions. There are no automatic petrol pumps. LPG (gáz liquido) is widely available.

Low Emission Zone

There is a Low Emission Zone in operation in Lisbon. There are 2 different zones within the city. In zone 1 vehicles must meet European Emission Standard 2 (EURO 3) and in zone 2 vehicles must meet EURO 2 standard. For more information visit www.lowemissionzones.eu.

Mountain Roads and Passes

There are no mountain passes or tunnels in Portugal. Roads through the Serra da Estrela near Guarda and Covilha may be temporarily obstructed for short periods after heavy snow.

Parking

In most cases vehicles must be parked facing in the same direction as moving traffic. Parking is very limited in the centre of main towns and cities and 'blue zone' parking schemes operate. Illegally parked vehicles may be towed away or clamped. Parking in Portuguese is 'estacionamento'.

Priority

In general at intersections and road junctions, road users must give way to vehicles approaching from the right, unless signs indicate otherwise. At roundabouts vehicles already on the roundabout, i.e. on the left, have right of way.

Do not pass stationary trams at a tram stop until you are certain that all passengers have finished entering or leaving the tram.

Roads

Roads are surfaced with asphalt, concrete or stone setts. Main roads generally are well surfaced and may be three lanes wide, the middle lane being used for overtaking in either direction.

Roads in the south of the country are generally in good condition, but some sections in the north are in a poor state. Roads in many towns and villages are often cobbled and rough. Drivers entering Portugal from Zamora in Spain will notice an apparently shorter route on the CL527/N221 road via Mogadouro. Although this is actually the signposted route, the road surface is poor in places and this route is not recommended for trailer caravans. The recommended route is via the N122/IP4 to Bragança.

Road Signs and Markings

Road signs conform to international standards. Road markings are white or yellow. Signs on motorways (auto-estrada) are blue and on regional roads they are white with black lettering. Roads are classified as follows:

Code	Road Type
AE	Motorways
IP	Principal routes
IC	Complementary routes
EN	National roads
EM	Municipal roads
CM	Other municipal roads

Signs you might encounter are as follows:

Portuguese	English Translation
Atalho	Detour
Entrada	Entrance
Estacão de gasolina	Petrol station
Estacão de policia	Police station
Estacionamento	Parking
Estrada con portagem	Toll road
Saida	Exit

Speed Limits

	Open Road (km/h)	Motorway (km/h)
Car Solo	90-100	120
Car towing caravan/trailer	70-80	100
Motorhome under 3500kg	90-100	120
Motorhome 3500-7500kg	70-90	100

Drivers must maintain a speed between 40 km/h (25 mph) and 60 km/h (37 mph) on the 25th April Bridge over the River Tagus in Lisbon. Speed limits are electronically controlled.

Visitors who have held a driving licence for less than one year must not exceed 90 km/h (56 mph) on any road subject to higher limits.

In built-up areas there is a speed limit of 50 km/h.

It is prohibited to use a radar detector or to have one installed in a vehicle.

Towing

Motorhomes are permitted to tow a car on a four wheel trailer, i.e. with all four wheels of the car off the ground. Towing a car on an A-frame (two back wheels on the ground) is not permitted.

Traffic Jams

Traffic jams are most likely to be encountered around the two major cities of Lisbon and Porto and on roads to the coast, such as the A1 Lisbon-Porto and the A2 Lisbon-Setúbal motorways, which are very busy on Friday evenings and Saturday mornings. The peak periods for holiday traffic are the last weekend in June and the first and last weekends in July and August.

Around Lisbon bottlenecks occur on the bridges across the River Tagus, the N6 to Cascais, the A1 to Vila Franca de Xira, the N8 to Loures and on the N10 from Setúbal via Almada.

Around Porto you may find traffic jams on the IC1 on the Arribada Bridge and at Vila Nova de Gaia, the A28/IC1 from Póvoa de Varzim and near Vila de Conde, and on the N13, N14 and the N15.

Major motorways are equipped with suspended signs which indicate the recommended route to take when there is traffic congestion.

Traffic Lights

There is no amber signal after the red. A flashing amber light indicates 'caution' and a flashing or constant red light indicates 'stop'. In Lisbon there are separate traffic lights in bus lanes.

Violation of Traffic Regulations

Speeding, illegal parking and other infringements of traffic regulations are heavily penalised.

You may incur a fine for crossing a continuous single or double white or yellow line in the centre of the road when overtaking or when executing a left turn into or off a main road, despite the lack of any other 'no left turn' signs. If necessary, drive on to a roundabout or junction to turn, or turn right as directed by arrows.

The police are authorised to impose on the spot fines and a receipt must be given. Most police vehicles are now equipped with portable credit card machines to facilitate immediate payment of fines.

Motorways

Motorway Tolls

Portugal has more than 2,600km of motorways (auto-estradas), with tolls (portagem) payable on most sections. Take care not to use the 'Via Verde' green lanes reserved for motorists who subscribe to the automatic payment system – be sure to go through a ticket booth lane where applicable, or one equipped with the new electronic toll system.

Dual carriageways (auto vias) are toll free and look similar to motoways, but speed limits are lower.

It is permitted to spend the night on a motorway rest or service area with a caravan, although The Caravan Club does not recommend this practice for security reasons. It should be noted that toll tickets are only valid for 12 hours and fines are incurred if this period of time is exceeded.

Vehicle are classified for tolls as follows:

Class 1   Vehicle with or without trailer with height from front axle less than 1.10m.

Class 2 Vehicle with 2 axles, with or without trailer, with height from front axle over 1.10m.

Class 3 Vehicle or vehicle combination with 3 axles, with height from front axle over 1.10m.

Class 4* Vehicle or vehicle combination with 4 or more axles with height from front axle over 1.10m.

* Drivers of high vehicles of the Range Rover/Jeep variety, together with some MPVs, and towing a twin axle caravan pay Class 4 tolls.

Electronic Tolls

An electronic toll collecting system was introduced in Portugal during 2010. The following motorways have tolls but no toll booths: A27, A28, A24, A41, A42, A25, A29, A23, A13, A8, A19, A33, A22 and parts of the A17 and A4. Tolls for these motorways can be paid by one of the following options:

If you are crossing the border from Spain on the A24, A25 or A22 or the A28 (via the EN13) then you can use the EASYToll welcome points. You can input your credit card details and the machine reads and then matches your credit/debit card to your number-plate, tolls are deducted automatically from your credit card, and the EASYToll machine will issue you a 30 day receipt as proof that you have paid.

If you are entering Portugal on a road that does not have an EASYToll machine you can register on-line or at a CTT post office and purchase either €5, €10, €20 or €40 worth of tolls. You can purchase a virtual prepaid ticket up to 6 times a year. For more information visit www.ctt.pt – you can select 'ENG' at the top left of the screen to see the site in English.

Alternatively you can get a temporary device (DT) available from some motorway service stations, post offices and Via Verde offices. A deposit of €27.50 is payable when you hire the DT and this is refundable when you return it to any of the outlets mentioned above. If you use a debit card, toll costs will automatically be debited from your card. If you pay cash you will be required to preload the DT. For further information see www.visitportugal.com and see the heading 'All about Portugal' then 'Useful Information'.

On motorways where this system applies you will see a sign: 'Lanço Com Portagem' or 'Electronic Toll Only', together with details of the tolls charged. Drivers caught using these roads without a DT will incur a minimum fine of €25.

The toll roads A1 to A15 and A21 continue to have manned toll booths. Most, but not all, accept credit cards or cash.

Toll Bridges

25th April Bridge and Vasco da Gama Bridge
The 2km long 25th April Bridge in Lisbon crosses the River Tagus. Tolls are charged for vehicles travelling in a south-north direction only. Tolls also apply on the Vasco da Gama Bridge, north of Lisbon, but again only to vehicles travelling in a south-north direction. Overhead panels indicate the maximum permitted speed in each lane and, when in use, override other speed limit signs.

In case of breakdown, or if you need assistance, you should try to stop in the emergency hard shoulder areas, wait inside your vehicle and switch on your hazard warning lights until a patrol arrives. Emergency telephones are placed at frequent intervals. It is prohibited to carry out repairs, to push vehicles physically or to walk on the bridges.

Touring

Some English is spoken in large cities and tourist areas. Elsewhere a knowledge of French could be useful.

A Lisboa Card valid for 24, 48 or 72 hours, entitles the holder to free unrestricted access to public transport, including trains to Cascais and Sintra, free entry to a number of museums, monuments and other places of interest in Lisbon and surrounding areas, as well as discounts in shops and places offering services to tourists. These cards are obtainable from tourist information offices, travel agents, some hotels and Carris ticket booths, or by visiting www.welovecitycards.com.

Do ensure when eating out that you understand exactly what you are paying for; appetisers put on the table are not free. Service is included in the bill, but it is customary to tip 5 to 10% of the total if you have received good service. Rules on smoking in restaurants and bars vary according to the size of the premises. The areas where clients are allowed to smoke are indicated by signs and there must be adequate ventilation. Each town in Portugal devotes several days in the year to local celebrations which are invariably lively and colourful. Carnivals and festivals during the period before Lent, during Holy Week and during the grape harvest can be particularly spectacular.

Public Transport

A passenger and vehicle ferry crosses the River Sado estuary from Setúbal to Tróia and there are frequent ferry and catamaran services for cars and passengers across the River Tagus from various points in Lisbon including Belém and Cais do Sodré.

Both Lisbon and Porto have metro systems operating from 6am to 1am. For routes and fares information see www.metrolisboa.pt and www.metrodoporto.pt (English versions).

Throughout the country buses are cheap, regular and mostly on time, with every town connected. In Lisbon the extensive bus and tram network is operated by Carris, together with one lift and three funiculars which tackle the city's steepest hills. Buy single journey tickets on board from bus drivers or buy a rechargeable 'Sete Colinas' or Via Viagem card for use on buses and the metro.

In Porto buy a 'Euro' bus ticket, which can be charged with various amounts, from metro stations and transport offices. Validate tickets for each journey at machines on the buses. Also available is an 'Andante' ticket which is valid on the metro and on buses. Porto also has a passenger lift and a funicular so that you can avoid the steep walk to and from the riverside.

Taxis are usually cream in colour. In cities they charge a standard, metered fare; outside they may run on the meter or charge a flat rate and are entitled to charge for the return fare. Agree a price for your journey before setting off.

Parque Natural da Ria Formosa, Faro

ALANDROAL *C3* (13km S Rural) *38.60645, -7.34674*
Camping Rosário, Monte das Mimosas, Rosário,
7250-999 Alandroal [268 459566; info@campingrosario.com;
www.campingrosario.com] Fr E exit IP7/A6 at Elvas W
junc 9; at 3rd rndabt take exit sp Espanha, immed 1st R dir
Juromenha & Redondo. Onto N373 until exit Rosário. Fr W exit
IP7/A6 junc 8 at Borba onto N255 to Alandroal, then N373 E
sp Elvas. After 1.5km turn R to Rosário & foll sp to site. Sm,
hdstg, pt sl, pt shd; wc; chem disp; shwrs inc; EHU (6A) €2.35;
gas 2km; lndry; shop 2km; rest; bar; playgrnd; pool; lake sw
adj; boating; fishing; TV; wifi; dogs €1 (not acc Jul/Aug); Eng
spkn; adv bkg; quiet; red long stay/LS; CKE/CCI. "Remote site
beside Alqueva Dam; excel touring base; ltd to 50 people max;
excel site; idyllic; peaceful; clean & well maintained; v helpful
owner." 1 Mar-1 Oct. € 24.50   2014*

"I like to fill in the reports as I travel from site to site"

You'll find report forms at the back of
this guide, or you can fill them in online
at www.caravanclub.co.uk/europereport.

⊞ **ALBUFEIRA** *B4* (3km NE Urban) *37.10617, -8.25395*
Camping Albufeira, Estrada de Ferreiras, 8200-555
Albufeira [289 587629 or 289 587630; fax 289 587633;
geral@campingalbufeira.net or info@campingalbufeira.net;
www.campingalbufeira.net] Exit IP1/E1 sp Albufeira onto
N125/N395 dir Albufeira; camp on L, sp. V lge, some mkd
pitch, pt sl, pt shd; wc; chem disp; mv service pnt; shwrs inc;
EHU (10-12A) €3; gas; lndry; shop; supmkt; rest, snacks; bar;
playgrnd; 3 pools; sand beach 1.5km; tennis; sports park;
bike hire; games area; games rm; disco (soundproofed); wifi;
entmnt; TV; 20% statics; dogs; phone; bus adj; car wash; cash
machine; security patrols; poss v cr; Eng spkn; no adv bkg;
quiet; ccard acc; red long stay/LS/CKE/CCI. "Friendly, secure
site; excel pool area/rest/bar; some pitches lge enough for US
RVs; pitches on lower pt of site prone to flooding in heavy rain;
conv beach & town; poss lge rallies during Jan-Apr; camp bus
to town high ssn." ♦ € 24.60   2013*

⊞ **ALBUFEIRA** *B4* (12km W Urban) *37.11916, -8.35083*
Camping Canelas, Alcantarilha, 8365-908 Armação de Pêra
[282 312612; fax 282 314719; turismovel@mail.telepac.pt;
www.camping-canelas.com] Fr Lagos take N125, turn R
(S) at Alcantarilha twd Armação de Pêra, site in 1.5km on R.
Fr IP1/A22 Algarve coastal m'way, take Alcantarilha exit & turn
L on N125 into vill, turn R at rndabt. Site on R in 1.5km just
bef 2nd rndabt. V lge, hdg pitch, pt sl, shd; wc; chem disp; mv
service pnt; shwrs; EHU (5-10A) €3-3.50; gas; lndry; shop; rest
high ssn; snacks; bar; BBQ; playgrnd; 3 solar htd pools; sand
beach 1.5km; tennis; games area; games rm; entmnt; TV rm;
5% statics; dogs €2; bus; phone; poss cr; Eng spkn; red
LS/long stay; CKE/CCI. "Spacious, shady, much improved site;
v popular in winter; vg security at ent; excel cent for Algarve."
♦ € 19.00   2011*

⊞ **ALBUFEIRA** *B4* (15km W Urban/Coastal) *37.10916,
-8.35333* Camping Armação de Pêra, 8365-184 Armação
de Pêra [282 312260; fax 282 315379; geral@camping-
armacao-pera.com; www.camping-armacao-pera.com]
Fr Lagos take N125 coast rd E. At Alcantarilha turn S onto
N269-1 sp Armação de Pêra & Campismo. Site at 3rd rndabt
in 2km on L. V lge, hdg pitch, pt sl, shd; wc; chem disp; mv
service pnt; shwrs inc; EHU (6-10A) €3-4; gas; lndry (inc dryer);
shop, rest, snacks; bar; playgrnd; pool & paddling pool; sand
beach 500m; tennis; bike hire; games area; games rm; internet;
entmnt; TV rm; 25% statics; phone; bus adj; car wash; poss
cr; Eng spkn; quiet; red LS; CKE/CCI. "Friendly, popular &
attractive site; gd pool; min stay 3 days Oct-May; easy walk to
town; interesting chapel of skulls at Alcantarilha; birdwatching
in local lagoon; vg." ♦ € 20.50   2012*

⊞ **ALCACER DO SAL** *B3* (1km NW Rural) *38.38027, -8.51583*
Parque de Campismo Municipal de Alcácer do Sal, Olival
do Outeiro, 7580-125 Alcácer do Sal [265 612303;
fax 265 610079; cmalcacer@mail.telepac.pt] Heading S
on A2/IP1 turn L twd Alcácer do Sal on N5. Site on R 1km
fr Alcácer do Sal. Sp at rndabt. Site behind supmkt. Sm, hdg/
mkd pitch, pt sl, pt shd; wc; chem disp; mv service pnt; shwrs
inc; EHU (6-12A) €1.50; lndry; shops 100m, rest, snacks & bar
50m; BBQ; playgrnd; pool, paddling pool adj; rv 1km; sand
beach 24km; games area; internet; dogs; phone; bus 50m;
clsd mid-Dec to mid-Jan; poss cr; Eng spkn; quiet; red LS; ccard
acc; CKE/CCI. "Excel, clean facs; in rice growing area - major
mosquito prob; historic town; spacious pitches; poss full in
winter - rec phone ahead." ♦ ltd. € 10.40   2011*

ALVOR see Portimao *B4*

AMARANTE *C1* (3km NE Rural) *41.27805, -8.07027* Camping
Penedo da Rainha, Rua Pedro Alveollos, Gatão, 4600-099
Amarante [255 437630; fax 255 437353; ccporto@sapo.pt]
Fr IP4 Vila Real to Porto foll sp to Amarante & N15. On N15
cross bdge for Porto & immed take R slip rd. Foll sp thro junc &
up rv to site. Lge, some hdstg, pt sl, terr, shd; wc; chem disp;
mv service pnt; shwrs inc; EHU (4A) €1.50; gas 2km; lndry;
shop in ssn & 2km; rest; snacks 100m; bar; playgrnd; sm pool &
3km; rv adj; fishing; canoeing; cycling; games rm; entmnt; TV;
dogs; phone; bus to Porto fr Amarante; some Eng spkn; adv
bkg; quiet; red LS/CKE/CCI. "Well-run site in steep woodland/
parkland - take advice or survey rte bef driving to pitch; excel
facs but some pitches far fr facs; few touring pitches; friendly,
helpful recep; plenty of shd; conv Amarante old town & Douro
Valley; Sat mkt." ♦ 1 Feb-30 Nov. € 12.50   2009*

ARCO DE BAULHE *C1* (300m NE Rural) *41.48659, -7.95845*
Arco Unipessoal, Lugar das Cruzes, 4860-067 Arco de
Baúlhe (Costa Verde) [(351) 968176246; campismoarco@
hotmail.com] Dir A7 exit 12 Mondm/Cabeceiras, 2nd R at
rndabt dir Arco de Baulhe. Call and they will lead you in. V narr
rd access, no mv's over 7m. Med, terr, pt sl; wc; chem disp;
shwr; EHU (6A); lndry; rest; bar; BBQ; htd sw; paddling pool;
rv; TV in bar; dogs; Eng spkn; adv bkg. "New site run by couple
with 20 yrs experience; quiet; centrally located for historic
towns & nature parks; gd rest; lovely well maintained site with
view; excel facs; 100m fr vill cent; beautiful mountain area."
1 Apr-10 Oct. € 26.00   2014*

ARMACAO DE PERA see Albufeira *B4*

AVEIRO *B2* (14km SW Coastal) *40.59960, -8.74981* **Camping Costa Nova, Estrada da Vagueira, Quinta dos Patos, 3830-453 Ílhavo [234 393220; fax 234 394721; info@campingcostanova.com; www.campingcostanova.com]** Site on Barra-Vagueira coast rd 1km on R after Costa Nova. V lge, mkd pitch, unshd; htd wc; chem disp; mv service pnt; shwrs inc; EHU (2-6A) €2.40; gas; lndry (inc dryer); shop; rest in ssn; snacks; bar; BBQ; playgrnd; pool 4km; sand beach; fishing; bike hire; games area; games rm; internet; entmnt; TV rm; some statics; dogs €1.40; phone; poss cr; site clsd Jan; Eng spkn; adv bkg; quiet; ccard acc; red long stay; CKE/CCI. "Superb, peaceful site adj nature reserve; helpful staff; gd, modern facs; hot water to shwrs only; sm pitches; sep car park high ssn; vg." ♦ 21 Mar-31 Oct. € 23.00   2012*

⊞ **AVEIRO** *B2* (10km W Coastal) *40.63861, -8.74500* **Parque de Campismo Praia da Barra, Rua Diogo Cão 125, Praia da Barra, 3830-772 Gafanha da Nazaré [tel/fax (234) 369425; barra@cacampings.com; www.cacampings.com]** Fr Aveiro foll sp to Barra on A25/IP5; foll sp to site. Lge, mkd pitch, shd; wc (some cont); chem disp; mv service pnt; baby facs; shwrs inc; EHU (6-10A) €2.50; gas; lndry (inc dryer); shop; rest; bar; BBQ; playgrnd; pool 400m; sand beach 200m; bike hire; games area; games rm; internet; entmnt; TV rm; 90% statics; dogs €1.80; phone; bus adj; recep open 0900-2200; Eng spkn; adv bkg; quiet; red LS; CKE/CCI. "Well-situated site with pitches in pine trees; old san facs." ♦ € 22.60   2013*

AVEIRO *B2* (8km NW Coastal/Rural) *40.70277, -8.7175* **Camping ORBITUR, N327, Km 20, 3800-901 São Jacinto [234 838284; fax 234 838122; infosjacinto@orbitur.pt; www.orbitur.pt]** Fr Porto take A29/IC1 S & exit sp Ovar onto N327. (Note long detour fr Aveiro itself by rd - 30+ km.) Site in trees to N of São Jacinto. Lge, mkd pitch, hdstg, terr, shd; wc; chem disp; mv service pnt; baby facs; shwrs inc; EHU (5-15A) €3-4 (poss rev pol); gas; lndry; sm shop & 5km; rest, snacks; bar; BBQ; playgrnd; pool 5km; sand beach 2.5km; fishing; TV; some statics; dogs €1.50; phone; bus; car wash; Eng spkn; adv bkg; quiet; red LS/long stay/snr citizens; ccard acc; CKE/CCI. "Excel site; best in area; gd children's park; 15 min to (car) ferry; gd, clean san facs." ♦ 1 Jun-30 Sep. € 27.00   2014*

⊞ **AVIS** *C3* (2km W Rural) *39.05638, -7.91138* **Parque de Campismo da Albufeira do Maranhão, Clube Náutico de Avis, Albufeira do Maranhão, 7480-999 Avis [242 412452; fax 242 410099; parque_campismo@cm-avis.pt; www.cm-avis.pt/parquecampismo]** Fr N exit A23/IP6 at Abrantes onto N2 dir Ponte de Sor, then N244 to Avis. Fr S exit A6/IP7 N at junc 7 Estremoz or junc 4 Montemor onto N4 to Arraiolos, then onto N370 to Pavia & Avis. Site sp. V lge, mkd pitch, terr, pt shd; wc; chem disp; mv service pnt; shwrs inc; EHU (16A) €2.60; gas 1km; lndry rm; shop 1km; rest adj; snacks; bar; playgrnd; pool complex adj; lake fishing & shgl beach adj; watersports; tennis; games area; games rm; TV; dogs €1; bus 1km; Eng spkn; adv bkg; quiet; red long stay; CKE/CCI. "V pleasant site on lakeside; interesting, historic town; gd walking area." ♦ € 14.00   2009*

⊞ **BEJA** *C4* (2km S Urban) *38.00777, -7.86222* **Parque de Campismo Municipal de Beja, Avda Vasco da Gama, 7800-397 Beja [tel/fax 284 311911; cmb.dcd@iol.pt; www.cm-beja.pt]** Fr S (N122) take 1st exit strt into Beja. In 600m turn R at island then L in 100m into Avda Vasco da Gama & foll sp for site on R in 300m - narr ent. Fr N on N122 take by-pass round town then 1st L after Intermarche supmkt, then as above. Lge, hdstg, shd, gravel pitches; wc; chem disp; shwrs inc; EHU (6A) €1.85; supmkt 500m; rest 500m; snacks 200m; bar adj; pool; tennis & football stadium adj; bus 300m; rlwy stn 1.5km; poss noisy in ssn; red LS/CKE/CCI. "C'van storage facs; helpful staff; NH only." ♦ € 10.40   2013*

BRAGANCA *D1* (6km N Rural) *41.84361, -6.74722* **Inatel Parque Campismo Bragança, Estrada de Rabal, 5300-671 Meixedo [tel/fax 273 329409 or 001090; pc.braganca@inatel.pt]** Fr Bragança N for 6km on N103.7 twd Spanish border. Site on R, sp Inatel. Med, hdstg, pt sl, terr, pt shd; wc; chem disp; shwrs inc; EHU (6A) inc; gas; lndry rm; shop & 6km; rest in ssn; snacks; bar; playgrnd; fishing; bike hire; dogs; bus; poss cr; Eng spkn; quiet but barking dogs. "On S boundary of National Park; rv runs thro site; friendly staff; gd rest; vg facs but site a little scruffy (June 2010); lovely location by rv." 1 Jun-15 Sep. € 17.00   2014*

⊞ **BRAGANCA** *D1* (12km W Rural) *41.84879, -6.86120* **Cepo Verde Camping, Gondesende, 5300-561 Bragança [273 999371; fax 273 323577; cepoverde@montesinho.com; www.bragancanet.pt/cepoverde]** Fr IP4 fr W take N103 fr Bragança for 8km. Site sp fr IP4 ring rd. R off N103, foll lane & turn R at sp. NB Camping sp to rd 103-7 leads to different site (Sabor) N of city. Med, mkd pitch, hdstg, terr, pt shd; wc; chem disp; shwrs inc; EHU (6A) €2 (poss rev pol & long lead poss req); shop; rest, snacks; bar; playgrnd; pool; dogs €1; phone; wifi; bus 1km; Eng spkn; adv bkg; quiet; CKE/CCI. "Remote, friendly, v pleasant, scenic site adj Montesinho National Park; clean but poorly maintained facs; vg value." ♦ € 20.00   2014*

BUDENS see Vila do Bispo *B4*

CABANAS TAVIRA see Tavira *C4*

⊞ **CALDAS DA RAINHA** *B3* (8km NW Rural/Coastal) *39.43083, -9.20083* **Camping ORBITUR, Rua Maldonado Freitas, 2500-516 Foz do Arelho [262 978683; fax 262 978685; infofozarelho@orbitur.pt; www.orbitur.pt]** Take N360 fr Caldas da Raina twds Foz do Arelho. Site on L; well sp. Lge, mkd pitch, terr, shd; wc; chem disp; mv service pnt; shwrs; EHU (5-15A) €3-4; gas; lndry (inc dryer); shop; rest high ssn; snacks; bar; BBQ; playgrnd; htd pool high ssn; paddling pool; sand beach 2km; tennis; bike hire; games rm; wifi; entmnt; cab/sat TV; 25% statics; dogs €1.50; car wash; Eng spkn; adv bkg; quiet; ccard acc; red LS; CKE/CCI. "Óbidos Lagoon nr; interesting walled town; attractive area; well-maintained, well-run site; excel san facs; excel touring base." ♦ € 24.60   2011*

PORTUGAL

PORTUGAL

⊞ **CAMINHA** B1 (3km SW Coastal) 41.86611, -8.85888
Camping ORBITUR-Caminha, Mata do Camarido, N13,
Km 90, 4910-180 Caminha [258 921295; fax 258 921473;
infocaminha@orbitur.pt; www.orbitur.pt] Foll seafront rd
N13/E1 fr Caminha dir Viana/Porto, at sp Foz do Minho turn
R, site in approx 1km. Long o'fits take care at ent. Med, terr,
shd; wc; mv service pnt; chem disp; shwrs inc; EHU (5-15A)
€3-4; gas; lndry; shop (high ssn); rest (high ssn); snacks; bar;
playgrnd; pool 2.5km; sand beach 150m; fishing; bike hire;
wifi; TV rm; 5% statics; dogs €1.50; Eng spkn; adv bkg;
fairly quiet; ccard acc; red LS/long stay/snr citizens; CKE/CCI.
"Pleasant, woodland site; care in shwrs - turn cold water on 1st
as hot poss scalding; Gerês National Park & Viana do Castelo
worth visit; poss to cycle to Caminha; vg site, nr attractive
beach and sh walk to pleasant town." ♦ € 36.50   2014*

⊞ **CAMPO MAIOR** C3 (2km SE Rural) 39.00833, -7.04833
Camping Rural Os Anjos, Estrada da Senhora da Saúde,
7371-909 Campo Maior [268 688138 or 965 236625 (mob);
info@campingosanjos.com; www.campingosanjos.com]
Fr Elvas foll rd N373 to Campo Maior. Foll sm sp thro vill. Site
on L down country lane. Sm, some hdstg, terr, pt shd; wc;
chem disp; baby facs; shwrs inc; EHU (6A) €2.60; lndry; shop in
town; bar; communal BBQ; pool; lake sw, fishing & watersports
8km; games area; games rm; wifi; TV rm; dogs €1 (max 1);
phone; Eng spkn; adv bkg (15 Nov-15 Feb open with adv bkg
only); quiet; red LS/long stay; CKE/CCI. "Excel, lovely, peaceful
site; v helpful, friendly, Dutch owners; gd touring base for
unspoiled, diverse area; conv Spanish border, Badajoz & Elvas;
Campo Maior beautiful, white town; LS call or email bef arr; gd
walks & bike rides; v clean shwrs; modern facs; fantastic views;
excel." ♦ € 17.00   2015*

"We must tell The Club about
that great site we found"
Get your site reports in by mid-August
and we'll do our best to get your updates
into the next edition.

⊞ **CASCAIS** A3 (7km NW Coastal/Urban) 38.72166,
-9.46666 Camping ORBITUR-Guincho, Lugar de Areia,EN
247-6, Guincho 2750-053 Cascais [(214) 870450; fax
(214) 857413; infoguincho@orbitur.pt; www.orbitur.pt]
Fr Lisbon take A5 W, at end m'way foll sp twd Cascais. At 1st
rndabt turn R sp Birre & Campismo. Foll sp for 2.5km. Steep
traff calming hump - care needed. V lge, some hdg/mkd pitch,
terr, shd; wc; chem disp; mv service pnt; baby facs; shwrs
inc; EHU (6A) €3-4; gas; lndry (inc dryer); supmkt & 500m;
rest, snacks; bar; BBQ; playgrnd; pool; sand beach 800m;
watersports & fishing 1km; tennis; bike hire; horseriding 500m;
golf 3km; games rm; wifi; entmnt; cab/sat TV; 50% statics;
dogs on lead €1.50; phone; car wash; Eng spkn; adv bkg;
some rd noise; ccard acc; red LS/long stay/snr citizens; CKE/
CCI. "Sandy, wooded site behind dunes; poss stretched & v
busy high ssn; poss diff lge o'fits due trees; steep rd to beach;
gd san facs, gd value rest; vg LS; buses to Cascais for train to
Lisbon; beautiful coastline within 20 min walk." ♦ € 39.00
SBS - E10   2013*

⊞ **CASTELO BRANCO** C2 (6km N Rural) 39.85777, -7.49361
Camp Municipal Castelo Branco, Estrada Nacional 18,
6000-113 Castelo Branco [(272) 322577; fax (272) 322578;
albigec@sm-castelobranco.pt; www.cm-castelobranco.pt]
Fr IP2 take Castelo Branco Norte, exit R on slip rd, L at 1st
rndabt, site sp at 2nd rndabt. Turn L at T junc just bef Modelo
supmkt, site 2km on L, well sp. Lge, pt sl, shd; wc; shwrs; chem
disp; mv service pnt; EHU (12A) €2.25; gas; lndry; shop, rest,
bar 2km; playgrnd; pool 4km; lake 500m; bus 100m; Eng spkn;
quiet but some rd noise; CKE/CCI. "Useful NH on little used
x-ing to Portugal; gd site but rds to it poor." 2 Jan-15 Nov.
€ 9.00   2013*

"I need an on-site restaurant"
We do our best to make sure site
information is correct, but it is always best
to check any must-have facilities are still
available or will be open during your visit.

⊞ **CASTELO DE VIDE** C3 (7km SW Rural) 39.39805, -7.48722
Camping Quinta do Pomarinho, N246, Km 16.5, Castelo
de Vide [965-755341 (mob); info@pomarinho.co.uk;
www.pomarinho.com] On N246 at km 16.5 by bus stop,
turn into dirt track. Site in 500m. Sm, mkd pitch, hdstg, unshd;
wc; chem disp; shwrs inc; EHU (6-10A) €2.50-3.50; lndry; shop
5km; pool; bike hire; wifi; dogs; bus adj; Eng spkn; adv bkg;
quiet. "On edge of Serra de São Mamede National Park; gd
walking, fishing, birdwatching, cycling; vg." € 14.00   2009*

⊞ **CELORICO DE BASTO** C1 (700m NW Rural) 41.39026,
-8.00581 Parque de Campismo de Celorico de Basto,
Adaufe-Gemeos, 4890-361 Celorico de Basto
[(255) 323340 or 964-064436 (mob); fax (255) 323341;
geral@celoricodebastocamping.com; www.celoricode
bastocamping.com] E fr Guimarães exit A7/IC5 S sp Vila
Nune (bef x-ing rv). Foll sp Fermil & Celorico de Basto, site sp.
Rte narr and winding or take the N210 fr Amarente and foll
sp to site. Med, mkd pitch, some hdstg, shd; wc; chem disp;
mv service pnt; shwrs inc; EHU (6-16A) €2-3.20; gas; lndry
(inc dryer); shop; rest; bar; BBQ; playgrnd; pool 500m; rv sw
& fishing adj; games area; wifi; entmnt; TV rm; some statics;
dogs €1.80; phone; quiet; ccard acc; red long stay/CKE/CCI.
"Peaceful, well-run site; gd facs; gd cycling & walking; vg." ♦
€ 16.00   2014*

⊞ **CHAVES** C1 (6km S Rural) 41.70166, -7.50055
Camp Municipal Quinta do Rebentão, Vila Nova de Veiga,
5400-764 Chaves [tel/fax 276 322733; ccchaves@sapo.pt]
Fr o'skts Chaves take N2 S. After about 3km in vill of Vila
Nova de Veiga turn E at sp thro new estate, site in about
500m. Med, hdstg, terr, pt shd; wc; chem disp; mv service
pnt; shwrs inc; EHU (6A) €1.50; gas 4km; lndry rm; shop 1km;
rest, snacks; bar; BBQ; pool adj; rv sw & fishing 4km; bike hire;
dogs; wifi; phone; bus 800m; site clsd Dec; Eng spkn; adv bkg;
red CKE/CCI. "Gd site in lovely valley but remote; helpful staff;
facs block quite a hike fr some terr pitches; Chaves interesting,
historical Roman town." ♦ € 19.00   2014*

⊞ **COIMBRA** *B2* (6km SE Urban) *40.18888, -8.39944*
**Camping Municipal Parque de Campismo de Coimbra,
Rua de Escola, Alto do Areeiro, Santo António dos
Olivais, 3030-011 Coimbra [tel/fax 239 086902;
coimbra@cacampings.com; www.cacampings.com]**
Fr S on AP1/IP1 at junc 11 turn twd Lousa & in 1km turn
twd Coimbra on IC2. In 9.5km turn R at rndabt onto Ponte
Rainha, strt on at 3 rndabts along Avda Mendes Silva. Then
turn R along Estrada des Beiras & cross rndabt to Rua de
Escola. Or fr N17 dir Beira foll sp sports stadium/campismo.
Fr N ent Coimbra on IC2, turn L onto ring rd & foll Campismo
sps. V lge, terr, hdstg, pt sl, pt shd; htd wc; chem disp; mv
service pnt; sauna; baby facs; shwrs inc; EHU (6A) €2.70; gas;
lndry; shop; rest, snacks; bar; BBQ; playgrnd; pool adj; rv sw
300m; health club; tennis; bike hire; games area; games rm;
internet; TV rm; 10% statics; dogs €2.20; bus 100m; poss cr;
Eng spkn; adv bkg; ccard acc; red long stay/LS/CKE/CCI. "Vg
site & facs; v interesting, lively university town." ♦ € 16.00
(CChq acc)   2009*

⊞ **COIMBRAO** *B2* (500m NW Urban) *39.90027, -8.88805*
**Camping Coimbrão, 185 Travessa do Gomes, 2425-452
Coimbrão [tel/fax 244 606007; campingcoimbrao@web.de]**
Site down lane in vill cent. Care needed lge o'fits, but site
worth the effort. Sm, unshd; wc; chem disp; mv service pnt;
shwrs inc; EHU (6-10A) €2.20-3.30; lndry (inc dryer); shop &
snacks 300m; BBQ; playgrnd; pool; sw, fishing, canoeing 4km;
wifi; TV; no dogs; bus 200m; Eng spkn; quiet; office open
0800-1200 & 1500-2200; red long stay/LS. "Excel site; helpful
& friendly staff; gd touring base." ♦ € 13.00   2010*

CORTEGACA see Espinho *B1*

COSTA DE CAPARICA see Lisboa *B3*

⊞ **COVILHA** *C2* (7km W Rural) *40.28750, -7.52722* **Clube
de Campismo do Pião, Rua 6 de Setembro 35, 356200-036
Covilhã [tel/fax 275 314312; campismopiao@hotmail.com]**
App Covilhã, foll sp to cent, then sp to Penhas da Saúde/Seia;
after 4km of gd but twisting climbing rd; site on L. Lge, terr, pt
shd; wc; shwrs inc; EHU (4-6A) €1.40; gas; shop; rest, snacks;
bar; BBQ; playgrnd; pool; paddling pool; tennis; entmnt; TV;
many statics; phone; bus adj; poss cr; Eng spkn; CKE/CCI. "Gd
walking fr site; few touring pitches." ♦ € 11.00   2009*

DARQUE see Viana do Castelo *B1*

ELVAS *C3* (2km SW Urban) *38.87305, -7.1800* **Parque de
Campismo da Piedade, 7350-901 Elvas [268 628997 or
268 622877; fax 268 620729]** Exit IP7/E90 junc 9 or 12 &
foll site sp dir Estremoz. Med, mkd pitch, hdstg, mostly sl, pt
shd; wc; chem disp; shwrs inc; EHU (16A) inc; gas; lndry rm;
shop 200m; rest, snacks; bar; BBQ; dogs; phone; bus
500m; poss cr; CKE/CCI. "Attractive aqueduct & walls; Piedade
church & relics adj; traditional shops; pleasant walk to town;
v quiet site, even high ssn; adequate san facs; conv NH en rte
Algarve." 1 Apr-15 Sep. € 16.50   2014*

ENTRE AMBOS OS RIOS see Ponte da Barca *B1*

⊞ **ERICEIRA** *B3* (2km N Coastal) *38.98055, -9.41861* **Camp
Municipal Mil Regos, 2655-319 Ericeira [261 862706;
fax 261 866798; info@ericeiracamping.com; www.ericeira
camping.com]** On N247 coast rd, well sp N of Ericeira. V lge,
pt sl, pt shd; wc (some cont); own san rec; shwrs inc; EHU
(10A) €3.50; gas; shop; rest; playgrnd; 2 pools adj; beach
200m; fishing; internet; entmnt; 75% statics; phone; bus adj;
quiet. "Busy site with sea views; improvements in hand (2009);
uneven, sl pitches." ♦ € 24.50   2009*

⊞ **ERMIDAS SADO** *B4* (11km W Rural) *38.01805, -8.48500*
**Camping Monte Naturista O Barão (Naturist), Foros do
Barão, 7566-909 Ermidas-Sado [936710623 (mob);
info@montenaturista.com; www.montenaturista.com]**
Fr A2 turn W onto N121 thro Ermidas-Sado twd Santiago do
Cacém. At x-rds nr Arelãos turn R at bus stop (km 17.5) dir
Barão. Site in 1km along unmade rd. Sm, mkd pitch, pt sl, pt
shd; wc; chem disp; mv service pnt; baby facs; fam bthrm;
shwrs inc; EHU (6A) €3.20; lndry rm; shop 7.5km; meals on
request; bar; BBQ; pool; games area; wifi; TV; 10% statics;
dogs €1; bus 1.5km; Eng spkn; adv bkg; quiet; ccard acc; red
long stay; INF/CKE/CCI. "Gd, peaceful 'retreat-type' site in
beautiful wooded area; friendly atmosphere; spacious pitches -
sun or shd." ♦ € 16.00   2010*

⊞ **ESPINHO** *B1* (11km S Coastal) *40.9400, -8.65833*
**Camping Os Nortenhos, Praia de Cortegaça, 3885-278
Cortegaça [256 752199; fax 256 755177; clube.nortenhos@
netvisao.pt; http://cccosnortenhos.cidadevirtual.pt]**
Fr Espinho foll rd thro Esmoriz twd Aveiro to Cortegaça vill.
Turn R to beach (Praia), site on L at beach. At T-junc with
pedestrian precinct in front turn L, take 2nd R then 2nd L.
Other rtes diff. V lge, pt shd; wc (cont); shwrs; EHU (6A); gas;
shop; snacks; bar; playgrnd; sand beach adj; entmnt; TV;
95% statics; no dogs; phone; bus 500m; poss cr; quiet; ccard
acc; CKE/CCI. "Ltd tourer pitches & poss v cr high ssn; facs
ltd at w/end; conv Porto; guarded at ent; sun shelters over
pitches." ♦ € 7.00   2009*

ESTELA see Povoa De Varzim *B1*

⊞ **EVORA** *C3* (3km SW Urban) *38.55722, -7.92583* **Camping
Orbitur Evora, Estrada das Alcaçovas, Herdade Esparragosa,
7005-206 Évora [(266) 705190; fax (266) 709830;
evora@orbitur.pt; www.orbitur.pt]** Fr N foll N18 & by-pass,
then foll sps for Lisbon rd at each rndabt or traff lts. Fr town
cent take N380 SW sp Alcaçovas, foll site sp, site in 2km. NB
Narr gate to site. Med, mkd pitch, hdstg, pt sl, pt shd; wc;
chem disp; mv service pnt; shwrs inc; EHU (5-15A) €3.50-4.60
(long lead poss req); gas; lndry; shop; supmkt 500m; snacks;
bar; playgrnd; pool; paddling pool; tennis; games area; wifi; TV
rm; dogs €2.20; phone; car wash; bus; rlwy stn 2km; Eng spkn;
adv bkg; quiet; ccard acc; red LS/long stay/snr citizens; red CKE/
CCI. "Conv town cent, Évora World Heritage site with wealth
of monuments & prehistoric sites nrby; cycle path to town; free
car parks just outside town walls; poss flooding some pitches
after heavy rain." ♦ € 35.60 (CChq acc)   2014*

⊞ **EVORAMONTE** C3 (6km NE Rural) 38.79276, -7.68701
Camping Alentejo, Novo Horizonte, 7100-300 Evoramonte [268 959283 or 936 799249 (mob); info@campingalentejo. com; www.campingalentejo.com] Fr E exit A6/E90 junc 7 Estremoz onto N18 dir Evora. Site in 8km at km 236. Sm, terr, pt shd; wc; chem disp; mv service pnt; shwrs inc; EHU (16A) €8; lndry rm; BBQ; horseriding; wifi; pool; dogs €1; bus adj; Eng spkn; adv bkg; quiet - some rd noise; CKE/CCI. "Excel site; gd birdwatching, v friendly and helpful owner." ♦ € 16.00   2012*

⊞ **FAO** B1 (1km S Urban/Coastal) 41.50780, -8.77830
Parque de Campismo de Barcelos, Rua São João de Deus, 4740-380 Fão [253 981777; fax 253 817786; contacto@ccc barcelos.com; www.cccbarcelos.com] Exit A28/IC1 junc 8 fr S or junc 9 fr N onto N13 thro Fão twd coast. Site sp off rd M501. Sm, pt shd; wc; chem disp; mv service pnt; baby facs; shwrs inc; EHU (3A) €3; gas; lndry; shop, snacks, bar high ssn; playgrnd; pool 5km; sand beach 800m; entmnt; TV; many statics; no dogs; bus 800m; quiet. "Gd site; Barcelos mkt Thurs." ♦ € 15.60   2009*

FERRAGUDO see Portimao B4

FIGUEIRA DA FOZ B2 (6km S Coastal) 40.14055, -8.86277
Camping Foz do Mondego, Cabedelo-Gala, 3080-661 Figueira da Foz [233 402740/2; fax 233 402749; foz.mondego@fcmportugal.com; www.fcmportugal.com] Fr S on N109 turn L bef bdge sp Gala. Foll site sp. V lge, mkd pitch; htd wc; chem disp; mv service pnt; baby facs; shwrs inc; EHU (2A) inc; gas; lndry; shop 2km; rest, snacks; bar; BBQ; playgrnd; sand beach adj; fishing; surfing; TV; 40% statics; dogs €0.50; phone; bus 1km; CKE/CCI. "Wonderful sea views but indus est adj; NH only." ♦ 14 Jan-13 Nov. € 16.40 2009*

⊞ **FIGUEIRA DA FOZ** B2 (7km S Coastal/Urban) 40.11861, -8.85666 **Camping ORBITUR-Gala, N109, Km 4, Gala, 3090-458 Figueira da Foz [233 431492; fax 233 431231; infogala@orbitur.pt; www.orbitur.pt]** Fr Figueira da Foz on N109 dir Leiria for 3.5km. After Gala site on R in approx 400m. Ignore sp on R 'Campismo' after long bdge. Lge, mkd pitch, hdstg, terr, shd; wc; chem disp; mv service pnt; shwrs; EHU (6-10A) €3-4; gas; lndry; shop; rest, snacks; bar; BBQ; playgrnd; htd pool high ssn; paddling pool; sand beach 400m; fishing 1km; tennis; games rm; wifi; entmnt; TV rm; many statics; dogs €1.50; phone; car wash; Eng spkn; adv bkg; red LS/long stay/ snr citizens; ccard acc; CKE/CCI. "Gd, renovated site adj busy rd; luxury san facs (furthest fr recep); excel pool." ♦ € 29.00 (CChq acc)   2011*

FOZ DO ARELHO see Caldas da Rainha B3

FUZETA see Olhao C4

GAFANHA DA NAZARE see Aveiro B2

GERES C1 (2km N Rural) 41.73777, -8.15805 **Vidoeiro Camping, Lugar do Vidoeiro, 4845-081 Gerês [253 391289; aderepg@mail.telepac.pt; www.adere-pg.pt]** NE fr Braga take N103 twds Chaves for 25km. 1km past Cerdeirinhas turn L twds Gerês onto N308. Site on L 2km after Caldos do Gerês. Steep rds with hairpins. Cross bdge & reservoir, foll camp sps. Lge, mkd pitch, hdstg, terr, pt shd; wc; chem disp; shwrs inc; EHU (12A) €1.20; lndry rm; rest, bar 500m; BBQ; pool 500m, lake sw 500m; dogs €0.60; phone; quiet. "Attractive, wooded site in National Park; gd, clean facs; thermal spa in Gerês; diff access for lge o'fits, mountain rd." ♦ 15 May-15 Oct. € 17.00   2013*

⊞ **GERES** C1 (14km NW Rural) 41.76305, -8.19111
Parque de Campismo de Cerdeira, Rue de Cerdeira 400, Campo do Gerês, 4840-030 Terras do Bouro [(253) 351005; fax (253) 353315; info@parquecerdeira.com; www.parquecerdeira.com] Fr N103 Braga-Chaves rd, 28km E of Braga turn N onto N304 at sp to Poussada. Cont N for 18km to Campo de Gerês. Site in 1km; well sp. V lge, shd; wc; chem disp; shwrs; EHU (5-10A) €3.90-4.90; gas; lndry service; rest; bar; shop; playgrnd; lake sw; TV rm; bike hire; fishing 2km; canoeing; few statics; dogs €3; bus 500m; entmnt; poss cr; quiet; Eng spkn; ccard acc; CKE/CCI. "Beautiful scenery; unspoilt area; fascinating old vills nrby & gd walking; ltd facs LS." ♦ € 30.70   2013*

⊞ **GOUVEIA** C2 (7km NE Rural) 40.52083, -7.54149
Camping Quinta das Cegonhas, Nabainhos, 6290-122 Melo [tel/fax 238 745886; cegonhas@cegonhas.com; www.cegonhas.com] Turn S at 114km post fr N17 Seia-Celorico da Beira. Site sp thro Melo vill. Sm, pt shd; wc; chem disp; mv service pnt; shwrs; EHU (6-10A) €3; lndry; shop 300m; rest, snacks; bar; playgrnd; pool; entmnt; games rm; guided walks; TV; dogs €1.10; bus 400m; Eng spkn; adv bkg; quiet; red long stay/ LS; CKE/CCI. "Vg, well-run, busy site in grnds of vill manor house; friendly Dutch owners; beautiful location conv Torre & Serra da Estrella; gd walks; highly rec." ♦ € 18.00   2013*

⊞ **GUARDA** C2 (2km W Urban) 40.53861, -7.27944 **Camp Municipal da Guarda, Avda do Estádio Municipal, 6300-705 Guarda [271 221200; fax 271 210025]** Exit A23 junc 35 onto N18 to Guarda. Foll sp cent & sports cent. Site adj sports cent off rndabt. Med, hdstg, sl, shd; wc (some cont, own san rec); chem disp (wc); shwrs inc; EHU (15A) €1.45; gas; lndry rm; shop; rest, snacks, bar high ssn; BBQ; playgrnd; pool 2km; TV; phone; bus adj; Eng spkn; poss noise fr rd & nrby nightclub; CKE/CCI. "Access to some pitches diff for c'vans, OK for m'vans; poss run down facs & site poss neglected low/mid ssn; walking dist to interesting town - highest in Portugal & poss v cold at night; music festival 1st week Sep." ♦ € 12.00 2014*

GUIMARAES B1 (6km SE Rural) 41.42833, -8.26861 **Camping Parque da Penha, Penha-Costa, 4800-026 Guimarães [tel/fax 253 515912 or 253 515085; geral@turipenha.pt; www.turipenha.pt]** Take N101 SE fr Guimarães sp Felgueiras. Turn R at sp for Nascente/Penha. Site sp. Lge, hdstg, pt sl, terr, shd; wc; shwrs inc; EHU (6A) €1.80; gas; shop; rest adj; snacks; bar; playgrnd; pool; fishing; no dogs; phone; wifi; bus 200m, teleferic (cable car) 200m; car wash; poss cr; Eng spkn; adv bkg; poss noisy; CKE/CCI. "Excel staff; gd san facs; lower terrs not suitable lge o'fits; densely wooded hilltop site; conv Guimarães World Heritage site European City of Culture 2012; cable car down to Guimaraes costs Euros 4.20 return." ♦ ltd. 1 Apr-30 Sep. € 10.40 2011*

GUIMARAES *B1* (32km W Rural) *41.46150, -8.01120*
Quinta Valbom, Quintã 4890-505 Ribas [351 253 653 048;
info@quintavalbom.nl; www.quintavalbom.nl]
Fr Guimaraes take A7 SE. Exit 11 onto N206 Fafe/Gandarela.
Turn R bef tunnel twds Ribas. Foll blue & red signs of campsite.
Med, mkd pitch, terr, pt shd; wc; shwrs inc; EHU (10A); lndry;
bar; BBQ; pool; wifi; dogs; bus 2km; twin axles; Eng spkn;
poss cr; adv bkg; quiet; CCI. "Very nice site; friendly Dutch
owners; quiet surroundings; lots of space in beautiful setting;
if driving c'van, park at white chapel and call campsite for their
4WD assistance up last bit of steep hill." ◆ ltd. 1 Apr-1 Oct.
€ 22.70   2014*

⊞ **IDANHA A NOVA** *C2* (10km NE Rural) *39.95027, -7.18777*
Camping ORBITUR-Barragem de Idanha-a-Nova, N354-1,
Km 8, Barragem de Idanha-a-Nova, 6060 Idanha-a-Nova
[(277) 202793; fax (277) 202945; infoidanha@orbitur.pt;
www.orbitur.pt] Exit IP2 at junc 25 sp Lardosa & foll sp
Idanha-a-Nova on N18, then N233, N353. Thro Idanha &
cross Rv Ponsul onto N354 to site. Avoid rte fr Castelo Branco
via Ladoeiro as rd narr, steep & winding in places. Lge, mkd
pitch, hdstg, terr, shd; wc; chem disp; mv service pnt; baby
facs; shwrs inc; EHU (6A) €3-4; gas; lndry; shop; rest, snacks;
bar; BBQ; playgrnd; htd pool; paddling pool; lake sw, fishing;
watersports 150m; tennis; games rm; wifi; entmnt; cab/sat TV;
10% statics; dogs €1.50; phone; car wash; Eng spkn; adv bkg;
quiet; red long stay/LS/snr citizens. "Uphill to town & supmkts;
hot water to shwrs only; pitches poss diff - a mover req; level
pitches at top of site; excel." ◆ € 29.40   2013*

ILHAVO see Aveiro *B2*

⊞ **LAGOS** *B4* (1km SW Urban/Coastal) *37.09469, -8.67218*
Parque de Campismo da Trindade, Rossio da Trindade,
8601-908 Lagos [282 763893; fax 282 762885; info@camping
trindade.com] Fr Faro on N125 app Lagos, foll sp for Centro;
drive 1.5km along front past BP stn, up hill to traff lts; turn L &
foll Campismo sp to L. Cont to traff island & foll to bottom of
hill, ent on R. Site adj football stadium. Sm, hdstg, terr, pt shd;
wc; own san facs; chem disp; shwrs inc; EHU (12A) €3.50; gas;
lndry (inc dryer); shop; rest, snacks; bar; playgrnd; pool 500m;
sand beach 500m (steep steps); dogs €1; phone; poss cr; Eng
spkn; rd noise; ccard acc; red long stay; CKE/CCI. "Gd beaches
& cliff walks; clean san facs; gd size m'van pitches; conv walk
into Lagos." ◆ € 16.70   2010*

⊞ **LAGOS** *B4* (7km W Coastal/Urban) *37.10111, -8.71777*
Camping ORBITUR-Valverde, Estrada da Praia da Luz,
Valverde, 8600-148 Lagos [214 857400 or 282 789211;
fax 214 857410; infovalverde@orbitur.pt; www.orbitur.pt]
Foll coast rd N125 fr Lagos to Sagres for 3km. Turn L at traff
lts sp Luz, site 2km on R, well sp. V lge, hdg/mkd pitch, hdstg,
terr, pt shd; wc; chem disp; mv service pnt; baby facs; shwrs
inc; EHU (6A) €3.50-4.60; gas; lndry (inc dryer); supmkt; rest,
snacks; bar; BBQ; playgrnd; pool; paddling pool; sand beach
3km; tennis; sports facs; games area; games rm; wifi; entmnt;
cab/sat TV; many statics; dogs €2; bus; car wash; Eng spkn;
adv bkg; quiet; ccard acc; red LS/long stay/snr citizens/Orbitur
card; CKE/CCI. "Well-run site on mildly sl grnd; v busy high
ssn, spacious LS; friendly staff; modern, clean san facs; pitches
on sandy grnd, access poss tight due trees; narr, busy rd to
lovely beach/town; poss muddy in wet weather." ◆ € 38.00
(CChq acc)   2011*

⊞ **LAGOS** *B4* (7km W Rural/Coastal) *37.10095, -8.73220*
Camping Turiscampo, N125 Espiche, 8600-109 Luz-Lagos
[282 789265; fax 282 788578; info@turiscampo.com;
www.turiscampo.com] Exit A22/IC4 junc 1 to Lagos then
N125 fr Lagos dir Sagres, site 3km on R. Lge, hdg/mkd pitch,
some hdstg, pt sl, terr, shd; htd wc; chem disp; mv service
pnt; baby facs; shwrs inc; EHU (6A) inc - extra for 10A; gas;
lndry (inc dryer); supmkt; rest, snacks; bar; BBQ; playgrnds;
pool; paddling pool; fitness cent; sand beach 2km; fishing
2.5km; tennis 2km; bike hire; games rm; games area; wifi;
entmnt; TV rm; 25% statics; dogs €1.50; phone; bus to
Lagos 100m; Eng spkn; adv bkg; quiet; ccard acc; red long
stay/LS/CKE/CCI. "Superb, well-run, busy site; v popular for
winter stays & rallies; all facs (inc excel pool) open all yr; gd
san facs; helpful staff; lovely vill, beach & views; varied &
interesting area, Luz worth visit; vg." ◆ € 39.00 (CChq acc)
SBS - E07   2014*

See advertisement

⊞ **LAMAS DE MOURO** *C1* (2km S Rural) *42.04166, -8.20833* **Camping Lamas de Mouro, 4960-170 Lamas de Mouro [(251) 466041; geral@camping-lamas.com**Este endereço de e-mail foi protegido contra spambots. Você deve habilitar o JavaScript para visualizá-lo.**; www.camping-lamas.com]** Fr N202 at Melgaco foll sp Peneda-Gerês National Park, cont R to rd sp Porta de Lamas de Mouro. Cont 1km past park info office, site on L in pine woods. Med, pt shd; wc; chem disp; mv service pnt; shwrs inc; EHU (10A) €3; lndry rm; shop; rest, snacks; bar; cooking facs; playgrnd; natural pool; dog €2; phone; bus 1km; poss cr; quiet; CKE/CCI. "Ideal for walking in National Park." € 17.00   2013*

LAVRA see Porto *B1*

⊞ **LISBOA** *B3* (17km SW Coastal) *38.65111, -9.23777* **Camping ORBITUR-Costa de Caparica, Ave Afonso de Albuquerque, Quinta de S. António, 2825-450 Costa de Caparica [212 901366 or 903894; fax 212 900661; infocaparica@orbitur.pt; www.orbitur.pt]** Take A2/IP7 S fr Lisbon; after Rv Tagus bdge turn W to Costa de Caparica. At end of rd turn N twd Trafaria, & site on L. Well sp fr a'strada. Lge, hdg/mkd pitch, terr, shd; wc; chem disp; mv service pnt; shwrs inc; EHU (6A) €3; gas; lndry (inc dryer); shop; rest, snacks; bar; BBQ; playgrnd; pool 800m; sand beach 1km; fishing; tennis; games rm; wifi; entmnt; TV; 75% statics; dogs €1.50; phone; car wash; bus to Lisbon; Eng spkn; adv bkg; some rd noise; ccard acc; red LS/long stay/snr citizens/Orbitur card; CKE/CCI. "Gd, clean, well run site; heavy traff into city; rec use free parking at Monument to the Discoveries & tram to city cent; ferry to Belém; ltd facs LS; pleasant, helpful staff." ♦ € 34.40 (CChq acc)   2012*

⊞ **LISBOA** *B3* (9km W Urban) *38.72472, -9.20805* **Parque Municipal de Campismo de Monsanto, Estrada da Circunvalação, 1400-061 Lisboa [(217) 628200; fax (217) 628299; info@lisboacamping.com; www.lisboacamping.com]** Fr W on A5 foll sp Parque Florestal de Monsanto/Buraca. Fr S on A2, cross toll bdge & foll sp for Sintra; join expressway, foll up hill; site well sp; stay in RH lane. Fr N on A1 pass airport, take Benfica exit & foll sp under m'way to site. Site sp fr all major rds. Avoid rush hrs! V lge, mkd pitch, hdstg, pt sl, terr, pt shd; htd wc (cont); chem disp; mv service pnt; 80% serviced pitches; baby facs; fam bthrm; shwrs inc; EHU (6-16A) inc; gas; lndry; shop; rest, snacks; bar; playgrnd; pool; sand beach 10km; tennis; bank; PO; car wash; entmnt; TV rm; 5% statics; dogs free; frequent bus to city; rlwy stn 3km; poss cr; Eng spkn; adv bkg; some rd noise; red LS; ccard acc; red CKE/CCI. "Well laid-out, spacious, guarded site in trees; ltd mv service pnt; take care hygiene at chem disp/clean water tap; facs poss badly maintained & stretched when site full; friendly, helpful staff; in high ssn some o'fits placed on sl forest area (quiet); few pitches take awning; excel excursions booked at TO on site." ♦ € 32.00   2013*

⊞ **LOURICAL** *B2* (5km SW Rural) *39.99149, -8.78880* **Campismo O Tamanco, Rua do Louriçal 11, Casas Brancas, 3105-158 Louriçal [tel/fax 236 952551; tamanco@me.com; www.campismo-o-tamanco.com]** S on N109 fr Figuera da Foz S twds Leiria foll sp at rndabt Matos do Corrico onto N342 to Louriçal. Site 800m on L. Med, hdg/mkd pitch, hdstg, pt shd; wc; chem disp; mv service pnt; baby facs; shwrs inc; EHU (6-16A) €2.25-3.50; gas; lndry (inc dryer); rest, café; bar; BBQ; htd pool; paddling pool; sand beach 5km; lake sw adj; wifi; 5% statics; dogs; bus 500m; twin axles; poss cr; Eng spkn; adv bkg; quiet; red LS/long stay; CKE/CCI. "Excel; friendly Dutch owners; chickens & ducks roaming site; superb mkt on Sun at Louriçal; a bit of real Portugal; gd touring base; mkd walks thro pine woods; v clean; relaxed; sm farm animal area." ♦ € 21.00   2014*

⊞ **LUSO** *B2* (1.5km NW Rural) *40.38222, -8.38583* **Camping Luso, N336, Pampilhosa, Quinta do Vale do Jorge, 3050-246 Luso [231 930916; fax 231 930917; info@orbitur.pt]** S fr Luso on N336, sp. Lge, hdstg, pt sl, pt shd; wc; chem disp; mv service pnt; shwrs inc; EHU (5-15A) €2.50; gas; lndry; shop; rest, snacks; bar; playgrnd; pool 1km; sand beach 35km; tennis; games rm; TV rm; some statics; dogs €1.30; car wash; adv bkg; Eng spkn; quiet; red LS/long stay/snr citizens; ccard acc; CKE/CCI. "Excel site in wooded valley; vg san facs; some sm pitches unsuitable for c'vans + awnings; internet in vill; sh walk to interesting spa town; conv Coimbra." ♦ € 25.00   2011*

MARTINCHEL see Tomar *B2*

⊞ **MEDA** *C2* (0.5km N Urban) *40.96972, -7.25916* **Parque de Campismo Municipal, Av. Professor Adriano Vasco Rodrigues, 6430 Mêda [(351) 925 480 500 or (351) 279 883 270; campismo@cm-meda.pt; www.cm-meda.pt/turismo/Paginas/Parque_Camsimo.aspx]** Head N fr cent of town, take 1st R, take 1st L & site on L within the Meda Sports Complex. Sm, hdstg, pt shd; wc; chem disp; mv service pnt; child/baby facs; shwrs; rest; pool; bar; snacks; wifi; Eng spkn. "Pt of the Municipal Sports Complex with facs avail; conv for town cent." ♦ ltd. € 11.50   2014*

MEDAS GONDOMAR see Porto *B1*

MELO see Gouveia *C2*

⊞ **MIRA** *B2* (3km NW Rural) *40.44728, -8.75723* **Camping Vila Caia, Travessa Da Carreira Do Tiro, Lagoa 3070-176 Mira [231 451524; fax 231 451861; vlcaia@portugalmail.com; www.vilacaia.com]** S fr Aveiro on N109 for 29km; at Mira take N334 for 5km. Site sp on R 500m W of Lagoa de Mira. Lge, hdstg, pt shd; wc (some cont); chem disp; mv service pnt; shwrs inc; EHU (4A) €3; gas; lndry; shop; rest, snacks; bar; playgrnd; pool; paddling pool; sand beach 3km; fishing; tennis; bike hire; entmnt; TV; some statics; dogs €1.30; phone; bus adj; site clsd Dec; Eng spkn; no adv bkg; quiet, but poss noisy entmnt high ssn; ccard acc; red LS; CKE/CCI. "Gd site." ♦ € 20.00   2011*

PORTUGAL

MIRA *B2* (7km NW Coastal/Urban) *40.44472, -8.79888*
Camping ORBITUR-Mira, Estrada Florestal 1, Km 2,
Dunas de Mira, 3070-792 Praia de Mira [231 471234;
fax 231 472047; infomira@orbitur.pt; www.orbitur.pt]
Fr N109 in Mira turn W to Praia de Mira, foll site sp. Lge, hdg
pitch, hdstg, shd; wc; chem disp; mv service pnt; shwrs inc;
EHU (5-15A) €3-4 (poss rev pol); gas; lndry (inc dryer); shop
(in ssn); rest, snacks, bar high ssn; playgrnd; pool 7km; sandy,
surfing beach & dunes 800m; fishing; boating; wifi; entmnt; TV
rm; 5% statics; dogs €1.50; phone; site clsd Dec; Eng spkn; adv
bkg; poss noisy w/end; red LS/long stay/snr citizens; ccard acc;
CKE/CCI. "Friendly, helpful staff; gd, clean, attractive site; excel
surfing beach nr; suitable for cycling; nature reserve opp site."
◆ 1 Jan-16 Oct. € 26.70   2011*

MIRANDA DO DOURO *D1* (2km W Rural) *41.49861,*
-6.28444 **Campismo Municipal Santa Lúzia, Rua do Parque**
de Campismo, 5210-190 Miranda do Douro [273 431273
or 430020; fax 273 431075; mirdouro@mail.telepac.pt;
www.cm-mdouro.pt] Fr Spain on ZA324/N221, cross dam
& thro town, site well sp. Do not enter walled town. Lge, pt
sl, terr, pt shd; wc; chem disp; shwrs inc; EHU (5A) €1.50;
shop, rest & 1km; snacks, bar; playgrnd; pool 300m; phone;
bus 500m; Eng spkn; quiet; CKE/CCI. "Simple, peaceful site;
interesting ent into N Portugal; old walled town; spectacular
rv gorge; boat trips; unrel opening dates." ◆ 1 Jun-30 Sep.
€ 9.50   2011*

MOGADOURO *D1* (1.6km SW Rural) *41.33527, -6.71861*
Parque de Campismo da Quinta da Agueira, Complexo
Desportivo, 5200-244 Mogadouro [279 340231 or 936-
989202 (mob); fax 279 341874; campismo@mogadouro.pt;
www.mogadouro.pt] Fr Miranda do Douro on N221 or
fr Bragança on IP2 to Macedo then N216 to Mogadouro. Site
sp adj sports complex. Lge, shd; wc; chem disp; mv service pnt;
shwrs inc; EHU (15A) €2; gas; lndry rm; shop 1km; rest 200m;
snacks; bar; BBQ; playgrnd; pool adj; waterslide; beach 15km;
tennis; car wash; entmnt; internet; TV; dogs €1.50; phone;
bus 300m; Eng spkn; adv bkg; quiet. "Brilliant site in lovely
area; value for money; steep hill to town; gd touring base." ◆
1 Apr-30 Sep. € 11.50   2013*

MONCARAPACHO see Olhao *C4*

⊞ **MONCHIQUE** *B4* (9km S Rural) *37.27672, -8.54390*
Parque Rural Caldas de Monchique, Barracão 190,
8550-213 Monchique [282 911502; fax 282 911503;
valedacarrasqueira@sapo.pt; www.valedacarrasqueira.com]
Fr S exit A22 N onto N266, site sp on R in 11km. Fr N on N266
dir Portimão, thro Monchique, site on L. Well sp. M'vans only.
Sm, mkd pitch, hdstg, unshd; wc; chem disp; mv service pnt; all
serviced pitches; shwrs inc; EHU (16A); lndry; bar; BBQ; pool;
dogs; no adv bkg; Eng spkn; quiet. "Excel, peaceful, scenic,
clean site; excel san facs; helpful staff; poss taking c'vans in
future." € 15.00   2009*

MONTALEGRE *C1* (10km S Rural) *41.75722, -7.81016*
Camping Penedones, 5470-235 Montalegre [276 510220;
info@montalegre.com; www.montalegrehotel.com]
Fr N103 turn S at sp for Hotel Montalegre, site in 1km on
lakeside. Well sp. Lge, some hdstg, pt shd; htd wc; chem
disp; mv service pnt; shwrs inc; EHU (6A) €2.10; lndry rm;
rest, snacks; bar; playgrnd; lake sw; 10% statics; bus; quiet.
"Beautiful situation; vg." 1 Apr-30 Sep. € 17.00   2010*

⊞ **MONTARGIL** *B3* (4km N Rural) *39.10083, -8.14472*
Camping ORBITUR, Baragem de Montargil, N2, 7425-017
Montargil [242 901207; fax 242 901220; infomontargil@
orbitur.pt; www.orbitur.pt] Fr N251 Coruche to Vimiero rd,
turn N on N2, over dam at Barragem de Montargil. Fr Ponte
de Sor S on N2 until 3km fr Montargil. Site clearly sp bet rd &
lake. Med, mkd pitch, hdstg, terr, pt shd; wc; chem disp; mv
service pnt; shwrs inc; EHU (6-10A) €3-4; gas; lndry; shop &
3km; rest, snacks; bar; BBQ; playgrnd; pool; paddling pool;
rv beach adj; boating; watersports; fishing; tennis; games rm;
wifi; entmnt; cab/sat TV; 60% statics; dogs €1.50; phone; car
wash; Eng spkn; adv bkg; some rd noise; ccard acc; red LS/long
stay/snr citizens; CKE/CCI. "Friendly site in beautiful area." ◆
€ 26.70   2011*

⊞ **NAZARE** *B2* (2km N Rural) *39.62036, -9.05630* **Camping**
Vale Paraíso, N242, 2450-138 Nazaré [262 561800;
fax 262 561900; info@valeparaiso.com; www.valeparaiso.
com] Site thro pine reserve on N242 fr Nazaré to Leiria. V lge,
mkd pitch, hdstg, terr, shd; wc (some cont); chem disp; mv
service pnt; baby facs; shwrs inc; EHU (4-10A) €3; gas; lndry
(inc dryer); supmkt; rest, snacks; bar; playgrnd; pools; paddling
pool; sand beach 2km; lake 1km; fishing; games area; games
rm; bike hire; wifi; TV rm; 20% statics; dogs €2; bus; site clsd
19-26 Dec; Eng spkn; adv bkg; quiet; ccard acc; red LS/long
stay; CKE/CCI. "Gd, clean site; well run; gd security; pitches
vary in size & price, & divided by concrete walls, poss not
suitable lge o'fits, bus outside gates to Nazare, exit down steep
hill." ◆ € 23.00   2011*

NAZARE *B2* (2km E Rural) *39.59777, -9.05611* **Camping**
ORBITUR-Valado, Rua dos Combatentes do Ultramar
2, EN8, Km 5, Valado, 2450-148 Nazaré-Alcobaca
[262 561111; fax 262 561137; infovalado@orbitur.pt;
www.orbitur.pt] Site on N of rd to Alcobaça & Valado (N8-4),
opp Monte de São Bartolomeu. Lge, mkd pitch, terr, sl, shd;
wc; chem disp; mv service pnt; shwrs inc; EHU (6A) €3-4; gas;
lndry; shop & 2km; rest, snacks; bar; BBQ; playgrnd; pool;
sand beach 1.8km; tennis; games rm; wifi; TV rm; 10% statics;
dogs €1.50; phone; car wash; Eng spkn; adv bkg; red LS/long
stay/snr citizens; ccard acc. "Pleasant site in pine trees; v soft
sand - tractor avail; helpful manager; visits to Fátima, Alcobaça,
Balhala rec." ◆ 1 Jan-16 Oct. € 25.60 (CChq acc)   2010*

⊞ **ODEMIRA** *B4* (13km W Rural) *37.60565, -8.73786*
Zmar Eco Camping Resort & Spa, Herdade A-de-Mateus,
N393/1, San Salvador, 7630-011 Odemira [(707) 200626
or (283) 690010; fax (283) 690014; info@zmar.eu;
www.zmar.eu] Fr N on A2 take IC33 dir Sines. Just bef ent
Sines take IC4 to Cercal (sp Sul Algarve) then foll N390/393 &
turn R dir Zambujeira do Mar, site sp. Med, mkd pitch, hdstg,
pt shd; wc; chem disp; mv service pnt; baby facs; fam bthrm;
sauna; shwrs inc; private bthrms avail; EHU (10A) inc; lndry;
shop; rest, snacks; bar; BBQ; cooking facs; playgrnd; 2 pools
(1 htd, covrd); paddling pool; sand beach 7km; tennis; bike
hire; games area; wellness cent; fitness rm; wifi; excursions;
entmnt; TV rm; 17% statics; Eng spkn; adv bkg; dogs €2.50;
twin-axles acc (rec check in advy); quiet; red LS. "Superb new
site 2009 (eco resort) with excel facs; in national park; vg
touring base." ◆ € 46.00 (4 persons) (CChq acc)   2013*

⊞ **ODIVELAS** *B3* (8km NE Rural) *38.18361, -8.10361*
**Camping Markádia, Barragem de Odivelas, 7920-999
Alvito [(284) 763141; fax (284) 763102; markadia@
hotmail.com; www.markadia.com]** Fr Ferreira do Alentejo
on N2 N twd Torrão. After Odivelas turn R onto N257 twd
Alvito & turn R twd Barragem de Odivels. Site in 7km, clearly
sp. Med, hdstg, pt sl, pt shd; wc; chem disp; mv service
pnt; shwrs inc; EHU (16A) inc; gas; lndry (inc dryer); shop;
rest, snacks; bar; playgrnd; pool 50m; paddling pool; sand
beach, lake sw 500m; boating; fishing; horseriding; tennis;
no dogs Jul-Aug; phone; car wash; adv bkg; v quiet; red LS/
CKE/CCI. "Beautiful, secluded site on banks of reservoir;
spacious pitches; gd rest; site lighting low but san facs well
lit; excel walking, cycling, birdwatching; wonderful." ♦ ltd.
€ 32.00   2013*

⊞ **OLHAO** *C4* (2km NE Rural) *37.03527, -7.82250*
**Camping Olhão, Pinheiros do Marim, 8700-912 Olhão
[289 700300; fax 289 700390 or 700391; parque.
campismo@sbsi.pt; www.sbsi.pt]** Turn S twd coast
fr N125 1.5km E of Olhão by filling stn. Clearly sp on S side
of N125, adj Ria Formosa National Park. V lge, hdg/mkd
pitch, pt sl, shd; wc; chem disp; mv service pnt; shwrs inc;
EHU (6A) €1.90; gas; lndry inc dryers; supmkt; rest; bar;
playgrnd; pool; paddling pool; beach 1.5km; tennis; games
rm; games area; bike hire; horseriding 1km; internet; wifi;
TV; 75% statics; dogs €1.60; phone; bus adj; rlwy stn 1.5km;
sep car park for some pitches; car wash; security guard; Eng
spkn; adv bkg; some rlwy noise; ccard acc; red long stay/LS;
CKE/CCI. "Pleasant, helpful staff; excel pool; gd san facs;
v popular long stay LS; many sm sandy pitches, some diff
access for lge o'fits; gd for cycling, birdwatching; ferry to
islands." ♦ € 24.00   2014*

See advertisement opposite

"Satellite navigation makes touring much easier"

Remember most sat navs don't know if
you're towing or in a larger vehicle – always
use yours alongside maps and site directions.

⊞ **OLHAO** *C4* (8km NE Rural) *37.07245, -7.79928* **Campismo
Casa Rosa, Apt 209 8700 Moncarapacho [(289) 794400 or
(9191) 73132 (mob); fax (289) 792952; casarosa@sapo.pt;
www.casarosa.eu.com]** Fr A22 (IP1) E twd Spain, leave at
exit 15 Olhão/Moncarapacho. At rndabt take 2nd exit dir
Moncarapacho. Cont past sp Moncarapacho Centro dir Olhão.
In 1km at Lagoão, on L is Café Da Lagoão with its orange
awning. Just past café is sp for Casa Rosa. Foll sp. Sm, hdstg,
terr, unshd; htd wc ltd; chem disp; shwrs inc; EHU (6A) inc; gas
3km; lndry; rest; pool; shgl beach 6km; rv sw 6km; sat TV, wifi;
dogs; Eng spkn; adv bkg; noise fr construction yard adj; CKE/
CCI. "Excel CL-type site adj holiday apartments; adults only;
helpful, friendly, Norwegian owners; evening meals avail; ideal
for touring E Algarve; conv Spanish border; rec; 30% dep req,
no refunds if leaving early; insufficient san facs, but still a gd
site; drinkable water taps." ♦ ltd. € 13.50   2013*

⊞ **OLHAO** *C4* (12km NE Rural) *37.09504, -7.77430* **Camping
Caravanas Algarve, Sitio da Cabeça Moncarapacho, 8700-
618 Moncarapacho [(289) 791669]**
Exit IP1/A22 sp Moncarapacho. In 2km turn L sp Fuzeta. At
traff lts turn L sp Fuzeta. In 1km. Turn R at site
sp. Site on L. Sm, hdstg, pt sl, unshd; wc; chem disp; shwrs
inc; EHU (6A) inc; lndry; shop, rest, snacks, bar 1.5km; sand
beach 4km; 10% statics; dogs; poss cr; Eng spkn; adv bkg;
quiet; 10% red CKE/CCI. "Situated on a farm in orange groves;
pitches ltd in wet conditions; gd, modern san facs; gd security;
Spanish border 35km; National Park Ria Formosa 4km; lovely
popular site." € 10.00   2013*

⊞ **OLHAO** *C4* (11km E Coastal/Urban) *37.05294, -7.74484*
**Parque Campismo de Fuzeta, 2 Rua do Liberdade, 8700-019
Fuzeta [289 793459; fax 289 794034; camping@jf-fuseta.pt]**
Fr N125 Olhão-Tavira rd, turn S at traff lts at Alfandanga sp
Fuzeta & foll sp to site. Lge, some hdstg, pt shd; wc; chem disp;
shwrs €0.25; EHU (6-10A) inc; gas; lndry; shop & 1km; rest
adj; snacks; bar; BBQ; playgrnd adj; sand beach adj; internet;
5% statics; dogs; phone; train 500m; Eng spkn; no adv bkg;
noise fr rd & adj bars; red long stay. "Pleasant staff; popular
with long-stay m'vanners; elec cables run across site rds; poss
flooding after heavy rain; clean san facs; gd security; attractive
area & fishing port." ♦ ltd. € 16.70   2010*

⊞ **OLIVEIRA DO HOSPITAL** *C2* (9km SE Rural) *40.34647,
-7.80747* **Parque de Campisom de São Gião, 3400-570
São Gião [238 691154; fax 238 692451]**
Fr N17 Guarda-Coimbra rd turn S almost opp N230 rd to
Oliveira do Hospital, dir Sandomil. Site on R in about 3km over
rv bdge. Lge, shd; wc; chem disp; shwrs; EHU (6A) €1.50; gas;
lndry; shop; rest, snacks; bar; BBQ; playgrnd; pool 7km; fishing;
phone; 50% statics; no dogs; bus adj; quiet. "Facs basic but
clean; working water mill; app/exit long, steep, narr, lane."
€ 10.50   2009*

⊞ **OLIVEIRA DO HOSPITAL** *C2* (10km NW Rural) *40.40550,
-7.93100* **Camping Quinta das Oliveiras (Naturist), Rua de
Estrada Nova, Andorinha, 3405-498 Travanca de Lagos
[962 621287; fax 235 466007; campismo.nat@sapo.pt;
www.quinta-das-oliveiras.com]** Fr Oliveira do Hospital foll
N230 & N1314 to Travanca de Lagos. Then take N502 twd
Midões. After 2km turn R on N1313 to Andorinha. Site on R
1.5km after Andorinha. Sm, pt sl, terr, pt shd; wc; chem disp;
shwrs inc; EHU (6A) €3.50; BBQ; playgrnd; pool; dogs €2; poss
cr; Eng spkn; adv bkg; quiet; red LS; INF card. € 19.00   2009*

⊞ **ORTIGA** *C3* (5km SE Rural) *39.48277, -8.00305* **Parque
Campismo de Ortiga, Estrada da Barragem, 6120-525
Ortiga [241 573464; fax 241 573482; campismo@cm-macao.
pt]** Exit A23/IP6 junc 12 S to Ortiga. Thro Ortiga & foll site
sp for 1.5km. Site beside dam. Sm, mkd pitch, hdstg, terr, pt
shd; wc; chem disp; shwrs inc; EHU (10A) €1.50; lndry; shop
1km; rest, snacks, bar adj; BBQ; playgrnd; lake sw 100m;
watersports; TV; 50% statics; dogs free; bus 1.5km; poss cr;
Eng spkn; quiet; red LS; CKE/CCI. "Lovely site in gd position."
♦ € 11.00   2013*

Camping Olhão ★★★ Open All Year

Tennis
Football
Bar
Sw. Pools
Restaurant
Bungalows
Mobilehomes

parque.campismo@sbsi.pt Tel. 351 289 700 300

Algarve - Portugal

PENACOVA *B2* (3km N Rural) *40.27916, -8.26805* **Camp Municipal de Vila Nova, Rua dos Barqueiros, Vila Nova, 3360-204 Penacova [239 477946; fax 239 474857; penaparque2@iol.pt]** IP3 fr Coimbra, exit junc 11, cross Rv Mondego N of Penacova & foll to sp to Vila Nova & site. Med, pt shd; wc; shwrs inc; EHU (6A) €1; shop 50m; rest 150m; snacks; bar; BBQ; playgrnd; rv sw 200m; fishing; bike hire; TV; no dogs; phone; bus 150m; Eng spkn; red CKE/CCI. "Open, attractive site." 1 Apr-30 Sep. € 11.00   2011*

PENELA *B2* (500m SE Rural) *40.02501, -8.38900* **Parque Municipal de Campismo de Panela, Rua do Convento de Santo Antonio, 3230-284 Penela [239 569256; fax 239 569400]** Fr Coimbra S on IC2, L at Condeixa a Nova, IC3 dir Penela. Thro vill foll sp to site. Sm, hstg, pt sl, terr, pt shd; wc; chem disp; shwrs €0.50; EHU (6A) €0.50; shop, rest, snacks, bar 200m; pool 500m; some statics; no dogs; bus adj; some traff noise; CKE/CCI. "Attractive sm town; restful, clean, well-maintained site." ♦ ltd. 1 Jun-30 Sep. € 4.50   2009*

⊞ **PENICHE** *B3* (1.5km NW Urban/Coastal) *39.36944, -9.39194* **Camping Peniche Praia, Estrada Marginal Norte, 2520 Peniche [262 783460; fax 262 784140; geral@peniche praia.pt; www.penichepraia.pt]** Travel S on IP6 then take N114 sp Peniche; fr Lisbon N on N247 then N114 sp Peniche. Site on R on N114 1km bef Peniche. Med, hdg/mkd pitch, hdstg, unshd; wc; chem disp; mv service pnt; shwrs inc; EHU (6A) inc; lndry; shop 1.5km; rest, snacks, bar high ssn; BBQ; playgrnd; covrd pool; paddling pool; sand beach 1.5km; games rm; bike hire; internet; entmnt; TV; dog €2.10; 30% statics; phone; bus 2km; car wash; poss cr; Eng spkn; adv bkg rec; red long stay/LS/CKE/CCI. "Vg site in lovely location; some sm pitches; rec, espec LS." € 18.00   2013*

POCO REDONDO see Tomar *B2*

PONTE DA BARCA *B1* (11km E Rural) *41.82376, -8.31723* **Camping Entre-Ambos-os-Rios, Lugar da Igreja, Entre-Ambos-os-Rios, 4980-613 Ponte da Barca [258 588361; fax 258 452450; aderepg@mail.telepac.pt; www.adere-pg.pt]** N203 E fr Ponte da Barca, pass ent sp for vill. Site sp N twd Rv Lima, after 1st bdge. Lge, pt sl, shd; wc; shwrs inc; EHU (6A) €1.20; gas; lndry rm; shop, rest 300m; snacks; bar; playgrnd; canoeing; fishing; entmnt; TV; dogs €0.60; phone; bus 100m; adv bkg; CKE/CCI. "Beautiful, clean, well run & maintained site in pine trees; well situated for National Park; vg rest." 15 May-30 Sep. € 18.00   2014*

⊞ **PORTIMAO** *B4* (7km SE Coastal) *37.11301, -8.51096* **Camping Ferragudo, 8400-280 Ferragudo [282 461121; fax 282 461355; cclferragudo@clubecampismolisboa.pt; www.clubecampismolisboa.pt]** Leave N125 at sp Ferraguda, turn L at traff lts at end of Parchal vill onto N539. Foll sp to site. V lge, terr, pt shd; wc (some cont); mv service pnt; shwrs inc; EHU (6A) inc; gas; lndry rm; shop; rest, snacks; bar; playgrnd; pool; sw & fishing 800m; entmnt; TV; 90% statics; no dogs; phone; bus 1km; v cr Jul/Aug; red LS; CKE/CCI. "Helpful staff; bus to Portimão at ent; shop/recep 1.5km fr pitches; unsuitable lge m'vans; housing bet site & beach." € 26.00   2010*

⊞ **PORTIMAO** *B4* (7km W Rural) *37.13500, -8.59027* **Parque Campismo de Alvor (Formaly da Dourada), R Serpa Pinto 8500-053 Alvor [tel/fax (282) 459178; info@campingalvor. com; www.campingalvor.com]** Turn S at W end of N125 Portimão by-pass sp Alvor. Site on L in 4km bef ent town. V lge, pt sl, terr, shd; wc; chem disp; shwrs free; EHU (6-16A) €3-5; gas; lndry; shop high ssn; rest, snacks; bar; playgrnd; pool; paddling pool; sand beach 1km; fishing; sports area; entmnt; TV rm; dogs €2.50; bus adj; poss noisy fr adjoining properties; red long stay/LS; CKE/CCI. "Friendly & helpful, family-run site; office poss unattended in winter, ltd facs & site untidy; excel rest; lovely town & beaches; site much improved, never untidy (2013); v welcoming; popular with wintering Brits." ♦ € 21.50   2013*

⊞ **PORTO** *B1* (17km N Coastal) *41.2675, -8.71972* **Camping ORBITUR-Angeiras, Rua de Angeiras, Matosinhos, 4455-039 Lavra [229 270571 or 270634; fax 229 271178; infoangeiras@orbitur.pt; www.orbitur.pt]** Fr ICI/A28 take turn-off sp Lavra, site sp at end of slip rd. Site in approx 3km - app rd potholed & cobbled. Lge, pt sl, shd; wc (some cont); chem disp; mv service pnt; shwrs inc; EHU (6A) €3-4 (check earth); gas; lndry (inc dryer); shop; rest, snacks; bar; BBQ; playgrnd; pool; paddling pool; sand beach 400m; tennis; fishing; games area; games rm; wifi; entmnt; cab/sat TV; 70% statics; dogs €1.50; phone; bus to Porto at site ent; car wash; Eng spkn; adv bkg; red LS/long stay/snr citizens; ccard acc; CKE/CCI. "Friendly & helpful staff; gd rest; gd pitches in trees at end of site but ltd space lge o'fits; ssnl statics all yr; fish & veg mkt in Matosinhos; excel new san facs (2015); vg pool." ♦ € 29.00   2015*

⊞ **PORTO** *B1* (32km SE Rural) *41.03972, -8.42666*
**Campidouro Parque de Medas, Lugar do Gavinho,
4515-397 Medas-Gondomar [224 760162; fax 224 769082;
geral@campidouro.pt]** Take N12 dir Gondomar off A1.
Almost immed take R exit sp Entre-os-Rios. At rndabt pick up
N108 & in approx 14km. Sp for Medas on R, thro hamlet &
forest for 3km & foll sp for site on R. Long, steep app. New
concrete access/site rds. Lge, mkd pitch, hdstg, terr, pt shd; wc;
chem disp; mv service pnt; serviced pitches; shwrs inc; EHU (3-
6A) €2.73 (poss rev pol); gas; lndry; shop, rest (w/end only LS);
bar; playgrnd; pool & paddling pool; rv sw, fishing, boating;
tennis; games rm; entmnt; TV rm; wifi; 90% statics; phone;
bus to Porto; poss cr; quiet; ccard acc; red CKE/CCI. "Beautiful
site on Rv Douro; helpful owners; gd rest; clean facs; sm level
area (poss cr by rv & pool) for tourers - poss noisy at night &
waterlogged after heavy rain; bus to Porto (just outside site) rec
as parking diff (ltd buses at w/end)." € 27.00   2014*

"There aren't many sites open at this time of year"

If you're travelling outside peak season
remember to call ahead to check site opening
dates – even if the entry says 'open all year'.

⊞ **PORTO** *B1* (9km SW Coastal/Urban) *41.10777, -8.65611*
**Camping ORBITUR-Madalena, Rua do Cerro 608, Praia da
Madalena, 4405-736 Vila Nova de Gaia [(227) 122520;
fax (227) 122534; infomadalena@orbitur.pt; www.orbitur.
pt]** Fr Porto ring rd IC1/A44 take A29 exit dir Espinho. In 1km
take exit slip rd sp Madalena opp Volvo agent. Watch for either
'Campismo' or 'Orbitur' sp to site along winding, cobbled rd
(beware campismo sp may take you to another site nrby). Lge,
terr, pt sl, pt shd; wc (some cont); chem disp; mv service pnt;
baby facs; shwrs inc; EHU (6A) €4.60; gas; lndry; shop; rest,
snacks, bar in ssn; BBQ; playgrnd; pool; paddling pool; sand
beach 250m; tennis; games area; games rm; wifi; entmnt; TV
rm; 40% statics; dogs €2.20; phone; bus to Porto; car wash;
Eng spkn; adv bkg; ccard acc; red LS/long stay/snr citizens; CKE/
CCI. "Site in forest; restricted area for tourers; slight aircraft
noise; some uneven pitches; poss ltd facs LS; excel bus to Porto
cent fr site ent - do not take c'van into Porto; facs in need of
refurb (2013)." ◆ € 29.00   2014*

⊞ **POVOA DE VARZIM** *B1* (12km N Coastal) *41.46277,
-8.77277* **Camping ORBITUR-Rio Alto, EN13, Km 13,
Lugar do Rio Alto, Estela, 4570-275 Póvoa de Varzim
[252 615699; fax 252 615599; inforioalto@orbitur.pt;
www.orbitur.pt]** Fr A28 exit Póvoa onto N13 N; turn L 1km N
of Estela at yellow Golf sp by hotel, in 2km (cobbles) turn R to
camp ent. V lge, some hdg/mkd pitch, unshd; wc; chem disp;
mv service pnt; baby facs; shwrs inc; EHU (5-15A) €3-4; gas;
lndry (inc dryer); shop; rest, snacks; bar; BBQ; playgrnd; pool
high ssn; sand beach 150m; tennis; games area; games rm;
golf adj; wifi; entmnt; cab/sat TV; 50% static/semi-statics; dogs
€1.50; phone; bus 2km; car wash; poss cr; Eng spkn; adv bkg;
poss cr; red LS/long stay/snr citizens; ccard acc; CKE/CCI. "Excel
facs; helpful staff; vg rest on site; direct access to vg beach
(steep sl); strong NW prevailing wind; excel touring base." ◆
€ 29.00 (CChq acc)   2011*

PRAIA DE MIRA see Mira *B2*

PRAIA DE QUIAIOS *B2* (1km W Coastal) *40.2200, -8.88666*
**Camping ORBITUR, Praia de Quiaios, 3080-515 Quiaios
[233 919995; fax 233 919996; infoquiaios@orbitur.pt;
www.orbitur.pt]** Fr N109 turn W onto N109-8 dir Quiaios,
foll sp 3km to Praia de Quiaios & site. Lge, some mkd pitch,
pt shd; wc; chem disp; mv service pnt; shwrs inc; EHU (10A)
€3-4; gas; lndry; supmkt; rest, snacks; bar; BBQ; playgrnd; pool
500m; sand beach 500m; tennis; bike hire; games rm; TV;
entmnt; 20% statics; dogs €1.50; phone; car wash; Eng spkn;
adv bkg; quiet; ccard acc; red LS/snr citizens/long stay; CKE/
CCI. "Interesting historical area; vg touring base; peaceful site;
hot water to shwrs only; care needed some pitches due soft
sand." ◆ 1 Jan-16 Oct. € 21.00   2010*

⊞ **QUARTEIRA** *C4* (2km E Coastal/Urban) *37.06722,
-8.08666* **Camping ORBITUR-Quarteira, Estrada da Fonte
Santa, Ave Sá Carneira, 8125-618 Quarteira [289 302826
or 302821; fax 289 302822; infoquarteira@orbitur.pt;
www.orbitur.pt]** Fr E & IP1/A22 take exit junc 12 at Loulé
onto N396 to Quarteira; in 8.5km at rndabt by g'ge L along
dual c'way. In 1km at traff lts fork R into site. No advance sp
to site. V lge, mkd pitch, pt sl, terr, pt shd; wc; chem disp;
mv service pnt; shwrs inc; EHU (6A) €3-4 (long lead req some
pitches); gas; lndry (inc dryer); supmkt 200m; rest, snacks; bar;
BBQ; playgrnd; pool; paddling pool; waterslide; sand beach
600m; tennis; games rm; wifi; entmnt; TV rm; 40% statics (tour
ops); dogs €2; phone; bus 50m; car wash; Eng spkn; adv bkg;
aircraft noise fr Faro; red LS/long stay/snr citizens; ccard acc;
CKE/CCI. "Lovely site; popular winter long stay; narr site rds &
tight turns; some o'hanging trees; some pitches diff lge o'fits;
gd san facs; caterpillar problem Jan-Mar; easy walk to town;
mkt Wed." ◆ € 30.00   2010*

ROSARIO see Alandroal *C3*

⊞ **SAGRES** *B4* (1km N Coastal) *37.02305, -8.94555* **Camping
ORBITUR-Sagres, Cerro das Moitas, 8650-998 Vila de
Sagres [282 624371; fax 282 624445; infosagres@orbitur.pt;
www.orbitur.pt]** On N268 to Cape St Vincent; well sp. Lge,
hdg/mkd pitch, hdstg, pt shd; wc; chem disp; mv service pnt;
shwrs inc; EHU (6-10A) €3-4; gas; lndry (inc dryer); shop; rest,
snacks; bar; BBQ; playgrnd; sand beach 2km; bike hire; games
rm; wifi; TV rm; dogs €1.50; car wash; Eng spkn; adv bkg;
quiet; red long stay/LS/snr citizens; ccard acc. "Vg, clean, tidy
site in pine trees; helpful staff; hot water to shwrs only; cliff
walks." ◆ € 25.60 (CChq acc)   2012*

SANTIAGO DO CACEM *B4* (17km NW Coastal) *38.10777,
-8.78690* **Camping Lagoa de Santo Andre, Campismo Lago
de Santo Andre, Vila Nova de Santo Andre [269 708550;
fax 269 708559]** Take N261 sp Melides out of town & foll
sps to Lagoa de Santo Andre to site on L of rd. On shore but
fenced off fr unsafe banks of lagoon. Med, pt sl, pt shd; wc;
shwrs inc; shop; EHU inc (4-6A); rest; bar; sw; fishing; boating;
ltd facs LS. 18 Jan-18 Dec. € 17.70   2014*

You can now fill in site reports online

PORTUGAL

⊞ **SANTO ANTONIO DAS AREIAS** *C3* (Rural) *39.40992, -7.34075* **Camping Asseiceira, Asseiceira, 7330-204 Santo António das Areias [tel/fax (245) 992940 or (960) 150352 (mob); gary-campingasseiceira@hotmail.com; www.campingasseiceira.com]** Fr N246-1 turn off sp Marvão/ Santo António das Areias. Turn L to Santo António das Areias then 1st R on ent town then immed R again, up sm hill to rndabt. At rndabt turn R then at next rndabt cont strt on. There is a petrol stn on R, cont down hill for 400m. Site on L. Sm, pt sl, pt shd; wc; chem disp; shwrs inc; EHU (10A) €4; gas 500m; shop, rest 1km; snacks; bar; pool; wifi; dogs free; bus 1km; quiet; CKE/CCI. "Attractive area; peaceful, well-equipped, remote site among olive trees; clean, tidy; gd for walking, birdwatching; helpful, friendly, British owners; excel san facs, maintained to a high standard; nr Spanish border; excel; ideal cent for walking, cycling, visit hilltop castle Marvao." ♦ ltd. Apr-Sep. € 15.00   2013*

SAO GIAO see Oliveira do Hospital *C2*

SAO JACINTO see Aveiro *B2*

⊞ **SAO MARCOS DA SERRA** *B4* (5km SE Rural) *37.3350, -8.3467* **Campismo Rural Quinta Odelouca, Vale Grande de Baixo, CxP 644-S, 8375-215 São Marcos da Serra [282 361718; info@quintaodelouca.com; www.quintaodelouca.com]** Fr N (Ourique) on IC1 pass São Marcos da Serra & in approx 2.5km turn R & cross blue rlwy bdge. At bottom turn L & at cont until turn R for Vale Grande (paved rd changes to unmade). Foll sp to site. Fr S exit A22 junc 9 onto IC1 dir Ourique. Pass São Bartolomeu de Messines & at km 710.5 turn L & cross blue rlwy bdge, then as above. Sm, terr, pt sl; wc; chem disp; baby facs; shwrs inc; EHU (10A) €2.10; lndry; shop 3km; rest 2km; bar; BBQ; pool; lake sw; wifi; dogs €1; Eng spkn; adv bkg; quiet; CKE/CCI. "Helpful, friendly Dutch owners; phone ahead bet Nov & Feb; beautiful views; gd walks; vg; v little shd; access via bad rd." € 18.00   2015*

"That's changed – Should I let The Club know?"

If you find something on site that's different from the site entry, fill in a report and let us know. See www.caravanclub.co.uk/europereport.

⊞ **SAO MARTINHO DO PORTO** *B2* (1.5km NE Coastal) *39.52280, -9.12310* **Parque de Campismo Colina do Sol, Serra dos Mangues, 2460-697 São Martinho do Porto [(262) 989764; fax (262) 989763; parque.colina.sol@clix.pt or geral@colinadosol.net; www.colinadosol.net]** Leave A8/IC1 SW at junc 21 onto N242 W to São Martinho, by-pass town on N242 dir Nazaré. Site on L. Lge, mkd pitch, hdstg, terr, pt shd; wc; chem disp; mv service pnt; shwrs inc; EHU (6A) €2.75; gas; lndry; shop high ssn; rest, snacks; bar; BBQ; playgrnd; pool; paddling pool; sand beach 2km; fishing; games area; games rm; TV; mob homes/c'vans for hire; dogs €1; phone; bus 2km; site clsd at Xmas; poss cr; Eng spkn; adv bkg; quiet; ccard acc; CKE/CCI. "Gd touring base on attractive coastline; gd walking, cycling; vg san facs; excel site; san facs a bit tired (2013), water v hot." ♦ € 30.50 (CChq acc)   2013*

⊞ **SAO PEDRO DE MOEL** *B2* (1km E Urban/Coastal) *39.75861, -9.02583* **Camping ORBITUR-São Pedro de Moel, Rua Volta do Sete, São Pedro de Moel, 2430 Marinha Grande [244 599168; fax 244 599148; infospedro@orbitur. pt; www.orbitur.pt]** Site at end of rd fr Marinha Grande to beach; turn R at 1st rndabt on ent vill. Site S of lighthouse. V lge, some hdg/mkd pitch, hdstg, pt terr, shd; wc; chem disp; mv service pnt; shwrs inc; EHU (6A) €3-4 (poss rev pol); gas; lndry; shop; rest, snacks; bar; BBQ; playgrnd; htd pool; paddling pool; waterslide; sand beach 500m (heavy surf); fishing; tennis; bike hire; games rm; wifi; entmnt; cab/sat TV; some statics; dogs €1.50; phone; car wash; poss cr; Eng spkn; adv bkg; quiet; red LS/long stay/snr citizens; ccard acc; CKE/CCI. "Friendly, well-run, clean site in pine woods; easy walk to shops, rests; gd cycling to beaches; São Pedro smart resort; ltd facs LS site in attractive area and well run." ♦ € 28.60 SBS - W18   2011*

SAO TEOTONIO *B4* (7km W Coastal) *37.52560, -8.77560* **Parque de Campismo da Zambujeira, Praia da Zambujeira, 7630-740 Zambujeira do Mar [(283) 961172 or (935) 682790; fax (283) 961320; campingzambujeira@gmail.com; www.campingzambujeira.com.sapo.pt]** S on N120 twd Lagos, turn W when level with São Teotónio on unclassified rd to Zambujeira. Site on L in 7km, bet vill. V lge, pt sl, pt shd; wc; chem disp; mv service pnt; shwrs inc; EHU (6-10A) €3.50; gas; shop, rest, snacks & bar high ssn; playgrnd; sand beach 1km; tennis; TV; dogs €4; phone; bus adj; Eng spkn; some rd noise; red LS/long stay. "Welcoming, friendly owners; in pleasant rural setting; hot water to shwrs only; sh walk to unspoilt vill with some shops & rest; cliff walks." 31Mar-31Dec. € 25.00   2013*

⊞ **SAO TEOTONIO** *B4* (11km W Coastal) *37.49497, -8.78667* **Camping Monte Carvalhal da Rocha, Praia do Carvalhal, 7630-569 S Teotónio [282 947293; fax 282 947294; geral@montecarvalhalr-turismo.com; www.montecarval haldarocha.com]** Turn W off N120 dir Brejão & Carvalhal; site in 4.5km. Site sp. Med, shd; wc; shwrs inc; EHU (16A) inc; gas; lndry; shop, rest, snacks, bar high ssn; BBQ; playgrnd; sand beach 500m; fishing; bike hire; TV; some statics; no dogs; phone; bus 2km; car wash; Eng spkn; adv bkg; quiet; ccard acc; red LS. "Beautiful area; friendly, helpful staff." € 26.00   2012*

SATAO *C2* (12km N Rural) *40.82280, -7.6961* **Camping Quinta Chave Grande, Rua do Barreiro 462, Casfreires, Ferreira d'Aves, 3560-043 Sátão [tel/fax 232 665552; info@chavegrande.com; www.chavegrande.com]** Leave IP5 Salamanca-Viseu rd onto N229 to Sátão, site sp in Satão - beyond Lamas. Med, terr, pt shd; wc; chem disp; baby facs; shwrs inc; EHU (6A) €3.50; gas; lndry; shop 3km; rest 3km; snacks; bar; playgrnd; pool; paddling pool; tennis; games area; games rm; internet; TV; dogs leashed €2.50; Eng spkn; quiet; red long stay. "Warm welcome fr friendly Dutch owners; gd facs; well organised BBQ's - friendly atmosphere; gd touring base; gd walks fr site; excel." 15 Mar-31 Oct. € 20.50   2013*

⊞ **SERPA** *C4* (1km SW Urban) *37.94090, -7.60404* **Parque Municipal de Campismo Serpa, Rua da Eira São Pedro, 7830-303 Serpa [284 544290; fax 284 540109]** Fr IP8 take 1st sp for town; site well sp fr most dirs - opp sw pool. Do not ent walled town. Med, pt sl, pt shd; wc; chem disp; shwrs inc; EHU (6A) €1.25; gas; lndry; shop 200m; rest, snacks, bar 50m; BBQ; daily mkt 500m; supmkt nr; pool adj; rv sw 5km; 20% statics; dogs; phone; wifi; adv bkg; some rd noise; no ccard acc; CKE/CCI. "Popular gd site; simple, high quality facs; interesting, historic town." ♦ € 10.00   2014*

⊞ **SESIMBRA** *B3* (2km SW Coastal) *38.43580, -9.11658* **Camp Municipal Forte do Cavalo, Porto de Abrigo, 2970 Sesimbra [212 288508; fax 212 288265; geral@cm-sesimbra.pt; www.cm-sesimbra.pt]** Fr Lisbon S on A2/IP7 turn S onto N378 to Sesimbra. Turn R immed after town ent sp Campismo & Porto. Fork R again sp Porto; L downhill at traff lts to avoid town cent. Turn R at sea front to site by lighthouse. Steep uphill app. V lge, pt sl, terr, shd; wc; shwrs inc; EHU (6A) €2.15; gas; shop, rest 1km; snacks, bar 500m; BBQ; playgrnd; beach 800m; fishing; boating; no dogs; phone; bus 100m; poss cr; Eng spkn; no adv bkg; quiet; CKE/CCI. "Pitches ltd for tourers; gd views; lovely, unique fishing vill; castle worth visit; unrel opening dates (poss not open until Jun) - phone ahead." € 13.00   2010*

⊞ **SETUBAL** *B3* (5km W Coastal) *38.50299, -8.92909* **Parque de Campismo do Outão, Estrada de Rasca, 2900-182 Setúbal [265 238318; fax 265 228098]** Fr Setúbal take coast rd W twd Outão, site on L. V lge, mkd pitch, hdstg, pt shd; wc (some cont); chem disp; shwrs inc; EHU (5A) inc; gas; shop; rest; bar; playgrnd; sand beach adj; 90% statics; dogs €1.50; poss cr; Eng spkn; some rd noise; ccard acc; red LS; red CKE/CCI. "Few pitches for tourers; hdstg not suitable for awning; vacant static pitches sm & have kerb." ♦ € 20.00   2010*

⊞ **TAVIRA** *C4* (5km E Rural/Coastal) *37.14506, -7.60223* **Camping Ria Formosa, Quinta da Gomeira, 8800-591 Cabanas-Tavira [tel/fax 281 328887; info@camping riaformosa.com; www.campingriaformosa.com]** Fr spain onto A22 take exit junc 17 (bef tolls) Fr N125 turn S at Conceição dir 'Cabanas Tavira' & 'Campismo'. Cross rlwy line & turn L to site, sp. V lge, mkd pitch, hdstg, terr, pt shd; htd wc; chem disp; mv service pnt; baby facs; shwrs inc; EHU (16A) €3; gas; lndry (inc dryer); shop; rest, snacks, bar; BBQ; playgrnd; pool; paddling pool; bike hire; sand beach 1.2km; games area; wifi; TV rm; dogs €2; bus 100m; train 100m; car wash; Eng spkn; adv bkg; quiet; ccard acc; red long stay/CKE/CCI. "Excel, comfortable site; friendly, welcoming owner & staff; vg, modern san facs; various pitch sizes; cycle path to Tavira, excel facs." ♦ € 23.00   2014*

⊞ **TOCHA** *B2* (7km W Coastal) *40.32777, -8.84027* **Camping Praia da Tocha, Rua dos Pescadores, Nossa Sra da Tocha, Praia da Tocha, 3060-691 Tocha [231 447112; tocha@cacampings.com; www.cacampings.com]** Fr N or S on N109, turn W onto N335 to Praia da Tocha, site sp. Med, pt shd; wc; chem disp; baby facs; shwrs; EHU (4-6A) €1.85; gas; lndry (inc dryer); shop; rest, snacks, bar high ssn; playgrnd; sand beach 200m; watersports; bike hire; internet; TV rm; dogs €1.55; phone; bus adj; Eng spkn; adv bkg; quiet; CKE/CCI. "Well-maintained, pleasant site; helpful staff." ♦ € 12.00   2009*

TOMAR *B2* (9km NE Rural) *39.63833, -8.33694* **Camping Pelinos, Casal das Aboboreiras, 2300-093 Tomar [249 301814; pelinos1@hotmail.com; www.campingpelinos.com]** N fr Tomar on N110, turn R to Calçadas at traff lts opp g'ge, foll site sp. Steep descent to site. Sm, terr, pt shd; wc; shwrs inc; EHU (10A) €2; lndry; rest, snacks; bar; BBQ (winter only); playgrnd; pool; lake sw, watersports, fishing 7km; TV; dogs; phone; bus 100m; Eng spkn; adv bkg; quiet; red LS; CKE/CCI. "Owner will assist taking o'fits in/out; vg." 15 Feb-15 Oct. € 11.50   2010*

⊞ **TOMAR** *B2* (11km E Rural) *39.62538, -8.32166* **Camping Redondo, Rua do Casal Rei 6, 2300-035 Poço Redondo [tel/fax 249 376421; info@campingredondo.co.uk; www.campingredondo.com]** Fr N or S on N110, take IC3 for Tomar, then take exit at km97 Castelo do Bode/Tomar, dir Junceira. Foll site sp (red hearts) for 7km. Steep drop at site ent. Sm, pt sl, pt shd; wc; chem disp; mv service pnt; baby facs; shwrs inc; EHU (6A) €2-2.30; lndry; shop 2km; rest, snacks; bar; BBQ; playgrnd; pool; waterslide; lake beach 4.5km; sat TV; few statics; dogs €1; phone; bus; poss cr; Eng spkn; adv bkg; red LS; CKE/CCI. "Due steep drop at ent, site owner can tow c'vans out; peaceful site; friendly, helpful owners; excel walking area." € 13.60   2010*

TOMAR *B2* (15km SE Rural) *39.53963, -8.31895* **Camping Castelo do Bode, 2200 Martinchel [241 849262; fax 241 849244; castelo.bode@fcmportugal.com]** S fr Tomar on N110, in approx 7km L onto N358-2 dir Barragem & Castelo do Bode. Site on L in 6km immed after dam; sh, steep app to ent. Med, mkd pitch, hdstg, terr, pt shd; wc (some cont); chem disp; shwrs inc; EHU (6A) inc; supmkt 6km; rest, snacks 2km; bar; playgrnd; lake sw adj; boating; fishing; dogs €0.60; phone; bus to Tomar 1km; no adv bkg; quiet; CKE/CCI. "Site on edge of 60km long lake with excel watersports; old san facs, but clean; helpful staff; lge car park on ent Tomar - interesting town." ♦ 13 Jan-11 Nov. € 12.00   2011*

⊞ **TOMAR** *B2* (1km NW Urban) *39.60694, -8.41027* **Campismo Parque Municipal, 2300-000 Tomar [249 329824; fax 249 322608; camping@cm-tomar.pt; www.cm-tomar.pt]** Fr S on N110 foll sp to town cent at far end of stadium. Fr N (Coimbra) on N110 turn R immed bef bdge. Site well sp fr all dirs. Med, mkd pitch, pt shd; htd wc; chem disp; mv service pnt; baby facs; shwrs inc; EHU (10A) €1.40; lndry rm; shop, rest, snacks, bar in town; BBQ; playgrnd; pool adj; wifi; TV; dogs; phone adj; Eng spkn; adv bkg; quiet; red LS; ccard acc; CKE/CCI. "Useful base for touring Alcobaca, Batalha & historic monuments in Tomar; conv Fatima; Convento de Cristo worth visit; vg, popular, improved site; lovely walk to charming rvside town; easy access for lge vehicle, sh walk thro gdns to Knights Templar castle; free wifi nr recep; camp entry ticket gives free access to adj pool; v helpful, friendly staff." € 19.00   2014*

TRAVANCA DE LAGOS see Oliveira do Hospital *C2*

⊞ **VAGOS** *B2* (6km W Rural) *40.55805, -8.74527* **Camping ORBITUR-Vagueira, Rua do Parque de Campismo, 3840-254 Gafanha da Boa-Hora [234 797526; fax 234 797093; infovagueira@orbitur.pt; www.orbitur.pt]**
Fr Aveiro take N109 S twd Figuera da Foz. Turn R in Vagos vill. After 6km along narr poor rd, site on R bef reaching Vagueira vill. V lge, mkd pitch, shd; wc; chem disp; mv service pnt; baby facs; shwrs inc; EHU (6-16A) €3-4; gas; lndry; supmkt, rest, bar high ssn; playgrnd; pool 1km; sand beach 1.5km; fishing 1km; tennis; games area; games rm; bike hire; wifi; entmnt; 90% statics; dogs €1.50; bus 500m; Eng spkn; adv bkg; quiet; ccard acc; red LS/snr citizens; CKE/CCI. "V pleasant & well-run; friendly staff; poss diff access to pitches for lge o'fits; areas soft sand; gd touring base." ◆ € 21.00   2010*

VALVERDE see Lagos *B4*

⊞ **VIANA DO CASTELO** *B1* (4.6km S Coastal/Urban) *41.67888, -8.82583* **Camping ORBITUR-Viana do Castelo, Rua Diogo Álvares, Cabedelo, 4935-161 Darque [258 322167; fax 258 321946; infoviana@orbitur.pt; www.orbitur.pt]**
Exit IC1 junc 11 to W sp Darque, Cabedelo, foll sp to site in park. Lge, mkd pitch, pt sl, shd; wc; chem disp; mv service pnt; shwrs inc; EHU (5-15A) inc; gas; lndry; shop; rest, snacks; bar; BBQ; playgrnd; htd pool; lge sand beach adj; surfing; fishing; wifi; entmnt; TV; dogs €2.20; phone; car wash; Eng spkn; adv bkg; red LS/long stay/snr citizens; ccard acc; CKE/CCI. "Site in pine woods; friendly staff; gd facs; plenty of shd; major festival in Viana 3rd w/end in Aug; lge mkt in town Fri; sm passenger ferry over Rv Lima to town high ssn; Santa Luzia worth visit." ◆ 23 Mar-30 Sep. € 38.00   2013*

⊞ **VIANA DO CASTELO** *B1* (4.6km S Coastal) *41.67908, -8.82324* **Parque de Campismo Inatel do Cabedelo, Avda dos Trabalhadores, 4900-164 Darque [258 322042; fax 258 331502; pc.cabedelo@inatel.pt; www.inatel.pt]**
Exit IC1 junc 11 to W sp Darque, Cabedelo, foll sp to site. Lge, mkd pitch, hdstg, pt sl, pt shd; wc (some cont); shwrs inc; EHU (6A) inc; gas; lndry; shop high ssn; snacks; bar; sand beach adj; entmnt; 30% statics; no dogs; phone; bus 100m; site clsd mid-Dec to mid-Jan; adv bkg; quiet; CKE/CCI. "V secure; gd for children; hourly ferry to Viana; spacious pitches under pines; poss poor facs LS & in need of refurb." ◆ € 12.50   2009*

⊞ **VILA DO BISPO** *B4* (11km SE Coastal/Rural) *37.07542, -8.83133* **Quinta dos Carriços (Part Naturist), Praia de Salema, 8650-196 Budens [282 695201; fax 282 695122; quintacarrico@oninet.pt; www.quintadoscarricos.com]**
Take N125 out of Lagos twd Sagres. In approx 14km at sp Salema, turn L & again immed L twd Salema. Site on R 300m. Lge, pt terr (tractor avail), pt shd; htd wc; chem disp; mv service pnt; shwrs €0.75; EHU (6-10A) €3.90 (metered for long stay); gas; lndry; shop; rest, snacks; bar; playgrnd; pool 1km; sand beach 1.5km; golf 1km; TV; 8% statics; dogs €2.45; phone; bus; Eng spkn; adv bkg (ess high ssn); noise fr adj quarry; ccard acc; red long/CKE/CCI. "Naturist section in sep valley; apartments avail on site; ltd pitches for lge o'fits; friendly Dutch owners; tractor avail to tow to terr; area of wild flowers in spring; beach 30 mins walk; buses pass ent for Lagos, beach & Sagres; excel." ◆ € 28.00   2012*

⊞ **VILA FLOR** *C1* (3km SW Rural) *41.29420, -7.17180* **Camp Municipal de Vila Flor, Barragem do Peneireiro, 5360-303 Vila Flor [278 512350; fax 278 512380; cm.vila.flor@mail. telepac.pt; www.cm-vilaflor.pt]** Site is off N215, sp fr all dirs. V bumpy app rd - 12km. V lge, terr, pt shd; wc; chem disp (wc); shwrs inc; EHU (16A) €1.50; gas; lndry rm; shop; snacks; bar; BBQ; playgrnd; pool adj; tennis adj; TV rm; 10% statics; dogs; phone; clsd 2300-0700 (1800-0800 LS); poss v cr; adv bkg; noisy high ssn; CKE/CCI. "Friendly staff; access to pitches diff." ◆ ltd. € 9.40   2010*

VILA NOVA DE CACELA see Vila Real de Santo Antonio *C4*

VILA NOVA DE GAIA see Porto *B1*

⊞ **VILA NOVA DE MILFONTES** *B4* (1km N Coastal) *37.73194, -8.78277* **Camping Milfontes, Apartado 81, 7645-300 Vila Nova de Milfontes [(283) 996140; fax (283) 996104; reservas@campingmilfontes.com; www.campingmilfontes.com]** S fr Sines on N120/IC4 for 22km; turn R at Cercal on N390 SW for Milfontes on banks of Rio Mira; clear sp. V lge, hdg/mkd pitch, pt shd; wc; chem disp; mv service pnt; shwrs inc; EHU (6A) €3 (long lead poss req); gas; lndry; shop; supmkt & mkt 5 mins walk; rest, snacks, bar high ssn; playgrnd; sand beach 800m; TV; many statics; phone; bus 600m; poss cr; quiet; ccard acc; red CKE/CCI. "Pitching poss diff for lge o'fits due trees & statics; nr fishing vill at mouth Rv Mira with beaches & sailing on rv; pleasant site." ◆ € 27.00   2013*

VILA REAL *C1* (1km NE Urban) *41.30361, -7.73694* **Camping Vila Real, Rua Dr Manuel Cardona, 5000-558 Vila Real [259 324724]** On IP4/E82 take Vila Real N exit & head S into town. Foll 'Centro' sp to Galp g'ge; at Galp g'ge rndabt, turn L & in 30m turn L again. Site at end of rd in 400m. Site sp fr all dirs. Lge, pt sl, terr, pt shd; wc; chem disp; baby facs; shwrs inc; EHU (6A) €2; gas; sm shop adj; rest, snacks; bar; BBQ; playgrnd; pool complex adj; tennis; 10% statics; dogs; phone; bus 150m; poss cr; red CKE/CCI. "Conv upper Douro; gd facs ltd when site full; gd mkt in town; Lamego well worth a visit." ◆ 1 Mar-30 Nov. € 16.00   2011*

⊞ **VILA REAL DE SANTO ANTONIO** *C4* (14km W Rural) *37.18649, -7.55003* **Camping Caliço Park, Sitio do Caliço, 8900-907 Vila Nova de Cacela [281 951195; fax 281 951977; transcampo@mail.telepac.pt]** On N side of N125 Vila Real to Faro rd. Sp on main rd & in Vila Nova de Cacela vill, visible fr rd. Lge, some hdstg, terr, pt sl, shd; wc; chem disp; shwrs inc; EHU (6A) €2.80; gas; lndry (inc dryer); shop; rest, snacks; bar; playgrnd; pool; sand beach 4km; bike hire; wifi; many statics; dogs €1.60; phone; bus/train 2km; Eng spkn; adv bkg; noisy in ssn & rd noise; ccard acc; red long stay/LS; CKE/CCI. "Friendly staff; not suitable for m'vans or tourers in wet conditions - ltd touring pitches & poss diff access; gd NH." € 17.00   2010*

VILAR DE MOUROS see Caminha *B1*

ZAMBUJEIRA DO MAR see Sao Teotonio *B4*

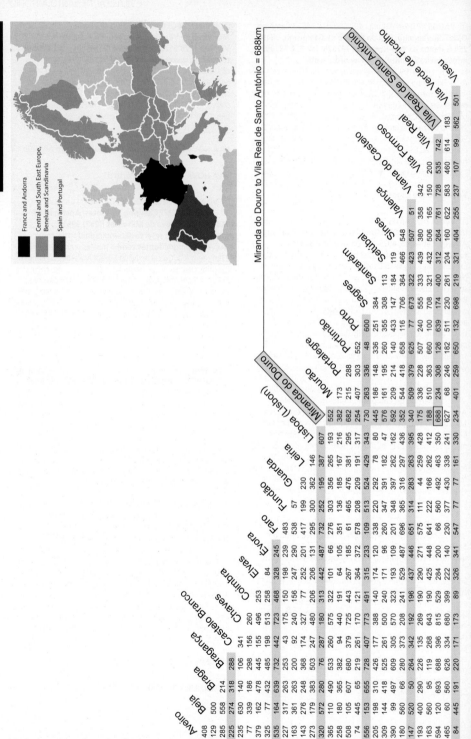

France and Andorra

Central and South East Europe, Benelux and Scandinavia

Spain and Portugal

Miranda do Douro to Vila Real de Santo António = 688km

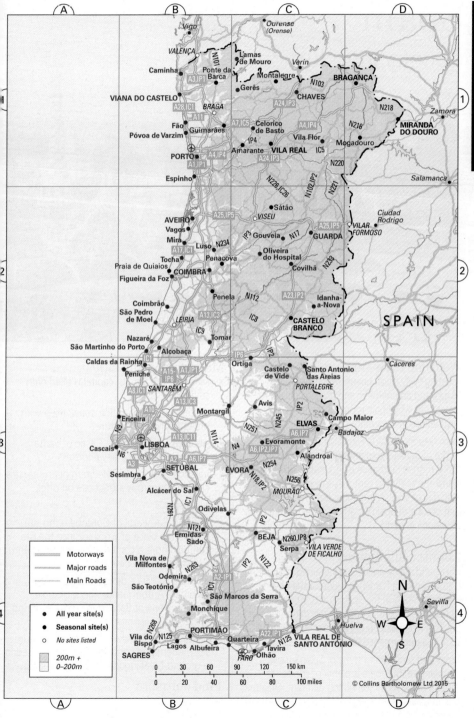

Spain
Country Introduction

Barcelona

Welcome to Spain

Boasting lively cities, beautiful beaches, a rich history and an energetic and diverse culture, it's easy to see why Spain is one of the most popular destinations in the world.

From Gaudi's Sagrada Familia in the bustling centre of Barcelona to ancient monuments in the rocky, rugged landscape of Andalusia, Spain has a landscape spanning centuries to explore. After a long day of sightseeing, what better way to relax that on one of Spain's many beaches, with a glass of Sangria in hand.

Country highlights

Music and dance are deeply ingrained in Spanish culture, and the flamenco is one of the best loved examples of the Spanish arts. Known for its distinctive flair and passion, this dance is now popular worldwide, but there is nowhere better to soak in a performance than in its homeland.

Tapas and sangria and some of Spain's most popular fare, but there is plenty of choice for those looking to try something different. Orxata is a refreshing drink made of tigernuts, water and sugar, and is served ice-cold in the summer.

Major towns and cities

- Madrid – this vibrant capital is filled with culture.
- Barcelona – a city on the coast, filled with breathtaking architecture.
- Alicante – home to the Castle of Santa Barbara, a huge medieval fortress.
- Valencia – set on the Mediterranean sea, this city has numerous attractions on offer.

Attractions

- Mosque-Cathedral of Córdoba – this site has been a place of worship since the 8th century and is a combination of Islamic and Christian art and design.
- Sagrada Familia – designed by Catalan architect, Antoni Gaudí, this incredible basilica is one of Barcelona's most enduring symbols.
- Guggenheim Museum, Bilbao – a museum for modern and contemporary art, housed in a ground-breaking 20th century building.

Find out more

www.spain.info
Tel: (0)9 13 43 35 00 Spain Tourist Office

Country Information

Population (approx): 47.7 million

Capital: Madrid (population approx 3.2 million)

Area: 510,000 sq km (inc Balearic & Canary Islands)

Bordered by: Andorra, France, Portugal

Terrain: High, rugged central plateau, mountains to north and south

Climate: Temperate climate; hot summers, cold winters in the interior; more moderate summers and cool winters along the northern and eastern coasts; very hot summers and mild/warm winters along the southern coast

Coastline: 4,964km

Highest Point (mainland Spain): Mulhacén (Granada) 3,478m

Languages: Castilian Spanish, Catalan, Galician, Basque

Local Time: GMT or BST + 1, i.e. 1 hour ahead of the UK all year

Currency: Euros divided into 100 cents; £1 = €1.42, €1 = £0.71 (September 2015)

Emergency numbers: Police 092; Fire brigade 080; Ambulance (SAMUR) 061. Operators speak English. Civil Guard 062. All services can be reached on 112.

Public Holidays 2016: Jan 1, 6; Mar 25; May 1; Aug 15; Oct 12; Nov 1; Dec 6 (Constitution Day), 8, 25.

Several other dates are celebrated for fiestas according to region. School summer holidays stretch from mid June to mid September.

Camping and Caravanning

There are more than 1,200 campsites in Spain with something to suit all tastes – from some of the best and biggest holiday parks in Europe, to a wealth of attractive small sites offering a personal, friendly welcome. Most campsites are located near the Mediterranean, especially on the Costa Brava and Costa del Sol, as well as in the Pyrenees and other areas of tourist interest. Campsites are indicated by blue road signs. In general pitch sizes are small at about 80 square metres.

Many popular coastal sites favoured for long winter stays may contain tightly packed pitches with long-term residents putting up large awnings, umbrellas and other structures. Many sites allow pitches to be reserved from year to year, which can result in a tight knit community of visitors who return every year.

If you're planning to stay on sites in the popular coastal areas between late spring and October, or in January and February, it is advisable to arrive early in the afternoon or to book in advance.

Although many sites claim to be open all year, if you're planning a visit out of season, always check first. It is common for many 'all year' sites to open only at weekends during the winter and facilities may be very limited.

Motorhomes

A number of local authorities now provide dedicated or short stay areas for motorhomes called 'Áreas de Servicio'.

For details see the websites www.lapaca.org or www.viajarenautocaravana.com for a list of regions and towns in Spain and Andorra which have at least one of these areas.

It is rare that yours will be the only motorhome staying on such areas, but take sensible precautions and avoid any that are isolated.

Some motorhome service points are situated in motorway service areas. Use these only as a last resort and do not be tempted to park overnight. The risk of a break-in is high.

Recent visitors to tourist areas on Spain's Mediterranean coast report that the parking of motorhomes on public roads and, in some instances, in public parking areas, may be prohibited in an effort to discourage 'wild camping'. Specific areas where visitors have encountered this problem include Alicante, Dénia, Palamós and the Murcian coast. Police are frequently in evidence moving parked motorhomes on and it is understood that a number of owners of motorhomes have been fined for parking on sections of the beach belonging to the local authority.

Cycling

There are around 2,200km of dedicated cycle paths in Spain, many of which follow disused railway tracks. Known as 'Vias Verdes' (Green Ways), they can be found mainly in northern Spain, in Andalucia, around Madrid and inland from the Costa Blanca. For more information see the website www.viasverdes.com or contact the Spanish Tourist Office.

There are cycle lanes in major cities and towns such as Barcelona, Bilbao, Córdoba, Madrid, Seville and Valencia. Madrid alone has over 100km of cycle lanes.

It is compulsory for all cyclists, regardless of age, to wear a safety helmet on all roads outside built-up areas. At night, in tunnels or in bad weather, bicycles must have front and rear lights and reflectors. Cyclists must also wear a reflective waistcoat or jacket while riding at night on roads outside built-up areas (to be visible from a distance of 150 metres) or when visibility is bad.

Strictly speaking, cyclists have right of way when motor vehicles wish to cross their path to turn left or right, but great care should always be taken. Do not proceed unless you are sure that a motorist is giving way.

Transportation of Bicycles
Spanish regulations stipulate that motor cycles or bicycles may be carried on the rear of a vehicle providing the rack to which the motorcycle or bicycle is fastened has been designed for the purpose. Lights, indicators, number plate and any signals made by the driver must not be obscured and the rack should not compromise the carrying vehicle's stability.

An overhanging load, such as bicycles, should not extend beyond the width of the vehicle but may exceed the length of the vehicle by up to 10% (up to 15% in the case of indivisible items). The load must be indicated by a 50cm x 50cm square panel with reflective red and white diagonal stripes. These panels may be purchased in the UK from motorhome or caravan dealers/accessory shops. There is currently no requirement for bicycle racks to be certified or pass a technical inspection.

If you are planning to travel from Spain to Portugal please note that slightly different official regulations apply. These are set out in the Portugal Country Introduction.

Electricity and Gas

The current on campsites should be a minimum of 4 amps but is usually more. Plugs have two round pins. Some campsites do not yet have CEE connections.

Campingaz is widely available in 901 and 907 cylinders. The Cepsa Company sells butane gas cylinders and regulators, which are available in large stores and petrol stations, and the Repsol Company sells butane cylinders at their petrol stations throughout the country.

French and Spanish butane and propane gas cylinders are understood to be widely available in Andorra.

Entry Formalities

Holders of valid British and Irish passports are permitted to stay up to three months without a visa. EU residents planning to stay longer are required to register in person at the Oficina de Extranjeros (Foreigners Office) in their province of residence or at a designated police station. You will be issued with a certificate confirming that the registration obligation has been fulfilled.

Dogs must be kept on a lead in public places and in a car they should be isolated from the driver by means of bars, netting or kept in a transport carrier.

Medical Services

Basic emergency health care is available free from practitioners in the Spanish National Health Service on production of a European Health Insurance Card (EHIC). Some health centres offer both private and state provided health care and you should ensure that staff are aware which service you require. In some parts of the country you may have to travel some distance to attend a surgery or health clinic operating within the state health service. It is probably quicker and more convenient to use a private clinic, but the Spanish health service will not refund any private health care charges.

In an emergency go to the casualty department (urgencias) of any major public hospital. Urgent treatment is free in a public ward on production of an EHIC; for other treatment you will have to pay a proportion of the cost.

Medicines prescribed by health service practitioners can be obtained from a pharmacy (farmacia) and there will be a charge unless you are an EU pensioner. In all major towns there is a 24 hour pharmacy.

Dental treatment is not generally provided under the state system and you will have to pay for treatment.

The Department of Health has two offices in Spain to deal with health care enquiries from British nationals visiting or residing in Spain. These are at the British Consultate offices in Alicante and Madrid, Tel: 965-21 60 22 or 917-14 63 00.

Opening Hours

Banks – Mon-Fri 8.30am/9am-2pm/2.30pm, Sat 9am-1pm (many banks are close Sat during summer).

Museums – Tue-Sat 9am/10am-1pm/2pm & 3pm/4pm-6pm/8pm. Sun 9am/10am-2pm; most close Mon.

Post Offices – Mon-Fri 8.30am-2.30pm & 5pm-8pm/8.30pm, Sat 9am/9.30am-1pm/1.30pm.

Shops – Mon-Sat 9am/10am-1.30pm/2pm & 4pm/4.30pm-8pm/8.30pm; department stores and shopping centres don't close for lunch.

Safety and Security

Street crime exists in many Spanish towns and holiday resorts. Keep all valuable personal items such as cameras or jewellery out of sight. The authorities have stepped up the police presence in tourist areas but nevertheless, you should remain alert at all times (including at airports, train and bus stations, and even in supermarkets and their car parks).

In Madrid particular care should be taken in the Puerto de Sol and surrounding streets, including the Plaza Mayor, Retiro Park and Lavapies, and on the metro. In Barcelona this advice also applies to the Ramblas, Monjuic, Plaza Catalunya, Port Vell and Olympic Port areas. Be wary of approaches by strangers either asking directions or offering any kind of help. These approaches are sometimes ploys to distract attention while they or their accomplices make off with valuables and/or take note of credit card numbers for future illegal use.

A few incidents have been reported of visitors being approached by a bogus police officer asking to inspect wallets for fake euro notes, or to check their identity by keying their credit card PIN into an official looking piece of equipment carried by the officer. If in doubt ask to see a police officer's official identification, refuse to comply with the request and offer instead to go to the nearest police station.

Spanish police have set up an emergency number for holidaymakers with English speaking staff and offering round the clock assistance - call 902 10 2 112. An English speaking operator will take a statement about the incident, translate it into Spanish and fax or email it to the nearest police station. You still have to report in person to a police station if you have an accident, or have been robbed or swindled, and the helpline operator will advise you where to find the nearest one.

Motorists travelling on motorways – particularly those north and south of Barcelona, in the Alicante region, on the M30, M40 and M50 Madrid ring roads and on the A4 and A5 – should be wary of approaches by bogus policemen in plain clothes travelling in unmarked cars. In all traffic related matters police officers will be in uniform. Unmarked vehicles will have a flashing electronic sign in the rear window reading 'Policía' or 'Guardia Civil' and will normally have blue flashing lights incorporated into their headlights, which are activated when the police stop you.

In non-traffic related matters police officers may be in plain clothes but you have the right to ask to see identification. Genuine officers may ask you to show them your documents but would not request that you hand over your bag or wallet. If in any doubt, converse through the car window and telephone the police on 112 or the Guardia Civil on 062 and ask them for confirmation that the registration number of the vehicle corresponds to an official police vehicle.

On the A7 motorway between the La Junquera and Tarragona toll stations be alert for 'highway pirates' who flag down foreign registered and hire cars (the latter have a distinctive number plate), especially those towing caravans. Motorists are sometimes targeted in service areas, followed and subsequently tricked into stopping on the hard shoulder of the motorway. The usual ploy is for the driver or passenger in a passing vehicle, which may be 'official-looking', to suggest by gesture that there is something seriously wrong with a rear wheel or exhaust pipe. If flagged down by other motorists or a motorcyclist in this way, be extremely wary. Within the Barcelona urban area thieves may also employ the 'punctured tyre' tactic at traffic lights.

In instances such as this, the Spanish Tourist Office advises you not to pull over but to wait until you reach a service area or toll station. If you do get out of your car when flagged down take care it is locked while you check outside, even if someone is left inside. Car keys should never be left in the ignition.

Spain shares with the rest of Europe an underlying threat from terrorism. Attacks could be indiscriminate and against civilian targets in public places including tourist areas.

The Basque terrorist organisation, ETA, has been less active in recent years and on 20 October 2011 announced a "definitive cessation of armed activity." However you should always be vigilant and follow the instructions of local police and other authorities.

Coast guards operate a beach flag system to indicate the general safety of beaches for swimming: red – danger / do not enter the water; yellow – take precautions; green – all clear. Coast guards operate on most of the popular beaches, so if in doubt, always ask. During the summer months stinging jellyfish frequent Mediterranean coastal waters.

There is a risk of forest fires during the hottest months and you should avoid camping in areas with limited escape routes. Take care to avoid actions that could cause a fire, e.g. disposal of cigarette ends.

Respect Spanish laws and customs. Parents should be aware that Spanish law defines anyone under the age of 18 as a minor, subject to parental control or adult supervision. Any unaccompanied minor coming to the attention of the local authorities for whatever reason is deemed to be vulnerable under the law and faces being taken into a minors centre for protection until a parent or suitable guardian can be found.

British Embassy & Consulate-General
TORRE ESPACIO, PASEO DE LA CASTELLANA 259D
28046 MADRID
Tel: 917 14 63 00
www.ukinspain.fco.gov.uk/en/

British Consulate-General
AVDA DIAGONAL 477-13, 08036 BARCELONA
Tel: 933 66 02 00

There are also British Consulates in Alicante and Málaga.

Irish Embassy
IRELAND HOUSE, PASEO DE LA CASTELLANA 46-4
28046 MADRID
Tel: 914 36 40 93
www.embassyofireland.es

There are also Irish Honorary Consulates in Alicante, Barcelona, Bilbao, El Ferrol, Málaga and Seville.

Customs Regulations
Alcohol and Tobacco
Under Spanish law the number of cigarettes which may be exported from Spain is set at eight hundred. Anything above this amount is regarded as a trade transaction which must be accompanied by the required documentation. Travellers caught with more than 800 cigarettes face seizure of the cigarettes and a large fine.

Documents
Driving Licence
The British EU format pink driving licence is recognised in Spain. Holders of the old style all green driving licence are advised to replace it with a photocard version. Alternatively, the old style licence may be accompanied by an International Driving Permit available from the AA, the RAC or selected Post Offices.

Passport
Visitors must be able to show some form of identity document if requested to do so by the police and you should carry your passport or photocard licence at all times.

Vehicle(s)

When driving in Spain it is compulsory at all times to carry your driving licence, vehicle registration certificate (V5C), insurance certificate and MOT certificate (if applicable). Vehicles imported by a person other than the owner must have a letter of authority from the owner.

Money

All bank branches offer foreign currency exchange, as do many hotels and travel agents.

The major credit cards are widely accepted as a means of payment in shops, restaurants and petrol stations. Smaller retail outlets in non commercial areas may not accept payments by credit card – check before buying. When shopping carry your passport or photocard driving licence if paying with a credit card as you will almost certainly be asked for photographic proof of identity.

Keep a supply of loose change as you could be asked for it frequently in shops and at kiosks.

Motoring in Spain

Drivers should take particular care as driving standards can be erratic, e.g. excessive speed and dangerous overtaking, and the accident rate is higher than in the UK. Pedestrians should take particular care when crossing roads (even at zebra crossings) or walking along unlit roads at night.

Accidents

The Central Traffic Department runs an assistance service for victims of traffic accidents linked to an emergency telephone network along motorways and some roads. Motorists in need of help should ask for 'auxilio en carretera' (road assistance). The special ambulances used are connected by radio to hospitals participating in the scheme.

It is not necessary to call the emergency services in case of light injuries. A European Accident Statement should be completed and signed by both parties and, if conditions allow, photos of the vehicles and the location should be taken. If one of the drivers involved does not want to give his/her details, the other should call the police or Guardia Civil.

Alcohol

The maximum permitted level of alcohol is 50 milligrams in 100 millilitres of blood, i.e. less than in the UK (80 milligrams) and it reduces to 30 milligrams for drivers with less than two years experience, drivers of vehicles with more than 8 passenger seats and for drivers of vehicles over 3,500kg. After a traffic accident all road users involved have to undergo a breath test. Penalties for refusing a test or exceeding the legal limit are severe and may include immobilisation of vehicles, a large fine and suspension of your driving licence. This limit applies to cyclists as well as drivers of private vehicles.

Breakdown Service

The motoring organisation, Real Automóvil Club de España (RACE), operates a breakdown service and assistance may be obtained 24 hours a day by telephoning the national centre in Madrid on 915 93 33 33. After hearing a message in Spanish press the number 1 to access the control room where English is spoken.

RACE's breakdown vehicles are blue and yellow and display the words 'RACE Asistencia' on the sides. This service provides on the spot minor repairs and towing to the nearest garage. Charges vary according to type of vehicle and time of day, but payment for road assistance must be made in cash.

Essential Equipment

Lights

Dipped headlights is now compulsory for all vehicles on all roads at night and in tunnels. Bulbs are more likely to fail with constant use and you are recommended to carry spares.

Dipped headlights must be used at all times on 'special' roads, e.g. temporary routes created at the time of road works such as the hard shoulder, or in a contra-flow lane.

Headlight flashing is only allowed to warn other road users about an accident or a road hazard, or to let the vehicle in front know that you intend to overtake.

Reflective Jacket/Waistcoat

If your vehicle is immobilised on the carriageway outside a built-up area at night, or in poor visibility, you must wear a reflective jacket or waistcoat when getting out of your vehicle. This rule also applies to passengers who may leave the vehicle, for example, to assist with a repair.

Reflectors/Marker Boards for Caravans

Any vehicle or vehicle combination, i.e. car plus caravan over 12 metres in length, must display at the rear of the towed vehicle two aluminium boards. These must have a yellow centre with a red outline, must be reflective and comply with ECE70 standards. These must be positioned between 50cm and 150cm off the ground and must be 500mm x 250mm or 565mm x 200mm in size. Alternatively a single horizontal reflector may be used measuring 1300mm x 250mm or 1130mm x 200mm.

To buy these aluminium marker boards (under Spanish regulations stickers are not acceptable) contact www.hgvdirect.co.uk, tel: 0845 6860008. Contact your local dealer or caravan manufacturer for advice on fitting them to your caravan.

Warning Triangles

All vehicles must carry warning triangles. They should be placed 50 metres behind and in front of broken down vehicles.

Child Restraint System

Children under the age of 12 years old and under the height of 1.35m must use a suitable child restraint system adapted for their size and weight (this does not apply to taxis in urban areas). Children measuring more than 1.35m in height may use an adult seatbelt.

Fuel

Credit cards are accepted at most petrol stations, but you should be prepared to pay cash if necessary in remote areas.

LPG (Autogas) can be purchased from some Repsol filling stations. Details of approximately 33 sales outlets throughout mainland Spain can be found on www.mylpg.eu.

Mountain Passes and Tunnels

Some passes are occasionally blocked in winter following heavy falls of snow. Check locally for information on road conditions.

Parking

Parking regulations vary depending on the area of a city or town, the time of day, the day of the week, and whether the date is odd or even. In many towns parking is permitted on one side of the street for the first half of the month and on the other side for the second half of the month. Signs marked '1-15' or '16-31' indicate these restrictions.

Yellow road markings indicate parking restrictions. Parking should be in the same direction as the traffic flow in one way streets or on the right hand side when there is two way traffic. Illegally parked vehicles may be towed away or clamped but, despite this, you will frequently encounter double and triple parking.

In large cities parking meters have been largely replaced by ticket machines and these are often located in areas known as 'zona azul', i.e. blue zones. The maximum period of parking is usually one and a half hours between 8am and 9pm. In the centre of some towns there is a 'zona O.R.A.' where parking is permitted for up to 90 minutes against tickets bought in tobacconists and other retail outlets.

In many small towns and villages it is advisable to park on the edge of town and walk to the centre, as many towns can be difficult to navigate due to narrow, congested streets.

Madrid

In Madrid, there is a regulated parking zone where parking spaces are shown by blue or green lines (called SER). Parking is limited to 1 or 2 hours in these areas for visitors and can be paid by means of ticket machines of by mobile phone.

Pedestrians

Jaywalking is not permitted. Pedestrians may not cross a road unless a traffic light is at red against the traffic, or a policeman gives permission. Offenders may be fined.

Priority and Overtaking

As a general rule traffic coming from the right has priority at intersections. When entering a main road from a secondary road drivers must give way to traffic from both directions. Traffic already on a roundabout (i.e. from the left) has priority over traffic joining it. Trams and emergency vehicles have priority at all times over other road users and you must not pass trams that are stationary while letting passengers on or off.

Motorists must give way to cyclists on a cycle lane, cycle crossing or other specially designated cycle track. They must also give way to cyclists when turning left or right.

You must use your indicators when overtaking. If a vehicle comes up behind you signalling that it wants to overtake and if the road ahead is clear, you must use your right indicator to acknowledge the situation.

Roads

There are approximately 16,200km of highways and dual carriageways. Roads marked AP (autopista) are generally toll roads and roads marked A (autovía) or N (nacional) are dual carriageways with motorway characteristics – but not necessarily with a central reservation – and are toll-free. In recent years some major national roads have been upgraded to Autovías and, therefore, have two identifying codes or have changed codes, e.g. the N-I from Madrid to Irún near the French border is now known as the A1 or Autovía del Norte. Autovías are often as fast as autopistas and are generally more scenic.

Roads managed by regional or local authorities are prefixed with the various identification letters such as C, CV, GR, L or T.

All national roads and roads of interest to tourists are generally in good condition, are well signposted, and driving is normally straightforward. Hills often tend to be longer and steeper than in parts of the UK and some of the coastal roads are very winding, so traffic flows at the speed of the slowest lorry.

As far as accidents are concerned the N340 coast road, especially between Málaga and Fuengirola, is notorious, as are the Madrid ring roads, and special vigilance is necessary.

Road humps are making an appearance on Spanish roads and recent visitors report that they may be high, putting low stabilisers at risk.

Andorra

The main road to Barcelona from Andorra is the C14/C1412/N141b via Ponts and Calaf. It has a good surface and avoids any high passes. The N260 along the south side of Andorra via Puigcerda and La Seo de Urgel also has a good surface.

Road Signs and Markings

Road signs conform to international standards. Lines and markings are white. Place names may appear both in standard (Castilian) Spanish and in a local form, e.g. Gerona/Girona, San Sebastián/Donostia, Jávea/Xàbio, and road atlases and maps usually show both.

You may encounter the following signs:

Spanish	English Translation
Carretera de peaje	Toll road
Ceda el paso	Give way
Cuidado	Caution
Curva peligrosa	Dangerous bend
Despacio	Slow
Desviación	Detour
Dirección única	One-way street
Embotellamiento	Traffic jam
Estacionamiento prohibido	No parking
Estrechamiento	Narrow lane
Gravillas	Loose chippings/gravel
Inicio	Start
Obras	Roadworks
Paso prohibido	No entry
Peligro	Danger
Prioridad	Right of way
Salida	Exit
Todas direcciones	All directions

Many non motorway roads have a continuous white line on the near (verge) side of the carriageway. Any narrow lane between this line and the side of the carriageway is intended primarily for pedestrians and cyclists and not for use as a hard shoulder.

A continuous line also indicates 'no stopping' even if it is possible to park entirely off the road and it should be treated as a double white line and not crossed except in a serious emergency. If your vehicle breaks down on a road where there is a continuous white line along the verge, it should not be left unattended as this is illegal and an on the spot fine may be levied.

Many road junctions have a continuous white centre line along the main road. This line must not be crossed to execute a left turn, despite the lack of any other 'no left turn' signs. If necessary, drive on to a 'cambio de sentido' (change of direction) sign to turn.

Traffic police are keen to enforce both the above regulations.

Watch out for traffic lights which may be mounted high above the road and hard to spot. The international three colour traffic light system is used in Spain. Green, amber and red arrows are used on traffic lights at some intersections.

Speed Limits

	Open Road (km/h)	Motorway (km/h)
Car Solo	90-100	120
Car towing caravan/trailer	70-80	80
Motorhome under 3500kg	80-90	100
Motorhome 3500-7500kg	80	90

In built-up areas speed is limited to 50km/h (31mph) except where signs indicate a lower limit. Reduce your speed to 20km/h (13mph) in residential areas. On motorways and dual carriageways in built-up areas, speed is limited to 80km/h (50mph) except where indicated by signs.

Outside built-up areas motorhomes under 3500kg are limited to 100km/h (62mph) and those over 3500kg are limited to 90km/h (56 mph) on motorways and dual carriageways. On other main roads motorhomes under 3500kg are limited to 80-90km/h (50-56mph) and those over 3500kg are limited to 80km/h (50mph).

It is prohibited to own, transport or use radar detectors.

Foreign Registered Vehicles

When a radar camera detects a foreign registered vehicle exceeding the speed limit, a picture of the vehicle and its number plate will be sent not only to the relevant traffic department, but also to the nearest Guardia Civil mobile patrol. The patrol will then stop the speeding vehicle and impose an on the spot fine which non-residents must pay immediately, otherwise the vehicle will be confiscated until the fine is paid.

This is to prevent offenders flouting the law and avoiding paying their fines, as pursuing them is proving costly and complicated for the Spanish authorities.

Towing

Motorhomes are prohibited from towing a car unless the car is on a special towing trailer with all four wheels of the car off the ground.

Any towing combination in excess of 10 metres in length must keep at least 50 metres from the vehicle in front except in built-up areas, on roads where overtaking is prohibited, or where there are several lanes in the same direction.

Traffic Jams

Roads around the large cities such as Madrid, Barcelona, Zaragoza, Valencia and Seville are extremely busy on Friday afternoons when residents leave for the mountains or coast, and again on Sunday evenings when they return. The coastal roads along the Costa Brava and the Costa Dorada may also be congested. The coast road south of Torrevieja is frequently heavily congested as a result of extensive holiday home construction.

Summer holidays extend from mid June to mid September and the busiest periods are the last weekend in July, the first weekend in August and the period around the Assumption holiday in mid August.

Traffic jams occur on the busy AP7 from the French border to Barcelona during the peak summer holiday period. An alternative route now exists from Malgrat de Mar along the coast to Barcelona using the C32 where tolls are lower than on the AP7.

The Autovía de la Cataluña Central (C25) provides a rapid east-west link between Gerona and Lleida via Vic, Manresa and Tàrrega. There is fast access from Madrid to La Coruña in the far north-west via the A6/AP6.

Information on road conditions, traffic delays, etc can be found on http://infocar.dgt.es/etraffic.

Violation of Traffic Regulations

The police are empowered to impose on the spot fines. Visiting motorists must pay immediately otherwise a vehicle will be confiscated until the fine is paid. An official receipt should be obtained. An appeal may be made within 15 days and there are instructions on the back of the receipt in English. RACE can provide legal advice – tel: 900 100 901.

Motorways

The Spanish motorway system has been subject to considerable expansion in recent years with more motorways under construction or planned. The main sections are along the Mediterranean coast, across the north of the country and around Madrid. Tolls are charged on most autopistas but many sections are toll-free, as are autovias. Exits on autopistas are numbered consecutively from Madrid. Exits on autovias are numbered according to the kilometre point from Madrid.

Many different companies operate within the motorway network, each setting their own tolls which may vary according to the time of day and classification of vehicles.

Avoid signposted 'Via T' lanes showing a circular sign with a white capital T on a blue background where toll collection is by electronic device only. Square 'Via T' signs are displayed above mixed lanes where other forms of payment are also accepted.

Rest areas with parking facilities, petrol stations and restaurants or cafés are strategically placed and are well signposted. Emergency telephones are located at 2km intervals.

Motorway signs near Barcelona are confusing. To avoid the city traffic when heading south, follow signs for Barcelona, but the moment signs for Tarragona appear follow these and ignore Barcelona signs.

Touring

A fixed price menu or 'menú del dia' invariably offers good value. Service is generally included in restaurant bills but a tip of approximately €1 per person up to 10% of the bill is appropriate if you have received good service. Smoking is not allowed in indoor public places, including bars, restaurants and cafés.

Spain is one of the world's top wine producers, enjoying a great variety of high quality wines of which cava, rioja and sherry are probably the best known. Local beer is low in alcohol content and is generally drunk as an aperitif to accompany tapas.

Perhaps due to the benign climate and long hours of sunshine, Spaniards tend to get up later and stay out later at night than their European neighbours. Out of the main tourist season and in 'non-touristy' areas it may be difficult to find a restaurant open in the evening before 9pm.

Taking a siesta is still common practice, although it is now usual for businesses to stay open during the traditional siesta hours.

Spain's many different cultural and regional influences are responsible for the variety and originality of fiestas held each year. Over 200 have been classified as 'of interest to tourists' while others have gained international fame, such as La Tomatina mass tomato throwing battle held each year in August in Buñol near Valencia. A full list of fiestas can be obtained from the Spanish Tourist Office, www.spain.info/uk or from provincial tourist offices. In addition, every year each town celebrates its local Saint's Day which is always a very happy and colourful occasion.

The Madrid Card, valid for one, two or three days, gives free use of public transport, free entry to various attractions and museums, including the Prado, Reina Sofia and Thyssen-Bornemisza collection, as well as free tours and discounts at restaurants and shows. You can buy the card from www.madridcard.com or by visiting the City Tourist Office in Plaza Mayor, or on Madrid Visión tour buses. Similar generous discounts can be obtained with the Barcelona Card, valid from two to five days, which can be purchased from tourist offices or online at www.barcelonacard.org. Other tourist cards are available in Burgos, Córdoba, Seville and Zaragoza.

The region of Valencia and the Balearic Islands are prone to severe storms and torrential rainfall between September and November and are probably best avoided at that time. Monitor national and regional weather on www.wmo.int.

Gibraltar

For information on Gibraltar contact:

GIBRALTAR GOVERNMENT TOURIST OFFICE
150 STRAND, LONDON WC2R 1JA
Tel: 020 7836 0777
www.gibraltar.gov.gi
info@gibraltar.gov.uk

There are no campsites on the Rock, the nearest being at San Roque and La Línea de la Concepción in Spain. The only direct access to Gibraltar from Spain is via the border at La Línea which is open 24 hours a day. You may cross on foot and it is also possible to take cars or motorhomes to Gibraltar.

A valid British passport is required for all British nationals visiting Gibraltar. Nationals of other countries should check entry requirements with the Gibraltar Government Tourist Office.

There is currently no charge for visitors to enter Gibraltar but Spanish border checks can cause delays and you should be prepared for long queues. As roads in the town are extremely narrow and bridges low, it is advisable to park on the outskirts. Visitors advise against leaving vehicles on the Spanish side of the border owing to the high risk of break-ins.

An attraction to taking the car into Gibraltar includes English style supermarkets and a wide variety of competitively priced goods free of VAT. The currency is sterling and British notes and coins circulate alongside Gibraltar pounds and pence, but note that Gibraltar notes and coins are not accepted in the UK. Scottish and Northern Irish notes are not generally accepted in Gibraltar. Euros are accepted but the exchange rate may not be favourable.

Disabled visitors to Gibraltar may obtain a temporary parking permit from the police station on production of evidence confirming their disability. This permit allows parking for up to two hours (between 8am and 10pm) in parking places reserved for disabled people.

Violence or street crime is rare but there have been reports of people walking from La Línea to Gibraltar at night being attacked and robbed.

If you need emergency medical attention while on a visit to Gibraltar, treatment at primary healthcare centres is free to UK passport holders under the local medical scheme. Non UK nationals need a European Health Insurance Card (EHIC). You are not eligible for free treatment if you go to Gibraltar specifically to be treated for a condition which arose elsewhere, e.g in Spain.

Public Transport

Madrid boasts an extensive and efficient public transport network including a metro system, suburban railways and bus routes. You can purchase a pack of ten tickets which offer better value than single tickets. In addition, tourist travel passes for use on all public transport are available from metro stations, tourist offices and travel agencies and are valid for one to seven days – you will need to present your passport when buying them. Single tickets must be validated before travel. For more information see www.ctm-madrid.es.

Metro systems also operate in Barcelona, Bilbao, Seville and Valencia and a few cities operate tram services including La Coruña, Valencia, Barcelona and Bilbao.
The Valencia service links Alicante, Benidorm and Dénia.

Various operators run year round ferry services from Spain to North Africa, the Balearic Islands and the Canary Islands. All enquiries should be made through their UK agent:

SOUTHERN FERRIES
22 SUSSEX STREET, LONDON SW1V 4RW
www.southernferries.co.uk
mail@southernferries.co.uk

ABEJAR *3C1* (800m NW Rural) *41.81645, -2.78869* **Camping El Concurso, Ctra Abejar-Molinos de Duero s/n, Km 1, N234, 42146 Abejar (Soria) [975-37 33 61; fax 975-37 33 96; info@ campingelconcurso.com; www.campingelconcurso.com]** N234 W fr Soria to Abejar. Turn onto rd CL117 dir Molinos de Duero, site on L. Lge, mkd pitch, pt sl, pt shd; wc; chem disp; mv service pnt; shwrs inc; EHU (5A) inc; gas; lndry; shop & 500m; rest, snacks; bar; BBQ; playgrnd; pool; paddling pool; lake 2km; some statics; dogs; phone; poss cr & noisy in ssn; ccard acc; CKE/CCI. "Nr lake & National Park; v beautiful; gd san facs; not suitable m'van due slope." ♦ ltd. Easter-12 Oct. € 19.50   2009*

⊞ **ABIZANDA** *3B2* (5km N Rural) *42.28087, 0.19740* **Fundación Ligüerre de Cinca, Ctra A138, Km 28, 22393 Abizanda (Huesca) [974-50 08 00; fax 974-50 08 30; info@liguerredecinca.com; www.liguerredecinca.com]** A138 N fr Barbastro, site sp at km 29, or S fr Ainsa site sp at km 27, 18km S of Ainsa. Med, hdg/mkd pitch, terr, shd; wc; chem disp; shwrs inc; baby rm; EHU (10A) inc; gas; lndry; shop, rest, snacks, bar high ssn; playgrnd; pool; lake sw 1km; watersports; tennis; bike hire; games rm; horseriding; car wash; 10% statics; dogs; phone; poss cr; Eng spkn; adv bkg; quiet; ccard acc; red long stay; CKE/CCI. "Excel facs; ltd LS; highly rec; site in 2 parts sep by ravine, bottom terr muddy in wet; trees may be diff for lge o'fits; helpful staff; lovely site; nearest shops at Ainsa; conv Ordesa & Monte Perdido National Park." € 29.00   2010*

⊞ **AGER** *3B2* (300m W Rural) *42.00277, 0.76472* **Camping Val d'Àger, Calle Afores s/n, 25691 Ager (Lleida) [973-45 52 00; fax 973-45 52 02; iniciatives@valldager.com; www.campingvalldager.com/]** Fr C13 turn W onto L904/ C12 twd L'Ametlla & Àger. Cross Rv Noguera, site sp on L. Med, terr, pt shd; wc; chem disp; shwrs inc; EHU €5.70; lndry; shop & 800m; rest, snacks; bar; BBQ; playgrnd; pool high ssn; paddling pool; games area; games rm; wifi; some statics; dogs €3.60; adv bkg; quiet. "Mountain views; high o'fits rec to park nr recep (due trees); vg, peaceful site." ♦ € 22.00   2009*

"I like to fill in the reports as I travel from site to site"

You'll find report forms at the back of this guide, or you can fill them in online at www.caravanclub.co.uk/europereport.

⊞ **AGUILAR DE CAMPOO** *1B4* (27.8km SW Rural) *42.58977, -4.33260* **Camping Fuente De Los Caños, Fuente Los Canos,34400 Herrera De Pisuerga (Palencia) [639- 81 34 69]** Fr N take A67 take exit mkd Herrera de Pisuerga a Olmos de Ojeda/P-227, turn R onto Av de Eusebio Salvador Merino, turn R onto Lugar de la Fuente los Canos, site will be on the L. Sm site; pt shd; chem disp; wc; shwr; EHU (3A); rv adj; lndry rm; playgrnd; pool; fishing; bike hire; walking. "Suitable for a NH." € 19.00   2011*

⊞ **AGUILAR DE CAMPOO** *1B4* (3km W Rural) *42.78694, -4.30222* **Monte Royal Camping, Carretera Virgen del Llano 34800 Aguilar de Campóo (Palencia) [979-18 10 07; info@ campingmonteroyal.com; www.campingmonteroyal.com]** App site fr S on N611 fr Palencia. At Aguilar de Campóo turn W at S end of rv bdge at S end of town. Site on L in 3km; sp at edge of reservoir. Fr N take 3rd exit fr rndabt on N611. Do not tow thro town. Lge, mkd pitch, pt sl, shd; wc; chem disp (wc); baby facs; shwrs €0.60; EHU (6A) inc; gas; lndry; shops 3km; rest in ssn; bar; playgrnd; sand beach nr lake; watersports; horseriding; fishing; TV; 20% statics; dogs; phone; ccard acc; CKE/CCI. "Useful, peaceful NH 2 hrs fr Santander; ltd/basic facs LS & poss stretched high ssn - in need of maintenance (2010); barking dogs poss problem; friendly staff; gd walking, cycling & birdwatching in National Park; unrel opening dates LS." ♦ € 22.00   2014*

"We must tell The Club about that great site we found"

Get your site reports in by mid-August and we'll do our best to get your updates into the next edition.

⊞ **AGUILAS** *4G1* (4km NE Rural) *37.42638, -1.55083* **Camping Águilas, Ctra Cabo Cope, Los Geráneos, 30880 Águilas (Murcia) [968-41 92 05; fax 968-41 92 82; info@campingaguilas.es; www.campingaguilas.es]** Fr A7 N of Lorca take C3211 dir Águilas. On joining N332 turn L & foll sp L to Calabardina/Cabo Cope; site on L within 3km. Med, mkd pitch, pt shd; wc; chem disp; mv service pnt; shwrs inc; EHU (10A) €5; gas; lndry; shop high ssn; rest, snacks; bar; playgrnd; pool; sand beach 4km; tennis; wifi; 30% statics; dogs €1; phone; site poss clsd last 2 weeks May & Sep; Eng spkn; adv bkg; quiet; red LS/long stay; ccard acc; red LS; CKE/ CCI. "All pitches shd with trees or netting; clean facs; helpful staff; popular winter long stay; excel." € 39.00   2010*

⊞ **AGUILAS** *4G1* (2km SW Coastal) *37.3925, -1.61111* **Camping Bellavista, Ctra de Vera, Km 3, 30880 Águilas (Murcia) [tel/fax 968-44 91 51; info@campingbellavista.com; www.campingbellavista.com]** Site on N332 Águilas to Vera rd on R at top of sh, steep hill, 100m after R turn to El Cocon. Well mkd by flags. Fr S by N332 on L 400m after fuel stn, after v sharp corner. Sm, hdg pitch, hdstg, pt sl, pt shd; wc; chem disp; mv service pnt; shwrs inc; EHU (10A) €5.20 or metered; gas; lndry (inc dryer); sm shop; rest adj; snacks; BBQ; playgrnd; pool; sand beach 300m; bike hire; wifi; some statics; dogs €2.50; poss cr; Eng spkn; adv bkg; quiet; ccard acc; red long stay/LS; CKE/CCI. "Gd autumn/winter stay; clean, tidy site with excel facs; ltd pitches for lge o'fits; helpful owner; fine views; rd noise at 1 end; excel town & vg beaches; v secure site." € 33.60   2014*

⊞ **AINSA** *3B2* (2.5km N Rural) *42.43555, 0.13583* **Camping Peña Montañesa**, Ctra Ainsa-Bielsa, Km 2.3, 22360 Labuerda (Huesca) [974-50 00 32; fax 974-50 09 91; info@penamontanesa.com; www.penamontanesa.com] E fr Huesca on N240 for approx 50km, turn N onto N123 just after Barbastro twd Ainsa. In 8km turn onto A138 N for Ainsa & Bielsa. Or fr Bielsa Tunnel to A138 S to Ainsa & Bielsa, site sp. NB: Bielsa Tunnel sometimes clsd bet Oct & Easter due to weather. Lge, mkd pitch, shd; htd wc; chem disp; mv service pnt; baby facs; sauna; shwrs inc; EHU (6A) inc; gas; lndry (inc dryer); supmkt; rest, snacks; bar; BBQ (gas/elec only); playgrnd; htd pools (1 covrd); lake sw 2km; fishing; canoeing; tennis; bike hire; horseriding; games area; games rm; wifi; entmnt; TV; 30% statics; dogs €4.25; no o'fits over 10m; phone; adv bkg; quiet, poss some noise fr local festival mid-Aug; ccard acc; red LS; CKE/CCI. "Situated by fast-flowing rv; v friendly staff; Eng spkn; gd, clean san facs; pitching poss diff due trees; nr beautiful medieval town of Ainsa & Ordesa National Park; excel." ♦ € 39.00 SBS - E12 2014*

See advertisement

AINSA *3B2* (10km N Rural) *42.50916, 0.12777* **Camping Valle de Añisclo**, Ctra Añisclo, Km 2, 22363 Puyarruego (Huesca) [974-50 50 96; info@valleanisclo.com; www.staragon.com/campingvalleanisclo] N fr Ainsa on A138, at Escalona turn L onto HU631 dir Puyarruego. In 2km cross bdge, site on R at ent to vill. Med, mkd pitch, pt sl, pt shd; htd wc; chem disp; mv service pnt; baby facs; shwrs inc; EHU (6A) €4.55; lndry; shop; rest, snacks; bar; playgrnd; rv adj; wifi; dogs €1.65; phone; Eng spkn; adv bkg; quiet; red LS. "Excel walking & birdwatching - nightingales; helpful owners; excel." Easter-15 Oct. € 19.00 2011*

AINSA *3B2* (1km E Rural) *42.41944, 0.15111* **Camping Ainsa**, Ctra Ainsa-Campo, 22330 Ainsa (Huesca) [974-50 02 60; fax 974-50 03 61; info@campingainsa.com; www.campingainsa.com] Fr Ainsa take N260 E dir Pueyo de Araguás, cross rv bdge, site sp L in 200m. Foll lane to site. Sm, terr, pt shd; wc; baby facs; shwrs inc; EHU €4.75; gas; lndry; shop 1km; rest, snacks bar high ssn; playgrnd; pool; games rm; wifi; TV; 50% statics; dogs €2.20; phone; poss cr; some indus noise mornings; ccard acc; red LS; CKE/CCI. "Pleasant, welcoming, well-maintained site; fine view of old city & some pitches mountain views; vg san facs; not suitable lge o'fits; gd pool." Holy Week-30 Oct. € 24.00 2014*

⊞ **AINSA** *3B2* (6km NW Rural) *42.43004, 0.07881* **Camping Boltaña**, Ctra N260, Km 442, Ctra Margudgued, 22340 Boltaña (Huesca) [974-50 23 47; fax 974-50 20 23; info@campingboltana.com; www.campingboltana.com] Fr Ainsa head twd Boltaña, turn L over rv & foll sp. Site is 2km E of Boltaña, final 300m on single track rd. Med, mkd pitch, pt sl, terr, pt shd; htd wc; chem disp; mv service pnt; baby facs; shwrs inc; EHU (4-10A) €6.40; gas; lndry (inc dryer); shop & 2km; rest, snacks; bar; playgrnd; pool; paddling pool; fishing 600m; tennis 1km; bike hire; horseriding 500m; games area; adventure sports; wifi; 30% statics; dogs €3.25; phone; clsd 15 Dec-15 Jan; poss cr; Eng spkn; adv bkg; poss noisy; ccard acc; red LS. "Conv Ordesa National Park; san facs stretched high ssn; friendly, helpful staff; Ainsa old town worth visit; excel." ♦ ltd. € 29.00 2010*

ALBANYA *3B3* (2.4km W Rural) *42.30630, 2.70970* **Camping Bassegoda Park**, Camí Camp de l'Illa, 17733 Albanyà (Gerona) [972-54 20 20; fax 972-54 20 21; info@bassegodapark.com; www.bassegodapark.com] Fr France exit AP7/E15 junc 3 onto GI510 to Albanyà. At end of rd turn R, site on rvside. Fr S exit AP7 junc 4 dir Terrades, then Albanyà. App poss diff for lge o'fits. Med, hdg pitch, hdstg, pt shd; htd wc; chem disp; mv waste; baby facs; shwrs inc; EHU (10A) €6.75; lndry (inc dryer); shop; rest, snacks; bar; BBQ; playgrnd; pool; fishing; trekking; hill walking; mountain biking; bike hire; games area; games rm; wifi; entmnt; TV rm; 8% statics; dogs €4.75 (1 only); phone; Eng spkn; adv bkg; quiet; ccard add; red LS/snr citizens/CKE/CCI. "Excel site surrounded by woods, rvs & streams; excel san facs; well worth a detour." ♦ 1 Mar-11 Dec. € 28.60 (CChq acc) 2010*

ALBARRACIN *3D1* (2km E Rural) *40.41228, -1.42788* **Camp Municipal Ciudad de Albarracín**, Camino de Gea s/n, 44100 Albarracín (Teruel) [tel/fax 978-71 01 97 or 657-49 84 33 (mob); campingalbarracin5@hotmail.com; www.campingalbarracin.com] Fr Teruel take A1512 to Albarracín. Go thro vill, foll camping sps. Med, pt sl, pt shd; wc; chem disp; baby facs; shwrs inc; EHU (16A) €3.85; gas; lndry; shop & adj; snacks; bar; BBQ; playgrnd; pool adj in ssn; wifi; some statics; dogs; phone; poss cr; adv bkg; quiet; ccard acc; CKE/CCI. "Gd site; immac san facs; narr pitches poss diff for lge o'fits; sports cent adj; gd touring base & gd walking fr site; rec; friendly staff." 15 Mar-3 Nov. € 16.00 2013*

ALBERCA, LA *1D3* (2km N Rural) *40.50915, -6.12312* **Camping Al-Bereka**, Ctra Salamanca-La Alberca, Km 75.6, 37624 La Alberca (Salamanca) [923-41 51 95; www.albereka.com] Fr Salamanca S on N630/E803 take C515 to Mogarraz, then SA202 to La Alberca. Site on L at km 75.6 bef vill. Rte fr Ciudad Real OK but bumpy in places. Med, mkd pitch, terr, shd; wc; chem disp; shwrs inc; EHU (3-6A) €3.50; lndry; shop; rest, snacks; bar; BBQ; playgrnd; pool; paddling pool; TV; some statics; dogs; quiet; ccard acc; CKE/CCI. "Gd, quiet site; helpful owner; beautiful countryside; La Alberca medieval vill with abbey." ♦ 15 Mar-31 Oct. € 21.40   2009*

ALBERCA, LA *1D3* (6km N Rural) *40.52112, -6.13756* **Camping Sierra de Francia**, Ctra Salamanca-La Alberca, Km 73, 37623 El Caserito (Salamanca) [923-45 40 81; fax 923-45 40 01; info@campingsierradefrancia.com; www.campingsierradefrancia.com] Fr Cuidad Rodrigo take C515. Turn R at El Cabaco, site on L in approx 2km. Med, hdg/mkd pitch, shd; wc; shwrs; mv service pnt; EHU (3-6A) €3.75; gas; lndry; shop; rest; bar; BBQ; playgrnd; pool; paddling pool; bike hire; horseriding; wifi; some statics; dogs free; quiet; ccard acc. "Conv 'living history' vill of La Alberca & Monasterio San Juan de la Peña; excel views." ♦ ltd. Holy Week-15 Sep. € 18.40   2009*

⊞ **ALCALA DE LOS GAZULES** *2H3* (4km E Rural) *36.46403, -5.66482* **Camping Los Gazules**, Ctra de Patrite, Km 4, 11180 Alcalá de los Gazules (Cádiz) [956-42 04 86; fax 956-42 03 88; camping@losgazules.e.telefonica.net; www.campinglosgazules.com] Fr N exit A381 at 1st junc to Alcalá, proceed thro town to 1st rndabt & turn L onto A375/A2304 dir Ubriqu, site sp strt ahead in 1km onto CA2115 dir Patrite on v sharp L. Fr S exit A381 at 1st sp for Acalá. At rndabt turn R onto A375/A2304 dir Ubrique. Then as above. Med, mkd pitch, pt sl, pt shd; wc; chem disp (wc); mv service pnt; shwrs inc; EHU (10A) €5.25 (poss rev pol); lndry; shop; rest; bar; playgrnd; pool; bike hire; TV rm; 90% statics; dog €2; phone; adv bkg; red long stay/LS; CKE/CCI. "Well-maintained, upgraded site; take care canopy frames; sm pitches & tight turns & kerbs on site; friendly, helpful staff; ltd facs LS; ltd touring pitches; attractive town with v narr rds, leave car in park at bottom & walk; gd walking, birdwatching." € 35.00   2013*

⊞ **ALCANAR** *3D2* (4km NE Coastal) *40.53986, 0.52071* **Camping Estanyet**, Paseo del Marjal s/n 43870, Les Cases d'Alcanar (Catalonia) [tel/fax 977-73 72 68; http://fr.campings.com/camping-estanyet-les-cases-dalcanar] Leave Alcanar to N340 at ILes Cases D'Alcanar foll camping signs. Fr AP7 Junc 41 fr N or Junc 43 fr S. Med, hdg pitch; hdstg; pt shd; htd wc; chem disp (wc); shwrs inc; baby facs; EHU (10A) €6.50; lndry; ltd shop high ssn; rest, snacks; bar; BBQ (charcoal); playgrnd; pool high ssn; shgl beach adj; 10% statics; phone; dogs €3.50; poss cr; adv bkg; ccard acc; CKE/CCI. "Gd; friendly owners; but ltd facs esp LS." 1 Apr-30 Sep. € 40.40   2013*

⊞ **ALCARAZ** *4F1* (6km E Rural) *38.67301, -2.40462* **Camping Sierra de Peñascosa**, Ctra Peñascosa-Bogarra, Km 1, 02313 Peñascosa (Albacete) [967-38 25 21; info@campingsierra penascosa.com; www.campingsierrapenascosa.com] Fr N322 turn E bet km posts 279 & 280 sp Peñascosa. In vill foll site sp for 1km beyond vill. Gravel access track & narr ent. Sm, mkd pitch, hdstg, terr, shd; wc; chem disp; shwrs; EHU (6A) €4; gas; lndry; shop; rest high ssn; snacks; bar; playgrnd; pool; bike hire; dogs €2; open w/end in winter; v quiet; ccard acc; CKE/CCI. "Not suitable lge o'fits or faint-hearted; pitches sm, uneven & amongst trees - care needed when manoeuvring; historical sites nr." ♦ € 21.00   2009*

⊞ **ALCOSSEBRE** *3D2* (2.5km NE Coastal/Rural) *40.27016, 0.30646* **Camping Ribamar**, Partida Ribamar s/n, 12579 Alcossebre (Castellón) [964-76 11 63; fax 964-76 14 84; info@campingribamar.com; www.campingribamar.com] Exit AP7 at junc 44 into N340 & foll sp to Alcossebre, then dir Sierra de Irta & Las Fuentes. Turn in dir of sea & foll sp to site in 2km - pt rough rd. Med, hdg/mkd pitch, hdstg, pt sl, terr, pt shd; wc; chem disp; mv service pnt; baby facs; shwrs inc; EHU (10A) €4.40 (metered for long stay); gas; lndry (inc dryer); shop; supmkt 2km; rest; bar; playgrnd; pool; sand beach 100m; paddling pool; tennis; games area; games rm; wifi; entmnt; TV rm; 25% statics; dogs €1.70; poss cr; Eng spkn; adv bkg; quiet; red long stay/LS; CKE/CCI. "Excel, refurbished tidy site in 'natural park'; warm welcome; realistic pitch sizes; variable prices; excel san facs; beware caterpillars in spring - poss dangerous for dogs." ♦ € 42.50 SBS - W04   2011*

See advertisement

Check any essential information with the site before you travel   *Last year of report

SPAIN

⊞ **ALCOSSEBRE** *3D2* (2.5km S Coastal) *40.22138, 0.26888*
**Camping Playa Tropicana, Camino de l'atall s/n, 12579
Alcossebre (Castellón) [964-41 24 63; fax 964 41 28 05;
info@playatropicana.com; www.playatropicana.com]**
Fr AP7 exit junc 44 onto N340 dir Barcelona. After 3km at
km 1018 turn on CV142 twd Alcossebre. Just bef ent town
turn R sp 'Platjes Capicorb', turn R at beach in 2.5km, site on
R. Lge, mkd pitch, pt terr, pt shd; htd wc; chem disp; baby
facs; some serviced pitches; shwrs inc; EHU (10A) €4.50; gas;
lndry; supmkt; rest, snacks; bar; playgrnd; pool; sand beach
adj; watersports; bike & kayak hire; games area; beauty salon;
cinema rm; wifi; entmnt; TV; car wash; 10% statics; no dogs;
poss cr; Eng spkn; adv bkg rec high ssn; quiet; ccard acc; ACSI
acc red LS/long stay & special offers; various pitch prices. "Excel
facs & security; superb well-run site; vg LS; poss rallies Jan-Apr;
management v helpful; poss flooding after heavy rain; pitch
access poss diff lge o'fits due narr access rds & high kerbs; take
fly swat!" ♦ € 56.00   2013*

⊞ **ALGAMITAS** *2G3* (3km SW Rural) *37.01934, -5.17440*
**Camping El Peñon, Ctra Algámitas-Pruna, Km 3,
41661 Algámitas (Sevilla) [955-85 53 00; info@camping
algamitas.com]** Fr A92 turn S at junc 41 (Arahal) to Morón de
la Frontera on A8125. Fr Morón take A406 & A363 dir Pruna.
At 1st rndabt at ent Pruna turn L onto SE9225 to Algámitas.
Site on L in approx 10km - steep app rd. Sm, hdg/mkd pitch,
hdstg, pt shd; wc; chem disp (wc); mv service pnt; shwrs inc;
EHU (16A) €3.32; gas; lndry (inc dryer); shop 3km; rest; bar;
BBQ; playgrnd; pool; games area; 50% statics; dogs; site clsd
13-24 Nov; adv bkg; quiet; cc acc; CKE/CCI. "Conv Seville,
Ronda & white vills; walking, hiking & horseriding fr site; excel
rest; excel, clean san facs; vg site - worth effort to find." ♦ ltd.
€ 15.00   2009*

⊞ **ALHAMA DE MURCIA** *4F1* (6km NW Rural) *37.88888,
-1.49333* **Camping Sierra Espuña, El Berro, 30848 Alhama de
Murcia (Murcia) [968-66 80 38; fax 968-66 80 79; camping@
campingsierraespuna.com; www.campingsierraespuna.com]**
Exit A7 junc 627 or 631 to Alhama de Murcia & take C3315 sp
Gebas & Mula. Ignore 1st sp to site & after Gebas foll sp to site
sp El Berro, site on edge of vill. 15km by rd fr Alhama - narr,
twisty & steep in parts, diff for lge o'fits & m'vans over 7.5m.
Med, hdstg, terr, pt shd; wc; chem disp; baby facs; shwrs;
EHU (6A) €4.28 (poss rev pol); gas; lndry; shop 200m; rest in
vill; snacks; bar; playgrnd; pool; tennis; minigolf; organised
activities; wifi; 30% statics; dogs €2.14; phone; adv bkg; quiet
but poss noise w/end; red long stay; ccard acc; CKE/CCI. "In
Sierra Espu a National Park on edge of unspoilt vill; gd walking,
climbing, mountain biking area; friendly staff; highly rec." ♦
€ 17.00   2009*

⊞ **ALHAURIN DE LA TORRE** *2H4* (4km W Rural) *36.65174,
-4.61064* **Camping Malaga Monte Parc, 29130 Alhaurín de
la Torre (Málaga) [tel/fax 951-29 60 28; info@malagamonte
parc.com; www.malagamonteparc.com]** W fr Málaga on
AP7 or N340 take exit for Churriana/Alhaurín de la Torre. Thro
Alhaurín de la Torre take A404 W sp Alhaurín el Grande, site
on R, sp. Sm, hdg/mkd pitch, hdstg, pt sl, shd; htd wc (cont);
chem disp; shwrs inc; EHU (6A) inc; lndry; shop 4km; rest,
snacks; bar; BBQ; golf nrby; wifi; TV; some statics; dogs
€1.70; bus 200m; Eng spkn; adv bkg; quiet; ccard acc; red
LS; CKE/CCI. "Vg site; well-appointed, clean san facs; friendly
Welsh owner; all facs open all year; sm pitches; gd position to
tour Costa Del Sol." ♦ ltd. € 25.00   2014*

⊞ **ALICANTE** *4F2* (10km NE Coastal) *38.41333, -0.40556*
**Camping Bon Sol, Camino Real de Villajoyosa 35, Playa
Muchavista, 03560 El Campello (Alicante) [tel/fax 965-
94 13 83; bonsol@infonegocio.com; www.infonegocio.com/
bonsol]** Exit AP7 N of Alicante at junc 67 onto N332 sp Playa
San Juan; on reaching coast rd turn N twds El Campello; site
sp. Sm, mkd pitch, hdstg, pt shd, all serviced pitches; wc; chem
disp; shwrs; EHU (4A) €4.50; lndry; shop; rest; bar; sand beach;
50% statics; adv bkg; ccard acc; red long stay/LS; CKE/CCI.
"Diff ent for long o'fits; helpful staff; noisy at w/end; poss cold
shwrs; vg." ♦ € 31.50   2011*

⊞ **ALLARIZ** *1B2* (1.5km W Rural) *42.18443, -7.81811*
**Camping Os Invernadeiros, Ctra Allariz-Celanova, Km 3,
32660 Allariz (Ourense) [988-44 01 26; fax 988-44 20 06;
reatur@allariz.com]** Well sp off N525 Orense-Xinzo rd
& fr A52. Steep descent to site off rd OU300. Height limit
2.85m adj recep - use gate to R. Sm, pt shd; wc; shwrs inc;
EHU €4; gas; lndry; shop; snacks; bar; playgrnd; pool 1.5km;
horseriding; bike hire; some statics; dogs €2.80; bus 1.8km; Eng
spkn; quiet; red long stay; ccard acc; CKE/CCI. "Vg; steep
slope into site, level exit is avail; site combined with horseriding
stable; rv walk adj." € 21.00   2011*

ALMAYATE see Torre del Mar *2H4*

⊞ **ALMERIA** *4G1* (23km SE Coastal/Rural) *36.80187, -2.24471*
**Camping Cabo de Gata, Ctra Cabo de Gata s/n, Cortijo
Ferrón, 04150 Cabo de Gata (Almería) [950-16 04 43;
fax 950-91 68 21; info@campingcabodegata.com;
www.campingcabodegata.com]** Exit m'way N340/344/E15
junc 460 or 467 sp Cabo de Gata, foll sp to site. Lge, hdg/
mkd pitch, shd; wc; chem disp; baby facs; shwrs inc; EHU
(6-16A) €4.60; gas; lndry; supmkt high ssn; rest, snacks; bar;
BBQ; playgrnd; pool; diving cent; sand beach 900m; tennis;
games area; games rm; excursions; bike hire; wifi; TV; some
statics; dogs €2.80; bus 1km; Eng spkn; adv bkg; quiet; ccard
acc; red long stay/LS/CKE/CCI. "M'vans with solar panels/
TV aerials take care sun shades; gd cycling, birdwatching esp
flamingoes; popular at w/end; isolated, dry area of Spain
with many interesting features; warm winters; excel site." ♦
€ 41.00   2014*

⊞ **ALMERIA** *4G1* (4km W Coastal) *36.82560, -2.51685*
**Camping La Garrofa, Ctra N340a, Km 435.4, 04002
Almería [tel/fax 950-23 57 70; info@lagarrofa.com;
www.lagarrofa.com]** Site sp on coast rd bet Almería &
Aguadulce. Med, mkd pitch, pt sl, shd; wc; chem disp; mv
service pnt; shwrs inc; EHU (6-10A) €4.30-4.90; gas; lndry;
shop; rest, snacks; bar; playgrnd; shgl beach adj; games
area; wifi; 10% statics; dogs €2.40; phone; bus adj; sep car
park; quiet; red LS/long stay; CKE/CCI. "V pleasant site adj
eucalyptus grove; helpful staff; modern, clean facs; sm pitches,
not rec lge o'fits; vg." ♦ € 20.50   2014*

⊞ **ALMERIA** *4G1* (10km W Coastal) *36.79738, -2.59128*
Camping Roquetas, Ctra Los Parrales s/n, 04740 Roquetas de Mar (Almería) [950-34 38 09; fax 950-34 25 25; info@campingroquetas.com; www.campingroquetas.com]
Fr A7 take exit 429; ahead at rndabt A391 sp Roquetas. Turn L at rndabt sp camping & foll sp to site. V lge, pt shd; wc; chem disp; mv service pnt; shwrs inc; EHU (10-15A) €6.35-7.45; gas; lndry; shop; snacks; bar; 2 pools; paddling pool; shgl beach 400m; tennis; wifi; TV rm; 10% statics; dogs €2.25; phone; bus 1km; Eng spkn; adv bkg rec high ssn; quiet; ccard acc; red LS/long stay/CKE/CCI. "Double-size pitches in winter; helpful staff; gd clean facs; tidy site but poss dusty; artificial shd; many long term visitors in winter." ♦ € 32.00   2014*

⊞ **ALMUNECAR** *2H4* (6km W Coastal) *36.73954, -3.75358*
Nuevo Camping La Herradura, Paseo Andrés Segovia s/n (Peña Parda), 18690 La Herradura (Granada) [958-64 06 34; fax 958-64 06 42; laherradura@neuvocamping. com; www.nuevocamping.com] Turn S off N340 sp La Herradura & foll rd to seafront. Turn R to end of beach rd. Site not well sp. Avoid town cent due narr rds. Med, mkd pitch, pt terr, pt shd; wc; chem disp; mv service pnt; serviced pitches; shwrs inc; EHU (5A) €3.50; gas 500m; lndry; shop, rest, snacks, bar adj; playgrnd; shgl beach adj; 20% statics; dogs €1.50; phone; bus 300m; poss v cr; adv bkg; quiet; red LS/long stay; CKE/CCI. "Friendly, attractive site in avocado orchard; mountain views some pitches; height restriction lge m'vans; some sm pitches - v tight to manoeuvre; vg san facs but ltd LS; popular winter long stay." ♦ € 22.00   2010*

⊞ **ALTEA** *4F2* (4km S Coastal) *38.57751, -0.06440* **Camping Cap-Blanch, Playa de Albir, 03530 Altea (Alicante) [965-84 59 46; fax 965-84 45 56; capblanch@ctv.es; www.camping-capblanch.com]** Exit AP7/E15 junc 64 Altea-Collosa onto N332, site bet Altea & Benidorm, dir Albir. 'No entry' sps on prom rd do not apply to access to site. Lge, pt shd, hdstg; wc; chem disp; mv service pnt; baby facs; shwrs inc; EHU (5-10A) €3.50; gas; shop 100m; lndry (inc dryer); rest; bar; playgrnd; shgl beach adj; watersports; tennis; golf 5km; wifi; TV; some statics; carwash; poss cr; Eng spkn; no adv bkg; quiet; ccard acc; red LS/long stay. "V cr in winter with long stay campers; lge pitches; Altea mkt Tues; buses to Benidorm & Altea; handy for lovely beach; most pitches hdstg on pebbles."
♦ € 25.00   2011*

⊞ **AMETLLA DE MAR, L'** *3C2* (2.5km S Coastal) *40.86493, 0.77860* **Camping L'Ametlla Village Platja, Paratge de Santes Creus s/n, 43860 L'Ametlla de Mar (Tarragona) [977-26 77 84; fax 977-26 78 68; info@campingametlla.com; www.campingametlla.com]** Exit AP7 junc 39, fork R as soon as cross m'way. Foll site sp for 3km - 1 v sharp, steep bend. Lge, hdg/mkd pitch, hdstg, terr, pt shd; htd wc; chem disp; mv service pnt; baby facs; shwrs inc; EHU (5-10A) inc; gas; lndry; shop high ssn; rest, snacks; bar; BBQ; playgrnd; pool; paddling pool; shgl beach 400m; diving cent; games area; games rm; fitness rm; bike hire; wifi; entmnt; TV rm; some statics; dogs free; phone; Eng spkn; adv bkg; some rd & rlwy noise; ccard acc; red LS/long stay; CKE/CCI. "Conv Port Aventura & Ebro Delta National Park; excel site & facs; can cycle into vill with mkt." ♦ € 47.60   2013*

⊞ **ARANDA DE DUERO** *1C4* (3km N Rural) *41.70138, -3.68666* **Camping Costajan, Ctra A1/E5, Km 164-165, 09400 Aranda de Duero (Burgos) [947-50 20 70; fax 947-51 13 54; campingcostajan@camping-costajan.com]**
Sp on A1/E5 Madrid-Burgos rd, N'bound exit km 164 Aranda Norte, S'bound exit km 165 & foll sp to Aranda & site 500m on R. Med, pt sl, shd; htd wc; chem disp; mv service pnt; shwrs inc; EHU (10A) €5 (poss rev pol &/or no earth); gas; lndry; shop; supmkt 3km; rest high ssn; snacks; bar; BBQ; playgrnd; pool high ssn; tennis; games area; wifi; 10% statics; dogs €2; phone; bus 2km; Eng spkn; adv bkg; quiet, but some traff noise; red LS but ltd facs; CKE/CCI. "Lovely site under pine trees; poultry farm adj; diff pitch access due trees & sandy soil; friendly, helpful owner; site poss clsd LS - phone ahead to check; many facs clsd LS & gate clsd o'night until 0800; recep poss open evening only LS; poss cold/tepid shwrs LS; gd winter NH; vg site for dogs." € 27.00   2014*

⊞ **ARANJUEZ** *1D4* (1.5km NE Rural) *40.04222, -3.59944* **Camping International Aranjuez, Calle Soto del Rebollo s/n, 28300 Aranjuez (Madrid) [918-91 13 95; fax 918-92 04 06; info@campingaranjuez.com; www.campingaranjuez.com]** Fr N (Madrid) turn off A4 exit 37 onto M305. After ent town turn L bef rv, after petrol stn on R. Take L lane & watch for site sp on L, also mkd M305 Madrid. Site in 500m on R. (If missed cont around cobbled rndabt & back twd Madrid.) Fr S turn off A4 for Aranjuez & foll Palacio Real sp. Join M305 & foll sp for Madrid & camping site. Site on Rv Tajo. Warning: rd surface rolls, take it slowly on app to site & ent gate tight. Lge, hdg/mkd pitch, pt sl, unshd; htd wc; chem disp; mv service pnt; some serviced pitches; baby facs; shwrs inc; EHU (16A) €4 (poss no earth, rev pol); gas; lndry (inc dryer); shop; hypmkt 3km; rest, snacks; bar; playgrnd; pool & paddling pool; rv fishing; canoe & bike hire; games area; wifi; entmnt; some statics; dogs free; phone; quiet; ccard acc; red LS/long stay; CKE/CCI. "Well-maintained site; gd san facs; rest vg value; some lge pitches - access poss diff due trees; some uneven pitches - care req when pitching; pleasant town - World Heritage site; conv Madrid by train; excel site; free train to Royal Palace each morning." ♦ € 42.00   2014*

See advertisement on next page

ARBIZU *3B1* (2km S Rural) *42.89860, -2.03444* **Camping Arbizu eko, NA 7100 km 5, 31839 Arbizu [848-47 09 22; info@campingarbizu.com; www.campingarbizu.com]**
Fr A10 Irurtzun to Altsasu exit 17 onto NA-7100. Site on R in 1km. Med; wc; chem disp; baby facs; shwrs; EHU (16A); lndry; shop; rest; snacks; bar; BBQ; playgrnd; paddling pool; sandy beach; fishing; games rm; entmnt; wifi; TV; dogs; twin axles; Eng spkn; adv bkg; quiet; ccard acc. "Stunning views of mountains fr site; excel, clean shwr block; v helpful, friendly staff; lots to do in area; gd size pitches; best site." 7 Jan-23 Dec. € 28.00   2015*

SPAIN

⊞ **ARENAS DEL REY** *2G4* (5km N Rural) *36.99439, -3.88064* **Camping Los Bermejales, Km 360, Embalse Los Bermejales, 18129 Arenas del Rey (Granada) [958-35 91 90; fax 958-35 93 36; camping@losbermejales.com; www.losbermejales.com]** On A44/E902 S fr Granada, exit at junc 139 dir La Malahá onto A385. In approx 10km, turn L onto A338 dir Alhama de Granada & foll sp for site. Fr A92 foll sp Alhama de Granada, then Embalse Los Bermejales. Med, mkd pitch, hdstg, terr, pt shd; wc; chem disp; mv service pnt; shwrs inc; EHU (9A) €2.67; gas; lndry; shop; rest, snacks; bar; BBQ; playgrnd; pool; lake sw & sand/shgl beach adj; fishing (licence req); pedalos; tennis; TV rm; 50% statics; dogs; phone; poss cr high ssn; little Eng spkn; adv bkg; quiet. "Ideal base for touring Granada; Roman baths 12km at Alhama de Granada." ♦ € 16.70   2011*

ARENAS, LAS *1A4* (1km E Rural) *43.30083, -4.80500* **Camping Naranjo de Bulnes, Ctra Cangas de Onís-Panes, Km 32.5, 33554 Arenas de Cabrales (Asturias) [tel/fax 985-84 65 78; info@campingnaranjodebulnes.com; www.campingnaranjodebulnes.com]** Fr Unquera on N634, take N621 S to Panes, AS114 23km to Las Arenas. Site E of vill of Las Arenas de Cabrales, both sides of rd. V lge, mkd pitch, pt sl, pt terr, pt shd; wc; chem disp; baby facs; shwrs inc; EHU (10A) €3.50 (poss rev pol); gas; lndry; shop; rest, snacks; bar; playgrnd; internet; TV rm; bus 100m; poss cr; rd noise; ccard acc. "Beautifully-situated site by rv; delightful vill; attractive, rustic-style, clean san facs - hot water to shwrs only, not basins or sinks; wcs up steps; poss poor security; conv Picos de Europa; mountain-climbing school; excursions; walking; excel cheese festival last Sun in Aug; excel rest, bars in vill." 1 Apr-11 Oct. € 32.00   2015*

ARIJA *1A4* (1km N Rural) *43.00064, -3.94492* **Camping Playa de Arija, Avda Gran Via, 09570 Arija (Burgos) [942-77 33 00; fax 942-77 32 72; info@campingplayadearija Sodot null. Com; www.campingplayadearija.com]** Fr W on A67 at Reinosa along S side of Embalse del Ebro. Go thro Arija & take 1st L after x-ing bdge. Go under rlwy bdge, site well sp on peninsula N of vill on lakeside. Or fr E on N623 turn W onto BU642 to Arija & turn R to peninsula & site. NB Rd fr W under repair 2009 & in poor condition. Lge, shd; wc; chem disp; mv service pnt; baby facs; shwrs inc; EHU (5A) €3; lndry; shop; rest; bar; BBQ; playgrnd; lake sw & beach; watersports; games area; 10% statics; dogs; phone; bus 1km; quiet; CKE/CCI. "Gd new site; gd birdwatching; LS phone ahead for site opening times." Easter-15 Sep. € 14.00   2013*

⊞ **ARNES** *3C2* (1km NE Rural) *40.9186, 0.2678* **Camping Els Ports, Ctra Tortosa T330, Km 2, 43597 Arnes (Tarragona) [tel/fax 977-43 55 60; elsports@hotmail.com]** Exit AP7 at junc Tortosa onto C12 sp Gandesa. Turn W onto T333 at El Pinell de Brai, then T330 to site. Med, pt shd; htd wc; shwrs inc; EHU €4.20; lndry; rest; bar; pool; paddling pool; games area; bike hire; horseriding 3km; entmnt; TV rm; some statics; no dogs; phone; bus 1km; quiet; ccard acc. "Nr nature reserve & many sports activities; excel walking/mountain cycling; basic san facs; poss smells fr adj pig units (2009); rock pegs req." ♦ ltd. € 18.40   2009*

AURITZ *3A1* (3km SW Rural) *42.97302, -1.35248* **Camping Urrobi, Ctra Pamplona-Valcarlos, Km 42, 31694 Espinal-Aurizberri (Navarra) [tel/fax 948-76 02 00; info@camping urrobi.com; www.campingurrobi.com]** NE fr Pamplona on N135 twd Valcarlos thro Erro; 1.5km after Auritzberri (Espinal) turn R on N172. Site on N172 at junc with N135 opp picnic area. Med, pt shd; wc; chem disp; mv service pnt; shwrs inc; EHU (5A) €4.90; gas; lndry; shop; supmkt 1.5km; rest, snacks; bar; BBQ; playgrnd; pool; rv adj; tennis; bike hire; horseriding; wifi; 20% statics; phone; Eng spkn; adv bkg; quiet; ccard acc; CKE/CCI. "Excel, busy site & facs; solar htd water - hot water to shwrs only; walks in surrounding hills; ltd facs LS; poss youth groups." ♦ 1 Apr-31 Oct. € 20.00   2010*

AVIN see Cangas de Onis *1A3*

⊞ **AYERBE** *3B2* (1km NE Rural) *42.28211, -0.67536* **Camping La Banera, Ctra Loarre Km.1, 22800 Ayerbe (Huesca) [tel/fax 974-38 02 42 or 659-16 15 90 (mob); labanera@ gmail.com; www.campinglabanera.com]** Take A132 NW fr Huesca dir Pamplona. Turn R at 1st x-rds at ent to Ayerbe sp Loarre & Camping. Site 1km on R on A1206. Med, mkd pitch, terr, pt shd; wc; chem disp (wc); baby facs; fam bthrm; shwrs inc; EHU (6A) €2.60; gas; lndry; shop 1km; rest, snacks; bar; cooking facs; TV rm; dogs €2; some Eng spkn; adv bkg; quiet; ccard acc; red long stay; CKE/CCI. "Friendly, pleasant, well-maintained, peaceful, family-run site; facs clean; pitches poss muddy after rain; helpful owners; wonderful views; close to Loarre Castle; care req by high o'fits as many low trees; area famous for Griffon Vultures which inhabit tall cliffs nr Loarre." ♦ € 17.50   2014*

⊞ **AYERBE** *3B2* (10km NE Rural) *42.31989, -0.61848*
Camping Castillo de Loarre, Ctra del Castillo s/n, 22809 Loarre (Huesca) [tel/fax 974-38 27 22; info@campingloarre. com; www.campingloarre.com] NW on A132 fr Huesca, turn R at ent to Ayerbe to Loare sp Castillo de Loarre. Pass 1st site on R (La Banera) & foll sp to castle past Loarre vill on L; site on L. App rd steep & twisting. Med, pt sl, pt shd; wc; chem disp; shwrs inc; EHU (6A) €4.50; gas; lndry; shop; rest, snacks; bar; playgrnd; sm pool; bike hire; 10% statics; dogs; phone; site clsd Feb; poss cr; Eng spkn; quiet; ccard acc; CKE/CCI. "Elevated site in almond grove; superb scenery & views, esp fr pitches on far L of site; excel birdwatching - many vultures/eagles; site open w/end in winter; busy high ssn & w/ends; pitching poss diff lge o'fits due low trees; worth the journey; v pleasant, well maint site; san facs clean but dated." ♦ € 16.00 2015*

⊞ **BAIONA** *1B2* (5km NE Urban/Coastal) *42.13861, -8.80916*
Camping Playa América, Ctra Vigo-Baiona, Km 9.250, Aptdo. Correos 3105 - 36350 Nigrán (Pontevedra) [986-36 54 03 or 986-36 71 61; fax 986-36 54 04; oficina@campingplayaamerica.com; www.campingplayaamerica.com] Sp on rd PO552 fr all dirs (Vigo/Baiona) nr beach. Med, mkd pitch, pt shd; wc; chem disp; mv service pnt; baby facs; shwrs inc; EHU (6A) €5; gas; lndry; shop; rest, snacks; bar; BBQ; playgrnd; pool; paddling pool; sand beach 300m; bike hire; 60% statics; dogs; bus 500m; poss cr; Eng spkn; adv bkg; CKE/CCI. "Friendly staff; pleasant, wooded site; gd." ♦ 16 Mar-15 Oct. € 25.50 2013*

⊞ **BAIONA** *1B2* (1km E Coastal) *42.11416, -8.82611*
Camping Bayona Playa, Ctra Vigo-Baiona, Km 19, Sabarís, 36393 Baiona (Pontevedra) [986-35 00 35; fax 986-35 29 52; campingbayona@campingbayona.com; www.campingbayona.com] Fr Vigo on PO552 sp Baiona. Or fr A57 exit Baiona & foll sp Vigo & site sp. Lge, mkd pitch, pt shd; wc; chem disp; mv service pnt; shwrs inc; EHU (3A) €4.80; gas; lndry; shop; rest, snacks; bar; playgrnd; pool; waterslide; sand beach adj; 50% statics; dogs; phone; poss cr; adv bkg (ess high ssn); quiet; red LS/long stay; CKE/CCI. "Area of outstanding natural beauty with sea on 3 sides; well-organised site; excel, clean san facs; avoid access w/end as v busy; ltd facs LS; tight access to sm pitches high ssn; gd cycle track to town; replica of ship 'La Pinta' in harbour." ♦ € 28.40 2011*

⊞ **BALAGUER** *3C2* (8km N Rural) *41.86030, 0.83250*
Camping La Noguera, Partida de la Solana s/n, 25615 Sant Llorenç de Montgai (Lleida) [973-42 03 34; fax 973-42 02 12; info@campinglanoguera.com; www.campinglanoguera.com] Fr Lleida, take N11 ring rd & exit at km 467 onto C13 NE dir Andorra & Balaguer. Head for Balaguer town cent, cross rv & turn R onto LV9047 dir Gerb. Site on L in 8km thro Gerb. App fr Camarasa not rec. Lge, mkd pitch, hdstg, terr, pt shd; wc; chem disp; mv service pnt; baby facs; shwrs inc; EHU (6A) €5.15; gas; lndry; supmkt; rest, snacks; bar; BBQ; playgrnd; pool; games area; TV rm; 80% statics; dogs €3.50; phone; poss cr; Eng spkn; adv bkg; quiet; ccard acc; red long stay; CKE/CCI. "Next to lake & nature reserve; gd cycling; poss diff lge o'fits; friendly warden; gd facs." ♦ ltd. € 46.00 2014*

BANOS DE FORTUNA see Fortuna *4F1*

BANOS DE MONTEMAYOR see Béjar *1D3*

⊞ **BANYOLES** *3B3* (2km W Rural) *42.12071, 2.74690*
Camping Caravaning El Llac, Ctra Circumvallació de l'Estany s/n, 17834 Porqueres (Gerona) [tel/fax 972-57 03 05; info@campingllac.com; www.campingllac.com] Exit AP7 junc 6 to Banyoles. Go strt thro town (do not use by-pass) & exit town at end of lake in 1.6km. Use R-hand layby to turn L sp Porqueres. Site on R in 2.5km. Lge, mkd pitch, pt shd; chem disp; htd wc; shwrs; EHU €4.60; lndry; shop; snacks; bar; pool; lake sw; wifi; 80% statics; dogs €2.30; bus 1km; site clsd mid-Dec to mid-Jan; poss cr; quiet but noisy rest/disco adj in high ssn; red long stay/LS. "Immac, ltd facs LS & stretched high ssn; sm pitches bet trees; pleasant walk around lake to town; site muddy when wet." ♦ € 22.00 2009*

BARBATE see Vejer de la Frontera *2H3*

BARCELONA See sites listed under El Masnou, Gavà and Sitges.

BARREIROS/REINANTE see Foz *1A2*

⊞ **BEAS DE GRANADA** *2G4* (750m N Rural) *37.22416, -3.48805* **Camping Alto de Viñuelas, Ctra de Beas de Granada s/n, 18184 Beas de Granada (Granada) [958-54 60 23; fax 958-54 53 57; info@campingaltodevinuelas.com; www.campingaltodevinuelas.com]** E fr Granada on A92, exit junc 256 & foll sp to Beas de Granada. Site well sp on L in 1.5km. Sm, mkd pitch, terr, pt shd; htd wc; chem disp; mv service pnt; shwrs inc; EHU (5A) €3.50; lndry (inc dryer); shop; rest, snacks; bar; BBQ; playgrnd; pool; wifi; 10% statics; dogs; bus to Granada at gate; Eng spkn; red long stay; CKE/CCI. "In beautiful area; views fr all pitches; 4X4 trip to adj natural park; gd; conv for night halt." € 26.00 (CChq acc) 2014*

⊞ **BECERREA** *1B2* (16km E Rural) *42.83315, -7.06112*
Camping Os Ancares, Ctra NV1, Liber, 27664 Mosteiro-Cervantes (Lugo) [tel/fax 982-36 45 56] Fr A6 exit Becerreá S onto LU722 sp Navia de Suarna. After 10km in Liber turn R onto LU723 sp Doiras, site in 7km just beyond Mosteiro hamlet; site sp. Site ent steep & narr - diff lge o'fits & lge m'vans. Med, terr, shd; wc; shwrs inc; EHU (6A) €3; gas; lndry rm; rest, snacks; bar; playgrnd; pool; fishing; horseriding; some statics; dogs €1; poss cr; quiet; CKE/CCI. "Isolated, scenic site; gd rest & san facs; ltd facs LS; low trees some pitches; gd walking; friendly owner; 17km fr nearest town." € 21.00 2015*

⊞ **BEGUR** *3B3* (1.5km S Rural) *41.94040, 3.19890* **Camping Begur, Ctra d'Esclanyà, Km 2, 17255 Begur (Gerona) [972-62 32 01; fax 972-62 45 66; info@campingbegur.com; www.campingbegur.com]** Exit AP7/E15 junc 6 Gerona onto C66 dir La Bisbal & Palamós. At x-rds to Pals turn L dir Begur then turn R twd Esclanyà, site on R, clearly sp. Slope to site ent. Lge, mkd pitch, hdstg, shd; wc; chem disp; mv service pnt; baby facs; serviced pitches; shwrs inc; EHU (10A) inc; lndry; supmkt; rest, snacks; bar; BBQ; playgrnd; pool; paddling pool; sand/shgl beach 2km; tennis; bike hire; games area; games rm; gym; wifi; entmnt; 14% statics; dogs €6.50; phone; bus adj; Eng spkn; adv bkg; red long stay/snr citizens/CKE/CCI. "Excel, peaceful site; narr site rds poss diff lge o'fits; adj castle & magnificent views; excel touring base." ♦ 15 Apr-25 Sep. € 43.00 2010*

BEJAR *1D3* (6km S Rural) *40.36344, -5.74918* **Camping Cinco Castaños, Ctra de la Sierra s/n, 37710 Candelario (Salamanca) [923-41 32 04; fax 923-41 32 82; profetur@ candelariohotel.com; www.candelariohotel.com]** Fr Béjar foll sp Candelario on C515/SA220, site sp on N side of vill. Steep bends & narr app rd. Sm, mkd pitch, pt sl, pt shd; htd wc; chem disp (wc); baby facs; shwrs inc; EHU (6A) €3.15; gas; lndry; shop 500m; rest; bar; playgrnd; pool high ssn; no dogs; bus 500m; phone; quiet; CKE/CCI. "Mountain vill; friendly owner; no facs in winter; no lge o'fits as steep site." ♦ Holy Week-15 Oct. € 18.50   2011*

⊞ **BEJAR** *1D3* (15km SW Rural) *40.28560, -5.88182* **Camping Las Cañadas, Ctra N630, Km 432, 10750 Baños de Montemayor (Cáceres) [927-48 11 26; fax 927-48 13 14; info@campinglascanadas.com; www.campinglascanadas. com]** Fr S turn off A630 m'way at 437km stone to Heruns then take old N630 twd Béjar. Site at 432km stone, behind 'Hervas Peil' (leather goods shop). Fr N exit A66 junc 427 thro Baños for 3km to site at km432 on R. Lge, mkd pitch, pt sl; shd (net shdg); htd wc; chem disp; mv service pnt; baby facs; shwrs inc; EHU (5A) €4; gas; lndry; shop; rest, snacks; bar; playgrnd; pool; paddling pool; fishing; tennis; bike hire; games area; TV rm; 60% statics; dogs; poss cr; Eng spkn; quiet but rd noise; ccard acc; red long stay/LS; CKE/CCI. "Gd san facs but poss cold shwrs; high vehicles take care o'hanging trees; gd walking country; NH/sh stay." ♦ ltd. € 17.00 (CChq acc)   2009*

⊞ **BELLVER DE CERDANYA** *3B3* (2km E Rural) *42.37163, 1.80674* **Camping Bellver, Ctra N260, Km 193.7, 17539 Isòvol (Gerona) [973-51 02 39; fax 973-51 07 19; camping bellver@campingbellver.com; www.campingbellver.com]** On N260 fr Puigcerdà to Bellver; site on L, well sp. Lge, mkd pitch, shd; htd wc; chem disp (wc); shwrs inc; EHU (5A) €3.50; gas; lndry; rest, snacks; bar; playgrnd; pool; 90% statics; dogs; phone; poss cr; Eng spkn; quiet; ccard acc; CKE/CCI. "Friendly, helpful staff; lovely pitches along rv; san facs immac; v quiet LS; gd NH for Andorra." € 19.00   2011*

⊞ **BELLVER DE CERDANYA** *3B3* (1km W Rural) *42.37110, 1.73625* **Camping La Cerdanya, Ctra N260, Km 200, 25727 Prullans (Lleida) [973-51 02 62; fax 973-51 06 72; cerdanya@prullans.net; www.prullans.net/camping]** Fr Andorra frontier on N260, site sp. Lge, mkd pitch, shd; wc; baby facs; mv service pnt; shwrs inc; EHU (4A) €5.15; gas; lndry; shop; rest, snacks; playgrnd; pool; paddling pool; games area; internet; entmnt; 80% statics; dogs €3.45; phone; bus 1km; poss cr; adv bkg; quiet; red long stay; ccard acc. ♦ € 20.60   2011*

BENABARRE *3B2* (500m N Urban) *42.1103, 0.4811* **Camping Benabarre, 22580 Benabarre (Huesca) [974-54 35 72; fax 974-54 34 32; aytobenabarre@aragon.es]** Fr N230 S, turn L after 2nd camping sp over bdge & into vill. Ignore brown camping sp (pt of riding cent). Med, some hdstg, pt shd; wc; shwrs inc; EHU (10A) inc; shops 500m; bar; pool; tennis; bus 600m; phone; quiet. "Excel, friendly, simple site; gd facs; gd value for money; v quiet LS; warden calls 1700; mkt on Fri; lovely vill with excel chocolate shop; conv Graus & mountains - a real find." 1 Apr-30 Sep. € 14.50   2012*

⊞ **BENICARLO** *3D2* (1.5km NE Urban/Coastal) *40.42611, 0.43777* **Camping La Alegría del Mar, Ctra N340, Km 1046, Calle Playa Norte, 12580 Benicarló (Castellón) [964-47 08 71; info@campingalegria.com; www.camping alegria.com]** Sp off main N340 app Benicarló. Take slip rd mkd Service, go under underpass, turn R on exit & cont twd town, then turn at camp sp by Peugeot dealers. Sm, mkd pitch, pt shd; htd wc; shwrs; EHU (4-6A) €4.70; gas; lndry; shop 500m; rest, snacks; bar; playgrnd; sm pool; beach adj; games rm; wifi; some statics; dogs; phone; bus 800m; poss cr; quiet but rd noise at night & poss cockerels!; red long stay/LS; ccard acc. "British owners; access to pitches variable, poss diff in ssn; vg, clean san facs; Xmas & New Year packages; phone ahead to reserve pitch; excel." € 22.00   2009*

⊞ **BENICASSIM** *3D2* (500m NE Coastal) *40.05709, 0.07429* **Camping Bonterra Park, Avda de Barcelona 47, 12560 Benicàssim (Castellón) [964 30 00 07; fax 964 10 06 69; info@bonterrapark.com; www.bonterrapark.com]** Fr N exit AP7 junc 45 onto N340 dir Benicàssim. In approx 7km turn R to Benicàssim/Centro Urba; strt ahead to traff lts, then turn L, site on L 500m after going under rlwy bdge. Lge, mkd pitch, hdstg, pt sl, shd; htd wc; chem disp; mv service pnt; some serviced pitches; baby facs; shwrs inc; EHU (6-10) inc; gas; lndry (inc dryer); shop; rest, snacks; bar; BBQ; playgrnd; 2 pools (1 covrd & htd); paddling pool; sand beach 300m; tennis; bike hire; gym; entmnt; games area; wifi; games/TV rm; 15% statics; dogs €2.24 (not acc Jul/Aug); no o'fits over 10m; phone; train; sep car park; Eng spkn; adv bkg; rd noise; ccard acc; red long stay/LS/CKE/CCI. "Fabulous site at gd location; excel cycle tracks & public transport; lovely beach; reasonable sized pitches; well-kept & well-run; clean modern san facs; access to some pitches poss diff due to trees; sun shades some pitches; winter festival 3rd wk Jan; Harley Davidson rallies Jan & Sep, check in adv; highly rec; flat rd to town; excel facs; ACSI card acc." ♦ € 66.40 SBS - E19   2013*

⊞ **BENICASSIM** *3D2* (4.5km NW Coastal) *40.05908, 0.08515* **Camping Azahar, Ptda Villaroig s/n, 12560 Benicàssim (Castellón) [964-30 35 51; fax 964-30 25 12; info@camping azahar.es; www.campingazahar.es]** Fr AP7 junc 45 take N340 twd València; in 5km L at top of hill (do not turn R to go-karting); foll sp. Turn R under rlwy bdge opp Hotel Voramar. Lge, mkd pitch, pt sl, terr, unshd; htd wc; chem disp; mv service pnt; baby facs; shwrs inc; EHU (4-6A) €2.90 (long leads poss req); gas; lndry; rest, snacks; bar; playgrnd; pool; sand beach 300m across rd; tennis at hotel; bike hire; 25% statics; dogs €4.07; phone; bus adj; poss cr high ssn; Eng spkn; bus adj; adv bkg; ccard acc; red long stay/LS/snr citizens; CKE/CCI. "Popular site, esp in winter; poss noisy high ssn; access poss diff for m'vans & lge o'fits; poss uneven pitches; organised events; gd walking & cycling; gd touring base." ♦ ltd. € 40.00   2013*

⊞ **BENIDORM** *4F2* (2km N Coastal) *38.56926, -0.09328* **Camping Almafrá, Partida de Cabut 25, 03503 Benidorm (Alicante) [tel/fax 965-88 90 75; info@campingalmafra.es; www.campingalmafra.es]** Exit AP7/E15 junc 65 onto N332 N. Foll sp Alfaz del Pi, site sp. Lge, mkd pitch, unshd; htd wc; sauna; baby facs; sauna; private san facs avail; shwrs inc; EHU (16A); lndry (inc dryer); shop; rest, snacks; bar; BBQ; playgrnd; 2 htd pools (1 covrd); paddling pool; jacuzzi; tennis; wellness/fitness cent; games area; gym; wifi; entmnt; sat TV; 30% statics; no dogs; adv bkg; quiet; red long stay/LS/CKE/CCI. ♦ € 15.00 (CChq acc)   2010*

⊞ **BENIDORM** *4F2* (1.5km NE Urban) *38.54833, -0.09851*
Camping El Raco, Avda Dr Severo Ochoa, 19 Racó de Loix, 03503 Benidorm (Alicante) [965-86 85 52; fax 965-86 85 44; info@campingraco.com; www.campingraco.com] Turn off A7 m'way at junc 65 then L onto A332; take turning sp Benidorm Levante Beach; ignore others; L at 1st traff lghts; strt on at next traff lts, El Raco 1km on R. Lge, hdg/mkd pitch, hdstg, pt sl, pt shd; wc; chem disp; 50% serviced pitches; baby facs; shwrs inc; EHU (10A) metered; gas; lndry (inc dryer); shop; rest, snacks; bar; BBQ; playgrnd; 2 pools (1 htd, covrd); beach 1.5km; games area; Eng spkn; wifi; TV; dogs €1.15; 30% statics; bus; poss v cr in winter; quiet; red LS; CKE/CCI. "Excel site; popular winter long stay but strictly applied rules about leaving c'van unoccupied; EHU metered for long stay; friendly helpful staff; two pin adaptor needed for elec conn." ♦ € 34.00   2014*

⊞ **BENIDORM** *4F2* (3km NE Urban) *38.56024, -0.09844*
Camping Benisol, Avda de la Comunidad Valenciana s/n, 03500 Benidorm (Alicante) [965-85 16 73; fax 965-86 08 95; campingbenisol@yahoo.es; www.campingbenisol.com] Exit AP7/E15 junc 65 onto N332. Foll sp Benidorm, Playa Levante (avoid by-pass). Dangerous rd on ent to site & ent easy to miss. Lge, hdg pitch, hdstg, shd; wc; chem disp; serviced pitches; shwrs inc; EHU (4-6A) €2.80; gas; lndry; shop & rest (high ssn); snacks; bar; playgrnd; pool (hgh ssn); sand beach 4km; TV; 85% statics; dogs; phone; bus to Benidorm; poss cr; Eng spkn; adv bkg with dep; some rd noise; red long stay/LS; CKE/CCI. "Helpful staff; well-run, clean site; many permanent residents." ♦ € 27.00   2011*

⊞ **BENIDORM** *4F2* (3km NE Coastal) *38.54438, -0.10325*
Camping La Torreta, Avda Dr Severo Ochoa 11, 03500 Benidorm (Alicante) [965-85 46 68; fax 965-80 26 53; campinglatorreta@gmail.com] Exit AP7/E15 junc 65 onto N332. Foll sp Playa Levante, site sp. Lge, mkd pitch, hdstg, pt sl, terr, pt shd (bamboo shades); wc (some cont); chem disp; mv service pnt; shwrs inc; EHU (10A) €3.40; gas; lndry (inc dryer); shop; rest, snacks; bar; playgrnd; pool; paddling pool; sand beach 1km; wifi; 10% statics; dogs; bus; no adv bkg; quiet; red long stay; CKE/CCI. "Take care siting if heavy rain; some pitches v sm; popular with long stay winter visitors." ♦ € 29.00   2010*

⊞ **BENIDORM** *4F2* (3km NE Urban) *38.55523, -0.09585*
Camping Villamar, Ctra del Albir, Km 0.300, 03503 Benidorm (Alicante) [966-81 12 55; fax 966-81 35 40; camping@ampingvillamar.com; www.campingvillamar. com] Exit AP7 junc 65. Down hill twd town, turn L at traff lts into Ctra Valenciana, turn R where 2 petrol stns either side of rd, site on L. V lge, mkd pitch, terr, pt shd; wc; chem disp; serviced pitches; shwrs; EHU €3.50; gas; lndry; shop; rest; bar; playgrnd; 2 pools (1 covrd/htd); sand beach 2km; entmnt; games rm; sat TV; phone; no dogs; adv bkg; quiet; red long stay/LS. "Excel site, esp winter; gd security; v welcoming; gd walking area." ♦ € 28.00   2012*

See advertisement above

⊞ **BENIDORM** *4F2* (1km E Coastal) *38.5449, -0.10696*
Camping Villasol, Avda Bernat de Sarriá 13, 03500 Benidorm (Alicante) [965-85 04 22; fax 966-80 64 20; info@camping-villasol.com; www.camping-villasol.com] Leave AP7 at junc 65 onto N332 dir Alicante; take exit into Benidorm sp Levante. Turn L at traff lts just past Camping Titus, then in 200m R at lts into Avda Albir. Site on R in 1km. Care - dip at ent, poss grounding. V lge, mkd pitch, hdstg, shd; htd wc; chem disp; baby facs; shwrs inc; EHU (5A) €4.28; lndry; supmkt; rest, snacks; bar; playgrnd; 2 pools (1 htd, covrd); sand beach 300m; games area; wifi; sat TV all pitches; medical service; currency exchange; 5% statics; no dogs; phone; adv bkg; Eng spkn; quiet; ccard acc; red LS/long stay. "Excel, well-kept site espec in winter; some sm pitches; friendly staff." ♦ € 32.00   2013*

See advertisement opposite

⊞ **BERCEO** *1B4* (200m SE Rural) *42.33565, -2.85335*
Camping Berceo, El Molino s/n, 26327 Berceo (La Rioja) [941-37 32 27; fax 941-37 32 01; camping.berceo@fer.es] Fr E on N120 foll sp Tricio, San Millan de la Cogolla on LR136/LR206. Fr W foll sp Villar de Torre & San Millan. In Berceo foll sp sw pools & site. Med, hdg/mkd pitch, hdstg, pt sl, shd; htd wc; chem disp; baby facs; fam bthrm; shwrs inc; EHU (7A) €4.70; lndry (inc dryer); shop; rest, snacks; bar; playgrnd; pool; paddling pool; bike hire; wifi; TV; 50% statics; phone; bus 200m; adv bkg; quiet; red long stay; CKE/CCI. "Excel base for Rioja vineyards; gd site." ♦ € 30.60   2010*

SPAIN

BESALU *3B3* (2km E Rural) *42.20952, 2.73682* **Camping Masia Can Coromines, Ctra N260, Km 60, 17851 Maià del Montcal (Gerona) [tel/fax 972-59 11 08; coromines@ grn.es; www.cancoromines.com]** NW fr Gerona on C66 to Besalú. Turn R sp Figueras (N260) for 2.5km. At 60km sp turn into driveway on L opp fountain for approx 300m. Narr app & ent. Site is 1km W of Maià. Narr site ent poss diff lge o'fits. Sm, pt shd; wc; serviced pitch; shwrs €0.50; EHU (10-15A) €3; gas; lndry; shop 2.5km; rest high ssn; snacks; bar; playgrnd; pool; bike hire; internet; some statics; dogs €2.90; Eng spkn; adv bkg; quiet with some rd noise; ccard acc; CKE/CCI. "Friendly, family-run site in beautiful area; gd walks; facs poss stretched when site full." ♦ 1 Apr-4 Nov. € 20.40   2011*

BIELSA *3B2* (7km W Rural) *42.65176, 0.14076* **Camping Pineta, Ctra del Parador, Km 7, 22350 Bielsa (Huesca) [974-50 10 89; fax 974-50 11 84; info@campingpineta.com; www.campingpineta.com]** Fr A138 in Beilsa turn W & foll sp for Parador Monte Perdido & Valle de Pineta. Site on L after 8km (ignore previous campsite off rd). Lge, terr, pt sl, pt shd; wc; chem disp; mv service pnt; baby facs; shwrs inc; EHU (6A) €5. (poss rev pol); gas; lndry (inc dryer); shop & 8km; rest, snacks; bar; BBQ; playgrnd; pool; games area; bike hire; dog €2.50; some statics; phone; ccard acc; CKE/CCI. "Well-maintained site; clean facs; glorious location in National Park." 1 Apr-15 Oct. € 36.00   2013*

⊞ **BIESCAS** *3B2* (1km SE Rural) *42.61944, -0.30416* **Camping Gavín, Ctra N260, Km 502.5, 22639 Gavín (Huesca) [974-48 50 90 or 659-47 95 51; fax 974-48 50 17; info@campinggavin.com; www.campinggavin.com]** Take N330/A23/E7 N fr Huesca twd Sabiñánigo then N260 twd Biescas & Valle de Tena. Ignore all sp to Biescas on N260 until R turn at g'ge. Drive over blue bdge & foll sp Gavin & site. Site is at km 502.5 fr Huesca, bet Biescas & Gavín. Lge, mkd pitch, terr, pt shd; htd wc; chem disp; mv service pnt; baby facs; fam bthrm; shwrs inc; EHU (10A) inc; gas; lndry (inc dryer); shop; rest, snacks; bar; playgrnd; pool; tennis; bike hire in National Park; wifi; TV rm; dogs inc; phone; bus 1km; adv bkg; quiet; CKE/CCI. "Wonderful, scenic site nr Ordesa National Park; poss diff access to pitches for lge o'fits & m'vans; superb htd san facs; Eng spkn; immac kept site; excel; superb site inc rest pitches with views, gd for walking." ♦ € 37.00   2015*

⊞ **BILBAO** *1A4* (14km N Coastal) *43.38916, -2.98444* **Camping Sopelana, Ctra Bilbao-Plentzia, Km 18, Playa Atxabiribil 30, 48600 Sopelana (Vizcaya) [946-76 19 81 or 649-11 57 51; fax 944-21 50 10; recepcion@camping sopelana.com; www.campingsopelana.com]** In Bilbao cross rv by m'way bdge sp to airport, foll 637/634 N twd & Plentzia. Cont thro Sopelana & foll sp on L. Med, hdg pitch, sl, terr; wc (some cont); own san; chem disp; mv service pnt; baby facs; shwrs; EHU (10A) €4.50; gas; lndry; shop, rest (w/end only LS); snacks; bar; playgrnd; pool; sand beach 200m; 70% statics; metro 2km; poss cr; Eng spkn; adv bkg ess high ssn; quiet but noise fr disco adj; red long stay; CKE/CCI. "Poss stong sea winds; ltd space for tourers; pitches sm, poss flooded after heavy rain & poss diff due narr, steep site rds; ltd facs LS & poss unclean; poss no hot water for shwrs; helpful manager; site used by local workers; poor security in city cent/ Guggenheim car park; poss clsd LS - phone ahead to check; NH/sh stay only; check open dates." ♦ € 34.50   2013*

BLANES *3C3* (1km S Coastal) *41.65944, 2.77972* **Camping Bella Terra, Avda Vila de Madrid 35-40, 17300 Blanes (Gerona) [972-34 80 17 or 972-34 80 23; fax 972-34 82 75; info@campingbellaterra.com; www.campingbellaterra. com]** Exit A7 junc 9 via Lloret or junc 10 via Tordera. On app Blanes, all campsites are sp at rndabts; all sites along same rd. V lge, mkd pitch, hdstg, pt sl, shd; wc; chem disp; mv service pnt; baby facs; shwrs inc; EHU (5A) inc; gas; lndry (inc dryer); shop; rest, snacks; bar; BBQ; playgrnd; pools; sand beach adj; tennis; games area; games rm; bike hire; wifi; entmnt; TV rm; 15% statics; dogs €4.50; Eng spkn; quiet; ccard acc; red long stay/LS/CKE/CCI. "Split site - 1 side has pool, 1 side adj beach; pitches on pool side lger; vg site with excel facs." ♦ 27 Mar-26 Sep. € 42.40   2010*

⊞ **BLANES** *3C3* (1km S Coastal) *41.65933, 2.77000* **Camping Blanes, Avda Vila de Madrid 33, 17300 Blanes (Gerona) [972-33 15 91; fax 972-33 70 63; info@campingblanes.com; www.campingblanes.com]** Fr N on AP7/E15 exit junc 9 onto NII dir Barcelona & foll sp Blanes. Fr S to end of C32, then NII dir Blanes. On app Blanes, foll camping sps & Playa S'Abanell - all campsites are sp at rndabts; all sites along same rd. Site adj Hotel Blau-Mar. Lge, mkd pitch, shd; wc; chem disp; mv service pnt; shwrs inc; shop; EHU (5A) inc; gas; lndry; supmkt; snacks high ssn; bar; playgrnd; pool; solarium; dir access to sand beach; watersports; bike hire; games rm; wifi; entmnt; dogs; phone; bus; poss cr; Eng spkn; quiet; ccard acc; red LS. "Excel site, espec LS; helpful owner; narr site rds; easy walk to town cent; trains to Barcelona & Gerona." ♦ € 37.00   2011*

SPAIN

BLANES *3C3* (1km S Coastal) *41.6550, 2.77861* **Camping El Pinar Beach, Avda Villa de Madrid s/n, 17300 Blanes (Gerona) [972-33 10 83; fax 972-33 11 00; camping@elpinarbeach.com; www.elpinarbeach.com]** Exit AP7/E15 junc 9 dir Malgrat. On app Blanes, all campsites are sp at rndabts; all sites along same rd. V lge, mkd pitch, shd; wc; chem disp; mv service pnt; baby facs; shwrs inc; EHU (5A) inc; lndry; shop; rest, snacks; bar; BBQ; playgrnd; pool; paddling pool; sand beach adj; games area; entmnt; excursions; internet; TV; 10% statics; dogs €2; phone; adv bkg; ccard acc; red long stay/LS/CKE/CCI. "V pleasant site; gd facs; lovely beach; lots to do." ♦ ltd. 27 Mar-26 Sep. € 36.00   2010*

⊞ **BLANES** *3C3* (1.5km SW Urban/Coastal) *41.66305, 2.78083* **Camping La Masia, Calle Cristòfor Colon 44, 17300 Blanes (Gerona) [972-33 10 13; fax 972-33 31 28; info@campinglamasia.com; www.campinglamasia.com]** Fr A7 exit junc 9 sp Lloret de Mar, then Blanes. At Blanes foll sp Blanes Sur (Playa) & Campings, site immed past Camping S'Abanell, well sp. V lge, hdstg, pt shd; htd wc; chem disp; mv service pnt; 25% serviced pitches; sauna; steam rm; baby facs; shwrs inc; EHU (3-5A) lndry (inc dryer); shop; rest, snacks; bar; playgrnd; 2 pools (1 htd, covrd); paddling pool; sand beach nrby; watersports; tennis 500m; weights rm; wellness cent; games area; games rm; wifi; entmnt; TV rm; 90% statics; dogs; site clsd mid-Dec to mid-Jan; poss cr; Eng spkn; adv bkg; poss noisy at w/ends; red long stay/LS; CKE/CCI. "Well-maintained site; excel, clean facs; helpful staff." ♦ € 38.50 (CChq acc)   2009*

BLANES *3C3* (1.5km SW Coastal) *41.66206, 2.78046* **Camping Solmar, Calle Cristòfor Colom 48, 17300 Blanes (Gerona) [972-34 80 34; fax 972-34 82 83; campingsolmar@campingsolmar.com; www.campingsolmar.com]** Fr N on AP7/E15 exit junc 9 onto NII dir Barcelona & foll sp Blanes. Fr S to end of C32, then NII dir Blanes. On app Blanes, foll camping sps. Lge, hdg/mkd pitch, shd; wc; chem disp; mv service pnt; baby facs; shwrs inc; EHU (6A) inc; lndry (inc dryer); shop; rest, snacks; bar; BBQ; playgrnd; 2 pools; paddling pool; sand beach 150m; tennis; games area; games rm; wifi; entmnt; some statics; dogs free; bus 100m; adv bkg; quiet; ccard acc; red long stay/LS/CKE/CCI. "Excel site & facs." ♦ 2 Apr-12 Oct. € 39.40   2011*

BOCA DE HUERGANO see Riaño *1A3*

⊞ **BOCAIRENT** *4F2* (9km E Rural) *38.75332, -0.54957* **Camping Mariola, Ctra Bocairent-Alcoy, Km 9, 46880 Bocairent (València) [962-13 51 60; info@campingmariola.com; www.campingmariola.com]** Fr N330 turn E at Villena onto CV81. N of Banyeres & bef Bocairent turn E sp Alcoi up narr, steep hill with some diff turns & sheer drops; site sp. Lge, hdstg, pt shd; htd wc (cont); chem disp; child/baby fac; mv service pnt; shwrs inc; EHU (6A) inc; lndry; shop; rest, snacks; bar; BBQ; cooking facs; playgrnd; pool; paddling pool; games area; games rm; bicycles; entmnt; wifi; TV (bar); twin axle acc; Eng spkn; adv bkg acc; 50% statics; phone; ccard acc; CKE/CCI. "In Mariola mountains; gd walking; superb tranquil location in Sierra Mariola National Park, excel walking & cycling, great for dogs, friendly family atmosphere." ♦ ltd. € 22.00   2013*

BOLTANA see Ainsa *3B2*

BONANSA see Pont de Suert *3B2*

⊞ **BOSSOST** *3B2* (3km SE Rural) *42.74921, 0.70071* **Camping Prado Verde, Ctra de Lleida a Francia, N230, Km 173, 25551 Era Bordeta/La Bordeta de Vilamòs (Lleida) [tel/fax 973-64 71 72; info@campingpradoverde.es; www.campingpradoverde.es]** On N230 at km 173 on banks of Rv Garona. Med, shd; htd wc; mv service pnt; baby facs; shwrs; EHU (6A) €5.50; lndry (inc dryer); shop & 3km; rest, snacks; bar; playgrnd; pool; paddling pool; fishing; bike hire; wifi; TV; some statics; dogs; bus; quiet; ccard acc; CKE/CCI. "V pleasant NH." € 22.00   2010*

BROTO *3B2* (1.2km W Rural) *42.59779, -0.13072* **Camping Oto, Afueras s/n, 22370 Oto-Valle De Broto (Huesca) [974-48 60 75; fax 974-48 63 47; info@campingoto.com; www.campingoto.com]** On N260 foll camp sp on N o'skts of Broto. Diff app thro vill but poss. Lge, pt sl, pt shd; wc; chem disp; baby facs; shwrs inc; EHU (10A) €3.80 (poss no earth); gas; lndry; shop; snacks; bar; BBQ; playgrnd; pool; paddling pool; entmnt; adv bkg; quiet; ccard acc. "Excel, clean san facs; excel bar & café; friendly owner; pitches below pool rec; some noise fr adj youth site; conv Ordesa National Park; gd site, pleasant." 5 Mar-15 Oct. € 30.00   2013*

"I need an on-site restaurant"

We do our best to make sure site information is correct, but it is always best to check any must-have facilities are still available or will be open during your visit.

⊞ **BROTO** *3B2* (6km W Rural) *42.61576, -0.15432* **Camping Viu, Ctra N260, Biescas-Ordesa, Km 484.2, 22378 Viu de Linás (Huesca) [974-48 63 01; fax 974-48 63 73; info@campingviu.com; www.campingviu.com]** Lies on N260, 4km W of Broto. Fr Broto, N for 2km on rd 135; turn W twd Biesca at junc with Torla rd; site approx 4km on R. Med, sl, pt shd; htd wc; chem disp; mv service pnt; shwrs inc; EHU (5-8A) €4.20; gas; lndry; shop; rest; BBQ; playgrnd; games rm; bike hire; horseriding; walking, skiing & climbing adj; car wash; phone; adv bkg; quiet; ccard acc; CKE/CCI. "Friendly owners; gd home cooking; fine views; highly rec; clean, modern san facs; poss not suitable for lge o'fits." € 17.40   2011*

⊞ **BURGOS** *1B4* (4km E Rural) *42.34111, -3.65777* **Camp Municipal Fuentes Blancas, Ctra Cartuja Miraflores, Km 3.5, 09193 Burgos [tel/fax 947-48 60 16; info@campingburgos.com; www.campingburgos.com]** E or W on A1 exit junc 238 & cont twd Burgos. Strt over 1st rndabt, then turn R sp Cortes. Look for yellow sps to site. Fr N (N627 or N623) on entering Burgos keep in R hand lane. Foll signs Cartuja miraflores & yellow camp signs. Lge, mkd pitch, shd; some htd wc; chem disp; mv service pnt; baby facs; shwrs inc; EHU (6A) inc; gas; lndry; shop high ssn & 3km; rest, snacks; bar; playgrnd; pool high ssn; games area; wifi; 10% statics; dogs €2.17; phone; bus at gate; poss cr; Eng spkn; quiet; ccard acc; "Clean facs but refurb req (2015); neat, roomy, well-maintained site adj woodland; some sm pitches; ltd facs LS; poss v muddy in wet; easy access town car parks or cycle/rv walk; Burgos lovely town; NH." € 28.00   2015*

CABO DE GATA see Almería *4G1*

⊞ **CABRERA, LA** *1D4* (1km SW Rural) *40.85797, -3.61580*
Camping Pico de la Miel, Ctra A-1 Salida 57, 28751 La
Cabrera (Madrid) [918-68 80 82 or 918-68 95 07; fax 918-
68 85 41; pico-miel@picodelamiel.com or info@picodelamiel.
com; www.picodelamiel.com] Fr Madrid on A1/E5, exit junc
57 sp La Cabrera. Turn L at rndabt, site sp. Lge, mkd pitch,
pt sl, pt shd; htd wc; chem disp; shwrs inc; EHU (10A) €4.45;
gas; lndry (inc dryer); shop high ssn; supmkt 1km; rest, snacks,
bar high ssn & w/end; playgrnd; Olympic-size pool; paddling
pool; sailing; fishing; windsurfing; tennis; games area; squash;
mountain-climbing; car wash; 75% statics; dogs; phone; v cr
high ssn & w/end; some Eng spkn; adv bkg; quiet; ccard acc;
red long stay/LS/CKE/CCI. "Attractive walking country; conv
Madrid; ltd touring area not v attractive; some pitches have low
sun shades; excel san facs; ltd facs LS." ♦ ltd. € 43.00   2014*

"Satellite navigation makes touring much easier"

Remember most sat navs don't know if you're towing or in a larger vehicle – always use yours alongside maps and site directions.

CABRERA, LA *1D4* (15km SW Rural) *40.80821, -3.69106*
Camping Piscis, Ctra Guadalix de la Sierra a Navalafuente,
Km 3, 28729 Navalafuente (Madrid) [918-43 22 68; fax
918-43 22 53; campiscis@campiscis.com; www.campiscis.
com] Fr A1/E5 exit junc 50 onto M608 dir Guidalix de la
Sierra, foll sp to Navalafuente & site. Lge, hdg pitch, hdstg, pt
sl, pt shd; wc; chem disp; shwrs €0.30; EHU (5A) €4.85 (long
lead req); gas; lndry; shop 6km; rest, snacks; bar; playgrnd;
pool; paddling pool; watersports 10km; tennis; games area;
75% statics; quiet; adv bkg; Eng spkn; ccard acc; red LS;
CKE/CCI. "Mountain views; walking; bus to Madrid daily
outside gate; spacious pitches but uneven; rough site rds." ♦
15 Jun-15 Sep. € 24.00   2010*

⊞ **CACERES** *2E3* (4km NW Urban) *39.29190, -6.2446*
Camp Municipal Ciudad de Cáceres, Ctra N630, Km
549.5, 10005 Cáceres [927-23 31 00; fax 927- 23 58 96;
info@campingcaceres.com; www.campingcaceres.com]
Fr Cáceres ring rd take N630 dir Salamanca. At 1st rndbt
turn R sp Vía de Servicio with camping symbol. Foll sp 500m
to site. Or fr N exit A66 junc 545 onto N630 twd Cáceres.
At 2nd rndabt turn L sp Vía de Servicio, site on L adj football
stadium. Med, mkd pitch, hdstg, terr, unshd; wc; chem disp;
mv service pnt; individual san facs each pitch; shwrs inc; EHU
(10-16A) €4.50; gas; lndry; shop; rest, snacks; bar; BBQ;
playgrnd; pool high ssn; paddling pool; games area; wifi; TV;
15% statics; dogs; bus 500m over footbdge; Eng spkn; adv
bkg; distant noise fr indus est nrby; ccard acc; ACSI acc; red
LS/CKE/CCI. "Vg, well-run site; excel facs; vg value rest; gd
bus service to and fr interesting old town with many historical
bldgs; excel site with ensuite facs at each pitch; location not
pretty adj to football stadium & indus est; town to far to walk."
€ 32.00   2014*

CADAQUES *3B3* (1km N Coastal) *42.29172, 3.28260*
Camping Cadaqués, Ctra Port Lligat 17, 17488 Cadaqués
(Girona) [972-25 81 26; fax 972-15 93 83; info@camping
cadaques.com; www.spain.info] At ent to town, turn L at
rdbt (3rd exit) sp thro narr rds, site in about 1.5km on L. NB
App to Cadaqués on busy, narr mountain rds, not suitable lge
o'fits. If raining, rds only towable with 4x4. Lge, mkd pitch,
hdstg, sl, pt shd; wc; chem disp; shwrs; EHU (5A) €5.95; gas;
lndry; shop; rest, snacks; bar; playgrnd; pool; paddling pool;
shgl beach 600m; no dogs; sep car park; poss cr; Eng spkn; no
adv bkg; quiet; ccard acc. "Cadaqués home of Salvador Dali;
sm pitches; medical facs high ssn; san facs poss poor LS; fair,
red facs in LS next to m'way so poss noisy but gd for en-route
stop." Easter-17 Sep. € 35.00   2013*

CADAVEDO see Luarca *1A3*

⊞ **CALATAYUD** *3C1* (15km N Rural) *41.44666, -1.55805*
Camping Saviñan Parc, Ctra El Frasno-Mores, Km 7,
50299 Saviñan (Zaragoza) [tel/fax 976-82 54 23]
Exit A2/E90 (Zaragoza-Madrid) at km 255 to T-junc. Turn R to
Saviñan for 6km, foll sps to site 1km S. Lge, hdstg, terr, pt shd;
wc; chem disp; mv service pnt; shwrs inc; EHU (6-10A) €4.20;
gas; lndry; shop; playgrnd; pool high ssn; tennis; horseriding;
50% statics; dogs €2.70; phone; site clsd Jan; quiet; ccard acc;
CKE/CCI. "Beautiful scenery & views; some sm narr pitches; rec
identify pitch location to avoid stop/start on hill; terr pitches
have steep, unfenced edges; many pitches with sunscreen
frames & diff to manoeuvre long o'fits; modern facs block but
cold in winter & poss stretched high ssn; hot water to some
shwrs only; gates poss clsd LS - use intercom; site poss clsd
Feb." € 24.00   2014*

⊞ **CALDES DE MONTBUI** *3C3* (2km N Rural) *41.6442, 2.1564*
Camping El Pasqualet, Ctra Sant Sebastià de Montmajor,
Km 0.3, 08140 Caldes de Montbui (Barcelona) [938-65 46 95;
fax 938-65 38 96; elpasqualet@elpasqualet.com;
www.elpasqualet.com] N fr Caldes on C59 dir Montmajor,
site sp on L off rd BV1243. Med, terr, pt shd; wc; chem disp;
mv service pnt; baby facs; shwrs inc; EHU (4A) €6.90; gas;
lndry (inc dryer); shop 2km; rest, snacks; bar; playgrnd; pool;
games area; TV rm; 80% statics; dogs €2.60; bus 2km; site
clsd mid-Dec to mid-Jan; poss cr; adv bkg; quiet. "Beautiful
area; ltd touring pitches; facs poss stretched high ssn." ♦
€ 26.40   2010*

CALELLA *3C3* (2km NE Coastal) *41.61774, 2.67680* **Camping
Caballo de Mar, Passeig Maritim s/n, 08397 Pineda de
Mar (Barcelona)** [937-67 17 06; fax 937-67 16 15;
info@caballodemar.com; www.caballodemar.com]
Fr N exit AP7 junc 9 & immed turn R onto NII dir Barcelona.
Foll sp Pineda de Mar & turn L twd Paseo Maritimo. Fr S on
C32 exit 122 dir Pineda de Mar & foll dir Paseo Maritimo.
Lge site, sm mkd pitch, shd; wc; chem disp; baby facs; shwrs
inc; EHU (3-6A) €3.40-4.40; gas; lndry; shop high ssn; rest,
snacks; bar; BBQ; playgrnd; pool; sand beach adj; games area;
games rm; entmnt; internet; 25% statics; dogs €2.20; rlwy
stn 2km (Barcelona 30 mins); Eng spkn; adv bkg; quiet; ccard
acc; red long stay/CKE/CCI. "Excursions arranged; gd touring
base & conv Barcelona; gd, modern facs; excel; pitches sm for
twin axle; noise fr locals on site." ♦ 31 Mar-30 Sep. € 34.00
(CChq acc)   2012*

SPAIN

⊞ **CALELLA** *3C3* (1km S Coastal) *41.60722, 2.63973*
Camping Botànic Bona Vista Kim, Ctra N11, Km 665.8,
08370 Calella de la Costa (Barcelona) [937-69 24 88; fax
937-69 58 04; info@botanic-bonavista.net; www.botanic-
bonavista.net] A19/C32 exit sp Calella onto NII coast rd, site
is sp S of Calella on R. Care needed on busy rd & sp almost
on top of turning (adj Camp Roca Grossa). Lge, mkd pitch,
hdstg, terr, pt shd; shwrs inc; wc; chem disp; mv service pnt;
sauna; shwrs inc; EHU (6A) €7.80 (rev pol); lndry; supmkt; rest,
snacks; bar; BBQ/picnic area; playgrnd; pool; paddling pool;
sand beach adj; solarium; jacuzzi; TV; 20% statics; dogs €5.90;
phone; poss cr; Eng spkn; adv bkg; some rd noise; ccard acc;
CKE/CCI. "Steep access rd to site - owner prefers to tow c'vans
with 4x4; poss diff v lge m'vans; all pitches have sea view;
friendly owner; clean facs; train to Barcelona fr St Pol (2km)."
♦ € 31.00   2010*

CALELLA *3C3* (1km SW Coastal) *41.60635, 2.63890* **Camping
Roca Grossa, Ctra N-11, Km 665, 08370 Calella (Barcelona)
[937-69 12 97; fax 937-66 15 56; rocagrossa@rocagrossa.
com; www.rocagrossa.com]** Situated off rd N11 at km
stone 665, site sp. V steep access rd to site. Lge, sl, terr, shd;
wc; chem disp; mv service pnt; shwrs inc; EHU (6A) €6; gas;
lndry; shop & rest at ent; snacks; bar; games rm; TV rm; pool;
playgrnd; beach adj; windsurfing; tennis; statics; phone; dogs
€4.20; adv bkg; Eng spkn; ccard acc. "V friendly, family-run
site; steep - tractor pull avail - but level pitches; clean modern
facs; excel pool & playgrnd on top of hill; scenic drive to
Tossa de Mar; conv for Barcelona." 1 Apr-30 Sep. € 28.40
(CChq acc)   2010*

CALIG *3D2* (1km NW Rural) *40.45183, 0.35211* **Camping
L'Orangeraie, Camino Peniscola-Calig, 12589 Càlig
[34 964 765 059; fax 34 964 765 460; info@camping-
lorangeraie.es]** On AP7 exit 43 Benicarlo-Peniscola. 1st R at
rndabt to Calig then foll sp to campsite. Fr N340 exit N232
to Morella, then after 1.5km turn L to Calig CV135, foll sp to
campsite. Med, hdg/mkd pitch, terr, pt shd; wc; chem disp;
mv service pnt; baby facs; EHU (10A); lndry; shop; snacks; bar;
BBQ; playgrnd; pool; waterslide; paddling pool; sandy beach
8km; games area; entmnt; wifi; 15% statics; dogs €2.50; bus
1km; twin axles; Eng spkn; adv bkg; quiet. "Excel site." ♦ ltd.
1 Apr-12 Oct. € 41.00   2014*

⊞ **CALLOSA D'EN SARRIA** *4F2* (6km NE Rural) *38.65450,
-0.09246* **Camping Fonts d'Algar, Ptda Segarra, 03510
Callosa d'en Sarrià (Alicante) [639-52 03 65 or 699-11 26 88
(mob); campingalgar@hotmail.com; www.campingfonts
dalgar.co.uk]** Exit A7 junc 64 & take CV755 NW dir Alcoi to
Collosa. In Callosa take CV715 N & in 2km turn R at sp Fonts
d'Algar. Steep, narr rd bef site on R. Med, hdstg, terr, unshd;
wc; chem disp; shwrs inc; EHU (5-16A) €4.50; shop & shop
6km; rest, snacks; bar; BBQ; sand beach 15km; entmnt; some
statics; dogs; Eng spkn; quiet. "Mountain views; cactus garden
& waterfalls nr; site being improved (2010)." € 23.00   2010*

CALONGE see Playa de Aro *3B3*

⊞ **CALPE** *4F2* (300m NE Urban/Coastal) *38.64488, 0.05604*
Camping CalpeMar, Calle Eslovenia 3, 03710 Calpe
(Alicante) [tel/fax 965-87 55 76; info@campingcalpemar.
com; www.campingcalpemar.com] Exit AP7/E15 junc
63 onto N332 & foll sp, take slip rd sp Calpe Norte & foll
dual c'way CV746 round Calpe twd Peñón d'Ifach. At
rndabt nr police stn with metal statues turn L, then L at
next rndabt, over next rndabt, site 200m on R. Med, hdg/
mkd pitch, hdstg, unshd; htd wc; chem disp; baby facs; all
serviced pitches; shwrs inc; EHU (10A) inc (metered for long
stay); lndry (inc dryer); ice; shop 500m; rest, snacks; bar;
BBQ; playgrnd; pool; sand beach 300m; games area; games
rm; entmnt; Spanish lessons; car wash; dog wash; wifi; TV
rm; 3% statics; dogs free; phone; extra lge pitches avail at
additional charge; bus adj; sep car park; Eng spkn; adv bkg;
quiet; ccard acc; red long stay/LS; CKE/CCI. "High standard
site; well-kept & laid out; gd security; excel; gd for long stay,
friendly staff; close to beach and Lidl." ♦ € 36.00   2012*

See advertisement below

⊞ **CAMARASA** *3B2* (23km N Rural) *42.00416, 0.86583*
Camping Zodiac, Ctra C13, Km 66, La Baronia de Sant
Oïsme, 25621 Camarasa (Lleida) [tel/fax 973-45 50 03;
zodiac@campingzodiac.com; www.campingzodiac.com]
Fr C13 Lleida to Balaguer. N of Balaguer take C13 & foll sp for
Camarasa, then dir Tremp & site. Steep, winding but scenic app
rd. Med, hdstg, pt sl, terr, pt shd; wc; chem disp; baby facs;
shwrs; EHU (5A) €4.60; shop; lndry; rest, snacks; bar; playgrnd;
pool; rv sw adj; tennis; TV; 90% statics; phone; Eng spkn;
quiet; ccard acc. "Site on reservoir; poss untidy, shabby LS;
some sm pitches diff due trees; excel views & walks; Terradets
Pass 2km." ♦ ltd. € 19.00   2011*

CAMBRILS See also sites listed under Salou.

⊞ **CAMBRILS** 3C2 (1km N Rural) 41.07928, 1.06661
**Camping Àmfora d'Arcs, Ctra N340, Km 1145, 43391
Vinyols i Els Arcs (Tarragona) [977-36 12 11; fax 977-79 50 75;
info@amforadarcs.com; www.amforadarcs.com]** Exit AP7 junc 37 onto N340 E & watch for km sps, site bet 1145 & 1146km. Lge, hdg pitch, hdstg, pt shd; wc; chem disp; shwrs inc; EHU (5A) inc; gas; lndry; supmkt opp; rest high ssn; bar; playgrnd; pool; beach 1.5km; 60% statics; dogs €4.50; phone; bus 300m; site poss clsd Xmas; poss cr; Eng spkn; adv bkg; noisy espec at w/end; ccard acc; red long stay/LS; CKE/CCI. "Sm pitches." € 34.50   2009*

CAMBRILS 3C2 (1.5km N Urban/Coastal) 41.06500, 1.08361
**Camping Playa Cambrils Don Camilo, Carrer Oleastrum 2,
Ctra Cambrils-Salou, Km 1.5, 43850 Cambrils (Tarragona)
[977-36 14 90; fax 977-36 49 88; camping@playacambrils.
com; www.playacambrils.com]** Exit A7 junc 37 dir Cambrils & N340. Turn L onto N340 then R dir port then L onto coast rd. Site sp on L at rndabt after rv bdge 100m bef watch tower on R, approx 2km fr port. V lge, hdg/mkd pitch, shd; wc; chem disp; baby facs; shwrs inc; EHU (5A) inc; gas; lndry (inc dryer); supmkt; rest, snacks; bar; playgrnd; htd pool; paddling pool; sand beach adj; tennis; games rm; boat hire; bike hire; watersports; entmnt; children's club; cinema; wifi; TV rm; 25% statics; bus 200m; cash machine; doctor; 24-hr security; dogs €4.35; Eng spkn; adv bkg ess high ssn; some rd & rlwy noise; ccard acc; red long stay/LS/CKE/CCI. "Helpful, friendly staff; sports activities avail; Port Aventura 5km; vg site." ♦ 15 Mar-12 Oct. € 43.00 (CChq acc)   2011*

CAMBRILS 3C2 (2km S Coastal) 41.05533, 1.02333 **Camping
Joan, Urbanització La Dorada, Passeig Marítim 88, 43850
Cambrils (Tarragona) [977-36 46 04; fax 977-79 42 14;
info@campingjoan.com; www.campingjoan.com]** Exit AP7 junc 37 onto N340, S dir València. Turn off at km 1.141 & Hotel Daurada, foll site sp. Lge, hdg/mkd pitch, hdstg, terr, shd; htd wc; chem disp; mv service pnt; baby facs; shwrs inc; EHU (5A) €4.40; gas; lndry; supmkt; rest, snacks; bar; BBQ; playgrnd; pool & paddling pool; sand beach adj; watersports; fishing; bike hire; games area; games rm; wifi; entmnt; sat TV; 16% statics; dogs €3.10; phone; currency exchange; car wash; Eng spkn; adv bkg; quiet; red LS/long stay/CKE/CCI. "Conv Port Aventura; gd family site; v clean san facs; friendly welcome; some sm pitches; gd beach; vg." ♦ 27 Mar-5 Nov. € 30.00   2009*

CAMBRILS 3C2 (5km SW Coastal) 41.04694, 1.00361 **Camping
Oasis Mar, Ctra de València N340, Km 1139, 43892 Montroig
(Tarragona) [977-17 95 95; fax 977-17 95 16; info@oasismar.
com; www.oasismar.com]** Fr AP7 exit 37; N340 Tarragona-València rd, at Montroig, km 1139. Lge, mkd pitch, pt shd; wc; chem disp; shwrs inc; baby facs; EHU (5A) €5; gas; lndry; shop; rest, snacks; bar; BBQ; playgrnd; pool; sand beach adj; watersports; 30% statics; dogs €5.08; Eng spkn; red long stay/LS. "Excel site by super beach; friendly, helpful owners; gd facs; busy at w/end when statics occupied; vg." 1 Mar-31 Oct. € 30.00   2009*

CAMBRILS 3C2 (8km SW Coastal) 41.03333, 0.96777
**Playa Montroig Camping Resort, N340, Km1.136, 43300
Montroig (Tarragona) [977 810 637; fax 977 811 411;
info@playamontroig.com; www.playamontroig.com]** Exit AP7 junc 37, W onto N340. Site has own dir access onto N340 bet Cambrils & L'Hospitalet de L'Infant, well sp fr Cambrils. V lge, mkd pitch, pt sl, shd; htd wc; chem disp; mv service pnt; serviced pitches; baby facs; shwrs inc; EHU (10A) inc; gas; lndry; supmkt; rest, snacks; bars; playgrnd; 3 htd pools; sand beach adj; tennis; games area; games rm; skateboard track; many sports; bike hire; golf 3km; cash machine; doctor; wifi; entmnt; 30% statics; no dogs; phone; Eng spkn; adv bkg; some rd & rlwy noise; ccard acc; red snr citizens/LS/CKE/CCI. "Magnificent, clean, secure site; private, swept beach; some sm pitches & low branches; 4 grades pitch/price; highly rec." ♦ 1 Apr-30 Oct. € 53.00   2011*

⊞ **CAMBRILS** 3C2 (1.8km W Urban/Coastal) 41.06550,
1.04460 **Camping La Llosa, Ctra N340 Barcelona a Valencia,
Km 1143, 43850 Cambrils (Tarragona) [977-36 26 15; fax
977-79 11 80; info@camping-lallosa.com; www.camping-
lallosa.com]** Exit A7/E15 at junc 37 & join N340 S. Head S into Cambrils (ignore L turn to cent) & at island turn R. Site sp on L within 100m. Fr N exit junc 35 onto N340. Strt over at x-rds, then L over rlwy bdge at end of rd, strt to site. V lge, hdstg, shd; wc; shwrs inc; EHU (5A) €5; gas; lndry; shop; rest, snacks; bar; playgrnd; pool; sand beach; entmnt high ssn; car wash; 50% statics; dogs €3.50; phone; bus 500m; poss cr; Eng spkn; some rd & rlwy noise; ccard acc; red long stay/LS. "Interesting fishing port; gd facs; excel pool; gd supmkt nrby; poss diff siting for m'vans due low trees; excel winter NH." ♦ € 51.00   2014*

CAMBRILS 3C2 (8km W Coastal) 41.03717, 0.97622
**Camping La Torre del Sol, Ctra N340, Km 1.136,
Miami-Playa, 43300 Montroig Del Camp (Tarragona)
[977 810 486; fax 977-81 13 06; info@latorredelsol.com;
www.latorredelsol.com]** Leave A7 València/Barcelona m'way at junc 37 & foll sp Cambrils. After 1.5km join N340 coast rd S for 6km. Watch for site sp 4km bef Miami Playa. Fr S exit AP7 junc 38, foll sp Cambrils on N340. Site on R 4km after Miami Playa. Site ent narr, alt ent avail for lge o'fits. V lge, hdg/mkd pitch, shd; wc; chem disp; mv service pnt; baby facs; sauna; shwrs inc; EHU (6A) inc (10A avail); gas; lndry (inc dryer); supmkt; rest, snacks; bar; BBQ; playgrnd; 2 htd pools; paddling pool; whirlpool; jacuzzi; direct access private sand beach; tennis; squash; bike hire; gym; skateboard zone; golf 4km; cinema; disco; games rm; wifi; entmnt; TV; 40% statics; no dogs; poss v cr; Eng spkn; adv bkg; quiet, but some rd/rlwy noise & disco; ccard acc; red LS. "Attractive well-guarded site for all ages; sandy pitches; gd, clean san facs; steps to facs for disabled; access to pitches poss diff lge o'fits due trees & narr site rds; radios/TVs to be used inside vans only; conv Port Aventura, Aquaparc, Aquopolis; highly rec, can't praise site enough; excel." ♦ 15 Mar-30 Oct. € 52.00 SBS - E14   2011*

See advertisement on previous page

⊞ **CAMPELL** *4E2* (1km S Rural) *38.77672, -0.10529* **Camping Vall de Laguar, Carrer Sant Antoni 24, 03791 La Vall de Laguar (Alicante) [965-57 74 90 or 699-77 35 09; info@campinglaguar.com; www.campinglaguar.com]** Exit A7 junc 62 sp Ondara. Turn L to Orba onto CV733 dir Benimaurell & foll sp to Vall de Laguar. In Campell vill (narr rds) fork L & foll site sp uphill (narr rd). Steep ent to site. Lge o'fits ignore sp in vill & turn R to Fleix vill. In Fleix turn L to main rd, downhill to site sp at hairpin. Diff app. Med, mkd pitch, hdstg, terr, pt shd; htd wc; chem disp; shwrs inc; EHU (5-10A) €2.75; gas; lndry; shop 500m; rest, snacks; bar; BBQ; pool; sand beach 18km; 50% statics; dogs €1.30; phone; Eng spkn; adv bkg; quiet; ccard acc; red LS/long stay; CKE/CCI. "Sm pitches diff for lge o'fits; m'vans 7.5m max; excel home-cooked food in rest; ideal site for walkers; mountain views; friendly owners live on site; excel but rec sm o'fits & m'vans only." ♦ ltd. € 21.50   2009*

CAMPELLO, EL see Alicante *4F2*

> ## "There aren't many sites open at this time of year"
> If you're travelling outside peak season remember to call ahead to check site opening dates – even if the entry says 'open all year'.

⊞ **CAMPRODON** *3B3* (2km S Rural) *42.29010, 2.36230* **Camping Vall de Camprodón, Les Planes d'en Xenturri, Ctra Ripoll-Camprodón, C38, Km 7.5, 17867 Camprodón [972-74 05 07; fax 972-13 06 32; info@valldecamprodon.net; www.valldecamprodon.net]** Fr Gerona W on C66/C26 to Sant Pau de Segúries. Turn N onto C38 to Camprodón, site sp. Access over bdge weight limit 3,5000 kg. Lge, mkd pitch, pt shd; htd wc; mv service pnt; baby facs; shwrs; EHU (4-10) €4.20-9.10 (poss rev pol); lndry (inc dryer); shop; rest, snacks; bar; BBQ; playgrnd; pool; paddling pool; rv fishing; tennis; games area; horseriding; wifi; entmnt; TV; 90% statics; dogs €5; bus 200m; o'night m'van area (no san facs); adv bkg; quiet. "Camprodón attractive vill; lovely scenery; peaceful site; helpful staff; ltd facs LS." ♦ € 31.40   2011*

CANDAS see Gijon *1A3*

CANDELARIO see Béjar *1D3*

CANET DE MAR *3C3* (1.5km E Coastal) *41.59086, 2.59195* **Camping Globo Rojo, Ctra N11, Km 660.9, 08360 Canet de Mar (Barcelona) [tel/fax 937-94 11 43; camping@globo-rojo.com; www.globo-rojo.com]** On N11 500m N of Canet de Mar. Site clearly sp on L. Gd access. Med, hdg/mkd pitch, hdstg, shd; wc; chem disp; baby facs; shwrs; EHU (10A) €6; gas; lndry; shop; rest, snacks; bar; BBQ; playgrnd; pool; paddling pool; shgl beach & watersports adj; tennis; games area; horseriding 2km; bike hire; internet; TV rm; 80% statics; dogs €5.50; phone; sep car park; Eng spkn; adv bkg; rd noise; ccard acc; red LS/CKE/CCI. "Excel facs; friendly, family-run site; busy w/end; slightly run down area; conv Barcelona by train (40km)." ♦ 1 Apr-30 Sep. € 42.00   2010*

⊞ **CANGAS DE ONIS** *1A3* (16km E Rural) *43.33527, -4.94777* **Camping Picos de Europa, Avin-Onís, 33556 Avín, [985-84 40 70; fax 985-84 42 40; info@picos-europa.com; www.picos-europa.com]** E80, exit 307. Dir Posada A5-115. Loc on the rd Onis-Carrena, 15 km fr Cangas de Onis and 10 km fr Carrena, foll sps. Med, hdg/mkd pitch, terr, pt shd; wc; chem disp; baby facs; shwrs inc; EHU (6A) €3.80; gas; lndry (inc dryer); shop; rest, snacks; bar; pool; beach 20km; horseriding; canoeing on local rvs; some statics; phone; poss cr; Eng spkn; adv bkg; some rd noise & goat bells; ccard not acc; CKE/CCI. "Owners v helpful; beautiful, busy, well-run site; vg value rest; modern san facs; poss diff access due narr site rds & cr; some sm pitches - lge o'fits may need 2; conv local caves, mountains, National Park, beaches; highly rec." € 22.00   2013*

CANGAS DE ONIS *1A3* (3km SE Rural) *43.34715, -5.08362* **Camping Covadonga, 33589 Soto de Cangas (Asturias) [tel/fax 985-94 00 97; info@camping-covadonga.com; www.camping-covadonga.com]** N625 fr Arriondas to Cangas de Onis, then AS114 twds Covadonga & Panes, cont thro town sp Covadonga. At rndabt take 2nd exit sp Cabrales, site on R in 100m. Access tight. Med, mkd pitch, pt shd; wc; chem disp; shwrs; EHU (10A) €3.50 (no earth); lndry (inc dryer); shop; supmkt in town; rest, snacks; bar; bus adj; poss cr; adv bkg; quiet, but slight rd noise; red long stay; CKE/CCI. "Sm pitches; take care with access; site rds narr; 17 uneven steps to san facs; conv for Picos de Europa." Holy Week & 15 Jun-30 Sep. € 21.00   2009*

CAPMANY see Figueres *3B3*

CARAVIA ALTA see Colunga *1A3*

CARBALLINO *1B2* (3km SW Rural) *42.42341, -8.09854* **Camp Municipal Arenteiro, Parque Etnográfico do Arenteiro s/n, 32500 O Carballiño (Ourense) [988-27 38 09; camping@carballino.org; www.campingarenteiro.carballino.org]** N fr Ourense on N541, just beyond km 29, turn L at Godas do Rio at site sp. Site in 1km on L. Sm, mkd pitch, shd; wc; chem disp; mv service pnt; shwrs inc; EHU (10A) €2.50; lndry rm; shop & 1.5km; rest, snacks; bar; BBQ; playgrnd; dogs; Eng spkn; quiet; red CKE/CCI. "In Ribeiro wine area among well-wooded mountains; vg mkd walks; highly rec." ♦ 31 Mar-30 Sep. € 10.50   2010*

⊞ **CARBALLO** *1A2* (6km N Coastal) *43.29556, -8.65528* **Camping Baldayo, Ctra Coruña- Arteyo, 15684 Carballo (La Coruña) [981-73 95 29]** Loc in Rebordelos, access via AC-514. Sm, pt sl, terr, pt shd; wc; chem disp; shwrs; EHU €1.50; lndry; shop; snacks; bar; playgrnd; sand beach 500m; 95% statics; no dogs; phone; poss cr; quiet. "Sm pitches & narr camp rds poss diff lge o'fits; poss unkempt LS." € 15.00   2012*

CARCHUNA see Motril *2H4*

SPAIN

www.campingmasnou.com CASTELLÓ D'EMPÚRIES (GIRONA)

CARIDAD, LA (EL FRANCO) *1A3* (1km SE Coastal) *43.54795, -6.80701* **Camping Playa de Castelló, Ctra N634, Santander-La Coruña, Km 532, 33758 La Caridad (El Franca) (Asturias)** [985-47 82 77; contacto@ campingcastello.com; www.campingcastello.com] On N634/E70 Santander dir La Coruña, turn N at km 532. Site in 200m fr N634, sp fr each dir. Sm, mkd pitch, pt shd; wc; chem disp; baby facs; shwrs inc; EHU (2-5A) €3; gas; lndry; shop, bar high ssn only; BBQ; playgrnd; shgl beach 800m; internet; some statics; dogs €1; bus 200m; Eng spkn; adv bkg; quiet; red long stay/CKE/CCI. "A green oasis with character; gd." Holy Week & 1 Jun-30 Sep. € 23.00   2012*

"That's changed – Should I let The Club know?"

If you find something on site that's different from the site entry, fill in a report and let us know. See www.caravanclub.co.uk/europereport.

⊞ **CARIDAD, LA (EL FRANCO)** *1A3* (3.6km W Rural) *43.55635, -6.86218* **Camping A Grandella, Ctra N634, Km 536.9 (Desvío San Juan de Prendonés), 33746 Valdepares (Asturias)** [607-85 49 00 or 661-35 28 70 (mob); camping@ campingagrandella.com] Sp fr N634/E70. Med, pt shd; wc; chem disp; shwrs inc; EHU €3.50; lndry; snacks; bar; playgrnd; bus 200m; some statics; dogs €1; site clsd mid-Dec to mid-Jan; quiet. "Attractive little site; well-situated." € 18.00   2012*

⊞ **CARLOTA, LA** *2G3* (1km NE Rural) *37.68321, -4.91891* **Camping Carlos III, Ctra de Madrid-Cádiz Km 430.5, 14100 La Carlota (Córdoba)** [957-30 03 38; fax 957-30 06 97; camping@campingcarlosiii.com; www.campingcarlosiii. com] Approx 25km SW fr Córdoba on A4/E5, exit at km 432 turning L under autovia. Turn L at rndabt on main rd, site well sp on L in 800m. Lge, mkd pitch, hdstg, pt sl, pt shd; htd wc (some cont); chem disp; shwrs inc; EHU (5-10A) €4; gas; lndry; shop; rest; bar; BBQ; playgrnd; pool; horseriding; 30% statics; dogs; phone; Eng spkn; adv bkg; ccard acc; red long stay; CKE/ CCI. "V efficient, well-run site; less cr than Córdoba municipal site; excel pool; gd, clean facs; if pitched under mulberry trees, poss staining fr berries; bus to Córdoba every 2 hrs." ♦ € 21.00   2010*

⊞ **CARRION DE LOS CONDES** *1B4* (400m W Rural) *42.33694, -4.60638* **Camping El Edén, Ctra Vigo-Logroño, Km 200, 34120 Carrión de los Condes (Palencia)** [979-81 11 52; administracion@campingeleden.es; www.campingeleden.es] Exit A231 to Carrión, turn L immed onto N120 sp Burgos & ent town fr NE. Site sp E & W ents to town off N120 adj Rv Carrión at El Plantio. App poorly sp down narr rds to rv. Suggest park nr Café España & check rte on foot. Med, mkd pitch, pt shd; wc; shwrs; mv service pnt; EHU (5A) €3.50; gas; lndry; rest; bar; playgrnd; dogs; bus 500m; ccard acc. "Pleasant walk to town; basic rvside site; recep in bar/rest; site open w/ends only LS; fair NH; quite lively in high ssn." ♦ € 22.00   2014*

⊞ **CARTAGENA** *4G1* (10km SW Coastal/Rural) *37.58611, -1.0675* **Camping Naturista El Portús (Naturist), 30393 Cartagena (Murcia)** [968-55 30 52; fax 968-55 30 53; elportus@elportus.com; www.elportus.com] Fr N332 Cartagena to Mazarrón rd take E20 to Canteras. In Canteras turn R onto E22 sp Isla Plana & in 500m turn L onto E21 sp Galifa/El Portús. In 2km at rndabt, site ent on L. Lge, mkd pitch; some hdstg, pt shd; wc; chem disp; mv service pnt; shwrs inc; EHU (6A) inc; gas; lndry (inc dryer); shop; rest, snacks; bar; playgrnd; htd, covrd pool & paddling pool; shgl beach adj; tennis; games area; gym; spa; golf 15km; internet; entmnt; 30% statics; dogs €4.80; phone; bus 1km; poss cr; Eng spkn; ccard acc; red LS/ long stay; INF card req. "Restful LS; gd situation; many long-stay winter visitors; helpful staff; random pitching & poss untidy site; Cartagena interesting old town." ♦ ltd. € 41.00   2009*

CASPE *3C2* (12km NE Rural) *41.28883, 0.05733* **Lake Caspe Camping, Ctra N211, Km 286.7, 50700 Caspe (Zaragoza)** [976-63 41 74 or 689-99 64 30 (mob); fax 976-63 41 87; lakecaspe@lakecaspe.com; www.campinglakecaspe.com] Fr E leave AP2 or N11 at Fraga & foll N211 dir Caspe to site. Fr W take N232 fr Zaragoza then A1404 & A221 E thro Caspe to site in 16km on L at km 286.7, sp. Med, hdg/mkd pitch, hdstg, pt shd; wc; chem disp; baby facs; shwrs inc; EHU (5-10A) €5.60; gas; lndry; shop; rest, snacks; bar; playgrnd; pool high ssn; fishing; sailing; 10% statics; dogs €3.75; phone; poss cr; Eng spkn; adv bkg; quiet; CKE/CCI. "Gd, well-run, scenic site but isolated (come prepared); avoid on public hols; site rds gravelled but muddy after rain; sm pitches nr lake; gd watersports; mosquitoes; beware low branches." 1Mar-10 Nov. € 37.00   2013*

CASTANARES DE LA RIOJA see Haro *1B4*

CASTELLBO see Seo de Urgel *3B3*

CASTELLO D'EMPURIES *3B3* (4km NE Rural) *42.26460, 3.10160* **Camping Mas Nou, Ctra Mas Nou 7, Km 38, 17486 Castelló d'Empúries (Gerona) [972-45 41 75; fax 972-45 43 58; info@campingmasnou.com; www.campingmasnou.com]** On m'way A7 exit 3 if coming fr France & exit 4 fr Barcelona dir Roses (E) C260. Site on L at ent to Empuriabrava - use rndabt to turn. Lge, shd, mkd pitch; htd wc; chem disp; mv service point; baby facs; shwrs inc; EHU (10A) €4.90; lndry (inc dryer); shops 200m; rest, snacks; bar; BBQ; playgrnd; pool; beach 2.5km; tennis; games area; wifi; entmnt; TV; 5% statics; dogs €2.35; phone; Eng spkn; red long stay/LS; ccard acc; CKE/CCI. "Aqua Park 4km, Dali Museum 10km; gd touring base; helpful staff; well-run site; excel, clean san facs; sports activities & children's club; gd cycling; excel." ♦ 31 Mar-30 Sep. € 38.70 (CChq acc)   2011*

See advertisement opposite

CASTELLO D'EMPURIES *3B3* (4km SE Coastal) *42.20725, 3.10026* **Camping Nautic Almatá, Aiguamolls de l'Empordà, 17486 Castelló d'Empúries (Gerona) [972-45 44 77; fax 972-45 46 86; info@almata.com; www.almata.com]** Fr A7 m'way exit 3; foll sp to Roses. After 12km turn S for Sant Pere Pescador & site on L in 5km. Site clearly sp on rd Castelló d'Empúries-Sant Pere Pescador. Lge, pt shd; wc; chem disp; shwrs inc; EHU (10A) inc; rest; gas; shop; lndry; playgrnd; pool; sand beach adj; sailing school; tennis; games area; horseriding; bike hire; TV; disco bar on beach; entmnt; dogs €6.40; poss cr; adv bkg; quiet; red LS. "Excel, clean facs; ample pitches; sports facs inc in price; helpful staff; direct access to nature reserve; waterside pitches rec." ♦ 16 May-20 Sep. € 59.00   2011*

CASTELLO D'EMPURIES *3B3* (1km S Coastal) *42.25563, 3.13791* **Camping Castell Mar, Ctra Roses-Figueres, Km 40.5, Playa de la Rubina, 17486 Castelló d'Empúries (Gerona) [972-45 08 22; fax 972-45 23 30; cmar@camping parks.com; www.campingparks.com]** Exit A7 at junc 3 sp Figueres; turn L onto C260 to Roses, after traff lts cont twd Roses, turn R down side of rest La Llar for 1.5km, foll sp Playa de la Rubina. Lge, hdg/mkd pitch, pt shd; wc; chem disp; serviced pitches; baby facs; shwrs inc; EHU (6-10A) inc; gas; lndry (inc dryer); shop; rest, snacks; bar; BBQ; playgrnd; pool; paddling pool; sand beach 100m; games rm; entmnt; sat TV; 30% statics; dogs; phone; Eng spkn; adv bkg; quiet; red LS; CKE/CCI. "Pitches poss unsuitable lge o'fits; gd location; excel for families." ♦ 22 May-19 Sep. € 52.00   2013*

CASTELLO D'EMPURIES *3B3* (5km S Coastal) *42.23735, 3.12121* **Camping-Caravaning Laguna, Platja Can Turias, 17486 Castelló d'Empúries (Gerona) [972-45 05 53; fax 972-45 07 99; info@campinglaguna.com; www.campinglaguna.com]** Exit AP7 junc 4 dir Roses. After 12km at rndabt take 3rd exit, site sp. Site in 4km; rough app track. V lge, mkd pitch, pt shd; wc; chem disp; mv service pnt; some serviced pitches (inc gas); baby facs; shwrs inc; EHU (5A) inc; gas; lndry; supmkt; rest, snacks; bar; playgrnd; htd pool; sand beach; sailing; watersports; tennis; games area; multisports area; bike hire; horseriding; wifi; entmnt; 4% statics; dogs €2; Eng spkn; adv bkg; quiet; red snr citizens/ long stay/LS; ccard acc; CKE/CCI. "Clean, modern san facs; gd birdwatching; excel." ♦ 5 Apr-31 Oct. € 49.70   2010*

CASTRO URDIALES *1A4* (1km N Coastal) *43.39000, -3.24194* **Camping de Castro, Barrio Campijo, 39700 Castro Urdiales (Cantabria) [942-86 74 23; fax 942-63 07 25; info@campingdecastro.com]** Fr Bilbao turn off A8 at 2nd Castro Urdiales sp, km 151. Camp sp on R by bullring. V narr, steep lanes to site - no passing places, great care req. Lge, pt sl, pt terr, unshd; wc; shwrs inc; EHU (6A) €3; lndry; shop; rest; bar; playgrnd; pool; sand beach 1km; 90% statics; dogs; phone; bus; poss cr; Eng spkn; adv bkg; quiet; CKE/CCI. "Gd, clean facs; conv NH for ferries; ltd touring pitches; narr, long, steep single track ent; great views over Bilbao bay." ♦ ltd. 13 Feb-10 Dec. € 39.60   2014*

CASTROJERIZ *1B4* (1km NE Rural) *42.29102, -4.13165* **Camping Camino de Santiago, Calle Virgen del Manzano s/n, 09110 Castrojeriz (Burgos) [947-37 72 55 or 658-96 67 43 (mob); fax 947-37 72 36; info@campingcamino.com; www.campingcamino.com]** Fr N A62/E80 junc 40 dir Los Balbases, Vallunquera & Castrojeriz - narr, uneven rd. In 16 km ent Castrojeriz, sp fr BU400 where you turn onto BU404. Once on BU404 proceed for approx 500yds to next rndabt, take 2nd exit. Site 1m on the L. Fr S A62, exit 68 twds Torquemada, then take P412, then BU4085 to Castrojeriz. Do not go thro town, as rd are narr. Med, hdg/mkd pitch, pt sl, shd; wc (some cont); chem disp (wc); shwrs inc; EHU (5-10A) €4 (poss no earth); lndry (inc dryer); shop 1km; rest, snacks; bar; games area; games rm; internet; TV rm; dogs €2; bus 200m; some Eng spkn; quiet; CKE/CCI. "Lovely site; helpful owner; pilgrims' refuge on site; some diff sm pitches; vg; site ent narr; excel bird watching tours on req; san facs dated." ♦ ltd. 15 Mar-15 Nov. € 32.00   2014*

CASTROPOL see Ribadeo *1A2*

CEE *1A1* (6km NW Coastal) *42.94555, -9.21861* **Camping Ruta Finisterre, Ctra La Coruña-Finisterre, Km 6, Playa de Estorde, 15270 Cée (La Coruña) [tel/fax 981-74 63 02; www.rutafinisterre.com]** Foll sp thro Cée & Corcubión on rd AC445 twd Finisterre; site easily seen on R of rd (no thro rd). Lge, mkd pitch, terr, shd; wc; chem disp; shwrs inc; EHU (10A) €4; gas; lndry; shop & 1km; rest, snacks; bar; playgrnd; sand beach 100m; dogs €3.70; phone; bus adj; poss cr; Eng spkn; adv bkg; some rd noise; ccard acc; CKE/CCI. "Family-run site in pine trees - check access to pitch & EHU bef positioning; gd, clean facs; 5km to Finisterre; clean beach adj; peaceful." ♦ Holy Week & 1 Jun-10 Sep. € 23.00   2010*

CERVERA DE PISUERGA *1B4* (500m W Rural) *42.87135, -4.50332* **Camping Fuentes Carrionas, La Bárcena s/n, 34840 Cervera de Pisuerga (Palencia) [979-87 04 24; fax 979-12 30 76; campingfuentescarrionas@hotmail.com]** Fr Aguilar de Campóo on CL626 pass thro Cervera foll sp CL627 Potes. Site sp on L bef rv bdge. Med, mkd pitch, pt shd; wc; chem disp; shwrs inc; EHU €3.50; lndry; shop 500m; rest 500m; bar; tennis; games area; 80% statics; bus 100m; quiet; CKE/CCI. "Gd walking in nature reserve; conv Casa del Osos bear info cent." ♦ ltd. Holy Week-30 Sep. € 21.00   2009*

⊞ **CIUDAD RODRIGO** *1D3* (1.5km S Rural) *40.59206, -6.53445* **Camping La Pesquera, Ctra Cáceres-Arrabal, Km 424, Huerta La Toma, 37500 Ciudad Rodrigo (Salamanca) [tel/fax 923-48 13 48; campinglapesquera@hotmail.com; www.campinglapesquera.com]** Fr Salamanca on A62/E80 exit junc 332. Look for tent sp on R & turn R, then 1st L & foll round until site on rvside. Med, mkd pitch, pt shd; wc; shwrs inc; EHU (6A) inc; lndry; shop; snacks; rv sw, fishing adj; wifi; TV; dogs free; phone; poss cr; no adv bkg; quiet; ccard acc; CKE/CCI. "Medieval walled city worth visit - easy walk over Roman bdge; gd san facs; vg, improved site; friendly nice sm site next to rv, gd for NH; lovely town; v helpful staff." ♦ € 17.00   2014*

⊞ **CLARIANA** *3B3* (4km NE Rural) *41.95878, 1.60361* **Camping La Ribera, Pantà de Sant Ponç, 25290 Clariana de Cardener (Lleida) [tel/fax 973-48 25 52; info@campinglaribera.com; www.campinglaribera.com]** Fr Solsona S on C55, turn L onto C26 at km 71. Go 2.7km, site sp immed bef Sant Ponç Dam. Lge, mkd pitch, hdstg, pt shd; wc; chem disp; baby facs; shwrs; EHU (4-10A) €4.60-8.45; lndry; shop; snacks; bar; playgrnd; pool; paddling pool; lake sw & beach 500m; tennis; games area; TV; 95% statics; dogs; bus 2.5km; phone; quiet. "Excel facs; gd site; narr pitches." ♦ € 27.40   2014*

⊞ **COLOMBRES** *1A4* (3 Km SW Rural) *43.37074, -4.56799* **Camping Colombres, Ctra El Peral A Noriega Kml - 33590 Colombres (Ribadedeva) [985 412 244; fax 985 413 056; campingcolombres@hotmail.com; www.campingcolombres.com]** E70/A8 Santander-Oviede, bet 283 & 284km markers, shop L turn opp petrol stn. Site to L 1km. Med, mkd pitch, terr, pt shd; htd wc; chem disp dedicated point; mv service pnt; child/baby facs; shwr(s) inc; EHU (6A) €4.20; lndry (inc dryer); shop; rest, snacks; bar; BBQ sep area; playgrnd; pool; sandy beach (3km); games area; wifi; 5% statics; dogs free; twin axles; Eng spkn; quiet; ccard acc; red LS; CKE/CCI. "Quiet, peaceful site in rural setting with fine mountain views; v helpful owners; nice pool; excel san facs; well kept & clean; immac, modern san facs." ♦ € 37.70   2014*

COLUNGA *1A3* (1km N Coastal) *43.49972, -5.26527* **Camping Costa Verde, Playa La Griega de Colunga, 33320 Colunga (Asturias) [tel/fax 985-85 63 73]** N632 coast rd, fr E turn R twd Lastres in cent of Colunga; site 1km on R. Med, mkd pitch, unshd; wc; chem disp; mv service pnt; baby facs; shwrs; EHU (5A) €3.50 - €5.20 (poss rev pol); gas; lndry; shop; rest; bar; BBQ; playgrnd; sand beach 500m; games area; bike hire; 50% statics; dogs €3; bus 500m; adv bkg; quiet but some rd noise; ccard acc; CKE/CCI. "Beautiful sandy beach; lovely views to mountains & sea; poss noise some fr rd & resident static owners; some site access rds used for winter storage; gd, plentiful facs; ltd hot water LS; friendly, welcoming staff; pleasant town." Easter & 1 Jun-30 Sep. € 19.00   2011*

COLUNGA *1A3* (12km E Coastal) *43.47160, -5.18434* **Camping Arenal de Moris, Ctra de la Playa s/n, 33344 Caravia Alta (Asturias) [985-85 30 97; fax 985-85 31 37; camoris@desdeasturias.com; www.arenaldemoris.com]** Fr E70/A8 exit junc 337 onto N632 to Caravia Alta, site clearly sp. Lge, mkd pitch, terr, pt shd; wc; chem disp; shwrs inc; EHU (5A) €4.50; lndry; shop; rest, snacks; bar; playgrnd; sand beach 500m; tennis; 10% statics; bus 1.5km; adv bkg; quiet; ccard acc; CKE/CCI. "Lovely views to mountains & sea; well-kept, well-run site; excel, clean san facs." 27 Mar-25 Aug. € 34.00   2015*

COMA RUGA see Vendrell, El *3C3*

COMILLAS *1A4* (1km E Coastal) *43.38583, -4.28444* **Camping de Comillas, 39520 Comillas (Cantabria) [942-72 00 74; fax 942-21 52 06; info@campingcomillas.com; www.campingcomillas.com]** Site on coast rd CA131 at E end of Comillas by-pass. App fr Santillana or San Vicente avoids town cent & narr streets. Lge, hdg/mkd pitch, pt sl, pt shd; wc; chem disp; shwrs inc; EHU (5A) €3.85; lndry (inc dryer); shop; rest 1km; snacks; bar; playgrnd; sand beach 800m; TV; dogs; phone; poss cr; adv bkg; quiet; CKE/CCI. "Clean, ltd facs LS (hot water to shwrs only); vg site in gd position with views; easy walk to interesting town; gd but rocky beach across rd; helpful owner; pitches inbetween 2 rds." Holy Week & 1 Jun-30 Sep. € 34.00   2013*

COMILLAS *1A4* (3km E Rural) *43.38328, -4.24689* **Camping El Helguero, 39527 Ruiloba (Cantabria) [942-72 21 24; fax 942-72 10 20; reservas@campingelhelguero.com; www.campingelhelguero.com]** Exit A8 junc 249 dir Comillas onto CA135 to km 7. Turn dir Ruiloba onto CA359 & thro Ruiloba & La Iglesia, fork R uphill. Site sp. Lge, mkd pitch, pt sl, pt shd; htd wc; chem disp; mv service pnt; baby facs; shwrs inc; EHU (6A) €4.35; lndry (inc dryer); shop, rest, snacks, bar in ssn; playgrnd; pool; paddling pool; sand beach 3km; tennis 300m; bike hire; wifi; many statics; dogs; night security; poss v cr high ssn; Eng spkn; poss noisy high ssn; ccard acc; CKE/CCI. "Attractive site, gd touring cent; clean facs but some in need of refurb; helpful staff; sm pitches poss muddy in wet." ♦ 1 Apr-30 Sep. € 39.50 (CChq acc)   2014*

COMILLAS *1A4* (3km W Rural/Coastal) *43.3858, -4.3361* **Camping Rodero, Ctra Comillas-St Vicente, Km 5, 39528 Oyambre (Cantabria) [942-72 20 40; fax 942-72 26 29; rodero@campingrodero-oyambre.es; www.campingrodero-oyambre.es]** Exit A8 dir San Vicente de la Barquera, cross bdge over estuary & take R fork nr km27.5. Site just off C131 bet San Vicente & Comillas, sp. Lge, mkd pitch, pt sl, terr, pt shd; wc; chem disp; mv service pnt; shwrs inc; EHU (6A) €3; gas; lndry; shop; rest, snacks; bar; playgrnd; pool; sand beach 200m; games area; wifi; 10% statics; no dogs; phone; bus 200m; poss v cr; adv bkg; ccard acc; CKE/CCI. "Lovely views; on top of hill; friendly owners; site noisy but happy - owner puts Dutch/British in quieter pt; sm pitches; poss run down LS." ♦ 15 Mar-30 Sep. € 29.00   2014*

⊞ **CONIL DE LA FRONTERA** *2H3* (3km N Coastal) *36.30206, -6.13082* **Camping Cala del Aceite (Naturist), Ctra del Puerto Pesquero, Km 4, 11140 Conil de la Frontera (Cádiz) [956-44 29 50; fax 956-44 09 72; info@caladelaceite.com; www.caladelaceite.com]** Exit A48 junc 26 dir Conil. In 2km at rndabt foll sp Puerto Pesquero along CA3208 & CA4202. Site sp. V lge, mkd pitch, pt shd; wc; chem disp; sauna; shwrs inc; EHU (10A) €5.50; gas; lndry; supmkt; rest, snacks; bar; playgrnd; pool; beach 500m; jacuzzi & steam rm; sep naturist area on site; dogs €3; phone; poss cr; Eng spkn; adv bkg; quiet; red long stay; CKE/CCI. "Friendly, helpful staff; interesting region; gd cliff-top walking; lge pitches; long stay winter offers; gd, modern san facs." ♦ Holy Week-31 Oct. € 30.60   2011*

⊞ **CONIL DE LA FRONTERA** *2H3* (3km NE Rural) *36.31061, -6.11276* **Camping Roche, Carril de Pilahito s/n, N340 Km 19.2, 11149 Conil de la Frontera (Cádiz) [956-44 22 16; fax 956-44 26 24; info@campingroche.com; www.campingroche.com]** Exit A48 junc 15 Conil Norte. Site sp on N340 dir Algeciras. Lge, mkd pitch, hdstg, pt shd; wc; chem disp; mv service pnt; EHU (10A) €5; lndry; shop; rest, snacks; bar; BBQ LS; playgrnd; pool; paddling pool; sand beach 2.5km; tennis; games area; games rm; TV; 20% statics; dogs €3.75; Eng spkn; adv bkg; quiet; ccard acc; red LS/long stay; special monthly rates. "V pleasant, peaceful site in pine woods; all-weather pitches; friendly, helpful staff; clean san facs; superb beaches nr; excel facs; lack of adequate management." ♦ € 36.60 SBS - W02 2014*

⊞ **CONIL DE LA FRONTERA** *2H3* (1.3km NW Rural/Coastal) *36.29340, -6.09626* **Camping La Rosaleda, Ctra del Pradillo, Km 1.3, 11140 Conil de la Frontera (Cádiz) [956-44 33 27; fax 956-44 33 85; info@campinglarosaleda.com; www.campinglarosaleda.com]** Exit A48 junc 26 dir Conil. In 2km at rndabt foll sp Puerto Pesquero along CA3208. Site sp on R. Lge, mkd pitch, some hdstg, pt sl, terr, pt shd; wc; chem disp; mv service pnt; shwrs inc; EHU (5-10A) inc; gas; lndry; shop & 1.3km; rest, snacks; bar; playgrnd; pool; sand beach 1.3km; entmnt; internet; 10% statics; no dogs 15 Jun-15 Sep, otherwise in sep area €5; phone; car wash; Eng spkn; adv bkg; quiet; red LS/long stay; CKE/CCI. "Well-run site; friendly, helpful staff; gd social atmosphere; poss noisy w/end; sm pitches not suitable lge o'fits but double-length pitches avail; poss travellers; pitches soft/muddy when wet; lge rally on site in winter; gd walking & cycling; sea views; historical, interesting area; conv Seville, Cádiz, Jerez, day trips Morocco; If low occupancy, facs maybe clsd and excursions cancelled." ♦ € 38.50 2013*

"I like to fill in the reports as I travel from site to site"

You'll find report forms at the back of this guide, or you can fill them in online at www.caravanclub.co.uk/europereport.

⊞ **CORDOBA** *2F3* (8km N Rural) *37.96138, -4.81361* **Camping Los Villares, Ctra Los Villares, Km 7.5, 14071 Córdoba (Córdoba) [957-33 01 45; fax 957-33 14 55; campingvillares@latinmail.com]** Best app fr N on N432: turn W onto CP45 1km N of Cerro Muriano at km 254. Site on R after approx 7km shortly after gd club. Last 5-6km of app rd v narr & steep, but well-engineered. Badly sp, easy to miss. Or fr city cent foll sp for Parador until past municipal site on R. Shortly after, turn L onto CP45 & foll sp Parque Forestal Los Villares, then as above. Sm, hdstg, sl, shd; wc; chem disp; shwrs inc; EHU (15A) €4.30 (poss rev pol); gas; lndry rm; shop; rest & bar (high ssn); some statics; no dogs; bus 1km; quiet; red long stay; CKE/CCI. "In nature reserve; peaceful; cooler than Córdoba city with beautiful walks, views & wildlife; sm, close pitches; basic facs (v ltd & poss unclean LS); mainly sl site in trees; strictly run; suitable as NH; take care electrics; poss no drinking water/hot water." ♦ € 17.70 2014*

⊞ **CORDOBA** *2F3* (1km NW Urban) *37.90053, -4.78760* **Camp Municipal El Brillante, Avda del Brillante 50, 14012 Córdoba [957-40 38 36; fax 957-28 21 65; elbrillante@campings.net; www.campingelbrillante.com]** Fr N1V take Badejoz turning N432. Take rd Córdoba N & foll sp to Parador. Turn R into Paseo del Brillante which leads into Avda del Brillante; white grilleblock wall surrounds site. Alt, foll sp for 'Macdonalds Brilliante.' Site on R 400m beyond Macdonalds on main rd going uphill away fr town cent. Site poorly sp. Med, hdg/mkd pitch, pt shd; wc; chem disp; mv service pnt; serviced pitches; shwrs inc; EHU (6-10A) €5.50 (poss no earth); gas; lndry (inc dryer); shop; hypmkt nrby; rest, snacks high ssn; bar; playgrnd; pool adj in ssn; dogs free; phone; bus adj; poss cr; Eng spkn; no adv bkg; quiet but traff noise & barking dogs off site; ccard not acc; CKE/CCI. "Well-run, busy, clean site; rec arr bef 1500; friendly staff; sun shades over pitches; easy walk/gd bus to town; poss cramped pitches - diff lge o'fits; poss travellers LS (noisy); gd for wheelchair users; highly rec; easy walk to beautiful city." ♦ € 39.50 2014*

CORUNA, A see Coruña, La *1A2*

CORUNA, LA *1A2* (5km E Coastal) *43.34305, -8.35722* **Camping Bastiagueiro, Playa de Bastiagueiro, 15110 Oleiros (La Coruña) [981-61 48 78; fax 981-26 60 08]** Exit La Coruña by NVI twd Betanzos. After bdge, take AC173 sp Santa Cruz. At 3rd rndabt, take 3rd exit sp Camping. In 100m, turn R up narr rd. Site on R in 150m. Sm, pt shd; wc (some cont); chem disp; shwrs inc; EHU (6A) €4; gas; lndry; shop; snacks; bar; playgrnd; sand beach 500m; dogs; phone; bus 300m; o'night area for m'vans; poss cr; adv bkg; quiet; CKE/CCI. "Friendly owners; lovely views of beach; care req thro narr ent gate, sharp turn & steep exit; poss feral cats on site & facs poss unclean in winter; some refurb needed." Easter & 1 Jun-30 Sep. € 20.00 2010*

CORUNA, LA *1A2* (9km E Rural) *43.34806, -8.33592* **Camping Los Manzanos, Olieros, 15179 Santa Cruz (La Coruña) [981-61 48 25; info@camping-losmanzanos.com; www.camping-losmanzanos.com]** App La Coruña fr E on NVI, bef bdge take AC173 sp Santa Cruz. Turn R at 2nd traff lts in Santa Cruz cent (by petrol stn), foll sp, site on L. Fr AP9/E1 exit junc 3, turn R onto NVI dir Lugo. Take L fork dir Santa Cruz/La Coruña, then foll sp Meiras. Site lge, pt shd; wc; chem disp; shwrs; EHU (6A) €4.80; gas; lndry (inc dryer); shop; rest, snacks; bar; playgrnd; pool; TV; 10% statics; dogs free; phone; adv bkg (day bef arr only); ccard acc; CKE/CCI. "Lovely site; steep slope into site, level exit is avail; helpful owners; hilly 1km walk to Santa Cruz for bus to La Coruña or park at Torre de Hércules (lighthouse) & take tram; gd rest; conv for Santiago de Compostela; excel." Easter-30 Sep. € 25.60 2013*

⊞ **COTORIOS** *4F1* (2km E Rural) *38.05255, -2.83996* **Camping Llanos de Arance, Ctra Sierra de Cazorla/Beas de Segura, Km 22, 23478 Cotoríos (Jaén) [953-71 31 39; fax 953-71 30 36; arancell@inicia.es; www.llanosdearance.com]** Fr Jaén-Albecete rd N322 turn E onto A1305 N of Villanueva del Arzobispo sp El Tranco. In 26km to El Tranco lake, turn R & cross over embankment. Cotoríos at km stone 53, approx 25km on shore of lake & Río Guadalaquivir. App fr Cazorla or Beas definitely not rec if towing. Lge, shd; wc; shwrs; EHU (5A) €3.21; gas; shops 1.5km; rest, snacks; bar; BBQ; playgrnd; pool; 2% statics; no dogs; phone; poss cr; quiet; ccard acc; red LS; CKE/CCI. "Lovely site; excel walks & bird life, boar & wild life in Cazorla National Park." € 21.40 2014*

SPAIN

⊞ **COVARRUBIAS** *1B4* (500m E Rural) *42.05944, -3.51527* Camping Covarrubias, Ctra Hortigüela, 09346 Covarrubias (Burgos) [947-40 64 17; fax 983-29 58 41; proatur@proatur. com; www.proatur.com] Take N1/E5 or N234 S fr Burgos, turn onto BU905 after approx 35km. Site sp on BU905. Lge, mkd pitch, pt sl, pt shd; wc; shwrs; EHU (12A) €3.90; gas; lndry; shop 500m; rest; bar; playgrnd; pool & paddling pool; 90% statics; phone; poss cr; "Ltd facs LS; pitches poss muddy after rain; charming vill; poss vultures; phone to confirm if open." € 18.50   2013*

CREIXELL *3C3* (2.9km E Coastal) *41.16512, 1.45800* Camping La Plana, Ctra N340, Km 1182, 43839 Creixell (Tarragona) [977-80 03 04; fax 977-66 36 63] Site sp at Creixell off N340. Med, hdstg, shd; wc; chem disp; shwrs inc; EHU inc; gas; lndry; shop; rest, snacks; bar; sand beach adj; poss cr; Eng spkn; adv bkg; some rlwy noise. "Vg, v clean site; v helpful & pleasant owners." 1 May-30 Sep. € 21.00   2011*

CREIXELL *3C3* (1km S Coastal) *41.15714, 1.44137* Camping Gavina Platja, Ctra N340, Km 1181, Platja Creixell, 43839 Creixell de Mar (Tarragona) [977-80 15 03; fax 977-80 05 27; info@gavina.net; www.gavina.net] Exit AP7 junc 31 (Coma-Ruga) onto N340 dir Tarragona. At km 1181 turn R twd Playa de Creixel via undergnd passage. Site 1km S of Creixell, adj beach - foll sp Creixell Platja. Lge, mkd pitch, pt shd; wc; chem disp; baby facs; fam bthrm; shwrs inc; EHU (6A) €4.50; gas; lndry; shop; rest, snacks; bar; playgrnd; sand beach adj; watersports; tennis; wifi; entmnt; 20% statics; dogs; poss cr; adv bkg rec Jul/Aug; some train noise; ccard acc; red long stay; CKE/CCI. "Rest o'looks beach; Port Aventura 20km." ◆ 4 Apr-31 Oct. € 34.50   2011*

"We must tell The Club about that great site we found"

Get your site reports in by mid-August and we'll do our best to get your updates into the next edition.

CREVILLENT see Elche *4F2*

⊞ **CREVILLENT** *4F2* (8km S Rural) *38.17770, -0.80876* Marjal Costa Blanca Eco Camping Resort, AP-7 Salida 730, 03330 Crevillent (Comunidad Valenciana) [965-48 49 45; camping@marjalcostablanca.com; www.marjalcostablanca.com] Fr A7/E15 merge onto AP7 (sp Murcia), take exit 730; site sp fr exit. V lge, hdg/mkd pitch, hdstg, pt shd; wc; chem disp; baby facs; shwrs; serviced pitches; EHU (16A) inc; gas; lndry (inc dryer); supmkt; rests; snacks; bar; BBQ; playgrnd; htd pool complex; wellness cent with fitness studio, htd pools, saunas, physiotherapy & spa; lake sw; tennis; car wash; hairdresser; doctor's surgery; games area; games rm; bike hire; entmnt; wifi; TV; 30% statics; tour ops; dogs €2.20; phone; Eng spkn; twin axle acc; adv bkg; ccard acc; lge pitches extra charge; red LS; CCI. "Superb site; gd security; excel facs; new site, trees and hedges need time to grow; excel, immac san facs." ◆ € 47.50 SBS - W05   2015*

⊞ **CUBILLAS DE SANTA MARTA** *1C4* (4km S Rural) *41.80511, -4.58776* Camping Cubillas, Ctra N620, Km 102, 47290 Cubillas de Santa Marta (Valladolid) [983-58 50 02; fax 983-58 50 16; info@campingcubillas.com; www.campingcubillas.com] A-62 Exit 102 Cubillas de Santa Marta. Fr N foll slip rd and cross rd to Cubillas de Santa Marta the site is on the R in 200m. Fr S take exit 102 take 5th exit off rndabt, cross over m'way and then 1st L. Site on R in 200m. Lge, some hdg/mkd pitch, pt sl, unshd; wc; chem disp; mv service pnt; shwrs inc; EHU (6-10A) €4-5.80; gas; lndry; sm shop; rest; snacks & bar in ssn; BBQ; playgrnd; pool; entmnt; 50% statics; dogs €2; phone; site clsd 18 Dec-10 Jan; Eng spkn; ccard acc; red long stay/LS; CKE/CCI. "Ltd space for tourers; conv visit Palencia & Valladolid; rd & m'way, rlwy & disco noise at w/end until v late; v ltd facs LS; NH only." ◆ ltd. € 26.00   2014*

CUDILLERO *1A3* (2.5km SE Rural) *43.55416, -6.12944* Camping Cudillero, Ctra Playa de Aguilar, Aronces, 33150 El Pito (Asturias) [tel/fax 985-59 06 63; info@campingcudillero.com; www.campingcudillero.com] Exit N632 (E70) sp El Pito. Turn L at rndabt sp Cudillero & in 300m at end of wall turn R at site sp, cont for 1km, site on L. Do not app thro Cudillero; streets v narr & steep; much traffic. Med, hdg/mkd pitch, pt shd; wc; chem disp; baby facs; shwrs inc; EHU (3-5A) €4.05; gas; lndry; shop; snacks high ssn; bar; playgrnd; htd pool; sand beach 1.2km; games area; entmnt high ssn; wifi; TV; dogs €2.15; phone; bus 1km; adv bkg; quiet; CKE/CCI. "Excel, well-maintained, well laid-out site; some generous pitches; gd san facs; steep walk to beach & vill; v helpful staff; excel facs; vill worth a visit, parking on quay but narr rds." ◆ 11 Apr-15 Sep. € 32.00   2014*

CUDILLERO *1A3* (2km S Rural) *43.55555, -6.13777* Camping L'Amuravela, El Pito, 33150 Cudillero (Asturias) [tel/fax 985-59 09 95; camping@lamuravela.com; www.lamuravela.com] Exit N632 (E70) sp El Pito. Turn L at rndabt sp Cudillero & in approx 1km turn R at site sp. Do not app thro Cudillero; streets v narr & steep; much traffic. Med, mkd pitch, pt sl, unshd; wc; chem disp; mv service pnt; shwrs inc; EHU €4.10; gas; shop; snacks; bar; pool; paddling pool; sand beach 2km; 50% statics (sep area); dogs €1; poss cr; ccard acc high ssn. "Pleasant, well-maintained site; gd clean facs; hillside walks into Cudillero, attractive fishing vill with gd fish rests; red facs LS & poss only open w/ends, surroundings excel." Holy Week & 1 Jun-30 Sep. € 24.60   2011*

CUENCA *3D1* (8km N Rural) *40.12694, -2.14194* Camping Cuenca, Ctra Tragacete, Km8, 16147 Cuenca [tel/fax 969-23 16 56; info@campingcuenca.com; www.campingcuenca.com] Fr Madrid take N400/A40 dir Cuenca & exit sp 'Ciudad Encantada' & Valdecabras on CM2110. In 7.5km turn R onto CM2105, site on R in 1.5km. Foll sp 'Nalimiento des Rio Jucar'. Lge, pt sl, pt terr, pt shd; wc; chem disp; mv service pnt; shwrs inc; EHU (6-10A) €4; gas; lndry; shop; snacks; bar; playgrnd; pool high ssn; jacuzzi; tennis; games area; 15% statics; dogs €1; phone; poss cr esp Easter w/end; Eng spkn; adv bkg; quiet; CKE/CCI. "Pleasant, well-kept, green site; gd touring cent; friendly, helpful staff; excel san facs but ltd LS; interesting rock formations at Ciudad Encantada." ◆ 19 Mar-11 Oct. € 21.00   2013*

CUEVAS DEL ALMANZORA see Garrucha *4G1*

DEBA *3A1* (6km E Coastal) *43.29436, -2.32853* **Camping Itxaspe, N634, Km 38, 20829 Itziar (Guipúzkoa) [tel/fax 943-19 93 77; itxaspe@hotmail.es; www.campingitxaspe. com]** Exit A8 junc 13 dir Deba; at main rd turn L up hill, in 400m at x-rds turn L, site in 2km - narr, winding rd. NB Do not go into Itziar vill. Sm, mkd pitch, pt sl, pt shd; wc; chem disp; baby facs; shwrs; EHU (5A) €4; gas; shop; rest, bar adj; BBQ; playgrnd; pool; solarium; shgl beach 4km; wifi; some statics; bus 2km; adv bkg; quiet; red LS; CKE/CCI. "Excel site; helpful owner; w/ends busy; sea views; Coastal geology is UNESCO site, walking fr site superb." ♦ ltd. 1 Apr-30 Sep. € 35.60   2012*

DEBA *3A1* (5km W Coastal) *43.30577, -2.37789* **Camping Aitzeta, Ctra Deba-Guernica, Km. 3.5, C6212, 20930 Mutriku (Guipúzkoa) [943-60 33 56; fax 943-60 31 06; www.campingseuskadi.com/aitzeta]**
On N634 San Sebastián-Bilbao rd thro Deba & on o'skts turn R over rv sp Mutriku. Site on L after 3km on narr & winding rd up sh steep climb. Med, mkd pitch, terr, pt shd; wc; chem disp (wc); shwrs inc; EHU (4A) €3; gas; lndry rm; sm shop; rest 300m; snacks; bar; playgrnd; sand beach 1km; dogs; bus 500m; phone; quiet; CKE/CCI. "Easy reach of Bilbao ferry; sea views; gd, well-run, clean site; not suitable lge o'fits; ltd pitches for tourers; helpful staff; walk to town." ♦ ltd. 1 May-30 Sep. € 21.00   2010*

DELTEBRE *3D2* (8km E Coastal) *40.72041, 0.84849* **Camping L'Aube, Afores s/n, 43580 Deltebre (Tarragona) [977-26 70 66; fax 977-26 75 05; campinglaube@hotmail.com; www.campinglaube.com]** Exit AP7 junc 40 or 41 onto N340 dir Deltebre. Fr Deltebre foll T340 sp Riumar for 8km. At info kiosk branch R, site sp 1km on R. Lge, mkd pitch, hdstg, pt shd; wc; chem disp; mv service pnt; shwrs inc; EHU (3-10A) €2.80-5; lndry; shop; rest; bar; snacks; pool; playgrnd; phone; sand beach adj; 40% statics; poss cr LS; red long stay; CKE/CCI. "At edge of Ebro Delta National Park; excel birdwatching; ltd facs in winter." ♦ ltd. 1 Mar-31 Oct. € 16.00   2011*

"I need an on-site restaurant"

We do our best to make sure site information is correct, but it is always best to check any must-have facilities are still available or will be open during your visit.

DELTEBRE *3D2* (10km SE Coastal) *40.65681, 0.77971* **Camping Eucaliptus, Playa Eucaliptus s/n, 43870 Amposta (Tarragona) [tel/fax 977-47 90 46; eucaliptus@ campingeucaliptus.com; www.campingeucaliptus.com]** Exit AP7/E15 at junc 41. Foll sp to Amposta but do not go into town. Take sp for Els Muntells on TV3405 then Eucaliptus beach. Site on R 100m fr beach. Lge, mkd pitch, pt shd; wc; chem disp; shwrs; EHU (5A) €4.30; gas; lndry; shops; rest, snacks; bar; BBQ area; playgrnd; pool; paddling pool; sand beach adj; fishing; watersports; cycling; entmnt; 40% statics; dogs €2.40; poss cr; adv bkg; noisy w/end & high ssn; red long stay; CKE/CCI. "Vg, well-run, peaceful site; gd facs; gd bar/rest; excel birdwatching; poss mosquito prob." ♦ Holy Week-27 Sep. € 24.00   2009*

⊞ **DENIA** *4E2* (3.5km SE Coastal) *38.82968, 0.14767* **Camping Los Pinos, Ctra Dénia-Les Rotes, Km 3, Les Rotes, 03700 Dénia (Alicante) [tel/fax 965-78 26 98; lospinosdenia@gmail.com; www.lospinosdenia.com]** Fr N332 foll sp to Dénia in dir of coast. Turn R sp Les Rotes/ Jávea, then L twrds Les Rotes. Foll site sp turn L into narr access rd poss diff lge o'fits. Med, mkd pitch, pt shd; wc; chem disp; shwrs inc; EHU (6-10A) €3.20; gas; lndry; shop adj; BBQ; cooking facs; playgrnd; shgl beach adj; internet; TV rm; 25% statics; dogs €3; phone; bus 100m; poss cr; Eng spkn; adv bkg; quiet; red long stays/LS; ccard acc; CKE/CCI. "Friendly, well-run, clean, tidy site but san facs tired (Mar 09); excel value; access some pitches poss diff due trees - not suitable lge o'fits or m'vans; many long-stay winter residents; cycle path into Dénia; social rm with log fire; naturist beach 1km, private but rocky shore." ♦ € 26.40   2012*

⊞ **DENIA** *4E2* (7km W Coastal) *38.87264, -0.02031* **Camping Los Patos, Playa de Les Deveses, Vergel, 03700 Dénia (Alicante) [tel/fax 965-75 52 93; info@camping-lospatos. com; www.camping-lospatos.com]** Exit A7/E15 junc 61 onto N332. Foll site sp. Med, hdg/mkd pitch, pt shd; htd wc; chem disp; mv service pnt; shwrs inc; EHU (6A); gas; lndry; shop; rest, snacks; bar; BBQ; playgrnd; sand beach adj; golf 1km; wifi; dogs; twin axles; poss cr; Eng spkn; adv bkg; quiet; red long stay/LS. "Gd site." € 14.50   2015*

⊞ **DENIA** *4E2* (9km W Rural/Coastal) *38.86750, -0.01615* **Camping Los Llanos, Partida Deveses 32, 03700 Dénia (Alicante) [965-75 51 88 or 649-45 51 58; fax 965-75 54 25; losllanos@losllanos.net; www.losllanos.net]** Exit AP7 junc 62 dir Dénia onto CV725. At lge rndabt turn L & foll sp to site along N332a. Med, pt shd; wc; chem disp; mv service pnt; shwrs inc; EHU (10A) €3.50; lndry; shop & 2km; rest 500m; snacks; bar; playgrnd; pool; paddling pool; sand beach 150m; wifi; 30% statics; dogs €2; phone; bus 100m; poss cr; adv bkg; quiet; ccard acc; red long stay. "Pleasant site; gd, modern san facs; gd touring base; friendly, helpful staff; vg." € 25.00   2009*

DOS HERMANAS *2G3* (1km W Urban) *37.27731, -5.93722* **Camping Villsom, Ctra Sevilla/Cádiz A4, Km 554.8, 41700 Dos Hermanas (Sevilla) [tel/fax 954-72 08 28; campingvillsom@hotmail.com]** On main Seville-Cádiz NIV rd travelling fr Seville take exit at km. 555 sp Dos Hermanos-Isla Menor. At the rndabt turn R (SE-3205 Isla Menor) to site 80 m. on R. Lge, hdg/mkd pitch, hdstg, pt sl, pt shd; wc (some cont); chem disp; shwrs inc; EHU (10A) €3.65 (poss no earth); gas; lndry; sm shop; hypmkt 1km; snacks in ssn; bar; playgrnd; pool in ssn; wifi; bus to Seville 300m (over bdge & rndabt); site clsd 25 Dec-9 Jan; poss cr; Eng spkn; adv bkg; rd noise; ccard acc; CKE/CCI. "Adv bkg rec Holy Week; helpful staff; clean, tidy, well-run site; vg, san facs, ltd LS; height barrier at Carrefour hypmkt - ent via deliveries; no twin axles; wifi only in office & bar area." 10 Jan-23 Dec. € 35.50   2014*

SPAIN

⊞ **ELCHE** *4F2* (10km SW Urban) *38.24055, -0.81194*
**Camping Las Palmeras, Ctra Murcia-Alicante, Km 45.3,
03330 Crevillent (Alicante) [965-40 01 88 or 966-68 06 30;
fax 966-68 06 64; laspalmeras@laspalmeras-sl.com;
www.laspalmeras-sl.com]** Exit A7 junc 726/77 onto N340
to Crevillent. Immed bef traff lts take slip rd into rest parking/
service area. Site on R, access rd down side of rest. Med,
mkd pitch, hdstg, pt shd; wc; chem disp; shwrs inc; EHU (6A)
inc; lndry; supmkt adj; rest, snacks; bar; pool; paddling pool;
10% statics; dogs free; ccard acc; CKE/CCI. "Useful NH; report
to recep in hotel; helpful staff; gd cent for touring Murcia; gd
rest in hotel; gd, modern san facs; excel." € 45.00   2011*

⊞ **ESCALA, L'** *3B3* (2km SE Coastal) *42.11048, 3.16378*
**Camping Cala Montgó, Avda Montgó s/n, 17130 L'Escala
(Gerona) [972-77 08 66; fax 972-77 43 40; calamontgo@
betsa.es; www.betsa.es]** Exit AP7 junc 4 Figueres onto
C31 dir Torroella de Montgri. Foll sp L'Escala & Montgó to
site. V lge, pt sl, pt shd; wc; chem disp; baby facs; shwrs inc;
EHU (5A) €4.10; gas; lndry; shop; rest; bar; playgrnd; pool;
paddling pool; sand beach 200m; fishing; sports area; bike hire;
30% statics; dogs; poss cr; adv bkg; quiet; ccard not acc; red
LS; CKE/CCI. "Nr trad fishing vill; facs ltd/run down; quiet LS;
exposed, poss windy & dusty site." ♦ € 36.00   2009*

> ## "Satellite navigation makes touring much easier"
>
> Remember most sat navs don't know if
> you're towing or in a larger vehicle – always
> use yours alongside maps and site directions.

ESCALA, L' *3B3* (1km S Coastal) *42.1134, 3.1443* **Camping
Maite, Avda Montó, Playa de Riells, 17130 L'Escala
(Gerona) [tel/fax 972-77 05 44; www.campingmaite.com]**
Exit A7 junc 5 dir L'Escala. Thro town dir Riells to rndabt with
supmkts on each corner, turn R to site. Lge, mkd pitch, some
terr, shd; wc; chem disp; mv service pnt; shwrs inc; EHU (6A)
€4.30; gas; shop adj; rest; bar; playgrnd; beach 200m; TV; bus
1km; adv bkg; red long stay; ccard acc; CKE/CCI. "Well-run
site; quiet oasis in busy resort; steep site rds; some pitches narr
access." ♦ 1 Jun-15 Sep. € 21.00   2011*

ESCALA, L' *3B3* (2km S Coastal) *42.11027, 3.16555* **Camping
Illa Mateua, Avda Montgó 260, 17130 L'Escala (Gerona)
[972-77 02 00 or 77 17 95; fax 972-77 20 31; info@
campingillamateua.com; www.campingillamateua.com]**
On N11 thro Figueras, approx 3km on L sp C31 L'Escala;
in town foll sp for Montgó & Paradis. Lge, terr, pt shd; wc;
chem disp; mv service pnt; baby facs; shwrs inc; EHU (5A) inc;
gas; lndry; shop; rest; bar; playgrnd; 2 pools; sand beach adj;
watersports; tennis; games area; entmnt; 5% statics; dogs
€3.60; Eng spkn; adv bkg ess high ssn; quiet; red LS/long
stay; CKE/CCI. "V well-run site; spacious pitches; excel san
facs; gd beach; no depth marking in pool; excel rest." ♦ ltd.
11 Mar-20 Oct. € 58.40   2013*

ESCALA, L' *3B3* (3km S Coastal) *42.10512, 3.15843*
**Camping Neus, Cala Montgó, 17130 L'Escala (Gerona)
[972-77 04 03 or 972-20 86 67; fax 972-77 27 51 or 972-
22 24 09; info@campingneus.com; www.campingneus.
com]** Exit AP7 junc 5 twd L'Escala then turn R twd Cala
Montgó & foll sp. Med, mkd pitch, pt sl, pt terr, shd; wc;
chem disp; mv service pnt; baby facs; shwrs inc; EHU (6A)
€4; gas; lndry; shop; snacks; bar; playgrnd; pool; paddling
pool; sand beach 850m; fishing; tennis; car wash; internet;
entmnt; TV rm; 15% statics; dogs €2; phone; bus 500m; Eng
spkn; adv bkg; quiet; ccard acc; red LS/long stay; CKE/CCI.
"Pleasant, clean site in pine forest; gd san facs; lge pitches;
vg." 28 May-19 Sep. € 39.00   2009*

See advertisement

ESCALA, L' *3B3* (500m S Urban/Coastal) *42.1211, 3.1346*
**Camping L'Escala, Camí Ample 21, 17130 L'Escala (Gerona)
[972-77 00 84; fax 972-77 00 08; info@campinglescala.com;
www.campinglescala.com]** Exit AP7 junc 5 onto GI623 dir
L'Escala; at o'skts of L'Escala, at 1st rndabt (with yellow sign
GI623 on top of rd dir sp) turn L dir L'Escala & Ruïnes Empúries;
at 2nd rndabt go str on dir L'Escala-Riells, then foll site sp. Do
not app thro town. Med, hdg/mkd pitch, pt shd; wc; chem
disp; all serviced pitches; baby facs; shwrs inc; EHU (6A) inc;
gas; lndry; supmkt; rest 100m; snacks; bar; BBQ; playgrnd;
beach 300m; TV; 20% statics; no dogs; phone; car wash;
poss cr; Eng spkn; adv bkg; quiet; red LS; CKE/CCI. "Access
to sm pitches poss diff lge o'fits; helpful, friendly staff; vg,
modern san facs; Empúrias ruins 5km; vg." ♦ 12 Apr-21 Sep.
€ 44.50   2014*

⊞ ESCORIAL, EL *1D4* (6km NE Rural) *40.62630, -4.09970*
Camping-Caravaning El Escorial, Ctra Guadarrama
a El Escorial, Km 3.5, 28280 El Escorial (Madrid)
[918 90 24 12 or 02 01 49 00; fax 918 96 10 62; info@
campingelescorial.com; www.campingelescorial.com]
Exit AP6 NW of Madrid junc 47 El Escorial/Guadarrama, onto
M505 & foll sp to El Escorial, site on L at km stone 3,500 -
long o'fits rec cont to rndabt (1km) to turn & app site on R.
V lge, mkd pitch, some hdstg, pt shd; htd wc; chem disp;
baby facs; shwrs inc; EHU (5A) inc (long cable rec); gas; lndry;
shop, rest, snacks & bar in ssn & w/end; BBQ; hypmkt 5km;
BBQ; playgrnd; 3 pools high ssn; tennis; horseriding 7km;
games rm; cash machine; wifi; entmnt; TV; 80% statics (sep
area); dogs free; o'fits over 8m must reserve lge pitch with
elec, water & drainage; adv bkg; some Eng spkn; poss cr &
noisy at w/end; ccard acc. "Excel, busy site; mountain views;
helpful staff; clean facs; gd security; sm pitches poss diff due
trees; o'head canopies poss diff for tall o'fits; facs ltd LS;
trains & buses to Madrid nr; Valle de Los Caídos & Palace at
El Escorial well worth visit; easy parking in town for m'vans
if go in early; mkt Wed; stunning scenery, nesting storks." ♦
€ 50.50 SBS - E13   2014*

See advertisement

ESCULLOS, LOS see Nijar *4G1*

ESPINAL see Auritz *3A1*

ESPOT *3B2* (850m SE Rural) *42.57223, 1.09677* Camping
Sol I Neu, Ctra Sant Maurici s/n, 25597 Espot (Lleida)
[973-62 40 01; fax 973-62 41 07; camping@solineu.com;
www.solineu.com] N fr Sort on C13 turn L to Espot on rd
LV5004, site on L in approx 6.5km by rvside. Med, mkd pitch,
pt shd; wc; chem disp; baby facs; shwrs inc; EHU (6-10A)
€5.80; gas; lndry; shop, bar high ssn; playgrnd; pool; paddling
pool; TV; dogs; quiet; ccard acc; CKE/CCI. "Excel facs; beautiful
site nr National Park (Landrover taxis avail - no private vehicles
allowed in Park); suitable sm o'fits only; poss unrel opening
dates; 10 mins walk to vill, many bars & rest." 1 Jul-31 Aug.
€ 25.60   2015*

ESTARTIT, L' *3B3* (500m Urban/Coastal) *42.04808, 3.1871*
Camping La Sirena, Calle La Platera s/n, 17258 L'Estartit
(Gerona) [972-75 15 42; fax 972-75 09 44; info@camping-
lasirena.com; www.camping-lasirena.com]
Fr Torroella foll sp to L'Estartit on rd GI641. On o'skts of vill
turn R at Els Jocs amusements, site on L 200m. Lge, pt shd;
wc; chem disp; baby facs; shwrs inc; EHU (6-10A) €5 (poss
long lead req); gas; lndry (inc dryer); shop; rest, snacks; bar;
BBQ; playgrnd; htd pool; paddling pool; sand beach adj; scuba
diving; internet; money exchange; car wash; TV; 10% statics;
dogs €2.50; bus adj; Eng spkn; quiet; red long stay/LS; CKE/
CCI. "Sm pitches, diff lge o'fits; poss long walk to beach;
v ltd facs LS; gd value boat trips; nature reserve adj." ♦
Easter-12 Oct. € 26.00   2009*

SPAIN

ESTARTIT, L' *3B3* (1.2km NE Coastal) *42.05670, 3.19785*
Camping Estartit, Calle Villa Primevera 12, 17258
L'Estartit (Gerona) [972-75 19 09; fax 972-75 09 91;
www.campingestartit.com] Exit AP7 junc 6 onto C66, then
take G642 dir Torroella de Montgri & L'Estartit; fork L on ent
L'Estartit, foll site sps. Med, pt sl, shd; htd wc; chem disp;
baby facs; shwrs; EHU (6A) €3.73; gas; lndry; shop; rest adj;
snacks; bar; playgrnd; htd pool; paddling pool; sand beach
400m; entmnt; 15% statics; no dogs 20/6-20/8; phone; poss
cr; Eng spkn; red long stay. "Friendly staff; 100m fr vill cent; gd
security; gd walks adj nature reserve; bar/rest & night club adj;
facs poss stretched high ssn." 1 Apr-30 Sep. € 24.00   2011*

ESTARTIT, L' *3B3* (1km S Coastal) *42.04972, 3.18416*
Camping El Molino, Camino del Ter, 17258 L'Estartit
(Gerona) [tel/fax 972-75 06 29] Fr N11 junc 5, take rd to
L'Escala. Foll sp to Torroella de Montgri, then L'Estartit. Ent
town & foll sp, site on rd Gl 641. V lge, hdg pitch, pt sl, pt shd;
wc; mv service pnt; shwrs; EHU (6A) €3.60; gas; lndry; supmkt
high ssn & 2km; rest; bar; playgrnd; sand beach 1km; games
rm; internet; bus 1km; poss cr; adv bkg. "Site in 2 parts - 1 in
shd, 1 at beach unshd; gd facs; quiet location outside busy
town." 1 Apr-30 Sep. € 28.00   2014*

⊞ **ESTARTIT, L'** *3B3* (2km S Coastal) *42.04250, 3.18333*
Camping Les Medes, Paratge Camp de l'Arbre s/n,
17258 L'Estartit (Gerona) [972-75 18 05; fax 972-75 04 13;
info@campinglesmedes.com; www.campinglesmedes.com]
Fr Torroella foll sp to L'Estartit. In vill turn R at town name
sp (sp Urb Estartit Oeste), foll rd for 1.5km, turn R, site well
sp. Lge, mkd pitch, shd; htd wc; chem disp; mv service
pnt; serviced pitches; baby facs; sauna; shwrs inc; EHU
(6A) €4.60; gas; lndry; shop; rest, snacks; bar; playgrnd;
htd indoor/outdoor pools; sand beach 800m; watersports;
solarium; tennis; games area; horseriding 400m; bike hire;
car wash; games rm; wifi; entmnt; TV; 7% statics; no dogs
high ssn otherwise €2.60; phone; poss cr; Eng spkn; adv bkg;
quiet; red long stay/LS (pay on arr); CKE/CCI. "Excel, popular,
family-run & well organised site; helpful staff; gd clean facs
& constant hot water; gd for children; no twin-axle vans high
ssn - by arrangement LS; conv National Park; well mkd foot &
cycle paths; ACSI acc." ♦ € 46.00   2015*

See advertisement

ESTARTIT, L' *3B3* (1km W Coastal) *42.05035, 3.18023*
Camping Castell Montgri, Ctra de Torroella, Km 4.7,
17258 L'Estartit (Gerona) [972-75 16 30; fax 972-75 09 06;
cmontgri@campingparks.com; www.campingparks.com]
Exit A7 junc 5 onto Gl 623 dir L'Escala. Foll sp on rd C252
fr Torroella de Montgri to L'Estartit. Site on L clearly sp. V lge,
hdg pitch, terr, hdstg, shd; wc; mv service pnt; chem disp; baby
facs; shwrs inc; EHU (10A) inc; gas; lndry (inc dryer); shop; rest,
snacks; bar; playgrnd; 3 pools; waterslide; beach 1km; tennis;
games area; watersports; wifi; entmnt; TV; car wash; money
exchange; 30% statics; dogs free; phone; poss cr; adv bkg; red
long stay/LS. "Gd views; help given to get to pitch; excel site."
♦ 12 May-30 Sep. € 62.00   2011*

ESTARTIT, L' *3B3* (1km W Coastal) *42.04907, 3.18385*
Camping L'Empordà, Ctra Torroella-L'Estartit, Km 4.8,
17258 L'Estartit (Gerona) [972-75 06 49; fax 972-75 14 30;
info@campingemporda.com; www.campingemporda.com]
Exit AP7 junc 5 onto Gl623 dir L'Escala. Bef L'Escala turn S
onto C31 dir Torroella de Montgri, then at Torroella take rd
Gl641 dir L'Estartit. Site bet L'Estartit & Torroella, opp Castell
Montgri. Lge, hdg/mkd pitch, pt shd; wc; chem disp; shwrs
inc; baby facs; EHU (6A) €4.70; gas; lndry; shop; snacks;
bar; playgrnd; pool; paddling pool; sand beach 1km; tennis;
entmnt; organised walks; wifi; TV; dogs €2.80; phone; bus
70m; car wash; poss cr; adv bkg; quiet; red LS/long stay; CKE/
CCI. "Family-run, pleasant & helpful; easy walking dist town
cent; lge pitches." ♦ 2 Apr-12 Oct. € 26.00   2011*

⊞ **ESTELLA** *3B1* (2km S Rural) *42.65695, -2.01761* Camping
Lizarra, Paraje de Ordoiz s/n, 31200 Estella (Navarra)
[948-55 17 33; fax 948-55 47 55; info@campinglizarra.com;
www.campinglizarra.com] N111 Pamplona to Logroño.
Leave N111 sp Estella, turn R at T-junc, bear R at traff lts &
turn R immed after rd tunnel, site sp. Pass factory, site on L
in 1.5km. Well sp thro town. Lge, mkd pitch, wide terr, pt sl,
unshd; htd wc; chem disp; mv service pnt; baby facs; shwrs
inc; EHU (6A) inc; gas; lndry; shop high ssn; rest, snacks; bar;
BBQ; playgrnd; pool; 80% w/end statics; phone; bus at w/
end; site clsd mid-Dec to early Jan; poss cr; Eng spkn; noisy;
ccard acc; CKE/CCI. "Poss school parties; no hdstg; poss
muddy when wet; interesting old town; excel birdwatching
in hills; on rte Camino de Compostela; unrel opening LS." ♦
€ 25.00   2011*

⊞ **ESTEPAR** *1B4* (2km NE Rural) *42.29233, -3.85097*
Camping Cabia, Ctra Burgos-Valladolid, Km 15.2, 09192
Cabia/Cavia (Burgos) [947-41 20 78] Site 15km SW of
Burgos on N side of A62/E80, adj Hotel Rio Cabia. Ent via
Campsa petrol stn, W'bound exit 17, E'bound exit 16, cross
over & re-join m'way. Ignore camp sp at exit 18 (1-way). Med,
pt shd; wc; chem disp; shwrs inc; EHU (6A) inc; shops 15km
& basic supplies fr rest; rest; bar; playgrnd; few statics; dogs;
constant rd noise; ccard acc; CKE/CCI. "Friendly, helpful owner;
gd rest; conv for m'way for Portugal but poorly sp fr W; poss v
muddy in winter; refurbed san facs; NH only." € 14.00   2012*

⊞ **ESTEPONA** *2H3* (7km E Coastal) *36.45436, -5.08105*
Camping Parque Tropical, Ctra N340, Km 162, 29680
Estepona (Málaga) [tel/fax 952-79 36 18; parquetropical
camping@hotmail.com; www.campingparquetropical.com]
On N side of N340 at km 162, 200m off main rd. Med, hdg/
mkd pitch, terr, pt shd; wc; chem disp; mv service pnt; serviced
pitch; shwrs inc; EHU (10A) €4; gas; lndry; shop; rest, snacks;
bar; sm playgrnd; htd, covrd pool; sand/shgl beach 1km; golf,
horseriding nrby; wildlife park 1km; 10% statics; dogs €2;
phone; bus 400m; poss cr; Eng spkn; adv bkg; rd noise; red LS/
long stay; CKE/CCI. "Site run down (Feb 09); facs in need of
update; helpful owners." ♦ € 27.00   2009*

⊞ **ETXARRI ARANATZ** *3B1* (2km N Rural) *42.91255, -2.07919*
Camping Etxarri, Parase Dambolintxulo, 31820 Etxarri-
Aranatz (Navarra) [tel/fax 948-46 05 37; info@campingetxarri.
com; www.campingetxarri.com] Fr N exit A15 at junc 112
to join A10 W dir Vitoria/Gasteiz. Exit at junc 19 onto NA120;
go thro Etxarri vill, turn L & cross bdge, then take rd over
rlwy. Turn L, site sp. Med, hdg pitch, pt shd; wc; chem disp;
shwrs inc; EHU (6A) €5.50; gas; lndry; shop; rest; bar; BBQ;
pool; playgrnd; sports area; archery; horseriding; cycling; wifi;
entmnt; 90% statics; dogs €2.15; phone; poss cr; Eng spkn;
ccard acc; red LS; CKE/CCI. "Gd, wooded site; gd walks;
interesting area; helpful owner; conv NH to/fr Pyrenees; youth
hostel & resident workers on site; san facs gd; various pitch
sizes & shapes, some diff lge o'fits; NH only." 1 Mar-5 Oct.
€ 38.00   2014*

EUSA see Pamplona *3B1*

FARGA DE MOLES, LA see Seo de Urgel *3B3*

⊞ **FIGUERES** *3B3* (1km N Urban) *42.28311, 2.94978* **Camping**
Pous, Ctra N11A, Km 8.5, 17600 Figueres (Gerona) [972-
67 54 96; fax 972-67 50 57; hostalandrol@wanadoo.es]
Fr N exit AP7/E15 at junc 3 & join N11. Then foll N11A S twd
Figueres. Site on L in 2km, ent adj Hostal Androl. Fr S exit junc
4 onto NII to N of town. At rndabt (access to AP7 junc 3) foll
NII S, then as above. Site recep in hotel. No access to N11A
fr junc 4. Med, mkd pitch, pt sl, shd; wc; chem disp; shwrs
inc; EHU (10A) €3; shop 1km; rest, snacks; bar; playgrnd; few
statics; dogs €3; bus adj; Eng spkn; quiet with some rd noise;
ccard acc. "Gd, clean site but san facs slightly run down & ltd/
unisex LS; easy access; pleasant owner; excel rest; 30 min walk
to town (busy main rd, no pavements) & Dali museum; 18km fr
Roses on coast." ♦ € 25.00   2014*

⊞ **FIGUERES** *3B3* (12km N Rural) *42.37305, 2.91305* **Camping**
Les Pedres, Calle Vendador s/n, 17750 Capmany (Gerona)
[972-54 91 92 or 686 01 12 23 (mob); info@campinglespedres.
net; www.campinglespedres.net] S fr French border on N11,
turn L sp Capmany, L again in 2km at site sp & foll site sp.
Med, mkd pitch, pt sl, pt shd; htd wc; chem disp; shwrs inc;
EHU (6-10A) €4.50; lndry rm; shop 1km; rest, snacks; bar; pool;
sand beach 25km; 20% statics; dogs; phone; Eng spkn; adv
bkg; quiet; ccard acc; red LS; CKE/CCI. "Helpful Dutch owner;
lovely views; gd touring & walking cent; gd winter NH." ♦
€ 39.40   2013*

FIGUERES *3B3* (8km NE Rural) *42.33902, 3.06758* **Camping**
Vell Empordà, Ctra Roses-La Jonquera s/n, 17780
Garriguella (Gerona) [972-53 02 00 or 972-57 06 31 (LS);
fax 972-55 23 43; vellemporda@vellemporda.com;
www.vellemporda.com] On A7/E11 exit junc 3 onto N260
NE dir Llançà. Nr km 26 marker, turn R sp Garriguella, then L
at T-junc N twd Garriguella. Site on R shortly bef vill. Lge, hdg/
mkd pitch, hdstg, terr, shd; htd wc; chem disp; mv service pnt;
baby facs; shwrs inc; EHU (6-10A) inc; gas; lndry; shop; rest,
snacks; bar; BBQ; playgrnd; pool; paddling pool; sand beach
6km; games area; games rm; entmnt; internet; TV; 20% statics;
dogs €4.50; phone; Eng spkn; adv bkg; quiet; ccard acc; red
long stay/LS; CKE/CCI. "Conv N Costa Brava away fr cr beaches
& sites; 20 mins to sea at Llançà; o'hanging trees poss diff high
vehicles; excel." ♦ 1 Feb-15 Dec. € 35.40   2011*

⊞ **FIGUERES** *3B3* (15km NW Rural) *42.31444, 2.77638*
Camping La Fradera, Pedramala, 17732 Sant Llorenç de la
Muga (Gerona) [tel/fax 972-54 20 54; camping.fradera@
teleline.es; www.terra.es/personal2/camping.fradera]
Fr cent Figueres take N260 W dir Olot. After 1km turn R at
mini-rndabt (supmkt on L), pass police stn to rd junc, strt on
& cross over A7 m'way & pass thro Llers & Terrades to Sant
Llorenç. Site 1km past vill on L. Med, mkd pitch, pt shd; wc;
chem disp; shwrs inc; EHU (6A) €2.67; lndry; shop 2km;
snacks; rest in vill; playgrnd; htd pool; rv sw 1km; few statics;
poss cr; Eng spkn; adv bkg; quiet; ccard acc; red long stay.
"Vg site in delightful vill in foothills of Pyrenees; fiesta 2nd w/
end Aug; pleasant staff; gates clsd LS - phone owner." ♦ ltd.
€ 19.00   2011*

FORNELLS DE LA SELVA see Gerona *3B3*

⊞ **FORTUNA** *4F1* (3km N Rural) *38.20562, -1.10712* **Camping**
Fuente, Camino de la Bocamina s/n, 30709 Baños de
Fortuna (Murcia) [968-68 50 17; fax 968 68 51 25;
info@campingfuente.com; www.campingfuente.com]
Fr Murcia on A7/E15 turn L onto C3223 sp Fortuna. After
19km turn onto A21 & foll sp Baños de Fortuna, then sp
'Complejo Hotelero La Fuente'. Avoid towing thro vill, if poss.
Med, mkd pitch, hdstg, pt sl, unshd; htd wc; chem disp; private
san facs some pitches; shwrs; EHU (10-16A) €2.20 or metered;
poss rev pol; gas; lndry (inc dryer); shop; rest, snacks; bar; BBQ;
playgrnd; htd pool, spa, jacuzzi; wifi; some statics; dogs €1.10;
phone; bus 200m; adv bkg; ccard acc; red long stay; CKE/CCI.
"Gd san facs; excel pool & rest; secure o'flow parking area;
many long-stay winter visitors - adv bkg rec; ltd recep hrs LS;
poss sulphurous smell fr thermal baths." ♦ € 19.00   2015*

⊞ **FORTUNA** *4F1* (3km N Rural) *38.20666, -1.11194*
**Camping Las Palmeras, 30709 Baños de Fortuna (Murcia)
[tel/fax 968-68 60 95]** Exit A7 junc 83 Fortuna; cont on
C3223 thro Fortuna to Los Baños; turn R & foll sp. Concealed R
turn on crest at beg of vill. Med, mkd pitch, pt shd; wc; chem
disp (wc); shwrs; EHU (6-10A) €2.20-3 or metered; gas; lndry;
shops 300m; rest, snacks; bar; natural hot water mineral pool
200m; some statics; dogs €0.54; poss cr; quiet; adv bkg acc;
red long stay; ccard acc; CKE/CCI. "Gd value, friendly site; gd,
modern san facs; gd rest; lge pitches; poss tatty statics; thermal
baths also at Archena (15km)." ♦ ltd. € 12.00   2010*

⊞ **FOZ** *1A2* (7km E Coastal) *43.55416, -7.17000* **Camping
Playa Reinante Anosa Casa, Estrada da Costa 42, 27279
Barreiros/Reinante (Lugo) [tel/fax 982-13 40 05; info@
campinganosacasa.com; www.campinganosacasa.com]**
E fr Barreiros on N634, exit rd at Reinante opp Hotel Casa
Amadora, turn R at beach, site on R. Sm, unshd; wc; chem
disp; shwrs €1; EHU €4.50; gas; lndry; shop, rest, snacks, bar
500m; BBQ; sand beach adj; wifi; 10% statics; dogs €5; bus/
train 900m; quiet. "Owners & location make up for basic facs
in need of upgrading; excel coastal walking fr site." ♦ ltd.
€ 18.00   2009*

⊞ **FOZ** *1A2* (11.9km E Coastal) *43.55525, -7.20019*
**Camping Benquerencia, 27792 Benquerencia-Barreiros
(Lugo) [982-12 44 50 or 679-15 87 88 (mob); contactol@
campingbenquerencia.com; www.campingbenquerencia.
com]** Fr junc of N642 & N634 S of Foz; E twd Ribadeo; in 1km
past Barreiros at km stone 566 turn L at site sp. Site on R in
1.5km. Med, mkd pitch, pt sl, pt shd; wc; shwrs inc; EHU (6A)
€3.50; gas; lndry; shop in ssn & 2km; rest; bar; playgrnd; sand
beach 400m; tennis; games area; phone; quiet; ccard acc; CKE/
CCI. "Hot water to shwrs only; NH only." € 18.50   2009*

FOZ *1A2* (2.5km NW Coastal/Rural) *43.58678, -7.28356*
**Camping San Rafael, Playa de Peizas, 27789 Foz (Lugo)
[tel/fax 982-13 22 18; info@campingsanrafael.com;
www.campingsanrafael.com]** N fr Foz on N642, site sp on
R. Med, pt sl, unshd; wc; chem disp; mv service pnt; shwrs
inc; EHU (5A) €4.50; gas; lndry; shop; rest, snacks; bar; sand
beach adj; games area; wifi; dogs €1; bus 200m; poss cr; adv
bkg; quiet; 15% red long stay; ccard acc; CKE/CCI. "Peaceful,
spacious site; basic facs; hot water to shwrs only; take care
electrics; pay night bef dep." 1 Apr-30 Sep. € 17.50   2009*

⊞ **FRAGA** *3C2* (1km SE Urban) *41.51738, 0.35553* **Camping
Fraga, Calle Major 22, Km 437, Ptda Vincanet s/n, 22520
Fraga (Huesca) [974-34 52 12; info@campingfraga.com;
www.campingfraga.com]** Fr W pass thro Fraga town on
N11. After about 500m turn R at mini rbdt into indus est just
past petrol stn. Turn R again in indus est, foll site sp. Fr E turn L
into indus est at mini rdbt just bef petrol stn. NB steep app poss
v diff lge o'fits. Sm, mkd pitch, hdstg, terr, pt shd; wc; chem
disp; mv service pnt; shwrs inc; EHU (6A) €3.20 (rev pol & poss
long lead req); lndry; hypmkt 1km; rest, snacks; bar; playgrnd;
pool; TV rm; some statics; dogs €2.70; phone; bus 1km;
poss cr; adv bkg; red LS; CKE/CCI. "Conv NH bet Zaragoza &
Tarragona; unspoilt town in beautiful area; rec not to hook-up
if in transit - ltd reliable EHU; chem disps placed bet pitches; NH
only." ♦ € 22.70   2011*

FRANCA, LA *1A4* (1km NW Coastal) *43.39250, -4.57722*
**Camping Las Hortensias, Ctra N634, Km 286, 33590
Colombres/Ribadedeva (Asturias) [985-41 24 42;
fax 985-41 21 53; lashortensias@campinglashortensias.com;
www.campinglashortensias.com]** Fr N634 on leaving vill
of La Franca, at km286 foll sp 'Playa de la Franca' & cont past
1st site & thro car park to end of rd. Med, mkd pitch, pt sl, pt
terr, pt shd; wc; chem disp; baby facs; shwrs inc; EHU (6-10A)
€5; gas; lndry; shop; rest, snacks, bar adj; playgrnd; sand beach
adj; tennis; bike hire; phone; dogs (but not on beach) €5;
bus 800m; poss cr; Eng spkn; adv bkg; ccard acc; red LS/CKE/
CCI. "Beautiful location nr scenic beach; sea views fr top terr
pitches; vg." 5 Jun-30 Sep. € 28.50   2011*

FRESNEDA, LA *3C2* (2.5km SW Rural) *40.90705, 0.06166*
**Camping La Fresneda, Partida Vall del Pi, 44596 La
Fresneda (Teruel) [978-85 40 85; info@campinglafresneda.
com; www.campinglafresneda.com]** Fr Alcañiz S on N232
dir Morella; in 15km turn L onto A231 thro Valjunquera to La
Fresneda; cont thro vill; in 2.5km turn R onto site rd. Site sp
fr vill. Sm, hdg/mkd pitch, terr, pt shd; wc; chem disp; baby
facs; shwrs inc; EHU (6A) inc; gas 2.5km; lndry; rest, snacks;
bar; plunge pool; wifi; no dogs; phone; poss cr; Eng spkn;
quiet; ccard acc; red long stay; CKE/CCI. "Narr site rds, poss
diff lge o'fits; various pitch sizes; gd; adv bkg adv; v helpful
owners." ♦ 15 Mar-15 Oct. € 24.50   2012*

> "There aren't many sites
> open at this time of year"
>
> If you're travelling outside peak season
> remember to call ahead to check site opening
> dates – even if the entry says 'open all year'.

⊞ **FUENGIROLA** *2H4* (9km W Coastal) *36.48943, -4.71813*
**Camping Los Jarales, Ctra N340, Km 197 Calahonda,
29650 Mijas-Costa (Málaga) [tel/fax 952-93 00 03;
www.campinglosjarales.com]** Fr Fuengirola take N340 W twd
Marbella, turn at km 197 stone; site located to N of rd. Lge, mkd
pitch, hdstg, pt sl, pt shd; wc; chem disp; serviced pitch; shwrs inc;
EHU (5A) €3.25; gas; lndry; shop adj; rest, snacks; bar; playgrnd;
pool; sand beach 400m; tennis; TV; no dogs; bus adj; poss cr; Eng
spkn; adv bkg; rd noise; red long stay/CKE/CCI. "Well-run site;
buses to Marbella & Fuengirola." ♦ € 21.50   2011*

⊞ **FUENTE DE PIEDRA** *2G4* (700m S Rural) *37.12905, -4.73315*
**Camping Fuente de Pedra, Calle Campillos 88-90, 29520
Fuente de Piedra (Málaga) [952-73 52 94; fax 952-73 54 61;
info@camping-rural.com; www.camping-rural.com]**
Turn off A92 at km 132 sp Fuente de Piedra. Sp fr vill cent.
Or to avoid town turn N fr A384 just W of turn for Bobadilla
Estación, sp Sierra de Yeguas. In 2km turn R into nature
reserve, cont for approx 3km, site on L at end of town. Sm,
mkd pitch, hdstg, pt sl, terr, pt shd; wc; shwrs inc; EHU (10A)
€5; gas; lndry rm; shop; rest, snacks; bar; BBQ; playgrnd; pool
in ssn; internet; 25% statics; dogs €3; phone; bus 500m; Eng
spkn; poss noise fr adj public pool; ccard acc; red long stay/LS/
CKE/CCI. "Mostly sm, narr pitches, but some avail for o'fits up
to 7m; gd rest; san facs dated & poss stretched; adj lge lake
with flamingoes; gd." ♦ ltd. € 22.00   2009*

FUENTE DE SAN ESTABAN, LA 1D3 (1km E Rural) 40.79128, -6.24384 **Camping El Cruce, 37200 La Fuente de San Estaban (Salamanca) [923-44 01 30; campingelcruce@ yahoo.es; www.campingelcruce.com]**
On A62/E80 (Salamanca-Portugal) take exit 293 into vill & foll signs immed behind hotel on S side of rd. Fr E watch for sp 'Cambio de Sentido' to cross main rd. Med, pt shd; wc; chem disp; shwrs; EHU (6A) €3.50 (poss no earth); rest adj; snacks; bar; playgrnd; wifi; Eng spkn; some rd noise; ccard acc; CKE/CCI. "Conv NH/sh stay en rte Portugal; friendly." ♦ 1 May-30 Sep. € 15.00   2013*

⊞ **FUENTEHERIDOS** 2F3 (600m SW Rural) 37.9050, -6.6742 **Camping El Madroñal, Ctra Fuenteheridos-Castaño del Robledo, Km 0.6, 21292 Fuenteheridos (Huelva) [959-50 12 01; castillo@campingelmadronal.com; www.campingelmadronal.com]** Fr Zafra S on N435n turn L onto N433 sp Aracena, ignore first R to Fuenteheridos vill, camp sp R at next x-rd 500m on R. At rndabt take 2nd exit. Avoid Fuenteheridos vill - narr rds. Med, mkd pitch, pt sl, pt shd; wc; chem disp; shwrs; EHU €3.20; gas; lndry rm; shop & 600m; snacks, bar high ssn; BBQ; 2 pools; bike hire; horseriding; 80% statics; dogs; phone; bus 1km; car wash; quiet; CKE/CCI. "Tranquil site in National Park of Sierra de Aracena; pitches among chestnut trees - poss diff lge o'fits or m'vans & poss sl & uneven; o'hanging trees on site rds; scruffy, pitches not clearly mkd; beautiful vill 1km away, worth a visit." € 13.00   2014*

GALENDE see Puebla de Sanabria 1B3

⊞ **GALLARDOS, LOS** 4G1 (4km N Rural) 37.18448, -1.92408 **Camping Los Gallardos, 04280 Los Gallardos (Almería) [950-52 83 24; fax 950-46 95 96; reception@ campinglosgallardos.com; www.campinglosgallardos.com]** Fr N leave A7/E15 at junc 525; foll sp to Los Gallardos; take 1st R after approx 800m pass under a'route; turn L into site ent. Med, mkd pitch, hdstg, pt shd; wc; chem disp; serviced pitch; mv service pnt; shwrs inc; EHU (10A) €3; gas; lndry; supmkt; rest (clsd Thurs); snacks; bar; pool; sand beach 10km; 2 grass bowling greens; golf; tennis adj; dogs €2.25; 40% statics; poss v cr; m'way noise; adv bkg; reds long stay/LS; ccard acc; CKE/CCI. "British owned; 90% British clientele LS; gd social atmosphere; sep drinking water supply nr recep; prone to flooding wet weather; facs tired; poss cr in winter; friendly staff." ♦ € 20.00   2014*

⊞ **GANDIA** 4E2 (4km NE Coastal) 38.98613, -0.16352 **Camping L'Alqueria, Avda del Grau s/n; 46730 Grao de Gandía (València) [962-84 04 70; fax 962-84 10 63; lalqueria@lalqueria.com; www.lalqueria.com]** Fr N on A7/AP7 exit 60 onto N332 dir Grao de Gandía. Site sp on rd bet Gandía & seafront. Fr S exit junc 61 & foll sp to beaches. Lge, mkd pitch, hdstg, pt shd; htd wc; chem disp; mv service pnt; baby facs; shwrs inc; EHU (10A) €5.94; gas; lndry; shop; rest adj; snacks; bar; playgrnd; htd, covrd pool; jacuzzi; sand beach 1km; games area; bike hire; wifi; entmnt; 30% statics inc disabled accessible; sm dogs (under 10kg) €1.90; phone; bus; adv bkg; quiet; ccard acc; red long stay/ snr citizens; CKE/CCI. "Pleasant site; helpful, friendly family owners; lovely pool; easy walk to town & stn; excel beach nrby; bus & train to Valencia; shop & snacks not avail in Jul; gd biking; htd pool avail; m'van friendly; site scruffy (2015)." ♦ € 42.00   2015*

⊞ **GARGANTILLA DEL LOZOYA** 1C4 (2km SW Rural) 40.9503, -3.7294 **Camping Monte Holiday, Ctra C604, Km 8.8, 28739 Gargantilla del Lozoya (Madrid) [tel/fax 918-69 52 78; monteholiday@monteholiday.com; www.monteholiday. com]** Fr N on A1/E5 Burgos-Madrid rd turn R on M604 at km stone 69 sp Rascafría; in 8km turn R immed after rlwy bdge & then L up track in 300m, foll site sp. Do not ent vill. Lge, terr, pt sl, pt shd; wc; chem disp; mv service pnt; baby facs; shwrs inc; EHU (7A) €4.30 (poss rev pol); lndry (inc dryer); shop 6km; rest; bar; pool; wifi; 80% statics; bus 500m; phone; little Eng spkn; adv bkg; quiet; ccard acc; red CKE/CCI. "Interesting, friendly site; vg san facs; gd views; easy to find; some facs clsd LS; lovely area but site isolated in winter & poss heavy snow; conv NH fr m'way & for Madrid & Segovia; excel wooded site; v rural but well worth the sh drive fr the N1 E5; clean; lovely surroundings." ♦ € 41.70 (CChq acc) SBS - E04   2014*

GARRIGUELLA see Figueres 3B3

⊞ **GARRUCHA** 4G1 (6km N Coastal) 37.23785, -1.79911 **Camping Cuevas Mar, Ctra Garrucha-Villaricos s/n, 04618 Palomares-Cuevas de Almanzora (Almería) [tel/fax 950-46 73 82; www.campingcuevasmar.com]** Exit A7 at junc 537 sp Cuevas del Almanzora & take A1200 sp Vera. In 2km turn L onto AL7101 (ALP118) sp Palomares & take 2nd exit at rndabt immed bef Palomares, site on L in 1.5km. Fr S exit A7 at junc 520, by-pass Garrucha, site on L in 6km. Med, hdg/mkd pitch, hdstg, pt shd; wc; chem disp; mv service pnt; baby facs; shwrs inc; EHU (6A) €4.20; gas 3km; lndry (inc dryer); shop; rest 500m; bar; BBQ; playgrnd; pool; jacuzzi; sand/shgl beach 350m; wifi; 10% statics; dogs €2; bus adj; poss cr; adv bkg; red LS/long stay; CKE/CCI. "Immac, well-maintained site; lge pitches; friendly owner; vg san facs; only 1 tap for drinking water; cycle track adj; beautiful coastline; mosquito problem; Fri mkt Garrucha; popular long stay site." ♦ ltd. € 33.00   2011*

⊞ **GAVA** 3C3 (5km S Coastal) 41.27245, 2.04250 **Camping Tres Estrellas, C31, Km 186.2, 08850 Gavà (Barcelona) [936-33 06 37; fax 936-33 15 25; info@camping3estrellas.com; www.camping3estrellas.com]** Fr S take C31 (Castelldefels to Barcelona), exit 13. Site at km 186.2 300m past rd bdge. Fr N foll Barcelona airport sp, then C31 junc 13 Gavà-Mar slip rd immed under rd bdge. Cross m'way, turn R then R again to join m'way heading N for 400m. Lge, mkd pitch, pt sl, pt shd; htd wc; chem disp; mv service pnt; baby facs; shwrs inc; EHU (5A) €6.56 (poss rev pol &/or no earth); gas; lndry (inc dryer); shop; rest, snacks; bar; BBQ; playgrnd; htd pool; sand beach adj; tennis; internet; entmnt; TV; 20% statics; dogs €4.90; phone; bus to Barcelona 400m; poss cr; Eng spkn; adv bkg; aircraft & rd noise & w/end noise fr disco nrby; ccard acc; red snr citizens/CKE/CCI. "20 min by bus to Barcelona cent; poss smells fr stagnant stream in corner of site; poss mosquitoes." ♦ 15 Mar-15 Oct. € 52.50   2013*

GERONA *3B3* (8km S Rural) *41.9224, 2.82864* **Camping Can Toni Manescal, Ctra de la Barceloneta, 17458 Fornells de la Selva (Gerona) [972-47 61 17; fax 972-47 67 35; campinggirona@campinggirona.com; www.campinggirona.com]** Fr N leave AP7 at junc 7 onto N11 dir Barcelona. In 2km turn L to Fornells de la Selva; in vill turn L at church (sp); over rv; in 1km bear R & site on L in 400m. NB Narr rd in Fornells vill not poss lge o'fits. Sm, mkd pitch, pt sl, pt shd; wc; chem disp; baby facs; shwrs inc; EHU (5A) inc (poss long lead req); gas; lndry; shop, rest 2km; snacks, bar 4km; playgrnd; pool; sand beach 23km; dogs; bus 1.5km; train nr; Eng spkn; adv bkg; quiet; ccard acc; CKE/CCI. "Pleasant, open site on farm; gd base for lovely medieval city Gerona - foll bus stn sp for gd, secure m'van parking; welcoming & helpful owners; lge pitches; ltd san facs; excel cycle path into Gerona, along old rlwy line; Gerona mid-May flower festival rec; gd touring base away fr cr coastal sites." 1 Jun-30 Sep. € 23.00   2012*

GETAFE see Madrid *1D4*

⊞ **GIJON** *1A3* (9.5km NW Coastal) *43.58343, -5.75713* **Camping Perlora, Ctra Candás, Km 12, Perán, 33491 Candás (Asturias) [tel/fax 985-87 00 48; recepcion@ campingperlora.com; www.campingperlora.com]** Exit A8 dir Candás; in 9km at rndabt turn R sp Perlora (AS118). At sea turn L sp Candás, site on R. Avoid Sat mkt day. Med, mkd pitch, pt sl, terr, unshd; wc; chem disp; some serviced pitches; shwrs inc; EHU (5A) €3.50; gas; lndry (inc dryer); shop; rest; playgrnd; sand beach 1km; tennis; watersports; fishing; wifi; 80% statics; dogs free; phone; bus adj; poss cr; Eng spkn; quiet; ccard not acc; red long stay. "Excel; helpful staff; attractive, well-kept site on dramatic headland; ltd space for tourers; vg san facs, ltd LS; easy walk to Candás; gem of a site; train (5 mins)." ♦ € 21.00   2014*

GIJON *1A3* (13km NW Coastal) *43.57575, -5.74530* **Camping Buenavista, Ctra Dormon-Perlora s/n, Carreño, 33491 Perlora (Asturias) [tel/fax 985-87 17 93; buenavista@ campingbuenavista.com; www.campingbuenavista.com]** Fr Gijón take AS19 sp Tremañes & foll rd for approx 5km. On sharp L bend take exit on R (Avilés) & immed L onto AS239 sp Candás/Perlora, site sp. Med, terr, pt shd; wc; chem disp; shwrs; EHU inc; gas; lndry; shop; rest, snacks; bar; playgrnd; sand beach 500m; 70% statics; bus 200m; site open w/end only out of ssn & clsd Dec & Jan; poss cr; noisy; CKE/CCI. "Oviedo historic town worth a visit; quite steep pull-out, need gd power/weight ratio." 15 Jun-15 Sep. € 22.70   2011*

GIRONELLA *3B3* (500m S Rural) *42.01378, 1.87849* **Camping Gironella, Ctra C16/E9, Km 86.750 Entrada Sud Gironella, 08680 Gironella (Barcelona) [938-25 15 29; fax 938-22 97 37; informacio@campinggironella.com; www.campinggironella.cat]** Site is bet Berga & Puig-reig on C16/E9. Well sp. Med, hdg/mkd pitch, hdstg, pt shd; wc; chem disp; serviced pitch; baby facs; shwrs inc; EHU (3-10A) €2.75-7; gas; lndry; shop; rest, snacks; bar; playgrnd; htd pool; games rm; entmnt; TV rm; 90% statics; dogs €1; phone; bus 600m; poss cr; Eng spkn; adv bkg; quiet; CKE/CCI. "Pleasant site; friendly staff; ltd touring pitches (phone ahead); conv NH." ♦ Holy Week, 1 Jul-15 Sep & w/ends low ssn. € 18.00   2011*

GORLIZ *1A4* (700m N Coastal) *43.41782, -2.93626* **Camping Arrien, Uresarantze Bidea, 48630 Gorliz (Bizkaia) [946-77 19 11; fax 946-77 44 80; recepcion@campinggorliz.com; www.campinggorliz.com]** Fr Bilbao foll m'way to Getxo, then 637/634 thro Sopelana & Plentzia to Gorliz. In Gorliz turn L at 1st rndabt, foll sps for site, pass TO on R, then R at next rndabt, strt over next, site on L adj sports cent/running track. Not sp locally. Lge, pt sl, pt shd; wc; chem disp; shwrs inc; EHU (3-5A) €4.20; lndry; gas; shop; rest, snacks; bar; BBQ; playgrnd; sand beach 700m; 60% statics; dogs €1; phone; bus 150m; poss cr; Eng spkn; ccard acc; red long stay/CKE/CCI. "Useful base for Bilbao & ferry (approx 1hr); bus to Plentzia every 20 mins, fr there can get metro to Bilbao; friendly, helpful staff; poss shortage of hot water." 1 Mar-31 Oct. € 31.00   2013*

GRANADA *2G4* (4km N Rural) *37.24194, -3.63333* **Camping Granada, Cerro de la Cruz s/n, 18210 Peligros (Granada) [tel/fax 958-34 05 48; pruizlopez1953@yahoo.es]** S on A44 fr Jaén twd Granada; take exit 121 & foll sp Peligros. Turn L at rndabt after 1km by Spar shop, site access rd 300m on R. Single track access 1km. Med, hdstg, terr, pt shd; wc; chem disp; shwrs inc; EHU (5A) €4.32; gas; lndry; shop; rest; bar; playgrnd; pool; tennis; dogs €1.30; bus 1km; poss cr; some Eng spkn; adv bkg; quiet; ccard acc; CKE/CCI. "Friendly, helpful owners; well-run site in olive grove; vg facs; superb views; gd access for m'vans but poss diff for v lge o'fits; pitches poss uneven & muddy after rain; site rds & access steep; conv Alhambra - book tickets at recep." ♦ ltd. Holy Week & 1 Jul-30 Sep. € 24.60   2009*

"I like to fill in the reports as I travel from site to site"

You'll find report forms at the back of this guide, or you can fill them in online at www.caravanclub.co.uk/europereport.

⊞ **GRANADA** *2G4* (4km N Urban) *37.19832, -3.61166* **Camping Motel Sierra Nevada, Avda de Madrid 107, 18014 Granada [958-15 00 62; fax 958-15 09 54; campingmotel@terra.es; www.campingsierranevada.com]** App Granada S-bound on A44 & exit at junc 123, foll dir Granada. Site on R in 1.5km just beyond bus stn & opp El Campo supmkt, well sp. Lge, shd; wc; chem disp; mv service pnt; baby facs; shwrs inc; EHU (6A) €4.20; gas; lndry (inc dryer); supmkt opp; rest, snacks; BBQ; playgrnd; 2 pools adj; sports facs; wifi; dogs; bus to city cent 500m; poss cr (arr early); Eng spkn; noisy at w/end; ccard acc; CKE/CCI. "V helpful staff; excel san facs, but poss ltd LS; motel rms avail; can book Alhambra tickets at recep (24 hrs notice); conv city; excel site." ♦ € 40.00   2014*

GRANADA *2G4* (9km E Rural) *37.16083, -3.45555* **Camping Cubillas, Ctra Bailén-Motril, Km 115, 18220 Albolote (Granada) [958-45 34 08]** Exit A44/E902 junc 116 dir El Chaparral, site sp. Sm, mkd pitch, pt sl, pt shd; wc; chem disp; mv service pnt; shwrs inc; EHU (5-10A) €2.50; gas; shop; snacks; bar; lake sw; playgrnd; boating & fishing adj; dogs; quiet; 10% red long stay & CKE/CCI. "Useful NH for Granada; some birdwatching; friendly staff; ltd facs LS." ♦ 9 May-13 Dec. € 17.00   2009*

⊞ **GRANADA** *2G4* (13km E Rural) *37.16085, -3.45388*
**Camping Las Lomas, 11 Ctra de Güejar-Sierra, Km 6, 18160
Güejar-Sierra (Granada) [958-48 47 42; fax 958-48 40 00;
info@campinglaslomas.com; www.campinglaslomas.com]**
Fr A44 exit onto by-pass 'Ronda Sur', then exit onto A395 sp
Sierra Nevada. In approx 4km exit sp Cenes, turn under A395
to T-junc & turn R sp Güejar-Sierra, Embalse de Canales. After
approx 3km turn L at sp Güejar-Sierra & site. Site on R 6.5km
up winding mountain rd. Med, hdg/mkd pitch, terr, pt shd;
htd wc; chem disp; mv service pnt; baby facs; fam bthrm;
shwrs inc; EHU (10A) €4 (poss no earth/rev pol); gas; lndry (inc
dryer); shop; rest, snacks; bar; playgrnd; pool; paddling pool;
waterskiing nrby; wifi; dogs free; bus adj; poss cr; Eng spkn;
adv bkg ess; quiet; red long stay; ccard acc; CKE/CCI. "Helpful,
friendly owners; well-run site; conv Granada (bus at gate);
access poss diff for lge o'fits; excel san facs; gd shop & rest;
beautiful mountain scenery; excel site." ♦ ltd. € 40.00   2014*

⊞ **GRANADA** *2G4* (3km SE Urban) *37.12444, -3.58611*
**Camping Reina Isabel, Calle de Laurel de la Reina, 18140
La Zubia (Granada) [958-59 00 41; fax 958-59 11 91; info@
reinaisabelcamping.com; www.reinaisabelcamping.com]**
Exit A44 nr Granada at junc sp Ronda Sur, dir Sierra Nevada,
Alhambra, then exit 2 sp La Zubia. Foll site sp approx 1.2km on
R; narr ent set back fr rd. Med, hdg pitch, hdstg, pt shd; htd
wc; chem disp; mv service pnt; baby facs; shwrs inc; EHU (5A)
poss rev pol €4.20; gas; lndry; shop; supmkt 1km; snacks; bar;
pool high ssn; internet; TV; dogs free; phone; bus to Granada
cent; Eng spkn; poss cr; adv bkg rec at all times; quiet except
during festival in May; ccard acc; red long stay/LS; red CKE/CCI.
"Well-run, busy site; poss shwrs v hot/cold - warn children;
helpful staff; ltd touring pitches & sm; poss student groups;
conv Alhambra (order tickets at site), shwr block not htd." ♦
€ 25.00   2011*

⊞ **GRANADA** *2G4* (12km S Rural) *37.06785, -3.65176* **Camping
Suspiro del Moro, 107 Avda de Madrid, 18630 Otura
(Granada) [tel/fax 958-55 54 11; info@campingsuspirodelmoro.
com; www.campingsuspirodelmoro.com]** On A44/E902 dir
Motril, exit junc 139. Foll camp sp fr W side of rndabt; site
visible at top of slight rise on W side of A44, 1km S of Otura.
Med, mkd pitch, hdstg, shd; wc; chem disp; mv service pnt;
shwrs inc; EHU (5A) €3 (poss no earth); gas; lndry rm; shop;
snacks & rest in ssn; bar; playgrnd; lge pool; tennis; games
area; 10% statics; phone; bus to Granada adj; Eng spkn;
rd noise & noisy rest at w/end; red LS; ccard acc; CKE/CCI.
"Decent site; reasonable pitches; quiet LS; clean facs but
inadequate for site this size." ♦ ltd. € 19.00   2011*

⊞ **GRAUS** *3B2* (6km S Rural) *42.13069, 0.30980* **Camping
Bellavista & Subenuix, Embalse de Barasona, Ctra Graus
N123, Km 23, 22435 La Puebla de Barasona (Huesca) [974-
54 51 13; fax 974 34 70 71; info@hotelcampingbellavista.
com; www.hotelcampingbellavista.com]**
Fr E on N230/N123 ignore 1st sp for Graus. Cont to 2nd sp 'El
Grado/Graus' & turn R. Site on L in 1km adj hotel. Med, mkd
pitch, terr, pt shd; htd wc; chem disp; shwrs inc; EHU (10A)
€4.50; gas; lndry; shop; rest, snacks; bar; playgrnd; pool; lake
sw adj; watersports; boat hire; fishing; tennis; horseriding; wifi;
entmnt; TV rm; 50% statics; dogs €1; phone; Eng spkn; adv
bkg; noisy at w/end; red LS; ccard acc; CKE/CCI. "Helpful staff;
sm pitches; excel rest; beautiful position above lake with sandy
beach; mountain views; gd NH." € 18.60   2011*

GRAUS *3B2* (5km SW Rural) *42.13130, 0.30871* **Camping
Lago Barasona, Ctra Barbastro-Graus, N123A, Km 25,
22435 La Puebla de Castro (Huesca) [974-54 51 48 or
974-24 69 06; fax 974-54 52 28; info@lagobarasona.com;
www.lagobarasona.com]** Fr E on N123, ignore 1st sp for
Graus. Cont to 2nd sp 'El Grado/Graus/Benasque' & turn R. Site
on L in 2km. Lge, hdg/mkd pitch, hdstg, sl, terr, shd; htd wc;
chem disp; mv service pnt; baby facs; shwrs inc; EHU (6A) inc;
gas; lndry (inc dryer); shop; rest, snacks; bar; BBQ; playgrnd;
2 pools; paddling pool; lake beach & sw 100m; watersports;
sailing; tennis; fitness rm; horseriding 1km; wifi; entmnt; TV
rm; 15% statics; dogs €3; Eng spkn; adv bkg; quiet; ccard acc;
red long stay; CKE/CCI. "Excel, well-equipped site; lge pitches;
helpful staff; adj reservoir water levels likely to drop; highly
rec." ♦ 1 Mar-12 Dec. € 37.00   2011*

GUADALUPE *2E3* (1.5km S Rural) *39.44232, -5.31708*
**Camping Las Villuercas, Ctra Villanueva-Huerta del Río,
Km 2, 10140 Guadalupe (Cáceres) [927-36 71 39; fax
927-36 70 28; www.campinglasvilluercasguadalupe.es]**
Exit A5/E90 at junc 178 onto EX118 to Guadalupe. Do not
ent town. Site sp on R at rndabt at foot of hill. Med, shd; wc;
shwrs; EHU €2.50 (poss no earth/rev pol); lndry; shop; rest; bar;
playgrnd; pool; tennis; ccard acc. "Vg; helpful owners; ltd facs
LS; some pitches sm & poss not avail in wet weather; nr famous
monastery." 1 Mar-15 Dec. € 14.50   2012*

⊞ **GUARDAMAR DEL SEGURA** *4F2* (2km N Rural/Coastal)
38.10916, -0.65472 **Camping Marjal, Ctra N332, Km 73.4,
03140 Guardamar del Segura (Alicante) [966-72 70 70; fax
966-72 66 95; camping@marjal.com; www.campingmarjal.
com]** Fr N exit A7 junc 72 sp Aeropuerto/Santa Pola; in 5km
turn R onto N332 sp Santa Pola/Cartagena, U-turn at km 73.4,
site sp on R at km 73.5. Fr S exit AP7 at junc 740 onto CV91
twd Guardamar. In 9km join N332 twd Alicante, site on R at
next rndabt. Lge, hdg/mkd pitch, hdstg, pt shd; all serviced
pitches; wc; chem disp; baby facs; sauna; shwrs inc; EHU (16A)
€3 or metered; gas; lndry (inc dryer); supmkt; rest; snacks &
bar; BBQ; playgrnd; 2 htd pools (1 covrd); tropical water park;
sand beaches 1km (inc naturist); lake sw 15km; tennis; sports
cent; bike hire; wifi; entmnt; TV rm; 18% statics; dogs €2.20;
phone; recep 0800-2300; adv bkg rec; Eng spkn; quiet; red
long stay/LS; ccard acc; CKE/CCI. "Fantastic facs; friendly,
helpful staff; excel family entmnt & activities; excel; well signposted; lge shwr cubicles; highly rec." ♦ € 65.00   2014*

GUARDIOLA DE BERGUEDA *3B3* (3.5km SW Rural) *42.21602,
1.83705* **Camping El Berguedà, Ctra B400, Km 3.5, 08694
Guardiola de Berguedà (Barcelona) [938-22 74 32;
info@campingbergueda.com; www.campingbergueda.com]**
On C16 S take B400 W dir Saldes. Site is approx 10km S
of Cadí Tunnel. Med, mkd pitch, some hdstg, terr, pt shd;
wc; chem disp; baby facs; shwrs; EHU (6A) €3.90 (poss rev
pol); gas; lndry; shop; rest, snacks; bar; BBQ; playgrnd; pool;
paddling pool; games area; games rm; TV; some statics; phone;
dogs; Eng spkn; quiet; CKE/CCI. "Helpful staff; vg clean san
facs; beautiful, remote situation; gd walking; poss open w/
ends in winter; highly rec; spectacular mountains/scenery; gd
touring area; rec Gaudi's Garden in La Pobla." ♦ 1 Apr-1 Nov.
€ 39.00   2014*

GUEJAR SIERRA see Granada *2G4*

GUITIRIZ *1A2* (1km N Rural) *43.17850, -7.82640* **Camping El Mesón, 27305 Guitiriz (Lugo) [982-37 32 88; fax 626 50 91 40; elcampingelmeson@gmail.com; http://elmesoncamping.wix.com/campingelmeson.]** On A6 NW fr Lugo, exit km 535 sp Guitiriz, site sp. Sm, mkd pitch, pt sl, pt shd; wc; chem disp (wc); baby facs; shwrs inc; EHU (10A) €4.50; lndry (inc dryer); gas; supmkt 1km; snacks; bar; BBQ; playgrnd; rv sw 500m; phone; bus adj; quiet. "Vg site." 15 Jun-15 Sep. € 17.00   2014*

HARO *1B4* (450m N Urban) *42.57900, -2.85153* **Camping de Haro, Avda Miranda 1, 26200 Haro (La Rioja) [941-31 27 37; fax 941-31 20 68; campingdeharo@fer.es; www.campingdeharo.com]** Fr N or S on N124 take exit sp A68 Vitoria/Logrono & Haro. In 500m at rndabt take 1st exit, under rlwy bdge, cont to site on R immed bef rv bdge. Fr AP68 exit junc 9 to town; at 2nd rndabt turn L onto LR111 (sp Logroño). Immed after rv bdge turn sharp L & foll site sp. Avoid cont into town cent. Med, hdg/mkd pitch, pt shd; htd wc; chem disp; mv service pnt; shwrs inc (am only in winter); EHU (6A) €4.40; gas; lndry (inc dryer); shop & 600m; snacks; bar; BBQ; playgrnd; htd pool high ssn; wifi; 70% statics; dogs €3; phone; bus 800m; car wash; site clsd 9 Dec-13 Jan; poss cr; Eng spkn; adv bkg; quiet (not w/end), some rv noise; red LS; ccard acc; CKE/CCI. "Clean, tidy, well run site - peaceful LS; friendly owner; some sm pitches & diff turns; excel facs; statics busy at w/ends; conv Rioja 'bodegas' & Bilbao & Santander ferries; recep clsd 1300-1500 no entry then due to security barrier; excel & conv NH for Santander/Bilbao; lge o'night area with electric." ♦ 30 Jan-8 Dec. € 30.00 SBS - E02   2015*

⊞ **HARO** *1B4* (10km SW Rural) *42.53017, -2.92173* **Camping De La Rioja, Ctra de Haro/Santo Domingo de la Calzada, Km 8.5, 26240 Castañares de la Rioja (La Rioja) [941-30 01 74; fax 941-30 01 56; info@campingdelarioja.com]** Exit AP68 junc 9, take rd twd Santo Domingo de la Calzada. Foll by-pass round Casalarreina, site on R nr rvside just past vill on rd LR111. Lge, hdg pitch, pt shd; htd wc; chem disp; shwrs; EHU (4A) €3.90 (poss rev pol); gas; lndry (inc dryer); sm shop; rest, snacks; bar; pool high ssn; tennis; bike hire; entmnt; dogs; clsd 10 Dec-8 Jan; 90% statics; dogs; bus adj; site clsd 9 Dec-11 Jan; poss cr; adv bkg; noisy high ssn; ccard acc. "Fair site but fairly isolated; basic san facs but clean; ltd facs in winter; sm pitches; conv for Rioja wine cents; Bilbao ferry." € 27.00   2009*

⊞ **HECHO** *3B1* (1km S Rural) *42.73222, -0.75305* **Camping Valle de Hecho, Ctra Puente La Reina-Hecho s/n, 22720 Hecho (Huesca) [974-37 53 61; fax 976-27 78 42; campinghecho@campinghecho.com; www.campinghecho.com]** Leave Jaca W on N240. After 25km turn N on a A176 at Puente La Reina de Jaca. Site on W of rd, o'skts of Hecho/Echo. Med, mkd pitch, pt sl, pt shd; htd wc; chem disp; mv service pnt; shwrs inc; EHU (5-15A) €4.20; gas; lndry; shop; rest, snacks; bar; playgrnd; pool; games area; 50% statics; dogs; phone; bus 200m; quiet; ccard acc; CKE/CCI. "Pleasant site in foothills of Pyrenees; excel, clean facs but poss inadequate hot water; gd birdwatching area; Hecho fascinating vill; shop & bar poss clsd LS except w/end; v ltd facs LS; not suitable lge o'fits." € 22.00   2010*

HERRADURA, LA see Almuñécar *2H4*

HONDARRIBIA see Irun *3A1*

⊞ **HORCAJO DE LOS MONTES** *2E4* (200m E Rural) *39.32440, -4.6358* **Camping Mirador de Cabañeros, Calle Cañada Real Segoviana s/n, 13110 Horcajo de los Montes (Ciudad Real) [926 77 54 39; fax 926 77 50 03; info@campingcabaneros.com; www.campingcabaneros.com]** At km 53 off CM4103 Horcajo-Alcoba rd, 200m fr vill. CM4106 to Horcajo fr NW poor in parts. Med, mkd pitch, hdstg, terr, pt shd; htd wc; chem disp; mv service pnt; baby facs; shwrs; EHU (6A) €4.20; gas; shop 500m; rest; bar; BBQ; playgrnd; pool; rv sw 12km; games area; games rm; tennis 500m; bike hire; entmnt; TV; 10% statics; dogs €2; phone; adv bkg rec high ssn; quiet; red long stay/LS; ccard acc; CKE/CCI. "Beside Cabañeros National Park; beautiful views; rd fr S much better." ♦ € 32.40   2013*

HORNOS *4F1* (9km SW Rural) *38.18666, -2.77277* **Camping Montillana Rural, Ctra Tranco-Hornos A319, km 78.5, 23292 Hornos de Segura (Jaén) [953-12 61 94 or 680-15 21 10; jrescalvor@hotmail.com; www.campingmontillana.es]** Fr N on N322 take A310 then A317 S then A319 dir Tranco & Cazorla. Site nr km 78.5, ent by 1st turning. Fr S on N322 take A6202 N of Villanueva del Arzobispo. In 26km at Tranco turn L onto A319 & nr km 78.5 ent by 1st turning up slight hill. Sm, mkd pitch, hdstg, terr, pt shd; wc; chem disp; shwrs inc; EHU (10A) €3.20; lndry; shop; rest, snacks; bar; pool; lake adj; 5% statics; dogs; phone; some Eng spkn; adv bkg; quiet; CKE/CCI. "Beautiful area; conv Segura de la Sierra, Cazorla National Park; much wildlife; friendly, helpful staff; gd site." 19 Mar-30 Sep. € 16.00   2013*

HOSPITAL DE ORBIGO *1B3* (1.3km N Urban) *42.4664, -5.8836* **Camp Municipal Don Suero, 24286 Hospital de Órbigo (León) [987-36 10 18; fax 987-38 82 36; camping@hospitaldeorbigo.com; www.hospitaldeorbigo.com]** N120 rd fr León to Astorga, km 30. Site well sp fr N120. Narr streets in Hospital. Med, hdg pitch, pt shd; wc; shwrs; EHU (6A) €1.90; lndry (inc dryer); shop, bar high ssn; rest adj; BBQ; pool adj; bus to León nr; 50% statics; dogs; bus 1km; poss open w/end only mid Apr-May; phone; poss cr; Eng spkn; ccard acc; CKE/CCI. "Statics v busy w/ends, facs stretched; poss noisy; phone ahead to check site open if travelling close to opening/closing dates." ♦ Holy Week-30 Sep. € 14.40   2009*

⊞ **HOSPITALET DE L'INFANT, L'** *3C2* (2km S Coastal) *40.97750, 0.90361* **Camping Cala d'Oques, Via Augusta s/n, 43890 L'Hospitalet de l'Infant (Tarragona) [977-82 32 54; fax 977-82 06 91; info@caladoques.com; www.caladoques.com]** Exit AP7 junc 38 onto N340. Take rd sp L'Hospitalet de l'Infant at km 1128. Lge, terr, shd; htd wc; mv service pnt; baby facs; shwrs; EHU (10A) €4.95; gas; lndry; shop; rest; bar; playgrnd; sand/shgl beach adj (naturist beaches nr); wifi; entmnt; dogs €3.40; poss cr; Eng spkn; some rlwy & rd noise; ltd facs LS; red snr citizens/long stay/LS; CKE/CCI. "Friendly, relaxing site; clean, modern san facs; well kept site; vg rest; sea views; poss v windy; conv Aquapolis & Port Aventura; mkd mountain walks; vg NH & longer stay." € 38.00   2011*

HOSPITALET DE L'INFANT, L' *3C2* (2km S Coastal)
40.97722, 0.90083 **Camping El Templo del Sol (Naturist),**
Polígon 14-15, Playa del Torn, 43890 L'Hospitalet de
l'Infant (Tarragona) [977-82 34 34; fax 977-82 34 64;
info@eltemplodelsol.com; www.eltemplodelsol.com]
Leave A7 at exit 38 or N340 twds town cent. Turn R (S)
along coast rd for 2km. Ignore 1st camp sp on L, site 200m
further on L. Lge, hdg/mkd pitch, pt sl, pt shd; wc; chem
disp; serviced pitch; shwrs inc; EHU (6A) inc; gas; lndry;
shop, rest, snacks; bar; playgrnd; pools; solar-energy park;
jacuzzi; official naturist sand/shgl beach adj; cinema/theatre;
TV rm; 5% statics; poss cr; Eng spkn; adv bkg (dep); some
rlwy noise rear of site; ccard acc; red long stay/LS; INF card.
"Excel naturist site; no dogs, radios or TV on pitches; lge
private wash/shwr rms; pitches v tight - take care o'hanging
branches; conv Port Aventura; mosquito problem; poss
strong winds - take care with awnings." ♦ 1 Apr-22 Oct.
€ 43.00   2009*

See advertisement

HOYOS DEL ESPINO *1D3* (4km E Rural) *40.34313, -5.13131*
Camping Navagredos, Ctra de Valdecasas, 05635
Navarredonda de Gredos (Ávila) [920-20 74 76;
fax 983-29 58 41; proatur@proatur.com] Fr N take N502
S. Then W on C500 twd El Barco. Site sp in Navarredonda on
L in 2km, just bef petrol stn. Steep app rd with bends. Med,
pt sl, pt shd; wc; chem disp; mv service pnt; baby facs; shwrs
inc; EHU (10A) €3.90; lndry; shops 2km; rest & snacks in ssn;
bar; BBQ; internet; phone; quiet. "Excel walking in Gredos
mountains; some facs poorly maintained LS; steep slope to
san facs; site open w/ends until mid-Nov." ♦ Easter-12 Oct.
€ 17.00   2010*

HOYOS DEL ESPINO *1D3* (1.5km S Rural) *40.34055, -5.17527*
Camping Gredos, Ctra Plataforma, Km.1.8, 05634 Hoyos del
Espino (Ávila) [920-20 75 85; campingredos@campingredos.
com; www.campingredos.com] Fr N110 turn E at El Barco
onto AV941 for approx 41km; at Hoyos del Espino turn S twd
Plataforma de Gredos. Site on R in 1.8km. Or fr N502 turn W
onto AV941 dir Parador de Gredos to Hoyos del Espino, then
as above. Sm, pt sl, pt shd; wc; chem disp; shwrs inc; EHU
€2.90; gas; lndry; shop 1km; snacks; playgrnd; rv sw adj; bike
hire; horseriding; adv bkg; quiet; CKE/CCI. "Lovely mountain
scenery; beautiful loc in forest nr rv, san facs basic, mountain
walks." ♦ Holy Week & 1 May-1 Oct. € 16.00   2012*

HUESCA *3B2* (1.7km SW Urban) *42.13725, -0.41900*
**Camping San Jorge, Calle Ricardo del Arco s/n, 22004
Huesca [tel/fax 974-22 74 16; contacto@campingsanjorge.
com; www.campingsanjorge.com]** Exit A23 S of town at
km 568 & head N twd town cent. Site well sp adj municipal
pool & leisure facs. Med, shd; wc; chem disp (wc); shwrs inc;
EHU (10A) €4; lndry; shop; snacks; bar; 2 pools; internet; dogs;
bus 300m; ccard acc; CKE/CCI. "Grassy pitches poss flooded
after heavy rain; san facs gd but poss stretched high ssn; vg
pool; friendly; conv town cent; gd supmkt 250m; gd NH."
15 Mar-15 Oct. € 22.00   2015*

⊞ **HUMILLADERO** *2G4* (500m S Rural) *37.10750, -4.69611*
**Camping La Sierrecilla, Avda de Clara Campoamor s/n,
29531 Humilladero (Málaga) [951-19 90 90 or 693-
82 81 99 (mob); fax 952-83 43 73; info@lasierrecilla.com;
www.lasierrecilla.com]** Exit A92 junc 138 onto A7280 twd
Humilladero. At vill ent turn L at 1st rndabt, site visible. Med,
mkd pitch, terr, hdstg, pt sl, pt shd; htd wc; chem disp; mv
service pnt; fam bathrm; baby facs; serviced pitches; shwrs
inc; EHU (16A) €3.50; lndry; shop 1km; rest, snacks; bar; BBQ;
playgrnd; htd pool; paddling pool; wifi; entmnt; 10% statics;
dogs €1.50; Eng spkn; adv bkg; quiet; CKE/CCI. "Excel new
site; gd modern, san facs; vg touring base; gd walking;
horseriding, caving, archery high ssn; Fuentepiedra lagoon
nrby; new trees planted, still need a year or so to give much
shd, but attractive none the less." ♦ € 32.00   2014*

⊞ **IRUN** *3A1* (2km N Rural) *43.36638, -1.80436* **Camping
Jaizkibel, Ctra Guadalupe Km 22, 20280 Hondarribia
(Guipúzcoa) [943-64 16 79; fax 943-64 26 53; jaizkibel@
campingseuskadi.com; www.campingseuskadi.com/
jaizkibel]** Fr Hondarribia/Fuenterrabia inner ring rd foll sp to
site below old town wall. Do not ent town. Med, hdg pitch, pt
hdstg, terr, pt shd; wc; baby facs; shwrs; EHU (6A) €4.35 (check
earth); lndry; rest; bar; BBQ; playgrnd; sand beach 1.5km; tennis;
wifi; 90% statics; no dogs; phone; bus 1km; Eng spkn; adv bkg;
quiet; red LS; ccard acc; CKE/CCI. "Easy 20 mins walk to historic
town; scenic area; gd walking; gd touring base but ltd turning
space for tourers; clean facs; gd rest & bar." € 31.00   2014*

⊞ **IRUN** *3A1* (3km S Rural) *43.31540, -1.87419* **Camping
Oliden, Ctra NI Madrid-Irún, Km 470, 20180 Oiartzun
(Guipúzcoa) [943-49 07 28; oliden@campingseuskadi.com]**
On S side of N1 at E end of vill. Lge, pt sl, pt shd; wc; chem
disp; mv service pnt; shwrs; EHU (5A) €3.53; lndry (inc dryer);
shops adj; rest; bar; playgrnd; pool in ssn; beach 10km; bus
200m; some statics; rlwy & factory noise; red CKE/CCI. "Steps
to shwrs; grass pitches v wet LS; NH only." € 18.00   2009*

⊞ **IRUN** *3A1* (6km W Coastal) *43.37629, -1.79939* **Camping
Faro de Higuer, Ctra. Del Faro, 58, 20280 Hondarribia
[943 64 10 08; fax 943 64 01 50; faro@campingseuskadi.
com; www.campingseuskadi.com]** Fr AP8 exit at junc 2 Irun.
Foll signs for airport. At rndabt take 2nd exit, cross two
more rndabts. 2nd exit at next 2 rndabts. Cont uphill to lighthouse
& foll signs for Faro. Med, hdg/mkd pitch, pt sl, terr, unshd; wc;
chem disp; mv service pnt; baby facs; fam bthrm; shwrs; EHU
(10A) €5.20; lndry (inc dryer); shop; rest; snacks; bar; BBQ; cooking
facs; playgrnd; pool; waterslide; paddling pool; beach adj; games
area; games rm; bike hire; entmnt; wifi; TV rm; 50% statics; dogs
€1.20; phone; poss cr; Eng spkn; adv bkg; noisy. "Vg site on top of
winding rd, is v busy outside; sep ent & exit; exit has low stone arch,
be careful when leaving." ♦ € 26.00   2014*

⊞ **ISABA** *3B1* (13km E Rural) *42.86618, -0.81247* **Camping
Zuriza, Ctra Anso-Zuriza, Km 14, 22728 Ansó (Huesca)
[tel/fax 974-37 01 96; campingzuriza@valledeanso.com;
http://campingzuriza.valledeanso.com]** On NA1370 N
fr Isaba, turn R in 4km onto NA2000 to Zuriza. Foll sp to site.
Fr Ansó, take HUV2024 N to Zuriza. Foll sp to site; narr, rough
rd not rec for underpowered o'fits. Lge, pt sl, pt shd; wc;
some serviced pitches; shwrs inc; EHU €6; lndry; shop; rest;
bar; playgrnd; 50% statics; phone; quiet; ccard acc; CKE/CCI.
"Beautiful, remote valley; no vill at Zuriza, nearest vills Isaba
& Ansó; no direct rte to France; superb location for walking."
€ 18.00   2011*

ISLA *1A4* (4km SW Rural) *43.46446, -3.60773* **Camping
Los Molinos de Bareyo, 39170 Bareyo [942-67 05 69;
losmolinosdebareyo@ceoecant.es; www.campingsonline.
com/molinosdebareyo]** Exit A8 at km 185 & foll sp for
Beranga, Noja. Bef Noja at rndabt take L for Ajo, site sp on L
up hill. Do not confuse with Cmp Los Molinos in Noja. V lge,
mkd pitch, terr, pt shd; htd wc; chem disp; shwrs inc; EHU
(3A) €3.60; lndry; shop; rest; snacks; bar; BBQ; playgrnd; htd
pool; sand beach 4km; tennis; games area; TV rm; 60% statics;
dogs; phone; bus 1km; site clsd mid Dec-end Jan; poss cr;
Eng spkn; adv bkg; CKE/CCI. "Vg site on hill with views of
coast; lively but not o'crowded high ssn." ♦ 1 Jun-30 Sep.
€ 22.50   2010*

ISLA *1A4* (1km NW Coastal) *43.50261, -3.54351* **Camping
Playa de Isla, Calle Ardanal 1, 39195 Isla [tel/fax 942-
67 93 61; consultas@playadeisla.com; www.playadeisla.
com]** Turn off A8/E70 at km 185 Beranga sp Noja & Isla. Foll
sp Isla. In town to beach, site sp to L. Then in 100m keep R
along narr seafront lane (main rd bends L) for 1km (rd looks
like dead end). Med, mkd pitch, pt sl, terr, pt shd; wc; chem
disp; shwrs inc; EHU (3A) €4.50; gas; lndry; shop & 1km;
snacks; bar; playgrnd; sand beach adj; 90% statics; no dogs;
phone; bus 1km; poss cr; quiet; ccard acc; CKE/CCI. "Beautiful
situation; ltd touring pitches; busy at w/end." Easter-30 Sep.
€ 26.40   2013*

⊞ **ISLA CRISTINA** *2G2* (4km E Coastal) *37.20555, -7.26722*
**Camping Playa Taray, Ctra La Antilla-Isla Cristina,
Km 9, 21430 La Redondela (Huelva) [959-34 11 02; fax 959-
34 11 96; www.campingtaray.com]** Fr W exit A49 sp Isla
Cristina & go thro town heading E. Fr E exit A49 at km 117 sp
Lepe. In Lepe turn S on H4116 to La Antilla, then R on coast rd
to Isla Cristina & site. Lge, pt shd; wc; mv service pnt; shwrs;
EHU (10) €4.28; gas; lndry; shop; bar; rest; playrnd; sand beach
adj; some statics; phone; dogs; bus; quiet; ccard acc; red long
stay/LS; CKE/CCI. "Gd birdwatching, cycling; less cr than other
sites in area in winter; poss untidy LS & ltd facs; poss diff for lge
o'fits; friendly, helpful owner." ♦ € 19.00   2011*

ISLA PLANA see Puerto de Mazarrón *4G1*

ISLARES see Oriñón *1A4*

ITZIAR see Deba *3A1*

⊞ **IZNATE** *2G4* (1km NE Rural) *36.78449, -4.17442* **Camping Rural Iznate, Ctra Iznate-Benamocarra s/n, 29792 Iznate (Málaga) [tel/fax 952-53 56 13; info@campingiznate.com; www.campingiznate.com]** Exit A7/E15 junc 265 dir Cajiz & Iznate. Med, mkd pitch, hdstg, unshd; wc; chem disp; shwrs; EHU (5-16A) €3-3.50 (poss no earth); gas; lndry; shop; rest, snacks; bar; pool; shgl beach 8km; wifi; some statics; dogs €2.10; bus adj; Eng spkn; quiet; red long stay/LS. "Beautiful scenery & mountain villages; conv Vélez-Málaga & Torre del Mar; pleasant owners; many ssnl static c'vans - scruffy LS."
€ 18.00   2010*

⊞ **JACA** *3B2* (2km W Urban) *42.56416, -0.57027* **Camping Victoria, Avda de la Victoria 34, 22700 Jaca (Huesca) [974-35 70 08; fax 974-35 70 09; victoria@campings.net; www.campingvictoria.es]** Fr Jaca cent take N240 dir Pamplona, site on R. Med, mkd pitch, pt shd; wc; chem disp; mv service pnt; shwrs inc; EHU (10A) €5; lndry; snacks; bar; BBQ; playgrnd; htd pool high ssn; 80% statics; dogs; bus adj; quiet. "Basic facs, but clean & well-maintained; friendly staff; conv NH/sh stay Somport Pass." € 22.00   2012*

JARANDILLA DE LA VERA *1D3* (2km W Rural) *40.12723, -5.69318* **Camping Yuste, Ctra EX203, Km 47, 10440 Aldeaneuva de la Vera (Cáceres) [927-57 26 59]** Fr Plasencia head E on EX203 following sp for Parador, site at km stone 47 in Aldeaneuva de la Vera. Clearly sp down narr rd. Med, pt sl, pt shd; wc; shwrs; EHU (5A) inc; gas; lndry rm; shop; rest, snacks; bar; BBQ; pool; rv fishing; tennis; games rm; TV; bus 500m; phone; quiet. "Simple, well-maintained, attractive site." 15 Mar-15 Sep. € 25.00   2010*

⊞ **JAVEA/XABIA** *4E2* (1km S Rural) *38.78333, 0.17294* **Camping Jávea, Camí de la Fontana 10, 03730 Jávea (Alicante) [965-79 10 70; fax 966-46 05 07; info@camping javea.es; www.camping-javea.com]** Exit N332 for Jávea on A132, cont in dir Port on CV734. At rndabt & Lidl supmkt, take slip rd to R immed after rv bdge sp Arenal Platjas & Cap de la Nau. Strt on at next rndabt to site sp & slip rd 100m sp Autocine. If you miss slip rd go back fr next rndabt. Lge, mkd pitch, pt shd; wc ltd; chem disp; baby facs; shwrs inc; EHU (8A) €4.56 (long lead rec); gas; lndry; shop 500m; rest, snacks; bar; BBQ; playgrnd; pool; paddling pool; sand beach 1.5km; tennis; games area; internet; 15% statics; dogs €2; adv bkg; quiet; red LS/long stay; ccard acc; CKE/CCI. "Excel site & rest; variable pitch sizes/prices; some lge pitches - lge o'fits rec phone ahead; gd, clean san facs; mountain views; helpful staff; m'vans beware low trees; gd cycling." ♦ € 27.00   2012*

⊞ **JAVEA/XABIA** *4E2* (3km S Coastal) *38.77058, 0.18207* **Camping El Naranjal, Cami dels Morers 15, 03730 Jávea (Alicante) [965-79 29 89; fax 966-46 02 56; delfi@ campingelnaranjal.com; www.campingelnaranjal.com]** Exit A7 junc 62 or 63 onto N332 València/Alicante rd. Exit at Gata de Gorgos to Jávea. Foll sp Camping Jávea/Camping El Naranjal. Access rd by tennis club, foll sp. Med, mkd pitch, hdstg, pt shd; htd wc; chem disp; mv service pnt; baby facs; shwrs inc; EHU (10A) €4.05 (poss rev pol); gas; lndry (inc dryer); shop; rest, snacks; bar; BBQ; playgrnd; pool; paddling pool; sand beach 500m; tennis 300m; bike hire; games rm; golf 3km; wifi; TV rm; 35% statics; dogs free; phone; bus 500m; adv bkg; Eng spkn; quiet; ccard acc; red long stay/LS/CKE/CCI. "Gd scenery & beach; pitches poss tight lge o'fits; excel rest; immac facs; tourist info - tickets sold; rec." ♦ € 26.00   2010*

LABUERDA see Ainsa *3B2*

LAREDO *1A4* (2km W Coastal) *43.41176, -3.45329* **Camping Playa del Regatón, El Sable 8, 39770 Laredo (Cantabria) [tel/fax 942-60 69 95; info@campingplayaregaton.com; www.campingplayaregaton.com]** Fr W leave A8 junc 172, under m'way to rndabt & take exit sp Calle Rep Colombia. In 800m turn L at traff lts, in further 800m turn L onto tarmac rd to end, passing other sites. Fr E leave at junc 172, at 1st rndabt take 2nd exit sp Centro Comercial N634 Colindres. At next rndabt take exit Calle Rep Colombia, then as above. Lge, mkd pitch; pt shd; wc; chem disp; mv service pnt; shwrs inc; EHU (6A) €4.30; gas; lndry; shop; rest; bar; sand beach adj & 3km; horseriding mr; wifi; 75% statics; no dogs; bus 600m; Eng spkn; adv bkg; quiet; ccard acc; red long stay/CKE/CCI. "Clean site; sep area for tourers; wash up facs (cold water) every pitch; gd, modern facs; gd NH/sh stay (check opening times of office for EHU release)." ♦ 1 Apr-25 Sep. € 30.00   2011*

LAREDO *1A4* (500m W Urban/Coastal) *43.40888, -3.43277* **Camping Carlos V, Avnda Los Derechos Humanos 15, Ctra Residencial Playa, 39770 Laredo (Cantabria) [tel/fax 942-60 55 93]** Leave A8 at junc 172 to Laredo, foll yellow camping sp, site on W side of town. Med, mkd pitch, pt shd; wc; mv service pnt; baby facs; shwrs inc; EHU €2.60; gas; lndry; shop & 100m; rest; bar; playgrnd; sand beach 200m; dogs €2.14; bus 100m; poss cr; noisy; CKE/CCI. "Well sheltered & lively resort; sm area for tourers; gd, clean, modern facs." 6 May-30 Sep.
€ 25.00   2012*

LEKEITIO *3A1* (3km S Coastal) *43.35071, -2.49260* **Camping Leagi, Calle Barrio Leagi s/n, 48289 Mendexa (Vizcaya) [946-84 23 52; fax 946-24 34 20; leagi@campingleagi.com; www.campingleagi.com]** Fr San Sebastian leave A8/N634 at Deba twd Ondarroa. At Ondarroa do not turn into town, but cont on BI633 beyond Berriatua, then turn R onto BI3405 to Lekeitio. Fr Bilbao leave A8/N634 at Durango & foll BI633 twd Ondarroa. Turn L after Markina onto BI3405 to Lekeitio - do not go via Ondarroa, foll sp to Mendexa & site. Steep climb to site & v steep tarmac ent to site. Only suitable for o'fits with v high power/weight ratio. Med, mkd pitch, pt sl, unshd; wc; chem disp; mv service pnt; serviced pitch; shwrs inc; EHU (5A) €3.90 (rev pol); lndry; shop; rest, snacks; bar; playgrnd; sand beach 1km; many statics; dogs; bus 1.5km; cr & noisy high ssn; ccard acc (over €50); CKE/CCI. "Ltd facs LS; tractor tow avail up to site ent; beautiful scenery; excel local beach; lovely town; gd views; gd walking; san facs under pressure due to many tents; bus to Bilbao & Gurnika." 28 Feb-9 Nov.
€ 36.00   2014*

LEKUNBERRI *3A1* (500m SE Rural) *43.00043, -1.88831* **Aralar Camping, Plazaola 9, 31870 Lekunberri (Navarra) [tel/fax 948-50 40 11 or 948-50 40 49; info@campingaralar. com; www.campingaralar.com]** Exit fr AP15 at junc 124 dir Lukunberri & foll sp for site. Site on R after v sharp downhill turn. Med, all hdstg, pt sl, terr, pt shd; htd wc; chem disp; shwrs inc; EHU (4A) €4.65; gas; lndry; shop; rest, snacks; bar; playgrnd; pool; bike hire; horseriding; TV; dogs €2.95; 70% statics; phone; some Eng spkn; quiet; ccard acc. "Beautiful scenery & mountain walks; only 14 sm touring pitches; avoid Pamplona mid-Aug during bull-run; site also open at w/end & long w/end all year except Jan/Feb." Holy Week & 1 Jun-30 Sep. € 22.50   2009*

LEON 1B3 (7km SE Urban) 42.5900, -5.5331 **Camping Ciudad de León**, Ctra N601, 24195 Golpejar de la Sobarriba [tel/fax 987-26 90 86; camping_leon@yahoo.es; www.vivaleon.com/campingleon.htm] SE fr León on N601 twds Valladolid, L at top of hill at rndabt & Opel g'ge & foll site sp Golpejar de la Sobarriba; 500m after radio masts turn R at site sp. Narr track to site ent. Sm, pt sl, shd; wc; chem disp; shwrs inc; EHU inc (6A) €3.60; gas; lndry; shop; rest, snacks; bar; playgrnd; pool; paddling pool; tennis; bike hire; wifi; dogs €1.50; bus 200m; quiet; adv bkg; poss cr; Eng spkn; CKE/CCI. "Clean, pleasant site; helpful, welcoming staff; access some sm pitches poss diff; easy access to León; shwrs need refurb (2015)." ♦ 1 Jun-20 Sep. € 19.00   2015*

LEON 1B3 (12km SW Urban) 42.51250, -5.77472 **Camping Camino de Santiago**, Ctra N120, Km 324.4, 24392 Villadangos del Páramo (León) [tel/fax 987-68 02 53; info@campingcaminodesantiago.com; www.campingcaminode santiago.com] Access fr N120 to W of vill, site sp on R (take care fast, o'taking traff). Fr E turn L in town & foll sp to site. Lge, mkd pitch, pt shd; wc; chem disp; mv service pnt; baby facs; shwrs inc; EHU €3.90; gas; lndry; shop; rest, snacks; bar; pool; wifi; 50% statics; dogs; phone; bus 300m; poss cr; adv bkg; rd noise; ccard acc; red long stay; CKE/CCI. "Poss no hot water LS; facs tired; pleasant, helpful staff; mosquitoes; vill church worth visit; gd NH." ♦ 23 Mar-30 Sep. € 18.60   2013*

⊞ **LINEA DE LA CONCEPCION, LA** 2H3 (S Urban/Coastal) 36.19167, -5.3350 **Camping Sureuropa**, Camino de Sobrevela s/n, 11300 La Línea de la Concepción (Cádiz) [956-64 35 87; fax 956-64 30 59; info@campingsureuropa.es; www.campingsureuropa.com] Fr AP7, ext junc 124. Use junc124 fr both dirs. Just bef Gibraltar turn R up lane, in 200m turn L into site. Fr N on AP7, exit junc 124 onto A383 dir La Línea; foll sp Santa Margarita thro to beach. Foll rd to R along sea front, site in approx 1km - no advance sp. App rd to site off coast rd poss floods after heavy rain. Med, hdg/mkd pitch, hdstg, pt shd; wc; chem disp; shwrs inc; EHU €4.30; lndry; bar; sand beach 500m; sports club adj; clsd 21 Dec-7 Jan; no dogs; phone; bus 1.5km; site clsd 20 Dec-7 Jan; poss cr; Eng spkn; adv bkg; quiet but noise fr adj sports club; no ccard acc; CKE/CCI. "Clean, flat, pretty site; vg, modern san facs; sm pitches & tight site rds poss diff twin-axles & l'ge o'fits; ideal for Gibraltar 4km; stay ltd to 4 days; wifi in recep only; sh stay only." ♦ € 18.60   2014*

LLAFRANC see Palafrugell 3B3

LLANES 1A4 (8km E Coastal) 43.39948, -4.65350 **Camping La Paz**, Ctra N634, Km 292, 33597 Playa de Vidiago (Asturias) [tel/fax 985-41 12 35; delfin@campinglapaz.com; www.campinglapaz.eu] Take Fr A8/N634/E70 turn R at sp to site bet km stone 292 & 293 bef Vidiago.Site access via narr 1km lane. Stop bef bdge & park on R, staff will tow to pitch. Narr site ent & steep access to pitches. Lge, mkd pitch, terr, shd; wc; chem disp; mv service pnt; baby facs; shwrs inc; EHU (9A) €4.82 (poss rev pol); gas; lndry (inc dryer); shop; rest; bar; BBQ; playgrnd; sand beach adj; fishing; watersports; horseriding; mountain sports; golf 4km; games rm; wifi; TV; dogs €2.51; phone; poss cr w/end; Eng spkn; adv bkg; quiet; ccard acc; CKE/CCI. "Exceptionally helpful owner & staff; sm pitches; gd, modern san facs; excel views; cliff top rest; superb beaches in area." ♦ Easter-30 Sep. € 42.00   2011*

LLANES 1A4 (3km W Coastal) 43.42500, -4.78944 **Camping Las Conchas de Póo**, Ctra General, 33509 Póo de Llanes (Asturias) [tel/fax 985-40 22 90 or 674-16 58 79(mob); campinglasconchas@gmail.com; www.campinglasconchas. com] Fr A8 at Llanes West junc 307 & foll sp. Site on rd AS263. Med, sl, terr, pt shd; wc; chem disp; baby facs; shwrs; EHU (6A) €3.20; lndry (inc dryer); shop (only in high ssn); rest; bar; playgrnd; sand beach adj; wifi; 50% statics; dogs; bus adj; phone; bus; quiet. "Pleasant site; footpath to lovely beach; lovely coastal walk to Celorio; stn in Póo vill." 1 Jun-15 Sep. € 20.00   2015*

LLANES 1A4 (5km W Coastal) 43.43471, -4.81810 **Camping Playa de Troenzo**, Ctra de Celerio-Barro, 33595 Celorio (Asturias) [985-40 16 72; fax 985-74 07 23; troenzo@telepolis.com] Fr E take E70/A8 exit at junc 300 to Celorio. At T-junc with AS263 turn L dir Celorio & Llanes. Turn L on N9 (Celorio) thro vill & foll sp to Barro. Site on R after 500m (after Maria Elena site). Lge, terr, pt shd; wc; chem disp; mv service pnt; shwrs inc; EHU (6A) €2.51; gas; lndry; rest, snacks; bar; playgrnd; sand beach 400m; 90% statics; dogs; phone; wifi; poss cr; Eng spkn; adv bkg; CKE/CCI. "Lovely, old town; most pitches sm; for pitches with sea views go thro statics to end of site; gd, modern facs; gd rests in town; nr harbour." 16 Feb-19 Dec. € 21.00   2014*

> ## "I need an on-site restaurant"
> We do our best to make sure site information is correct, but it is always best to check any must-have facilities are still available or will be open during your visit.

LLAVORSI 3B2 (8km N Rural) 42.56004, 1.22810 **Camping Del Cardós**, Ctra Llavorsí-Tavascan, Km 85, 25570 Ribera de Cardós (Lleida) [973-62 31 12; fax 973-62 31 83; info@campingdelcardos.com; www.campingdelcardos.com] Take L504 fr Llavorsi dir Ribera de Cardós for 9km; site on R on ent vill. Med, mkd pitch, pt shd; wc; chem disp; mv service pnt; shwrs; EHU (4-6A) €5.30; gas; lndry (inc dryer); shop; rest; playgrnd; pool; 2 paddling pools; fishing; games area; TV rm; 5% statics; dogs €3.60; Eng spkn; quiet; CKE/CCI. "By side of rv, v quiet LS; excel." 1 Apr-20 Oct. € 24.00   2009*

⊞ **LLAVORSI** 3B2 (9km N Rural) 42.56890, 1.23040 **Camping La Borda del Pubill**, Ctra de Tavescan, Km 9.5, 25570 Ribera de Cardós (Lleida) [973-62 30 80; fax 973-62 30 28; info@campinglabordadelpubill.com; www.campinglabordadelpubill.com] Fr France on A64 exit junc 17 at Montréjeau & head twd Spanish border. At Vielha turn E onto C28/C1412 to Llavorsí, then L504 to Ribera. Fr S take N260 fr Tremp to Llavorsí, then L504 to site. Lge, pt shd; htd wc; baby facs; shwrs; EHU €5.30; gas; lndry; shop, rest high ssn; snacks; bar; playgrnd; htd pool; paddling pool; rv sw & fishing; kayaking; trekking; adventure sports; quad bike hire; horseriding; skiing 30km; games area; games rm; TV; 10% statics; dogs €3; phone; car wash; adv bkg; quiet; ccard acc. "In beautiful area; excel walking; gd rest." ♦ € 24.00 (CChq acc)   2009*

LLORET DE MAR *3B3* (1km S Coastal) *41.6973, 2.8217* **Camping Tucan, Ctra Blanes-Lloret, 17310 Lloret de Mar (Gerona) [972-36 99 65; fax 972-36 00 79; info@campingtucan.com; www.campingtucan.com]** Fr N exit AP7 junc 9 onto C35 twd Sant Feliu then C63 on R sp Lloret de Mar. At x-rds foll sp Blanes, site on R. Fr S take last exit fr C32 & foll sp Lloret de Mar, site on L, sp. Lge, mkd pitch, terr, shd; wc; chem disp; baby facs; shwrs inc; EHU (3-6A) €3.40-4.40; gas; lndry; shop; rest, snacks; bar; BBQ; playgrnd; pool; paddling pool; sand beach 600m; games area; golf 500m; entmnt; internet; TV rm; 25% statics; dogs €2; phone; bus; car wash; Eng spkn; adv bkg; quiet; ccard acc; red long stay/snr citizens/CKE/CCI. "Well-appointed site; friendly staff." ♦ 1 Apr-30 Sep. € 28.00   2011*

⊞ **LLORET DE MAR** *3B3* (1km SW Coastal) *41.6984, 2.8265* **Camping Santa Elena-Ciutat, Ctra Blanes/Lloret, 17310 Lloret de Mar (Gerona) [972-36 40 09; fax 972-36 79 54; santaelana@betsa.es; www.betsa.es]** Exit A7 junc 9 dir Lloret. In Lloret take Blanes rd, site sp at km 10.5 on rd GI 682. V lge, pt sl; wc; baby facs; shwrs; EHU (5A) €3.90; gas; lndry; shop; rest, snacks; bar; playgrnd; pool; paddling pool; shgl beach 600m; games area; phone; cash machine; poss cr; Eng spkn; quiet LS; red facs LS; CKE/CCI. "Ideal for teenagers." ♦ € 34.60   2011*

⊞ **LOBOS, LOS** *4G1* (2km NE Rural) **Camping Hierbabuena, Los Lobos, 04610 Cuevas del Almanzora (Almería) [tel/fax 950-16 86 97 or 629-68 81 53 (mob)]** S fr Lorca on A7; at Cuevas del Almanzora turn L onto A332 to Los Lobos - do not ent vill; 400m after junc with A1201 (dir El Largo & Pulpí) turn L & foll gravel rd to site in 1km. Sm, mkd pitch, hdstg, pt shd; htd wc; chem disp; baby facs; shwrs inc; EHU (6-10A) inc; gas (Spanish only); lndry; supmkt & rest 5km; snacks & bar 500m; BBQ; playgrnd; sand beach 5km; 75% statics (sep area); dogs free; Eng spkn; adv bkg; quiet; ccard not acc; red long stay. "Gd for long winter stay; friendly British owners; lge pitches; pretty & interesting area; excel choice of beaches; gd walking, cycling & sightseeing; vg security; excel." ♦ € 25.50   2011*

⊞ **LOGRONO** *3B1* (500m N Urban) *42.47187, -2.45164* **Camping La Playa, Avda de la Playa 6, 26006 Logroño (La Rioja) [941-25 22 53; fax 941-25 86 61; info@campingla playa.com; www.campinglaplaya.com]** Leave Logroño by bdge 'Puente de Piedra' on N111, then turn L at rndabt into Camino de las Norias. Site well sp in town & fr N111, adj sports cent Las Norias, on N side of Rv Ebro. Med, hdg pitch, shd; wc; mv service pnt; shwrs inc; EHU (5A) €4.80; gas; lndry (inc dryer); shop; snacks, bar in ssn; playgrnd; pool; rv sw adj; tennis; 80% statics; dogs €2; red CKE/CCI. "Sh walk to town cent; ltd facs LS & site poss clsd; vg; nr rest." ♦ € 25.00   2014*

LOGRONO *3B1* (10km W Rural) *42.41613, -2.55169* **Camping Navarrete, Ctra La Navarrete-Entrena, Km 1.5, 26370 Navarrete (La Rioja) [941-44 01 69; fax 941-44 06 39; campingnavarrete@fer.es; www.campingnavarrete.com]** Fr AP68 exit junc 11, at end slip rd turn L onto LR137 to Navarette. Foll sp thro town for Entrena (S) on LR137 dir Entrena. Site 1km on R. Lge, mkd pitch, pt shd; wc; chem disp; mv service pnt; baby facs; shwrs inc; EHU (6A) €4.40; gas; lndry; shop; snacks; bar; BBQ; playgrnd; pool & paddling pool; tennis; horseriding; car wash; wifi; 95% statics; dogs €2.40; site clsd 10 Dec-12 Jan; bus 1.3km; Eng spkn; noisy at w/end; ccard acc; red LS/long stay. "Professionally run, clean, tidy site; excel san facs; helpful staff; some sm pitches; Bilbao ferry 2 hrs via m'way; gd NH; interesting area; highly rec." 16 Jan-14 Dec. € 42.00   2014*

⊞ **LORCA** *4G1* (8km W Rural) *37.62861, -1.74888* **Camping La Torrecilla, Ctra Granada-LaTorrecilla, 30817 Lorca (Murcia) [968-44 21 36; fax 968-44 21 96; campinglatorrecilla@hotmail.es]** Leave A7/E15 at junc 585. In 1km turn L, site well sp. Med, mkd pitch, hdstg, pt sl, pt shd; htd wc; chem disp; mv service pnt; shwrs inc; EHU (6A) €3.88; gas; lndry; shop 2km; rest, snacks; bar; BBQ; playgrnd; pool; tennis; games area; TV rm; 95% statics; dogs; phone; bus 1km; poss cr; Eng spkn; quiet; ccard acc; red long stay. "Ltd touring pitches & EHU; friendly, helpful staff; excel pool; vg san facs." ♦ € 20.00   2013*

⊞ **LUARCA** *1A3* (1km NE Coastal) *43.54914, -6.52426* **Camping Los Cantiles, Ctra N634, Km 502.7, 33700 Luarca (Asturias) [tel/fax 985-64 09 38; cantiles@camping loscantiles.com; www.campingloscantiles.com]** On A8 exit junc 467 (sp Luarca/Barcia/Almuña), At rndabt foll sp to Luarca, after petrol stn turn R, foll sp to site. Not rec to ent town fr W. Not rec to foll SatNav as may take you up v steep & narr rd. On leaving site, retrace to main rd - do not tow thro Luarca. Med, hdg pitch, pt shd; wc; chem disp; baby facs; shwrs inc; EHU inc (3-6A) €2-2.50; gas; lndry; shop; rest high ssn; snacks; bar; pool 300m; shgl beach at foot of cliff; dogs €1; phone; poss cr; Eng spkn; adv bkg; quiet; red long stay; CKE/CCI. "Site on cliff top; some narr site rds; pitches soft after rain; steep climb down to beach; 30 min walk to interesting town & port; wonderful setting; san fac's OK, water in shwrs v hot." ♦ € 29.40   2013*

⊞ **LUARCA** *1A3* (12km E Rural/Coastal) *43.54898, -6.38420* **Camping La Regalina, Ctra de la Playa s/n, 33788 Cadavedo (Asturias) [tel/fax 985-64 50 56; info@laregalina.com]** Fr N632 dir Cadavedo, km126. Site well sp. Med, pt shd; wc; chem disp; shwrs inc; EHU (5-8A) €2.30; gas; shop; rest, snacks; bar; pool; beach 1km; TV; 10% statics; dogs €3; phone; bus 600m; adv bkg; quiet; ccard acc high ssn; red long stay. "Scenic area; pretty vill; ltd facs LS; gd." € 21.00   2009*

LUARCA *1A3* (2km W Coastal) *43.55116, -6.55310* **Camping Playa de Taurán, 33700 Luarca (Asturias) [tel/fax 985-64 12 72 or 619-88 43 06 (mob); tauran@campingtauran. com; www.campingtauran.com]** Exit A8/N634 junc 471 sp Luarca, El Chano. Cont 3.5km on long, narr, rough access rd. Rd thro Luarca unsuitable for c'vans. Med, some hdg pitch, pt sl, pt shd; wc; chem disp; mv service pnt; baby facs; shwrs inc; EHU (10A) €3.50; gas; lndry; shop; rest, snacks; bar; BBQ; pool; paddling pool; shgl beach 200m; sand beach 2km; bike hire; phone; dogs €1; quiet; red long stays. "Sea & mountain views; off beaten track; conv fishing & hill vills; peaceful, restful, attractive, well-kept site; steep access to beach; excel." 1 Apr-30 Sep. € 18.50   2013*

LUGO *1B2* (25km S Rural) *42.78683, 7.84516* **A Peneda, Edil Luis Garcia Rojo 38, 27560 Monterroso [tel/fax 34 98 23 77 501; aged@aged-sl.com]** Fr Lugo on N540, take N640 sp to Monterroso. Sp in ctr of town, go down to rv. Sm, hdg pitch, pt shd; wc; chem disp; mv service pnt; baby facs; shwr inc; EHU (6A); rest; snacks; bar; playgrnd; 1% statics; poss cr; adv bkg; quiet; CCI. "Very pretty, nr rv and excel picnic facs; helpful staff, ltd Eng; excel site." ♦ 30 Mar-24 Sep. € 28.00   2014*

"That's changed – Should I let The Club know?"

If you find something on site that's different from the site entry, fill in a report and let us know. See www.caravanclub.co.uk/europereport.

LUMBIER *3B1* (1.3km S Rural) *42.65111, -1.30222* **Camping Iturbero, Ctra N240 Pamplona-Huesca, 31440 Lumbier (Navarra) [948-88 04 05; fax 948-88 04 14; iturbero@ campingiturbero.com; www.campingiturbero.com]** SE fr Pamplona on N240 twds Yesa Reservoir. In 30km L on NA150 twds Lumbier. In 3.5km immed bef Lumbier turn R at rndabt then over bdge, 1st L to site, adj sw pool. Well sp fr N240. Med, hdg/mkd pitch, some hdstg, pt shd; wc; chem disp; mv service pnt; shwrs inc; EHU (5A) €4.95; gas; lndry; shop 1km; rest, snacks; bar; BBQ; playgrnd; pool 100m; tennis; hang-gliding; 25% statics; dogs; bus 1km; quiet; CKE/CCI. "Beautiful, well-kept site; clean, basic facs; excel touring base; open w/end only Dec-Easter (poss fr Sep) but clsd 19 Dec-19 Feb; eagles & vultures in gorge & seen fr site; helpful staff; Lumbier lovely sm town." 15 Mar-15 Dec. € 26.50   2014*

MACANET DE CABRENYS *3B3* (1km S Rural) *42.37314, 2.75419* **Camping Maçanet de Cabrenys, Mas Roquet s/n, 17720 Maçanet de Cabrenys (Gerona) [667-77 66 48 (mob); info@campingmassanet.com; www.campingmassanet.com]** Fr N, exit AP7 junc 2 at La Jonquera onto N-II dir Figueres; at km 767 turn R onto GI-502/GI-503 dir Maçanet de Cabrenys; turn L 500m bef vill; site sp. Or fr S, exit AP7 junc 4 at Figueres onto N-II dir France; at km 766 turn L onto GI-502 dir Maçanet de Cabrenys; then as above. Sm, mkd pitch, some hdstg, sl, terr, pt shd; htd wc; chem disp; mv service pnt; baby facs; shwrs; EHU (10A) €6.50; gas; lndry; sm shop & 2km; ltd rest, snacks; bar; BBQ; playgrnd; pool; bike hire; cycle rtes fr site; games rm; wifi; TV; some statics; dogs €5.50; Eng spkn; quiet; adv bkg; ccard acc; red LS; CKE/CCI. ♦ 1 Mar-31 Dec. € 30.00   2013*

⊞ **MADRID** *1D4* (13km NE Urban) *40.45361, -3.60333* **Camping Osuna, Jardines de Aranjuez 1, 28042 Madrid [917-41 05 10; fax 913-20 63 65; camping.osuna.madrid@ microgest.es]** Fr M40, travelling S clockwise (anti-clockwise fr N or E) exit junc 8 at Canillejas sp 'Avda de Logroño'. Turn L under m'way, then R under rlwy, immed after turn R at traff lts. Site on L corner - white painted wall. Travelling N, leave M40 at junc 7 (no turn off at junc 8) sp Avda 25 Sep, U-turn at km 7, head S to junc 8, then as above. Med, hdg/mkd pitch, pt sl, pt shd; wc; chem disp; shwrs inc; EHU (6A) €4.85 (long lead rec); lndry; shop 600m; playgrnd; metro to town 600m; 10% statics; dogs free; phone; poss cr; rd & aircraft noise; Eng spkn; red LS; CKE/CCI. "Sm pitches poss diff lge o'fits; poss neglected LS & facs tired (June 2010); poss travellers; conv city cent; busy; gd basic facs; easy walk to metro with frequent svr into Madrid." ♦ ltd. € 33.00   2015*

⊞ **MADRID** *1D4* (13km S Urban) *40.31805, -3.68888* **Camping Alpha, Ctra de Andalucía N-IV, Km 12.4, 28906 Getafe (Madrid) [916-95 80 69; fax 916-83 16 59; info@campingalpha.com; www.campingalpha.com]** Fr S on A4/E5 twd Madrid, leave at km 12B to W dir Ocaña & foll sp. Fr N on A4/E5 at km 13B to change dir back onto A4; then exit 12B sp 'Polígono Industrial Los Olivos' to site. Lge, hdstg, hdg pitch, pt shd; wc; chem disp; mv service pnt; shwrs inc; EHU (15A) €5.90 (poss no earth); lndry; shop; rest, snacks; bar; playgrnd; pool high ssn; tennis; games area; 20% statics; dogs; phone; poss cr; Eng spkn; adv bkg; ccard acc; red CKE/ CCI. "Lorry depot adj; poss vehicle movements 24 hrs but minimal noise; bus & metro to Madrid 30-40 mins; sm pitches poss tight for space; vg, clean facs; helpful staff; NH or sh stay." € 28.00   2011*

⊞ **MADRIGAL DE LA VERA** *1D3* (500m E Rural) *40.14864, -5.35769* **Camping Alardos, Ctra Madrigal-Candeleda, 10480 Madrigal de la Vera (Cáceres) [tel/fax 927-56 50 66; mirceavd@hotmail.com; www.campingalardos.es]** Fr Jarandilla take EX203 E to Madrigal. Site sp in vill nr rv bdge. Med, mkd pitch, pt shd; wc; chem disp; shwrs inc; EHU (6-10A) €4; lndry; shop & 1km; rest, snacks; bar; BBQ; playgrnd; pool; rv sw adj; TV; 10% statics; no dogs; phone; poss cr Jul/Aug; Eng spkn; adv bkg; ccard not acc. "Friendly owners; superb site; ltd facs LS; beautiful scenery; excel touring area; ancient Celtic settlement at El Raso 5km." € 24.60   2013*

⊞ **MAMOLA, LA** *2H4* (500m W Coastal) *36.74062, -3.29976* **Camping Castillo de Baños, Castillo de Baños, 18750 La Mamola (Granada) [958-82 95 28; fax 958-82 97 68; info@campingcastillo.com; www.campingcastillo.com]** Fr E on A7/E15 exit km 360.4 sp Camping/Rest El Paraiso/ Castillo de Baños, site on L after rest at ent to vill. Fr W exit km 359.3. Lge, mkd pitch, hdstg, pt shd; wc; chem disp; mv service pnt; shwrs inc; EHU (5A) €4; gas; lndry (inc dryer); shop; rest, snacks; bar; playgrnd; pool; private shgl beach adj; fishing; bike hire; entmnt; internet; Eng spkn; dogs €2.50; bus 200m; adv bkg; ccard acc; quiet; red LS/CKE/CCI. "Poss rallies LS." ♦ € 23.50   2010*

⊞ **MANGA DEL MAR MENOR, LA** *4G2* (27.7km E Urban) *37.6244, -0.7447* Caravaning La Manga, Autovia Cartagena - La Manga, exit 11, E-30370 La Manga del Mar Menor [968-56 30 19; fax 968-543426; lamanga@ caravaning.es; www.caravaning.es] Take Autovia CT-32 fr Cartagena to La Manga; take exit 800B twds El Algar/ Murcia; keep L, merge onto Autovia MU312; cont to foll MU-312; cont onto Ctra a La Manga & cont onto Av Gran Via; site clearly sp. Lge, hdg, hdstg; pt shd; wc; chem disp; mv service pnt; serviced pitches; baby facs; shwrs inc; EHU (10A) inc; lndry (inc dryer); supmkt; rest, snacks; bar; BBQ; playgrnd; pools; beach; gym; sauna; jacuzzi; outdoor fitness course; tennis; watersports; bike hire & horseridng nrby; games rm; entmnt; wifi; some statics; dogs €1.45; Eng spkn; adv bkg; bus to Murcia and Cartagena; recep open 24 hrs; ccard acc. "Open air cinema & children's programme high ssn; lovely location & gd for golfers; Mar Menor well worth visiting; vg rest; helpful staff." € 38.00   2013*

See advertisement

⊞ **MANZANARES EL REAL** *1D4* (8km NE Rural) *40.74278, -3.81583* Camping La Fresneda, Ctra M608, Km 19.5, 28791 Soto del Real (Madrid) [tel/fax 918-47 65 23] Fr AP6/NV1 turn NE at Collado-Villalba onto M608 to Cerceda & Manzanares el Real. Foll rd round lake to Soto del Real, site sp at km 19.5. Med, shd; wc; chem disp; baby facs; shwrs €0.15; EHU (6A) €3.50; gas; lndry; shop; snacks; bar; playgrnd; pool; tennis; dogs €3; phone; rd noise; ccard acc. ◆ € 24.00   2009*

⊞ **MANZANERA** *3D2* (1km NE Rural) *40.06266, -0.82629* Camping Villa de Manzanera, Partida Las Bateas s/n, Ctra 1514, Km 10.5, 44420 Manzanera (Teruel) [978-78 18 19 or 978-78 17 48; fax 978-78 17 09; reservas@ campingmanzanera.com] Exit junc 76 fr A23 onto N234 dir Sarrión. Nr Mora turn onto A1514 at site sp. Site on L by petrol stn bef vill. Med, mkd pitch, unshd; htd wc; chem disp; baby facs; shwrs inc; EHU (10A) €4.20; gas; lndry; shop 1km; rest, snacks; bar; playgrnd; pool; 80% statics; no dogs; phone; bus 300m; poss cr; poss noisy; ccard acc; CKE/CCI. "Site v run down & unclean (Jan 2011); nr wintersports area; ltd touring pitches bet seasonal statics - some pitches worn & uneven; ltd facs in winter & site poss clsd; pay at filling stn adj; NH only if desperate." ◆ ltd. € 21.00   2011*

⊞ **MARBELLA** *2H3* (7km E Coastal) *36.50259, -4.80413* Camping La Buganvilla, Ctra N340, Km 188.8, 29600 Marbella (Málaga) [952-83 19 73 or 952-83 19 74; fax 952-83 56 21; info@campingbuganvilla.com; www.campingbuganvilla.com] E fr Marbella for 6km on N340/E15 twds Málaga. Pass site & cross over m'way at Elviria & foll site sp. Fr Málaga exit R off autovia immed after 189km marker. Lge, terr, shd; pt sl; wc; chem disp; shwrs; EHU (10A) €4.80; gas; lndry; shop & 250m; rest; bar & sun terr; playgrnd; pool; sand beach 350m; games rm; wifi; TV; phone; dogs €4 (not acc Jul/Aug); Eng spkn; adv bkg; poss noisy at w/end; red long stay/snr citizens; ccard acc; CKE/CCI. "Relaxed, conv site; helpful staff; excel beach; facs being upgraded (2014)." ◆ € 48.60   2014*

> ## "I like to fill in the reports as I travel from site to site"
>
> You'll find report forms at the back of this guide, or you can fill them in online at www.caravanclub.co.uk/europereport.

⊞ **MARBELLA** *2H3* (10km E Coastal) *36.49111, -4.76416* Camping Marbella Playa, Ctra N340, Km 192.8, 29600 Marbella (Málaga) [952-83 39 98; fax 952-83 39 99; recepcion@campingmarbella.com; www.campingmarbella. com] Fr Marbella on A7/N340 coast rd (not AP7/E15 toll m'way) & site is on R bef 193 km stone & just bef pedestrian bdge over A7/N340, sp 'to beach'. Fr Málaga U-turn on m'way as follows: pass 192km mark & immed take R slip rd to Elviria to turn L over bdge, back onto A7/N340. Turn R bef next bdge. Lge, mkd pitch, hdstg, pt shd; wc; chem disp; mv service pnt; baby facs; shwrs; EHU (10A) €4; gas; lndry service; supmkt; rest, snacks; bar; BBQ; playgrnd; pool; sand beach adj; watersports; tennis 50m; wifi; TV; dogs; phone; bus nr; poss v cr; rd noise; ccard acc; red LS/long stay/snr citizens/CKE/CCI. "Pitches tight; clean facs but tired; gd supmkt; friendly, helpful manager; gd base Costa del Sol; noisy peak ssn & w/ends, espec Sat nights." ◆ € 26.00   2010*

Check any essential information with the site before you travel

⊞ **MARBELLA** *2H3* (12km E Coastal) *36.48881, -4.74294*
**Kawan Village Cabopino, Ctra N340/A7, Km 194.7,
29600 Marbella (Málaga) [tel/fax 952-83 43 73;
info@campingcabopino.com; www.campingcabopino.
com]** Fr E site is on N side of N340/A7; turn R at km 195 'Salida
Cabopino' past petrol stn, site on R at rndabt. Fr W on A7 turn R
at 'Salida Cabopino' km 194.7, go over bdge to rndabt, site strt
over. NB Do not take sm exit fr A7 immed at 1st Cabopino sp. Lge,
mkd pitch, pt sl, pt shd; wc; chem disp; mv service pnt; baby facs;
shwrs inc; EHU (6-10A) inc (poss long lead req); lndry (inc dryer);
shop; rest, snacks; bar; BBQ (gas/elec); playgrnd; 2 pools (1 covrd);
sand beach/dunes 200m; watersports; marina 300m; games area;
archery; golf driving range; wifi; games/TV rm; 50% statics; dogs
€2; no o'fits over 11m high ssn; bus 100m; Eng spkn; rd noise & lge
groups w/enders; ccard acc; red LS; CKE/CCI. "V pleasant site set in
pine woodland; busy, particularly w/end; varied pitch size, poss diff
access lge o'fits; blocks req some pitches; gd, clean san facs; feral
cats on site (2009)." ♦ € 48.00 (CChq acc) SBS - E21   2014*

⊞ **MARIA** *4G1* (8km W Rural) *37.70823, -2.23609* **Camping
Sierra de María, Ctra María a Orce, Km 7, Paraje La Piza,
04838 María (Málaga) [950-16 70 45 or 660-26 64 74 (mob);
fax 950-48 54 16; info@campingsierrademaria.com;
www.campingsierrademaria.com]** Exit A92 at junc 408 to
Vélez Rubio, Vélez Blanco & María. Foll A317 to María & cont
dir Huéscar & Orce. Site on R. Med, mkd pitch, pt sl, pt shd;
wc; chem disp; shwrs; EHU (6-10A) €3.75; shop high ssn;
rest; bar; bike hire; horseriding; some statics; dogs; adv bkg;
quiet; ccard acc; CKE/CCI. "Lovely, peaceful, ecological site
in mountains; much wildlife; variable pitch sizes; facs poss
stretched high ssn; v cold in winter. ♦ € 16.00   2011*

⊞ **MARINA, LA** *4F2* (1.5km S Coastal) *38.12972, -0.65000*
**Camping Internacional La Marina, Ctra N332a, Km 76,
03194 La Marina (Alicante) [965-41 92 00; fax 965-41 91 10;
info@campinglamarina.com; www.campinglamarina.com]**
Fr N332 S of La Marina turn E twd sea at rndabt onto
Camino del Cementerio. At next rndabt turn S onto
N332a & foll site sp along Avda de l'Alegría. V lge, hdg/
mkd pitch, hdstg, terr, shd; htd wc; chem disp; mv service
pnt; 50% serviced pitches; baby facs; fam bthrm; sauna;
solarium; shwrs inc; EHU (10A) €3.21; gas; lndry (inc dryer);
supmkt; rest, snacks; bars; playgrnd; 2 pools (1 htd/covrd);
waterslides; sand beach 500m; fishing; watersports; tennis;
games area; games rm; fitness cent; entmnt; disco; wifi; TV
rm; 10% statics; dogs €2.14; phone; bus 50m; car wash;
security; Eng spkn; adv bkg; ccard acc; various pitch sizes/
prices; red long stay/LS; CKE/CCI. "Popular winter site -
almost full late Feb; v busy w/end; clean, high quality facs;
bus fr gate; gd security; excel rest; gd site; v helpful; hire cars
avail." ♦ € 61.50   2015*

See advertisement

⊞ **MASNOU, EL** *3C3* (750m W Coastal) *41.4753, 2.3033*
Camping Masnou, Ctra NII, Km 633, Carrer de Camil Fabra 33, 08320 El Masnou (Barcelona) [tel/fax 935-55 15 03; masnou@ campingsonline.es; www.campingmasnoubarcelona.com] App site fr N on N11. Pass El Masnou rlwy stn on L & go strt on at traff lts. Site on R on N11 after km 633. Not clearly sp. Med, pt sl, shd; wc; mv service pnt; shwrs inc; EHU €5.88; shop, snacks, bar high ssn; BBQ; playgrnd; pool high ssn; sand beach opp; internet; dogs; phone; bus 300m; train to Barcelona nr; poss v cr; Eng spkn; rd & rlwy noise; ccard acc; CKE/CCI. "Gd pitches, no awnings; some sm pitches, poss shared; facs vg, though poss stretched when site busy; no restriction on NH vehicle movements; well-run, friendly site but tired; gd service LS; rlwy line bet site & excel beach - subway avail; excel train service to Barcelona; excel pool." ♦ ltd. € 34.00   2015*

MATARO *3C3* (3km E Coastal) *41.55060, 2.48330* **Camping Barcelona, Ctra NII, Km 650, 08304 Mataró (Barcelona) [937-90 47 20; fax 937-41 02 82; info@campingbarcelona. com; www.campingbarcelona.com]** Exit AP7 onto C60 sp Mataró. Turn N onto NII dir Gerona, site sp on L after rndabt. Lge, mkd pitch, hdstg, shd; wc; chem disp; mv service pnt; baby facs; shwrs inc; EHU (6A) €5.50; gas; lndry; shop; rest, snacks; bar; playgrnd; pool; paddling pool; sand beach 1.5km; games area; games rm; animal farm; wifi; entmnt; TV; 5% statics; dogs €4; shuttle bus to beach & town; Eng spkn; adv bkg; rd noise; ccard acc; red long stay/LS; CKE/CCI. "Conv Barcelona 28km; pleasant site; friendly, welcoming staff." ♦ 4 Mar-1 Nov. € 45.70   2013*

⊞ **MAZAGON** *2G2* (10km E Coastal) *37.09855, -6.72650* **Camping Doñana Playa, Ctra San Juan del Puerto-Matalascañas, Km 34.6, 21130 Mazagón (Huelva) [959-53 62 81; fax 959-53 63 13; info@campingdonana.com; www.campingdonana.com]** Fr A49 exit junc 48 at Bullullos del Condado onto A483 sp El Rocio, Matalascañas. At coast turn R sp Mazagón, site on L in 16km. V lge, mkd pitch, hdstg, pt shd; wc; chem disp; shwrs inc; EHU (6A) €5.20; shop; rest, snacks; bar; playgrnd; pool; sand beach 300m; watersports; tennis; games area; bike hire; entmnt; some statics; dogs €4.10; bus 500m; site clsd 14 Dec-14 Jan; adv bkg; quiet but v noisy Fri/Sat nights; red LS; CKE/CCI. "Pleasant site amongst pine trees but lack of site care LS; ltd LS; lge pitches but poss soft sand; new (2014) lge shwr block on lower pt of site." ♦ € 48.00   2014*

MENDEXA see Lekeitio *3A1*

⊞ **MENDIGORRIA** *3B1* (500m SW Rural) *42.62416, -1.84277* **Camping El Molino, Ctra Larraga, 31150 Mendigorría (Navarra) [948-34 06 04; fax 948-34 00 82; info@camping elmolino.com; www.campingelmolino.com]** Fr Pamplona on N111 turn L at 25km in Puente la Reina onto NA601 sp Mendigorría. Site sp thro vill dir Larraga. Med, some mkd pitch, pt shd; wc; chem disp; serviced pitches; baby facs; shwrs inc; EHU (6A) inc; gas; lndry (inc dryer); shop; rest, snacks; bar; BBQ; playgrnd; pool; paddling pool; waterslide; canoe hire; tennis; games area; wifi; TV; statics (sep area); dogs; phone; poss cr at w/end; clsd 23 Dec-14 Jan & poss Mon-Thurs fr Nov to Feb, phone ahead to check; adv bkg; poss v noisy at w/end; ccard acc; CKE/CCI. "Gd clean san facs; solar water heating - water poss only warm; vg leisure facs; v ltd facs LS; for early am dep LS, pay night bef & obtain barrier key; friendly, helpful staff; lovely medieval vill." ♦ 7 Jan-22 Dec. € 38.00   2013*

⊞ **MEQUINENZA** *3C2* (Urban) *41.37833, 0.30555* **Camp Municipal Octogesa, Ctra Alcanyís-Fraga s/n, Km 314, 50170 Mequinenza (Zaragoza) [974-46 44 31; fax 974-46 50 31; rai@fuibol.e.telefonica.net; www.fuibol.net]** Exit AP2 junc 4 onto N211 S. On ent Mequinenza just past wooded area on L, turn L thro break in service rd, site well sp. Tight ent poss unsuitable lge o'fits. Med, hdg/mkd pitch, terr, pt shd; wc; chem disp (wc); shwrs inc; EHU (6A) €3.90; lndry; shop 1km; rest, snacks; bar; BBQ; playgrnd; 2 pools high ssn; tennis; dogs; phone; Eng spkn; adv bkg; quiet but noise fr arr of fishing parties; ccard acc; CKE/CCI. "Site pt of complex on bank of Rv Segre; base for fishing trips - equipment supplied; sm pitches unsuitable lge o'fits; NH only." 15 Feb-15 Nov. € 17.70   2009*

⊞ **MERIDA** *2E3* (5km NE Urban) *38.93558, -6.30426* **Camping Mérida, Avda de la Reina Sofia s/n, 06800 Mérida (Badajoz) [924-30 34 53; fax 924-30 03 98; proexcam@jet.es]** Fr E on A5/E90 exit junc 333/334 to Mérida, site on L in 2km. Fr W on A5/E90 exit junc 346, site sp. Fr N exit A66/E803 at junc 617 onto A5 E. Leave at junc 334, site on L in 1km twd Mérida. Fr S on A66-E803 app Mérida, foll Cáceres sp onto bypass to E; at lge rndabt turn R sp Madrid; site on R after 2km. Med, mkd pitch, pt sl, pt shd; wc; chem disp; shwrs inc; EHU (6A) €3.20 (long lead poss req & poss rev pol); gas; lndry; ltd shop high ssn & 3km; hypmkt 6km; rest, snacks; bar; pool; paddling pool; TV; some statics; dogs; wifi; phone; no bus; quiet but some rd noise; CKE/CCI. "Roman remains & National Museum of Roman Art worth visit; poss diff lge o'fits manoeuvring onto pitch due trees & soft grnd after rain; ltd facs LS; conv NH; taxi to town costs 5-9 euros; grass pitches; bread can be ordered fr rest; poss nightclub noise at w/ end." ♦ € 20.00   2015*

⊞ **MIAJADAS** *2E3* (10km SW Rural) *39.09599, -6.01333* **Camping-Restaurant El 301, Ctra Madrid-Lisbon, Km 301, 10100 Miajadas (Cáceres) [927-34 79 14; camping301@ hotmail.com]** Leave A5/E90 just bef km stone 301 & foll sp 'Via de Servicio' with rest & camping symbols; site in 500m. Med, pt shd; wc; chem disp; shwrs inc; EHU (8A) €4 (poss no earth); gas; lndry; shop; rest, snacks; bar; playgrnd; pool; TV; phone; m'way noise & dogs; ccard acc; CKE/CCI. "Well-maintained, clean site; grass pitches; OK wheelchair users but steps to pool; gd NH." € 16.00   2010*

MIJAS COSTA see Fuengirola *2H4*

MOIXENT *4E2* (12km N Rural) *38.96488, -0.79917* **Camping Sierra Natura (Naturist), Finca El Tejarico, Ctra Moixent-Navalón, Km 11.5, 46810 Enguera (València) [962-25 30 26; fax 962-25 30 20; info@sierranatura.com; www.sierranatura.com]** Exit A35 fr N exit junc 23 or junc 23 fr S onto CV589 sp Navalón. At 11.5km turn R sp Sierra Natura - gd rd surface but narr & some steep, tight hairpin bends (owners arrange convoys on request). Fr E on N340 exit junc 18 (do not take junc 14). Sm, pt sl, pt shd; wc; chem disp; baby facs; sauna; shwrs inc; EHU (10A) €5.20; lndry rm; shop & 12 km; rest, snacks; bar; playgrnd; pool; 10% statics; dogs €4.55; phone; poss cr; Eng spkn; adv bkg; quiet; red long stay. "Tranquil, family-run site in remote area; unusual architecture; stunning mountain scenery; nature walks on site; excel pool & rest complex." ♦ ltd. 1 Mar-30 Oct. € 19.00   2011*

⊞ **MOJACAR** *4G1* (3.5km S Coastal) *37.12656, -1.83250* Camping El Cantal di Mojácar, Ctra Garrucha-Carboneras, 04638 Mojácar (Almería) [950-47 82 04; fax 950-47 23 93; campingelcantal@hotmail.com] Fr N on coast rd AL5105, site on R 800m after Parador, opp 25km sp.Or exit A7 junc 520 sp Mojácar Parador. Foll Parador sps by-passing Mojácar, to site. Med, hdstg, pt shd; wc; chem disp; mv service pnt; shwrs inc; EHU (15A) €3; gas; lndry rm; shop 500m; shops adj; rest, snacks; bar adj; BBQ; sand beach adj; 5% statics; dogs; phone; bus; poss v cr; some rd noise; red long stay/LS; CKE/CCI. "Pitches quite lge, not mkd; lge o'fits rec use pitches at front of site; busy site; staff unhelpful, quite expensive; facs run down." ♦ € 30.00   2014*

⊞ **MOJACAR** *4G1* (9km S Rural) *37.06536, -1.86864* Camping Sopalmo, Sopalmo, 04638 Mojácar (Almería) [950-47 84 13; fax 950-47 30 02; info@campingsopalmoelcortijillo.com; www.campingsopalmoelcortijillo.com] Exit A7/E15 at junc 520 onto AL6111 sp Mojácar. Fr Mojácar turn S onto A1203/AL5105 dir Carboneras, site sp on W of rd about 1km S of El Agua del Medio. Sm, mkd pitch, hdstg, pt shd; wc; chem disp (wc); shwrs; EHU (15A) €3; gas; lndry; sm shop (high ssn); rest, snacks 6km; bar; shgl beach 1.7km; internet; 10% statics; dogs €1; Eng spkn; adv bkg; some rd noise; ccard not acc; red LS; CKE/CCI. "Clean, pleasant, popular site; remote & peaceful; friendly owner; gd walking in National Park; lovely san facs." ♦ € 29.00   2012*

⊞ **MOJACAR** *4G1* (4km SW Coastal) *37.08888, -1.85599* Camping Cueva Negra, Camino Lotaza, 2, 04638 Mojácar (Almería) [950-47 58 55; fax 950-47 57 11; info@camping cuevanegra.es; www.campingcuevanegra.es] Leave N340/E15 at junc 520 for AL151 twd Mojácar Playa. Turn R onto coastal rd. Site 500m fr Hotel Marina on R. App rd diff lge o'fits.m'vans due grounding. Take care dip at site ent. Med, hdg/mkd pitch, all hdstg, terr, unshd; wc; chem disp; mv service pnt; shwrs inc; EHU (22A) €3.30; gas; lndry; shop; rest, snacks; bar; covrd pool; jacuzzi; sand beach adj; entmnt; TV; 5% statics; dogs €1.90; poss cr; adv bkg; quiet; red 30+ days; CKE/CCI. "Well-kept, beautifully laid-out site; clean san facs but some basic; pleasant atmosphere; gd touring base; facs stretched when site full." ♦ € 28.60   2011*

⊞ **MOJACAR** *4G1* (5km W Rural) *37.16394, -1.89361* Canada Camping, 04639 Turre (Almería) [627-76 39 08 (mob); canadacampingmojacar@yahoo.co.uk] Exit A7/E15 at junc 525 & foll sp Los Gallardos on N340A. After approx 3km turn L at sp Turre & Garrucha onto A370. In 3.5km slow down at green sp 'Kapunda' & turn R in 300m at sp 'Casa Bruns'. Site in 100m - bumpy access. Sm, hdg/mkd pitch, hdstg, unshd; wc; chem disp; mv service pnt; shwrs inc; EHU (6A) €3.50; lndry rm; shop, rest, snacks, bar 4km; BBQ; dogs; adv bkg; quiet - some rd noise. "Gd, British-owned, adults-only site; friendly atmosphere; lge pitches; mountain views." € 10.00   2010*

⊞ **MOJACAR** *4G1* (500m W Rural) *37.14083, -1.85916* Camping El Quinto, Ctra Mojácar-Turre, 04638 Mojácar (Almería) [950-47 87 04; fax 950-47 21 48; campingel quinto@hotmail.com] Fr A7/E15 exit 520 sp Turre & Mojácar. Site on R in approx 13km at bottom of Mojácar vill. Sm, hdg/mkd pitch, hdstg, pt shd; wc; chem disp; mv service pnt; shwrs inc; EHU (6-10A) €3.21; gas; lndry; shop; rest 3km; snacks; bar; BBQ; playgrnd; pool; sand beach 3km; dogs €1; phone; poss cr; Eng spkn; adv bkg; quiet but some rd noise; red long stay; CKE/CCI. "Neat, tidy site; mkt Wed; close National Park; excel beaches; metered 6A elect for long winter stay; popular in winter, poss cr & facs stretched; security barrier; poss mosquitoes; drinking water ltd to 5L a time." ♦ € 20.50   2012*

⊞ **MONASTERIO DE RODILLA** *1B4* (800m NE Rural) *42.4604, -3.4581* Camping Picon del Conde, Ctra N1 Madrid-Irún, Km 263, 09292 Monasterio de Rodilla (Burgos) [tel/fax 947-59 43 55; info@picondelconde.com; www.picondelconde. com] Fr A1 join N1 at exit 2 or 3, site is on N1 at km marker 263 - behind motel. Easy to miss in heavy traff. Med, hdg/mkd pitch, shd; htd wc; chem disp; shwrs inc; EHU (5A) €3.60; gas; lndry rm; shop; rest, snacks; bar; playgrnd; pool; 75% statics; dogs; phone; rd noise; ccard acc; CKE/CCI. "Ltd facs LS; poss migrant workers; caution EHU; new grnd floor san facs 2009; site muddy in wet weather; friendly staff; 2 hrs drive fr Bilbao ferry; gd NH." ♦ € 14.60   2011*

⊞ **MONCOFA** *3D2* (2km E Coastal/Urban) *39.80861, -0.12805* Camping Mon Mar, Camino Serratelles s/n, 12593 Platja de Moncófa (Castellón) [950-47 58 85 92; campingmonmar@hotmail.com] Exit 49 fr A7 or N340, foll sp Moncófa Platja passing thro Moncófa & foll sp beach & tourist info thro 1-way system. Site sp, adj Aqua Park. Lge, hdg pitch, hdstg, pt shd; htd wc; chem disp; all serviced pitches; baby facs; shwrs inc; EHU (6A) inc; gas; lndry (inc dryer); shop & 1km; rest, snacks; bar; BBQ; playgrnd; pool; sand/shgl beach 200m; entmnt; internet; 80% statics; no dogs; phone; bus 300m; poss v cr; Eng spkn; adv bkg; quiet; ccard acc; red LS/ long stay; CKE/CCI. "Helpful owner & staff; rallies on site Dec-Apr; mini-bus to stn & excursions; sunshades over pitches poss diff high o'fits; excel clean, tidy site." ♦ € 27.00   2014*

⊞ **MONCOFA** *3D2* (2km S Coastal) *39.78138, -0.14888* Camping Los Naranjos, Camino Cabres, Km 950.8, 12593 Moncófa (Castellón) [964-58 03 37; fax 964-76 62 37; info@campinglosnaranjos.com] Fr N340 at km post 950.8 turn L at site sp, site 1km on R. Med, mkd pitch, hdstg, pt shd; wc; chem disp; mv service pnt; shwrs inc; EHU (10A) €5.35; gas; lndry; shop; rest, snacks; bar; playgrnd; pool; paddling pool; beach 300m; games area; 20% statics; phone; bus 1.5km; poss cr; adv bkg; quiet; red LS/long stay. "Gd." € 27.00   2010*

MONESTERIO *2F3* (3km S Rural) Camping Tentudia, CN 630 Km 727, 06260 Monesterio (Badajoz) [924-51 63 16; fax 924-51 63 52; ctentudia@turiex.com; www.camping-extremadura.com] On E803/A66 N Mérida-Sevilla take exit 722 and foll dir to Monesterio then Santa Olallio - don't take rd into Nature Park. Med, hdstg, mkd pitch, terr, shd; 30% serviced pitches; wc; shwrs; EHU (15A); rest, snacks; bar; shop; gas 5km; lndry; playgrnd; pool; bike hire; horseriding nr; quiet; adv bkg; 10% red 7+ days; Eng spkn; ccard acc; CKE/CCI. "Gd stopping place in quiet area; Sep '99 future of site uncertain, contact in advance; site a little run down; poss rd noise fr A66." ♦ Easter-15 Sep. € 20.00   2013*

⊞ **MONTBLANC** *3C2* (1.5km NE Rural) *41.37743, 1.18511* Camping Montblanc Park, Ctra Prenafeta, Km 1.8, 43400 Montblanc [977-86 25 44; fax 977-86 05 39; montblancpark@franceloc.fr; www.montblancpark.com] Exit AP2 junc 9 sp Montblanc; foll sp Montblanc/Prenafeta/ TV2421; site on L on TV2421. Med, hdg pitch, pt sl, terr, pt shd; htd wc; chem disp; mv service pnt; baby facs; shwrs inc; EHU (10A) inc; lndry; shop; rest, snacks; bar; BBQ; playgrnd; pool; paddling pool; wifi; entmnt; 50% statics; dogs €4.50; phone; Eng spkn; adv bkg; ccard acc; red long stay/snr citizens; CKE/CCI. "Excel site; excel facs; lovely area; many static pitches only suitable for o'fits up to 7m; Cistercian monestaries nrby; conv NH Andorra." ♦ ltd. € 39.50   2014*

You can now fill in site reports online

MONTERROSO *1B2* (1km S Rural) *42.78720, -7.84414* **Camp Municipal de Monterroso, A Peneda, 27560 Monterroso (Lugo) [982-37 75 01; fax 982-37 74 16; campingmonterroso@ aged-sl.com; www.campingmonterroso.com]** Fr N540 turn W onto N640 to Monterroso. Fr town cent turn S on LU212. In 100m turn sharp R then downhill for 1km; 2 sharp bends to site. Sm, hdg/mkd pitch, pt sl, pt shd; wc; chem disp; shwrs inc; EHU (10A) €3.50; shop; rest, snacks, bar 500m; pool adj; games area; internet; wifi; dogs; Eng spkn; quiet; CKE/CCI. "Helpful staff; v quiet & ltd facs LS; vg." ♦ 30 Marr-24 Sep. € 21.00   2015*

MONTROIG see Cambrils *3C2*

⊞ **MONZON** *3B2* (5.7km NE Rural) *41.93673, 0.24146* **Camping Almunia, Calle del Nao 10, 22420 Almunia de san Juan [696-77 18 51; camping-almunia@hotmail.com; www.camping-almunia.es]** Foll the A-22 to Monzón. Turn R onto the A-1237 to campsite. Sm, hdstg, terr, pt shd; wc; chem disp; mv service pnt; child/baby facs; fam bthrm; shwrs; EHU (6A) €4; lndry; BBQ; playgrnd; pool; wifi; twin axle acc; adv bkg acc; "Friendly German couple; Monzon splendid medieval castle to visit; conv NH." ♦ € 13.00   2013*

⊞ **MORATALLA** *4F1* (8km NW Rural) *38.21162, -1.94444* **Camping La Puerta, Ctra del Canal, Paraje de la Puerta, 30440 Moratalla (Murcia) [tel/fax 968-73 00 08; info@campinglapuerta.com; www.campinglapuerta.com]** Fr Murcia take C415 dir Mula & Caravaca. Foll sp Moratalla & site. Lge, mkd pitch, pt sl, terr, shd; htd wc; chem disp; shwrs inc; EHU (10A) €5.30; gas; lndry (inc dryer); shop; rest, snacks; bar; BBQ; playgrnd; pool; tennis; games area; internet; TV rm; statics; dogs €1.20; adv bkg; quiet; ccard acc. "Busy at w/ ends." ♦ € 19.00   2011*

⊞ **MORELLA** *3D2* (2km NE Rural) *40.62401, -0.09141* **Motor Caravan Parking, 12300 Morella (Castellón)** Exit N232 at sp (m'van emptying). Sm, hdstg, pt shd; chem disp; mv service pnt; water; quiet. "Free of charge; stay up to 72 hrs; clean; superb location; lge m'vans acc; excel Aire with fine views of hilltop town of Morella (floodlit at night), clean, well maintained."   2013*

⊞ **MOTILLA DEL PALANCAR** *4E1* (10km NW Rural) *39.61241, -2.10185* **Camping Pantapino, Paraje de Hontanar, s/n, 16115 Olmedilla de Alarcón (Cuenca) [969-33 92 33 or 676-47 86 11 (mob); fax 969-33 92 44; pantapina@hotmail. com]** Fr cent of Motilla foll NIII; turn NW onto rd CM2100 at sp for Valverde de Júcar; site on L just bef 12km marker. Med, mkd pitch, pt sl, pt shd; wc; chem disp; mv service pnt; serviced pitches; baby facs; shwrs inc; EHU (6A) €4; gas; lndry; shop; rest, bar high ssn; BBQ; playgrnd; pool; tennis; games area; horseriding; bike hire; 40% statics; dogs €1.50; adv bkg; quiet; ltd facs LS; ccard acc; 10% red CKE/CCI. "Clean, attractive site but tatty statics; poor facs; gd size pitches; resident owners hospitable; poss clsd in winter - phone ahead to check; vg; san facs old but clean; gd NH." ♦ € 18.00   2014*

⊞ **MOTRIL** *2H4* (12km SE Coastal) *36.70066, -3.44032* **Camping Don Cactus, N340, Km 343, 18730 Carchuna (Granada) [958-62 31 09; fax 958-62 42 94; camping@ doncactus.com; www.doncactus.com]** On N340 SE fr Motril 1km W of Calahonda. Foll site sp. Lge, hdg/mkd pitch, hdstg, shd; wc; chem disp; mv service pnt; shwrs; EHU (5A) €4.50; gas; lndry; supmkt; rest, snacks; bar; BBQ; playgrnd; pool; shgl beach adj; tennis; archery; golf 6km; wifi; entmnt; TV rm; 60% statics; dogs €2.50 (not acc Jul & Aug); poss cr; no adv bkg; quiet; ccard acc; red long stay/LS; CKE/CCI. "Many greenhouses around site (unobtrusive); some sm pitches not rec lge o'fits; clean san facs; gd pool & rest; helpful staff; popular winter long stay; gd NH." ♦ € 28.50   2010*

⊞ **MUNDAKA** *3A1* (1km S Coastal) *43.39915, -2.69620* **Camping Portuondo, Ctra Amorebieta-Bermeo, Km 43, 48360 Mundaka (Bilbao) [946-87 77 01; fax 946-87 78 28; recepcion@campingportuondo.com; www.camping portuondo.com]** Fr Bermeo pass Mundaka staying on main rd, do not enter Mundaka. Stay on BI-2235 sp Gernika. After approx 1km site on L down steep slip rd. Med, terr, pt shd; wc; shwrs inc; EHU (6A) €4.20; lndry; rest, snacks; bar; playgrnd; pool; paddling pool; beach 500m; 30% statics; site clsd end Jan-mid Feb; dogs; train 800m; poss v cr w/ends; adv bkg rec; ccard acc. "Excel clean, modern facs; pitches tight not suitable for lge o'fits; popular with surfers; conv Bilbao by train; site suitable sm m'vans only." ♦ € 35.00   2015*

MUROS *1B1* (3km SSW Coastal) *42.76072, -9.06222* **A'Vouga, Ctra Mouros-Finisterre, km 3 15291 Louro [tel/fax 34 98 18 26 115; avouga@hotmail.es]** On Coast rd fr Muros (3km) on L side. Med, mkd pitch, pt sl, unshd; htd wc; chem disp; mv service pnt; baby facs; shwrs inc; EHU (6A); lndry (inc dryer); shops 3km; rest; snacks; bar; BBQ; beach adj; games rm; entmnt; wifi; TV rm; 10% statics; dogs; phone; twin axles; poss cr; Eng spkn; adv bkg; quiet; ccard acc. "Excel site & rest; seaviews; friendly & helpful staff; rec; guided walking tours." 1 Mar-31 Oct. € 38.00   2014*

MUROS *1B1* (7km W Coastal) *42.76100, 9.11100* **Camping Ancoradoiro, Ctra Corcubión-Muros, Km.7.2, 15250 Louro (La Coruña) [981-87 88 97; fax 981-87 85 50; wolfgang@ mundo-r.com; www.rc-ancoradoiro.com/camping]** Foll AC550 W fr Muros. Site on L (S), well sp. Immed inside ent arch, to thro gate on L. Med, hdg/mkd pitch, terr, pt shd; wc; chem disp; shwrs inc; EHU (6-15A) €3.50; lndry; shop adj; rest; snacks, bar adj; playgrnd; sand beach 500m; watersports; entmnt; no dogs; bus 500m; phone; poss cr; adv bkg; quiet; CKE/CCI. "Excel, lovely, well-run, well-kept site; superb friendly site on headland bet 2 sandy beaches; welcoming owner; excel rest; excel san facs; poss diff for lge o'fits; beautiful beaches; scenic area." 15 Mar-15 Sep. € 22.00   2014*

MUROS *1B1* (500m W Coastal/Rural) *42.76176, -9.07365* **Camping San Francisco, Camino de Convento 21, 15291 Louro-Muros (La Coruña) [981-82 61 48; fax 981-57 19 16; campinglouro@yahoo.es; www.campinglouro.com]** Fr Muros cont on C550 coast rd for 3km to San Francisco vill. Site sp to R up narr rd. Med, mkd pitch, pt shd; htd wc; chem disp; mv service pnt; shwrs; EHU (5-8A) inc; gas; lndry; rest, snacks; bar; sand beach 200m; playgrnd; dogs; phone; bus 300m; Eng spkn; adv bkg; quiet; ccard acc; CKE/CCI. "Pleasant site in walled monastery garden; gd, clean facs; vg sm rest; sh walk to lovely beach; excel security; unspoilt area." ♦ 22 Jun-7 Sep. € 27.60   2009*

MUTRIKU see Deba *3A1*

⊞ **MUXIA** *1A1* (10km E Coastal) *43.1164, -9.1583* **Camping Playa Barreira Leis, Playa Berreira, Leis, 15124 Camariñas-Muxia (La Coruña) [tel/fax 981-73 03 04; playaleis@yahoo.es]** Fr Ponte do Porto turn L sp Muxia; foll camp sp. Site is 1st after Leis vill on R. Med, mkd pitch, terr, pt shd; wc; chem disp; shwrs inc; EHU €3.50; lndry; shop; rest; bar; BBQ; playgrnd; sand beach 100m; dogs €1; TV; quiet; ccard acc; CKE/CCI. "Beautiful situation on wooded hillside; dir acces to gd beach; ltd, poorly maintained facs LS; mkt in Muxia Thurs."
€ 16.00   2012*

NAJERA *3B1* (500m S Urban) *42.41183, -2.73168* **Camping El Ruedo, San Julián 24, 26300 Nájera (La Rioja) [941-36 01 02; www.campingslarioja.es]** Take Nájera town dirs off N120. In town turn L bef x-ing bdge. Site sp. Sm, pt shd; htd wc; chem disp; shwrs inc; EHU (10-16A) €3 (rev pol & poss no earth); gas; lndry; shop; rest, snacks; bar; playgrnd; pool 1km; entmnt; TV; phone; bus 200m; poss cr; adv bkg; quiet; ccard acc; CKE/CCI. "Pleasant site in quiet location, don't be put off by 1st impression of town; monastery worth visit, some pitches in former bullring." 1 Apr-10 Sep. € 21.00   2013*

⊞ **NAVAJAS** *3D2* (1km W Rural) *39.87489, -0.51034* **Camping Altomira, Carretera, CV-213 Navajas Km. 1, E-12470 Navajas (Castellón) [964-71 32 11; fax 964-71 35 12; reservas@campingaltomira.com; www.campingaltomira.com]** Exit A23/N234 at junc 33 to rndabt & take CV214 dir Navajas. In approx 2km turn L onto CV213, site on L just past R turn into vill, sp. Med, hdstg, terr, pt shd; htd wc; chem disp; serviced pitches; baby facs; shwrs; EHU (3-6A) €3.80; gas; lndry (inc dryer); shop; rest, snacks; bar; BBQ; playgrnd; pool; paddling pool; tennis; bike hire; wifi; TV; 70% statics; dogs; phone; bus 500m; adv bkg; poss noisy w/end & public hols; ccard acc; red LS/long stay/CKE/CCI. "Friendly welcome; panoramic views fr upper level (steep app) but not rec for lge o'fits due tight bends & ramped access/kerb to some pitches; gd birdwatching, walking, cycling; excel san facs; some sm pitches poss diff for lge o'fits without motor mover; poss clsd LS - phone ahead to check; useful NH & longer; excel." ♦
€ 25.50   2014*

NAVALAFUENTE see Cabrera, La *1D4*

NAVARREDONDA DE GREDOS see Hoyos del Espino *1D3*

NAVARRETE see Logroño *3B1*

⊞ **NEGRAS, LAS** *4G1* (1km N Coastal) *36.87243, -2.00674* **Camping Náutico La Caleta, Parque Natural Cabo de Gata, 04116 Las Negras (Almería) [tel/fax 950-52 52 37; campinglacaleta@gmail.com]** Exit N344 at km stone 487 twd Las Negras. Site sp at ent to vill on R. Med, hdg pitch, hdstg, shd; wc; chem disp; shwrs inc; EHU (10A) inc; gas; lndry; shop & 1km; rest, snacks; bar; playgrnd; pool (high ssn); sand/shgl beach adj; bike hire; dogs €3.20; phone; bus 300m; poss cr; quiet; red long stay/LS; CKE/CCI. "Lge o'fits need care on steep app rd; vans over 2.5m take care sun shades on pitches; gd walking area; lovely site in lovely area." ♦ € 31.00   2010*

⊞ **NERJA** *2H4* (4km E Rural) *36.76035, -3.83490* **Nerja Camping, Ctra Vieja Almeria, Km 296.5, Camp de Maro, 29787 Nerja (Málaga) [952-52 97 14; fax 952-52 96 96; nerjacamping5@hotmail.com]** On N340, cont past sp on L for 200m around RH corner, bef turning round over broken white line. Foll partly surfaced rd to site on hillside. Fr Almuñécar on N340, site on R approx 20km. Med, pt sl, terr, pt shd; wc; chem disp; shwrs inc; EHU (5A) €3.75 (check earth); gas; lndry rm; shops; rest, snacks; bar; playgrnd; sm pool; sand beach 2km; bike hire; site clsd Oct; Eng spkn; adv bkg rec; rd noise; red long stay/LS/CKE/CCI. "5 mins to Nerja caves; mkt Tue; annual carnival 15 May; diff access lge o'fits; gd horseriding; site rds steep but gd surface; gd views; friendly owners." ♦ ltd. € 24.00   2011*

⊞ **NIJAR** *4G1* (23km SE Coastal) *36.80298, -2.07768* **Camping Los Escullos San José, Paraje de los Escullos s/n, 04118 Los Escullos (Almería) [950-38 98 11; fax 950-38 98 10; info@losescullossanjose.com; www.losescullossanjose.com]** Fr E on E15/A7 exit 479 sp San Isidro; fr W exit junc 471 sp San José. Foll sp San José on AL3108 & after passing La Boca de los Frailes turn L onto AL4200 sp Los Escullos & site. After 3km turn R to site, ent on R in 1km - take care unmkd speed bumps. Lge, mkd pitch, hdstg, pt sl, shd; wc; chem disp; mv service pnt; baby facs; sauna; private san facs avail; shwrs inc; EHU (10A) €5.10; gas; lndry (inc dryer); shop; rest, snacks; bar; playgrnd; pool; beach 700m; watersports; diving; tennis; bike hire; fitness rm; wifi; entmnt; TV rm; 40% statics; dogs €2.60; Eng spkn; adv bkg; ccard acc; red long stay/CKE/CCI. "Well-run, rustic, attractive site in National Park; many secluded beaches & walks; excel for watersports; vg pool & rest; clean facs; helpful staff; pitches poss flood in heavy rain." ♦ € 30.00 (CChq acc)   2010*

⊞ **NOIA** *1B2* (5km SW Coastal) *42.77198, -8.93761* **Camping Punta Batuda, Playa Hornanda, 15970 Porto do Son (La Coruña) [981-76 65 42; camping@puntabatuda.com; www.puntabatuda.com]** Fr Santiago take C543 twd Noia, then AC550 5km SW to Porto do Son. Site on R approx 1km after Boa. Lge, mkd pitch, pt shd; wc; chem disp; shwrs inc; EHU (3A) €3.74 (poss rev pol); gas; lndry; shop; rest w/end only; snacks; bar; playgrnd; htd pool w/end only; sand beach adj; tennis; 50% statics; some Eng spkn; adv bkg; quiet; red long stay/LS; CKE/CCI. "Wonderful views; exposed to elements & poss windy; ltd facs LS; hot water to shwrs only; some pitches v steep &/or sm; gd facs; naturist beach 5km S." ♦ € 23.60   2012*

NOJA *1A4* (N Coastal) *43.48525, -3.53918* **Camping Los Molinos, Playa del Ris, 39180 Noja (Cantabria) [942-63 04 26; fax 942-63 07 25; campinglosmolinos@ campinglosmolinos.com; www.campinglosmolinos.com]** Exit A8 at km 185. Go N & foll sp to Noja, then L at Playa del Ris. Site sp. V lge, hdg pitch, pt shd; wc; chem disp; mv service pnt; shwrs; baby facs; EHU (3A) €3.60; gas; lndry; shop; rest, snacks; bar; BBQ; playgrnd; pool; paddling pool; sand beach 500m; tennis; car wash; entmnt; 75% statics; dogs; poss cr; Eng spkn; adv bkg; ccard not acc; CKE/CCI. "Gd site; lovely beach; some noise fr karting circuit until late evening but noise levels strictly curtailed at midnight." ♦ 1 Jun-30 Sep. € 30.00   2010*

NOJA *1A4* (1km NW Coastal) *43.49011, -3.53636* **Camping Playa Joyel, Playa del Ris, 39180 Noja (Cantabria) [942-63 00 81; fax 942-63 12 94; info@playayoyel.com; www.playajoyel.com]** Fr Santander or Bilbao foll sp A8/E70 (toll-free). Approx 15km E of Solares exit m'way junc 185 at Beranga onto CA147 N twd Noja & coast. On o'skirts of Noja turn L sp Playa del Ris, (sm brown sp) foll rd approx 1.5km to rndabt, site sp to L, 500m fr rndabt. Fr Santander take S10 for approx 8km, then join A8/E70. V lge, mkd pitch, pt sl, pt shd; wc; chem disp; mv service pnt; baby facs; shwrs inc; EHU (6A) inc; gas; lndry (inc dryer); supmkt; rest, snacks; bar; BBQ; playgrnd; pool; paddling pool; jacuzzi; direct access to sand beach adj; windsurfing; sailing; tennis; hairdresser; car wash; cash dispenser; wifi; entmnt; games/TV rm; 40% statics; no dogs; no o'fits over 8m high ssn; phone; recep 0800-2200; poss v cr w/end & high ssn; Eng spkn; adv bkg; ccard acc; quiet at night; red LS/snr citizens; CKE/CCI. "Well-organised site on sheltered bay; v busy high ssn; pleasant staff; gd, clean facs; superb pool & beach; some narr site rds with kerbs; midnight silence enforced; highly rec." ♦ 27 Mar-26 Sep. € 49.00 SBS - E05   2015*

⊞ **NOJA** *1A4* (1.9km NW Coastal) *43.49294, -3.5248* **Camping Playa de Ris, Paseo Maritimo 2, Avda de Ris, 39180 Noja [942-63 04 15]** Fr A8 take exit 185, at rdbt 3rd exit onto N634, at next rdbt take exit CA147, turn R CA452, turn R onto Barrio de Castillo San Pedro CA147, turn L onto Av de los Ris/CA451 turn R onto Paseo de Maritimo. Sm, pt shd; wc; chem disp (wc); shwr inc; lndry rm; shop 500m; snacks; bar; pool adj; sandy beach 200m; 50% statics; no dogs; poss cr; no twin-axles; CKE/CCI. "Conv for Santander ferry; poss tight for lge o'fits." € 24.00   2011*

NUEVALOS *3C1* (300m N Rural) *41.21846, -1.79211* **Camping Lago Park, Ctra De Alhama de Aragón a Cillas, Km 39, 50210 Nuévalos (Zaragoza) [tel/fax 976-84 90 38; info@campinglagopark.com; www.campinglagopark.com]** Fr E on A2/E90 exit junc 231 to Nuévalos, turn R sp Madrid. Site 1.5km on L when ent Nuévalos. Fr W exit junc 204, site well sp. Steep ent fr rd. V lge, hdg/mkd pitch, terr, pt shd; wc; chem disp; child/baby facs; shwrs inc; EHU (10A) €5.40; gas; lndry; shop 500m; rest, snacks high ssn; bar 500m; BBQ; playgrnd; pool; lake nrby; fishing; boating; games area; some statics; dogs free; bus 500m; poss cr; adv bkg; quiet but noisy w/end high ssn; red long stay; CKE/CCI. "Nr Monasterio de Piedra & Tranquera Lake; excel facs on top terr, but stretched high ssn & poss long, steepish walk; ltd facs LS; gd birdwatching; only site in area; gd; v friendly owner." 1 Apr-30 Oct. € 25.00 (CChq acc)   2015*

⊞ **O GROVE** *1B2* (2km SW Coastal) *42.48305, -8.89083* **Camping Moreiras, Reboredo 26, 36989 O Grove (Pontevedra) [986-73 16 91; campingmoreiras@campingmoreiras.com; www.campingmoreiras.com]** Exit AP9 junc 119 W onto AG41 dir Sangenjo to Pedriñán; then foll sp N to O Grove, site sp, adj aquarium. Med, hdg/mkd pitch, shd; htd wc; chem disp; mv service pnt; baby facs; shwrs; EHU €4.50; lndry (inc dryer); shop; rest, snacks; bar; BBQ; playgrnd; sand beach adj; watersports; bike hire; games area; golf 3km; wifi; some statics; no dogs; adv bkg; quiet. € 23.00   2010*

OCHAGAVIA *3A1* (7km S Rural) *42.85486, -1.09766* **Camping Murkuzuria, 31453 Esparza de Salazar [948-89 01 90 or 661-08 87 35; campingesparza@gmail.com; www.campingmurkuzuria.com]** Fr N or S on Pic d'Orhy rte thro Pyrenees, NA178(Spain)/D26(France). Situated in vill. Pamplona approx 80km. Med, mkd pitch, pt shd; wc; chem disp; shwrs; EHU; lndry; shop; rest; bar; BBQ; playgrnd; pool; TV; phone; bus adj; twin axles; Eng spkn; adv bkg; quiet. "Discounted forest passes avail for Foret d'Iraty; excel." 15 May-30 Oct. € 19.00   2015*

⊞ **OCHAGAVIA** *3A1* (500m S Rural) *42.90777, -1.08750* **Camping Osate, Ctra Salazar s/n, 31680 Ochagavia (Navarra) [tel/fax 948-89 01 84; info@campingosate.net; www.campingosate.net]** On N135 SE fr Auritz, turn L onto NA140 & cont for 24km bef turning L twd Ochagavia on NA140. Site sp in 2km on R, 500m bef vill. Med, mkd pitch, pt shd; wc; chem disp; some serviced pitches; shwrs inc; EHU (4A) €5.50; gas; lndry; shop; rest high ssn; snacks; bar; BBQ; Eng spkn; 50% statics; dogs €2; quiet but poss noise fr bar (open to public). "Attractive, remote vill; gd, well-maintained site; touring pitches under trees, sep fr statics; facs ltd & poss stretched high ssn; site clsd 3 Nov-15 Dec & rec phone ahead LS." € 22.50   2014*

⊞ **OLITE** *3B1* (2km S Rural) *42.48083, -1.67756* **Camping Ciudad de Olite, Ctra N115, Tafalla-Peralta, Km 2.3, 31390 Olite [948-74 10 14; fax 948-74 06 04; info@campingde olite.com; www.campingdeolite.com]** Fr Pamplona S on AP15 exit 50 twd Olite. At rndabt turn L, then in 300m turn R onto NA115, site sp on L past Netto in 2km. Lge, mkd pitch, pt shd; wc; chem disp; mv service pnt; serviced pitches; baby facs; shwrs inc; EHU (5A) inc; lndry; shop 2km; rest; bar; playgrnd; htd pool (caps ess); tennis; entmnt; games area; 95% statics; dogs €1; poss cr; Eng spkn; phone; poss noisy at w/ends; ccard acc; CKE/CCI. "Close to m'way; ltd space & facs for tourers; site mostly used by Spanish for w/ends; site bleak in winter; narr site rds; Olite historic vill with fairytale castle; neglected facs (2009); ltd EHU; NH only, 35 min walk thro fields to Olite, friendly owners." ♦ ltd. € 21.50   2011*

⊞ **OLIVA** *4E2* (2km E Coastal) *38.93278, -0.09778* **Camping Kiko Park, Calle Assagador de Carro 2, 46780 Playa de Oliva (València) [962-85 09 05; fax 962-85 43 20; kikopark@kikopark.com; www.kikopark.com]** Exit AP7/E15 junc 61; fr toll turn R at T-junc onto N332. At rndabt turn L foll sp Platjas; next rdbt take 1st exit sp Platja; next rndabt foll sp Kiko Park. Do not drive thro Oliva. Access poss diff on app rds due humps. Lge, hdg/mkd pitch, hdstg, shd; htd wc; chem disp; mv service pnt; some serviced pitches; baby facs; fam bthrm; shwrs inc; EHU (16A) inc; gas; lndry (inc dryer); supmkt; rest, snacks; bar; BBQ; playgrnd; 2 pools (1 covrd); paddling pool; whirlpool; spa; direct access to sand beach adj; watersports; windsurfing school; fishing; golf & horseriding nrby; tennis; games area; bike hire; games rm; beauty cent; cash machine; wifi; entmnt; dogs €3.10; phone; pitch price variable (lge pitches avail); Eng spkn; adv bkg; quiet; ccard acc; red snr cititzens/long stay/LS; red CKE/ CCI. "Gd, family-run site; v helpful staff; vg, clean san facs; excel rest in Michelin Guide; access tight to some pitches." ♦ € 66.00 SBS - E20   2014*

See advertisement on next page

⊞ **OLIVA** *4E2* (4km E Coastal) *38.90759, -0.06722* **Camping Azul**, 46780 Playa de Oliva (València) [962-85 41 06; fax 962-85 40 96; campingazul@ctv.es; www.campingazul.com] Exit A7/E15 junc 61; fr toll turn R at T-junc onto N332. Drive S thro Oliva, site sp, turn twds sea at km 209.8. Narr access rd. Med, mkd pitch, pt shd; wc; mv service pnt; shwrs inc; EHU (10A) €3.20; gas; lndry; shop; rest; bar; playgrnd; bike hire; games area; golf 1km; wifi; entmnt; 20% statics; dogs free; no adv bkg; ccard acc; red long stay/LS. "Gd site but constant barking dogs fr adj houses; san facs tired." ♦ 1 Mar-1 Nov. € 25.60   2010*

"I need an on-site restaurant"

We do our best to make sure site information is correct, but it is always best to check any must-have facilities are still available or will be open during your visit.

⊞ **OLIVA** *4E2* (3km SE Coastal) *38.90555, -0.06666* **Eurocamping**, Ctra València-Oliva, Partida Rabdells s/n, 46780 Playa de Oliva (València) [962-85 40 98; fax 962-85 17 53; info@eurocamping-es.com; www.eurocamping-es.com] Fr N exit AP7/E15 junc 61 onto N332 dir Alicante. Drive S thro Oliva & exit N332 km 209.9 sp 'urbanización'. At v lge hotel Oliva Nova Golf take 3rd exit at rndabt sp Oliva & foll camping sp to site. Fr S exit AP7 junc 62 onto N332 dir València, exit at km 209 sp 'urbanización', then as above. Lge, hdg/mkd pitch, hdstg, pt shd; htd wc; chem disp; mv service pnt; baby facs; shwrs inc; EHU (6-10A) €4.64-6.70; gas; lndry (inc dryer); shop; rest, snacks; bar; BBQ; playgrnd; sand beach adj; bike hire; wifi; entmnt; TV; dogs €2.16; phone; poss cr; quiet but some noise fr adj bar; ccard acc; red long stay/ LS/CKE/CCI. "Gd facs; busy, well-maintained, clean site adj housing development; helpful British owners; beautiful clean beach; gd rest; gd beach walks; cycle rte thro orange groves to town; pitch far fr recep if poss; night noise fr generators 1700-2400; recep clsd 1400-1600; highly rec; rest stretched; busy site." ♦ € 44.40 (CChq acc)   2012*

⊞ **OLIVA** *4E2* (3km S Coastal) *38.89444, -0.05361* **Camping Olé**, Partida Aigua Morta s/n, 46780 Playa de Oliva (València) [962-85 75 17; fax 962-85 75 16; campingole@ hotmail.com; www.camping-ole.com] Exit AP7/E15 junc 61 onto N332 dir Valencia/Oliva. At km 209 (bef bdge) turn R sp 'Urbanización'. At 1st rndabt, take 2nd exit past golf club ent, then 1st exit at next rndabt, turn L sp ' Camping Olé' & others. Site down narr rd on L. Lge, hdg/mkd pitch, hdstg, pt shd; htd wc; chem disp; baby facs; shwrs inc; EHU (6-10A) €5.74; gas; lndry (inc dryer); supmkt; rest, snacks; bar; BBQ; playgrnd; pool; sand beach adj; fishing; tennis 600m; bike hire; games rm; horseriding 2km; golf adj; wifi; entmnt; 15% statics; dogs €3.15; phone; Eng spkn; adv bkg; quiet; ccard acc; red long stay/LS; CKE/CCI. "Many sports & activities; direct access to beach; excel site; rest across rd v nice; gd value; pool only opens 1st July." ♦ € 50.00   2014*

⊞ **OLOT** *3B3* (3km SE Rural) *42.15722, 2.51694* **Camping Fageda**, Batet de la Serra, Ctra Olot-Santa Pau, Km 3.8, 17800 Olot (Gerona) [tel/fax 972-27 12 39; info@campinglafageda.com; www.campinglafageda.com] Fr Figueras exit A26 sp Olot E twd town cent. Pick up & foll sp Santa Pau on rd GI524. Site in 3.8km. Med, mkd pitch, pt sl, terr, pt shd; htd wc; chem disp; shwrs inc; EHU (10A) €3.50 (poss rev pol); gas; lndry; shop; snacks; rest & bar high ssn; playgrnd; htd pool high ssn; wifi; 90% statics (sep area); dogs; phone; Eng spkn; adv bkg; quiet; ccard acc; CKE/CCI. "In beautiful area with extinct volcanoes & forests; isolated, pretty site; few visitors LS; friendly, helpful staff; diff access to water pnts for m'vans." ♦ € 21.00   2011*

⊞ **OLVERA** *2H3* (4.2km E Rural) *36.93905, -5.21719* **Camping Pueblo Blanco**, Ctra N384, Km 69, 11690 Olvera (Cadiz) [619 45 35 34; fax 952 83 43 73; info@camping puebloblanco.com; www.campingpuebloblanco.com] Bet Antequera and Jerez de la Frontera, on the A384, at 69km marker. About 3km bef Olvera on the R. Wide driveway 600m to the top. Lge, terr, pt sl, unshd; wc; chem disp; mv service pnt; child/baby facs; shwrs, EHU (16A) €4; shop; rest, bar; BBQ; playgrnd; poolgames area; games rm; entmnt high ssn; wifi; TV rm; 12 bungalows; dog €1.50; Eng spkn; adv bkg acc; red long stay. "Site has 360 degree mountain views; ideal for walking; bird watching and Pueblo Blanco; vg site, but not quite finished." ♦ € 27.50 (CChq acc)   2013*

⊞ **ORGIVA** *2G4* (2km S Rural) *36.88852, -3.41837* **Camping Órgiva, Ctra A348, Km 18.9, 18400 Órgiva (Granada) [tel/fax 958-78 43 07; campingorgiva@descubrelaalpujarra. com; www.descubrelaalpujarra.com]** Fr N or S on Granada-Motril rd suggest avoid A348 via Lanjarón (narr & congested). Fr N323/A44 turn E nr km 179, 1km S of lge dam sp Vélez de Benaudalla, over multi-arch bdge, turn L sp Órgiva. Foll rd (easy climb) turn L after sh tunnel over rv bdge; site 2nd building on R. Sm, pt sl, pt shd; wc; chem disp; serviced pitches; baby facs; shwrs inc; EHU (10A) €3.82 (rev pol); gas; lndry; supmkt 2km; rest, snacks; bar; playgrnd; pool; shgl beach 30km; bus 2km; adv bkg; ccard acc; some Eng spkn; red LS/long stay; ccard acc; red long stay/CKE/CCI. "Immac san facs; excel, friendly site; some sm pitches; vg value rest open all yr; magnificent scenery; gd base for mountains & coast; Thurs mkt in town; fiesta 27 Sep-1 Oct; pleasant walk thro orange & almond groves to vill; loyalty discounts & gd red for longer stays." ♦ € 19.00 *2011**

⊞ **ORGIVA** *2G4* (2km NW Rural) *36.90420, -3.43880* **Camping Puerta de la Alpujarra, Ctra Lanjarón-Órgiva (Las Barreras), 18418 Órgiva (Granada) [tel/fax 958-78 44 50; puertalpujarra@ yahoo.es; www.campingpuertadelaalpujarra.com]** Fr Órgiva take A348 to Lanjarón. Site on L in 2km. Lanjarón poss diff for long o'fits. Med, mkd pitch, hdstg, terr, pt shd; wc; chem disp; mv service pnt; shwrs inc; EHU (16A) €3.50; gas 2km; lndry; shop; rest; bar; playgrnd; pool, paddling pool high ssn; entmnt; few statics; dogs free; phone; bus adj; poss cr; Eng spkn; adv bkg; quiet; ccard acc; 10% red 7+ days. "Scenic area with gd views fr site; steepish access to pitches; excel walking; ltd facs & staff LS." ♦ € 30.00 *2010**

ORIHUELA DEL TREMEDAL *3D1* (1km S Rural) *40.54784, -1.65095* **Camping Caimodorro, Camino Fuente de los Colladillos s/n, 44366 Orihuela del Tremedal (Teruel) [978-71 43 55 or 686-92 21 53 (mob); campingcaimodorro@ gmail.com; www.campingcaimodorro.com]** Fr Albarracin on A1512 head twd Orihuela. Turn R twd vill & R after petrol stn, sp. Sm, unshd; wc; shwrs; EHU €3.30; lndry (inc dryer); shop; snacks; bar; pool; paddling pool; wifi; dogs; some statics; phone; bus 600m; Eng spkn; ccard acc. "Elevated, breezy situation o'looking mountain vill; lovely scenery; gd touring base; friendly owner; v quiet LS." 1 Apr-31 Oct. € 13.40 *2009**

ORINON *1A4* (6km NE Coastal) *43.40361, -3.31027* **Camping Playa Arenillas, Ctra Santander-Bilbao, Km 64, 39798 Islares (Cantabria) [tel/fax 942-86 31 52 or 609-44-21-67 (mob); cueva@mundivia.es; www.campingplayaarenillas.com]** Exit A8 at km 156 Islares. Turn W on N634. Site on R at W end of Islares. Steep ent & sharp turn into site, exit less steep. Lge, mkd pitch, pt shd; wc; chem disp; mv service pnt; baby facs; shwrs inc; EHU (5A) €4.63 (poss no earth); gas; lndry; shop; rest adj; snacks; bar; BBQ; playgrnd; sand beach 100m; horseriding; bike hire; games area; TV; 40% statics; no dogs; phone; bus 500m; poss cr; adv bkg rec Jul/Aug; some rd noise; ccard acc; CKE/CCI. "Facs ltd LS & stretched in ssn; facs constantly cleaned; hot water to shwrs and washing up; rec arr early for choice of own pitch, and avoid Sat & Sun due to parked traffic; conv Guggenheim Museum; excel NH for Bilbao ferry; beautiful setting." 1 Apr-29 Sep. € 30.60 *2015**

ORINON *1A4* (500m NW Rural/Coastal) *43.39944, -3.32805* **Camping Oriñón, 39797 Oriñón (Cantabria) [tel/fax 942-87 86 30; info@campingorinon.com; www.campingorinon.com]** Exit A8/E70 at km 160 to Oriñón. Adj holiday vill. Med, mkd pitch, pt sl, unshd; wc; chem disp; mv service pnt; shwrs inc; EHU (4A) €4; gas; lndry (inc dryer); shop; rest, snacks; bar; playgrnd; sand beach adj; internet; TV; 90% statics; dogs; phone; bus 1km; Eng spkn; quiet; red long stay. "Excel surfing beach adj; clean site; no hot water to wash basins; helpful staff; conv Bilbao ferry." ♦ ltd. Holy Week & 1 Jun-30 Sep. € 20.00 *2009**

ORIO see Zarautz *3A1*

⊞ **OROPESA** *3D2* (4.2km N Coastal) *40.12125, 0.15848* **Camping Didota, Avenida de la Didota s/n, 12594 Oropesa del Mar (Castellón) [964 31 95 51; fax 964 31 98 47; info@campingdidota.es; www.campingdidota.es]** N on rd E-15 fr València to Barcelona, bear L at exit 45 sp Oropesa del Mar. Turn L onto N-340. Turn R at next exit, then cont strt at rndabt onto on Avenida La Ratlla. Foll camping signs. Med, pt shd; wc; shwrs inc; chem disp; EHU (6-10A) €4.30; child/baby facs; lndry; shop; rest, snacks; meals; gas; pool; sand beach; playgrnd; dogs; some statics; poss cr; ccard acc; adv bkg; "Gd site, helpful friendly staff; excel pool." ♦ € 33.70 *2014**

See advertisement

⊞ **OROPESA** *3D2* (3km NE Coastal) *40.12786, 0.16088*
Camping Torre La Sal 1, Camí L'Atall s/n, 12595 Ribera de Cabanes (Castellón) [964-31 95 96; fax 964-31 96 29; info@campingtorrelasal.com; www.campingtorrelasal.com] Leave AP7 at exit 44 or 45 & take N340 twd Tarragona. Foll camp sp fr km 1000.1 stone. Do not confuse with Torre La Sal 2 or Torre Maria. Lge, hdg/mkd pitch, hdstg, pt shd; htd wc; chem disp; mv service pnt; baby facs; shwrs inc; EHU (10A) €4.20; gas; lndry; shop adj; rest, snacks, bar; BBQ; playgrnd; htd, covrd pool; paddling pool; sand/shgl beach adj; tennis; games area; wifi; TV rm; 10% statics; dogs (except Jul/Aug); phone adj; bus 200m; poss cr; Eng spkn; adv bkg; quiet; ccard acc; red long stay/snr citizens; CKE/CCI. "Clean, well-maintained, peaceful site; elec metered for long stays; night security guard." ♦ ltd. € 24.00   2010*

⊞ **OROPESA** *3D2* (3.5km NE Coastal) *40.1275, 0.15972*
Camping Torre La Sal 2, Cami L'Atall s/n, 12595 Ribera de Cabanes (Castellón) [964-31 95 67; fax 964-31 97 44; camping@torrelasal2.com; www.torrelasal2.com] Leave AP7 at exit 45 & take N340 twd Tarragona. Foll camp sp fr km 1000 stone. Site adj Torre La Sal 1. Lge, hdg/mkd pitch, hdstg, pt shd; htd wc; chem disp; sauna; serviced pitch; shwrs inc; EHU (10A) inc; gas; lndry; shop; supmkt adj & 1km; rest, snacks; bar; playgrnd; shgl beach adj; 4 pools (2 htd & covrd); tennis; games area; wifi; entmnt; library; wifi; TV rm; some statics; dogs free; Eng spkn; adv bkg; quiet; red long stay/LS/snr citizens; CKE/CCI. "Vg, clean, peaceful, well-run site; lger pitches nr pool; more mature c'vanners v welcome; many dogs; poss diff for lge o'fits & m'vans; excel rest; excel beach with dunes; excel site, spotless facs, highly rec." ♦ € 51.00   2013*

⊞ **OSSA DE MONTIEL** *4E1* (10km SW Rural) *38.93717, -2.84744* **Camping Los Batanes, Ctra Lagunas de Ruidera, Km 8, 02611 Ossa de Montiel (Albacete)** [926-69 90 76; fax 926-69 91 71; camping@losbatanes.com; www.los batanes.com] Fr Munera twd Ossa de Montiel on N430. In Ossa foll sp in vill to site in 10km. Fr Manzanares on N430 app to Ruidera, cross bdge; turn immed R alongside lagoon, camp at 12km. Lge, pt shd; htd wc; chem disp; mv service pnt; shwrs; EHU (5A) €3.10; lndry; shops 10km; rest 200m; snacks; bar; playgrnd; pool, paddling pool high ssn; lake sw adj; bike hire; TV; 10% statics; dogs €2; phone; site clsd 28 Dec-2 Jan; Eng spkn; adv bkg; noisy at w/end; ccard acc; red CKE/CCI. "Lovely area of natural lakes; excel birdwatching & walking; friendly owners; LS phone to check open." ♦ € 24.00   2011*

OTURA see Granada *2G4*

PALAFRUGELL *3B3* (5km E Coastal) *41.9005, 3.1893* **Kim's Camping, Calle Font d'en Xeco s/n, 17211 Llafranc (Gerona)** [972-30 11 56; fax 972-61 08 94; info@campingkims.com; www.campingkims.com] Exit AP7 at junc 6 Gerona Nord if coming fr France, or junc 9 fr S dir Palamós. Foll sp for Palafrugell, Playa Llafranc. Site is 500m N of Llafranc. Lge, hdg/mkd pitch, hdstg, pl sl, terr, shd; wc; chem disp; baby facs; shwrs inc; EHU (6A) inc; gas; lndry; shop; rest, snacks; bar; BBQ (gas only); playgrnd; 2 pools; sand beach 500m; watersports; tennis 500m; games rm; games area; bike hire 500m; golf 10km; wifi; entmnt; excursions; TV; 10% statics; dogs; phone; guarded; poss cr; Eng spkn; adv bkg; quiet; ccard acc; red LS/long stay; red CKE/CCI. "Excel, well-organised, friendly site; steep site rds, new 2nd ent fr dual c'way fr Palafrugell to llafranc for lge o'fits & steps to rd to beach; discount in high ssn for stays over 1 wk; excel, modern san facs." ♦ 30 Mar-30 Sep. € 51.00   2013*

PALAFRUGELL *3B3* (5km SE Rural) *41.89694, 3.18250* **Camping La Siesta, Chopitea 110, 17210 Calella de Palafrugell (Gerona)** [972-61 51 16; fax 972-61 44 16; info@campinglasiesta.com; www.campingzodiac.com] Fr C66/C31 main rd Gerona-Palamós turn E at rndabt onto GI6546 & foll sp Calella - Avda del Mar. Site on R just bef Calella dir Llafranc. V lge, mkd pitch, pt sl, pt shd; wc; chem disp; shwrs inc; EHU (6A) inc; gas; lndry (inc dryer); shops; rest, snacks; 2 bars; no BBQ; playgrnd; 2 lge pools; waterslide; beach 1.3km; tennis; horseriding; wifi; entmnt; 80% statics; no dogs; bus; site open w/ends Nov-March & clsd Xmas to 8 Jan; Eng spkn; adv bkg; noisy at w/end; red LS. "Excel beaches at Llafranc & Calella de Palafrugell; mkt at Palafrugell; many beaches & coves adj; narr, winding paths thro pines to pitches; most vans have to be manhandled onto pitches." ♦ Easter-31 Oct. € 52.70   2011*

PALAFRUGELL *3B3* (5km S Coastal) *41.88831, 3.18013* **Camping Moby Dick, Carrer de la Costa Verda 16-28, 17210 Calella de Palafrugell (Gerona)** [972-61 43 07; fax 972-61 49 40; info@campingmobydick.com; www.campingmobydick.com] Fr Palafrugell foll sps to Calella. At rndabt just bef Calella turn R, then 4th L, site clearly sp on R. Med, hdstg, sl, terr, pt shd; wc; chem disp; mv service pnts; baby facs; shwrs inc; EHU (6-10A); €4.05; lndry; shop; supmkt 100m; rest 100m; snacks; bar; playgrnd; shgl beach 100m; TV; 15% statics; dogs €3.30; phone; bus 100m; poss cr; Eng spkn; adv bkg; quiet; ccard acc; CKE/CCI. ♦ 1 Apr-30 Sep. € 23.40   2009*

PALAMOS *3B3* (1km N Coastal) *41.85695, 3.13801* **Camping Internacional Palamós, Camí Cap de Planes s/n, 17230 Palamós (Gerona)** [972-31 47 36; fax 972-31 76 26; info@ internacionalpalamos.com; www.internacionalpalamos. com] Fr N leave AP7 at junc 6 to Palamós on C66. Fr Palafrugell turn L 16m after overhead sp to Sant Feliu-Palamós at sm sp La Fosca & camp sites. Winding app thro La Fosca. Fr S, take exit 9 dir Sant Feliu & Lloret, then C65/C31 to Santa Christina-Palamós, then La Fosca. Lge, pt shd; wc (mainly cont); chem disp; mv service pnt; baby facs; serviced pitches; private bthrms avail; shwrs inc; EHU; (5A) inc; lndry; shop; rest, snacks; bar; playgrnd; pool; paddling pool; sand beach 300m; solarium; windsurfing, sailing & diving 1km; bike hire; golf 15km; wifi; TV rm; car wash; 20% statics; phone; bus 600m; quiet. "Attractive site; superb san facs; some sm pitches on steep access rds - check bef pitching; highly rec; lovely area." ♦ 16 Apr-30 Nov. € 42.50 (CChq acc)   2011*

PALAMOS *3B3* (1km N Coastal) *41.85044, 3.13873* **Camping Palamós, Ctra La Fosca 12, 17230 Palamós (Gerona)** [972-31 42 96; fax 972-60 11 00; campingpal@grn.es; www.campingpalamos.com] App Palamós on C66/C31 fr Gerona & Palafrugell turn L 16m after overhead sp Sant Feliu-Palamós at sm sp La Fosca & campsites. Lge, pt sl, terr, pt shd; wc; shwrs; baby facs; EHU (4A) €2.70; gas; lndry; shop; rest 400m; playgrnd; 2 htd pools; shgl/rocky beach adj; tennis; golf; internet; 30% statics; dogs €2; phone; ccard acc. ♦ 27 Mar-30 Sep. € 40.00   2013*

PALAMOS *3B3* (2km N Coastal) *41.87277, 3.15055* **Camping Benelux, Paratge Torre Mirona s/n, 17230 Palamós (Gerona) [972-31 55 75; fax 972-60 19 01; cbenelux@ cbenelux.com; www.cbenelux.com]** Turn E off Palamós-La Bisbal rd (C66/C31) at junc 328. Site in 800m on minor metalled rd, twd sea at Playa del Castell. Lge, hdstg, pt sl, pt shd; wc; chem disp; mv service pnt; shwrs inc; EHU (6A) €4.30; gas; lndry; shop; supmkt; rest (w/end only LS); snacks; bar; playgrnd; pool; sand beach 1km; safe dep; car wash; currency exchange; TV; 50% statics; dogs; poss cr; Eng spkn; adv bkg; noisy at w/end; red LS/long stay; ccard acc; CKE/CCI. "In pine woods; many long stay British/Dutch; friendly owner; clean facs poss ltd LS; poss flooding in heavy rain; rough grnd." ♦ ltd. Easter-30 Sep. € 43.00   2012*

PALAMOS *3B3* (2km N Coastal) *41.86263, 3.14315* **Camping Caravanning Kings, Ctra de la Fosca, s/n 17230 Palamós (Gerona) [972-31 75 11; fax 972-31 77 42; info@campingkings.com; www.campingkings.com]** App Palamós on C66/C31 fr Gerona & Palafrugell, turn L immed after o'head sp Sant Felui-Palamós at sm sp La Fosca & campsites. Lge, pt sl, pt shd; wc; shwrs; EHU (6A) inc; lndry; supmkt; rest; bar; playgrnd; pool; spa; beach 200m; bike hire; games rm; wifi; entmnt; dogs €2.70; adv bkg; quiet; ccard acc; red LS. "Upmkt recep building; helpful staff; clean modern san facs; super pool; gd walking & cycling; thoroughly rec." 2 Apr-18 Sep. € 48.40   2010*

PALAMOS *3B3* (3km SW Coastal) *41.84598, 3.09460* **Camping Costa Brava, Avda Unió s/n, 17252 Sant Antoni de Calonge (Gerona) [tel/fax 972-65 02 22; campingcostabrava@ campingcostabrava.net; www.campingcostabrava.net]** Foll sp St Antoni de Calonge fr C31, site sp. Lge, mkd pitch, shd; wc; chem disp; baby facs; shwrs inc; EHU (4A) €3.80; lndry; shop adj; rest, snacks; bar; BBQ; playgrnd; pool & child pool; sand beach 300m; watersports; games rm; entmnt; car wash; dogs; phone; bus; poss cr; adv bkg; quiet; ccard acc. "Well-managed, family-run site; sm pitches; clean san facs; rec arr early high ssn to secure pitch; pleasant, helpful owners." ♦ 1 Jun-15 Sep. € 22.70   2011*

PALAMOS *3B3* (2.5km W Rural) *41.88194, 3.14083* **Camping Castell Park, Ctra C31 Palamós-Palafrugell, Km 328, 17253 Vall-Llobrega (Gerona) [tel/fax 972-31 52 63; info@ campingcastellpark.com; www.campingcastellpark.com]** Exit m'way at junc 6 & take C66/C31 to Palamós. Site on R sp after 40km marker. Lge, mkd pitch, terr, shd; wc (some cont); chem disp; baby facs; shwrs inc; EHU (3A) inc; gas; lndry; supmkt; rest, snacks; bar; BBQ; playgrnd; pool; paddling pool; sand beach 2.5km; bike hire; golf 11km; games rm; internet; entmnt; TV rm; some statics; dogs; bus 700m; Eng spkn; adv bkg; quiet; red long stay/LS/snr citizens; CKE/CCI. "Pleasant, quiet family site with friendly atmosphere & gd welcome; rallies & single c'vanners welcome; c'van storage avail." ♦ 27 Mar-12 Sep. € 34.00   2009*

PALAMOS 3B3 (3km W Coastal) 41.84700, 3.09861 **Eurocamping, Avda de Catalunya 15, 17252 Sant Antoni de Calonge (Gerona) [972-65 08 79; fax 972-66 19 87; info@euro-camping.com; www.euro-camping.com]** Exit A7 junc 6 dir Palamós on C66 & Sant Feliu C31. Take exit Sant Antoni; on ent Sant Antoni turn R at 1st rndabt. Visible fr main rd at cent of Sant Antoni. V lge, hdg/mkd pitch, shd; wc; chem disp; mv service pnt; 20% serviced pitches; baby facs; shwrs inc; EHU (5A) inc; lndry; supmkt; rest, snacks; bar; BBQ; playgrnd; 2 pools & paddling pool; waterpark; sand beach 300m; waterpark 5km; tennis; golf 7km; games area; games rm; fitness rm; doctor Jul & Aug; car wash; entmnt high ssn; wifi; TV rm; 15% statics; dogs €4; phone; Eng spkn; adv bkg; quiet; ccard acc; red long stay/LS. "Excel facs for families; lots to do in area; excel." ♦ 16 Apr-18 Sep. € 48.00   2010*

PALS 3B3 (6km NE Coastal) 41.98132, 3.20125 **Camping Inter Pals, Avda Mediterránea s/n, Km 45, 17256 Playa de Pals (Gerona) [972-63 61 79; fax 972-66 74 76; interpals@interpals.com; www.interpals.com]** Exit A7 junc 6 dir Palamós onto C66. Turn N sp Pals & foll sp Playa/Platja de Pals, pass Camping Neptune sp on L then Golf Aparthotel on R. At rndbt take 2nd exit, site clearly sp on L approx 500m. Lge, pt sl, terr, shd; htd wc; chem disp; mv service pnt; baby facs; shwrs inc; EHU (5-10A) inc; lndry (inc dryer); supmkt nr; rest, snacks; bar; playgrnd; pool; paddling pool; sand beach 600m (naturist beach 1km); watersports; tennis; bike hire; games area; golf 1km; wifi; entmnt; TV; 20% statics; dogs €3.50; phone; adv bkg; quiet; red snr citizens/CKE/CCI. "Lovely, well-maintained site in pine forest; poss diff lge o'fits - lge pitches at lower end of site; modern, well-maintained facs." ♦ 1 Apr-25 Sep. € 55.60 (CChq acc)   2014*

> ## "Satellite navigation makes touring much easier"
>
> Remember most sat navs don't know if you're towing or in a larger vehicle – always use yours alongside maps and site directions.

⊞ **PALS** 3B3 (1km E Rural) 41.95541, 3.15780 **Camping Resort Mas Patoxas, Ctra Torroella-Palafrugell, Km 339, 17256 Pals (Gerona) [972-63 69 28; fax 972-66 73 49; info@campingmaspatoxas.com; www.campingmaspatoxas.com]** AP7 exit 6 onto C66 Palamós/La Bisbal, turn L via Torrent to Pals. Turn R & site on R almost opp old town of Pals on rd to Torroella de Montgri. Or fr Palafrugell on C31 turn at km 339. Lge, mkd pitch, terr, shd; htd wc; 30% serviced pitches; chem disp; mv service pnt; baby facs; shwrs inc; EHU (5A) inc; gas; lndry; supmkt; rest, snacks; bar; playgrnd; pool; sand beach 4km; games area; entmnt; tennis; bike hire; golf 4km; TV; dogs €3.60; phone; site clsd 14 Dec-16 Jan; recep clsd Monday LS; Eng spkn; adv bkg ess high ssn; quiet; red long stay/LS; gd security; ccard acc; CKE/CCI. "Excel." ♦ € 47.00   2015*

See advertisement on previous page

PALS 3B3 (4km E Rural) 41.98555, 3.18194 **Camping Cypsela, Rodors 7, 17256 Playa de Pals (Gerona) [972-66 76 96; fax 972-66 73 00; info@cypsela.com; www.cypsela.com]** Exit AP7 junc 6, rd C66 dir Palamós. 7km fr La Bisbal take dir Pals & foll sp Playa/Platja de Pals, site sp. V lge, hdg/mkd pitch, hdstg, shd; wc; chem disp; mv service pnt; 25% serviced pitches; child/baby facs; private bthrms avail; shwrs inc; EHU (6-10A) inc; gas; lndry; supmkt; rest, snacks; bar; BBQ; playgrnd; pool; sand beach 1.5km; tennis; mini-golf & other sports; bike hire; golf 1km; games rm; wifi; entmnt; TV rm; free bus to beach; 30% statics; no dogs; Eng spkn; adv bkg; ccard acc; red long stay/LS/CKE/CCI. "Noise levels controlled after midnight; excel san facs; 4 grades of pitch/price (highest price shown); vg site." ♦ 14 May-15 Sep. € 58.00   2012*

⊞ **PAMPLONA** 3B1 (7km N Rural) 42.85776, -1.62250 **Camping Ezcaba, Ctra a Francia, km 2,5, 31194 Eusa-Oricain (Navarre) [948-33 03 15; fax 948-33 13 16; info@campingezcaba.com; www.campingezcaba.com]** Fr N leave AP15 onto NA30 (N ring rd) to N121A sp Francia/Iruña. Pass Arre & Oricáin, turn L foll site sp 500m on R dir Berriosuso. Site on R in 500m - fairly steep ent. Or fr S leave AP15 onto NA32 (E by-pass) to N121A sp Francia/Iruña, then as above. Med, mkd pitch, pt sl, pt shd; wc; shwrs inc; EHU (10A) €5.50; gas; lndry (inc dryer); shop; rest, snacks; bar; playgrnd; pool; horseriding; tennis; wifi; dogs €2.95; phone; bus 1km; poss cr; adv bkg; rd noise; red LS. "Helpful, friendly staff; sm pitches unsuitable lge o'fits & poss diff due trees, esp when site full; attractive setting; gd pool, bar & rest; ltd facs LS & poss long walk to san facs; in winter use as NH only; phone to check open LS; cycle track to Pamplona; quiet rural site; gd facs not htd." ♦ € 38.60   2013*

PEDROSILLO EL RALO see Salamanca 1C3

PELIGROS see Granada 2G4

PENAFIEL 1C4 (2km SW Rural) 41.59538, -4.12811 **Camping Riberduero, Avda Polideportivo 51, 47300 Peñafiel [tel/fax 983-88 16 37; camping@campingpenafiel.com; www.campingpenafiel.com]** Fr Valladolid 56km or Aranda de Duero 38km on N122. In Peñafiel take VA223 dir Cuéllar, foll sp to sports cent/camping. Med, mkd pitch, hdstg, shd; htd wc; chem disp; mv service pnt; baby facs; fam bthrm; shwrs inc; EHU (5A) €3.50; gas; lndry; shop; rest, snacks; bar; playgrnd; pool; rv 1km; bike hire; TV; 20% statics; dogs €3.60; phone; bus 1km; site open w/end only LS; poss cr; Eng spkn; adv bkg; quiet; ccard acc; 10% red 15 days. "Excel, well-kept site; interesting, historical area; ideal for wheelchair users; sm pitches and access diff due to trees." ♦ Holy Week & 1 Apr-30 Sep. € 18.50   2013*

PENASCOSA see Alcaraz 4F1

⊞ PENISCOLA *3D2* (500m N Coastal) *40.37694, 0.39222*
**Camping El Cid, Azagador de la Cruz s/n, 12598 Peñíscola
(Castellón) [964-48 03 80; fax 964-46 76 02; info@camping
elcid.com; www.campingelcid.com]** Exit A7 at junc 43. Take
N340 sp València for sh dist, turn L sp Peñíscola. Approx 2km
look for yellow sp to site. Narr site ent - rec loop o'fit rnd in rd
& ent thro R-hand site of security barrier. Med, mkd pitch, shd;
wc; chem disp; shwrs inc; EHU (10A) €4.50; gas; lndry; shop;
supmkt; rest, snacks; bar; playgrnd; pool; paddling pool; sand
beach 500m; 50% statics; poss cr; ccard acc; red long stay/
LS; CKE/CCI. "Vg, well-run site; popular with Spanish families;
friendly staff." € 27.00   2009*

⊞ PENISCOLA *3D2* (500m N Coastal) *40.36222, 0.39583*
**Camping Ferrer, Avda Estación 27, 12598 Peñíscola
(Castellón) [964-48 92 23; fax 964-48 91 44; campingferrer@
campingferrer.com; www.campingferrer.com]**
Exit AP7 onto CV141 twd Peñíscola, site sp on R, adj Consum
supmkt. Med, hdstg, terr, pt shd; htd wc; chem disp; mv
service pnt; baby facs; shwrs inc; EHU (6A) €3; lndry rm; shop
adj; rest, snacks; bar; BBQ; playgrnd; pool; sand beach 500m;
games rm; wifi; entmnt; some statics; dogs; bus 700m; adv
bkg; poss rd noise; cc acc; red long stay; CKE/CCI. "Conv NH;
vg, family run site; level pitches but access poss diff due trees."
€ 22.00   2010*

⊞ PENISCOLA *3D2* (3km NE Coastal) *40.37152, 0.40269*
**Camping El Edén, Ctra CS501 Benicarló-Peñíscola Km 6,
12598 Peñíscola (Castellón) [964-48 05 62; fax 964-48 98 28;
camping@camping-eden.com; www.camping-eden.com]**
Exit AP7 junc 43 onto N340 then CV141 to Peñíscola ctr. Take
3rd exit off rndabt at seafront, after 1km turn L after Hotel del
Mar. Rec avoid Sat Nav rte across marshes fr Peñíscola. Lge,
hdg/mkd pitch, pt shd; htd wc; chem disp; mv service pnt;
baby facs; shwrs inc; EHU (10A) inc; gas; service lndry; shop
300m; rest, snacks; bar; playgrnd; pool; paddling pool; sand/
shgl beach adj; wifi; 40% statics; dogs €0.75; bus adj; cash
dispenser; poss cr; no adv bkg; rd noise in ssn; ccard acc; red
long stay/LS; ACSI acc; "San facs refurbished & v clean; beach
adj cleaned daily; gd security; excel pool; easy access to sandy/
gravel pitches but many sm trees poss diff for awnings or high
m'vans; poss vicious mosquitoes at dusk; easy walk/cycle to
town; 4 diff sizes of pitch (some with tap, sink & drain) with
different prices; ltd facs LS; excel." ◆ € 53.00   2015*

⊞ PENISCOLA *3D2* (2km NW Rural) *40.40158, 0.38116*
**Camping Spa Natura Resort, Partida Villarroyos s/n,
Playa Montana, 12598 Peñíscola-Benicarló (Castellón)
[tel/fax 964-47 54 80; info@spanaturaresort.com;
www.spanaturaresort.com]** Exit AP7 junc 43, within 50m
of toll booths turn R immed then immed L & foll site sp twd
Benicarló (NB R turn is on slip rd). Fr N340 take CV141 to
Peñíscola. Cross m'way bdge & immed turn L; site sp. Med,
mkd pitch, hdstg, shd; htd wc; chem disp; mv service pnt;
serviced pitches; sauna; baby facs; shwrs inc; EHU (6A) inc; gas;
lndry (inc dryer); rest, snacks; bar; BBQ area; playgrnd; pool;
htd pool; waterslide; paddling pool; spa; wellness cent; jacuzzi;
sand beach 2.5km; tennis; bike hire; gym; games area; games
rm; wifi; entmnt; TV rm; 50% statics; dogs €3 (free LS); twin-
axles acc (rec check in adv); phone; bus 600m; c'van storage;
car wash; Eng spkn; adv bkg; some rd noise; ccard acc; red LS/
long stay/snr citizens/ CKE/CCI. "Vg site; helpful, enthusiastic
staff; gd clean san facs; wide range of facs; gd cycling." ◆
€ 40.00 (CChq acc) SBS - E23   2013*

⊞ PILAR DE LA HORADADA *4F2* (4km NE Coastal)
37.87916, -0.76555 **Lo Monte Camping & Caravaning,
Avenida Comunidada Valenciana No 157 CP 03190
[00 34 966 766 782; fax 00 34 966 746 536; info@campling
lomonte-alicante.es; www.campinglomonte-alicante.es]**
Exit 770 of AP7 dir Pilar de la Horadada; take the 1st L. Med,
mkd/hdg pitch; htd wc; chem disp; serviced pitches; baby
facs; shwrs inc; EHU (16) €0.40; lndry; shop; rest; bar; BBQ;
playgrnd; htd, covrd pool; beach 1km; bike hire; gym/wellness
cent; entmnt; wifi; dogs €1; adv bkg; ccard acc; CKE/CCI.
"New site; superb facs; great location - lots of golf & gd for
walking; rec; excel." ◆ € 35.00   2014*

PINEDA DE MAR see Calella *3C3*

PINEDA, LA see Salou *3C2*

PITRES *2G4* (500m SW Rural) *36.93178, -3.33268* **Camping
El Balcón de Pitres, Ctra Órgiva-Ugijar, Km 51, 18414
Pitres (Granada) [958-76 61 11; fax 958-80 44 53;
info@balcondepitres.com; www.balcondepitres.com]**
S fr Granada on A44/E902, turn E onto A348 for 22km. At
Órgiva take A4132 dir Trevélez to Pitres to site. Ask at rest in
vill for dirs. Sm, terr, shd; wc; chem disp; EHU (10A) €4.28;
gas; lndry; shop; rest, snacks; bar; playgrnd; pool; bike hire;
some statics; bus 600m; poss cr Aug; adv bkg; quiet; red long
stay; ccard acc; CKE/CCI. "Site in unspoilt Alpujarras region of
Sierra Nevada mountains; fine scenery & wildlife; site on steep
hillside, poss diff lge o'fits; san facs at top of hill - own san facs
saves climb." 1 Mar-31 Oct. € 32.00 (3 persons)   2011*

PLASENCIA *1D3* (4km NE Urban) *40.04348, -6.05751*
**Camping La Chopera, Ctra N110, Km 401.3, Valle del Jerte,
10600 Plasencia (Caceres) [tel/fax 927-41 66 60; lachopera@
campinglachopera.com; www.campinglachopera.com]**
In Plasencia on N630 turn E on N110 sp Ávila & foll sp indus est
& sp to site. Med, shd; wc; serviced pitches; chem disp; baby facs;
shwrs inc; EHU (6A) inc; gas; lndry; shop; rest; bar; BBQ; playgrnd;
pool; paddling pool; tennis; bike hire; wifi; dogs; quiet but w/end
disco; ccard acc; CKE/CCI. "Peaceful & spacious; much birdsong;
conv Manfragüe National Park (breeding of black/Egyptian
vultures, black storks, imperial eagles); excel pool & modern facs;
helpful owners." ◆ 1 Mar-30 Sep. € 30.00   2011*

⊞ **PLASENCIA** *1D3* (10km SE Rural) *39.94361, -6.08444*
**Camping Parque Natural Monfragüe, Ctra Plasencia-Trujillo,
Km 10, 10680 Malpartida de Plasencia (Cáceres) [tel/fax
927- 45 92 33 or 605 94 08 78 (mob); campingmonfrague@
hotmail.com; www.campingmonfrague.com]** Fr N on A66/
N630 by-pass town, 5km S of town at flyover junc take EXA1
(EX108) sp Navalmoral de la Mata. In 6km turn R onto EX208
dir Trujillo, site on L in 5km. Med, hdg pitch, pt sl, terr, pt shd;
htd wc; chem disp; mv service pnt; baby facs; shwrs inc; EHU
(5-15A) €4; gas; lndry (inc dryer); shop; rest, snacks; bar; BBQ;
playgrnd; pool high ssn; tennis; games area; archery; bike hire;
rambling; 4x4 off-rd; horseriding; wifi; TV rm; 10% statics;
dogs; phone; Eng spkn; no adv bkg; quiet; ccard acc; red long
stay/cash/CKE/CCI. "Friendly staff; vg, clean facs; gd rest; clean,
tidy, busy site but poss dusty - hoses avail; 10km to National
Park (birdwatching trips); many birds on site; excel year round
base; new san facs; staff helpful; discounted fees must be paid
in cash." ◆ € 28.00 (CChq acc)   2014*

PLAYA DE ARO *3B3* (2km N Coastal) *41.83116, 3.08366*
Camping Cala Gogo, Avda Andorra 13, 17251 Calonge
(Gerona) [972-65 15 64; fax 972-65 05 53; calagogo@
calagogo.es; www.calagogo.es] Exit AP7 junc 6 dir Palamós/
Sant Feliu. Fr Palamós take C253 coast rd S twd Sant Antoni,
site on R 2km fr Playa de Aro, sp. Lge, pt sl, pt terr, pt shd; wc;
chem disp; mv service pnt; serviced pitch; baby facs; shwrs inc;
EHU (10A) inc; gas; lndry (inc dryer); supmkt; rest; bar; snacks;
bar; BBQ; playgrnds; htd pool; paddling pool; sand beach adj;
boat hire; diving school; games area; games rm; tennis; bike hire;
golf 4km; wifi; entmnt; TV; no dogs 3/7-21/8 (otherwise €2); Eng
spkn; adv bkg; quiet; red long stay/LS. "Clean & recently upgraded
san facs; rest/bar with terr; site terraced into pinewood on steep
hillside; excel family site." ♦ 16 Apr-18 Sep. € 52.00   2011*

⊞ **PLAYA DE ARO** *3B3* (2km N Coastal) *41.83333, 3.08416*
Camping Internacional Calonge, Avda d'Andorra s/n,
Ctra 253, Km 47, 17251 Calonge (Gerona) [972-65 12 33 or
972-65 14 64; fax 972-65 25 07; info@intercalonge.com;
www.intercalonge.com] Fr A7 exit junc 6 onto C66 dir
La Bisbal, Palamós & Playa de Aro; 3km bef Palamós foll sp
St Antoni de Calonge. At 2nd rndbt bear R onto C253 dir Sant
Feliu, site on R in 3km. V lge, mkd pitch, terr, shd; htd wc; chem
disp; mv service pnt; some serviced pitches; baby facs; shwrs
inc; EHU (5A) inc; gas; lndry; supmkt; rest, snacks; bar; BBQ;
playgrnd; 2 pools; paddling pool; solarium; sand/shgl beach adj;
tennis; extensive sports facs; wifi; entmnt; TV rm; 30% statics;
phone; dogs €4.20; Eng spkn; adv bkg; poss noisy high ssn;
ccard acc; red LS/long stay; CKE/CCI. "On side of steep hill -
parking poss diff at times; conv Dali Museum; Roman ruins; gd
security; superb facs; excel site." ♦ € 49.00   2011*

PLAYA DE ARO *3B3* (2km N Coastal) *41.83666, 3.08722*
Camping Treumal, Ctra Playa de Aro/Palamós, C253,
Km 47.5, 17250 Playa de Arro (Gerona) [972-65 10 95;
fax 972-65 16 71; info@campingtreumal.com;
www.campingtreumal.com] Exit m'way at junc 6, 7 or 9
dir Sant Feliu de Guixols to Playa de Aro; site is sp at km 47.5
fr C253 coast rd SW of Palamós. Lge, mkd pitch, terr, shd;
wc; baby facs; shwrs inc; chem disp; mv service pnt; EHU
(10A) inc; gas; lndry; supmkt; rest, snacks; bar; playgrnd;
sm pool; sand beach adj; fishing; tennis 1km; games rm;
sports facs; bike hire; golf 5km; wifi; entmnt; 25% statics;
no dogs; phone; car wash; Eng spkn; adv bkg; quiet; ccard
acc; red LS; CKE/CCI. "Peaceful site in pine trees; excel san
facs; manhandling poss req onto terr pitches; gd beach." ♦
31 Mar-30 Sep. € 49.00   2011*

See advertisement opposite

PLAYA DE ARO *3B3* (2km N Rural) *41.81116, 3.01821*
Yelloh! Village Mas Sant Josep, Ctra Santa Cristina-Playa
de Aro, Km 2, 17246 Santa Cristina de Aro (Gerona) [972-
83 51 08; fax 972-83 70 18; info@campingmassantjosep.com;
www.campingmassantjosep.com or www.yellohvillage.
co.uk] Fr A7/E15 take exit 7 dir Sant Feliu de Guixols to Santa
Christina town. Take old rd dir Playa de Aro, site in 2km. V lge,
mkd pitch, shd; htd wc; chem disp; mv service pnt; baby facs;
serviced pitches; sauna; shwrs inc; EHU (10A) inc; gas; lndry (inc
dryer); shop; rest, snacks; bar; BBQ; playgrnd; lge pools; sand
beach 3.5km; tennis; games rm; games area; mini-golf & assorted
sports; bike hire; entmnt; golf 4km; internet; TV rm; 60% statics;
dogs €4; Eng spkn; adv bkg; quiet; ccard acc; red LS; CKE/CCI.
"Generous pitches; excel." ♦ 15 Apr-11 Sep. € 47.00   2010*

PLAYA DE ARO *3B3* (1km S Coastal) *41.81416, 3.04444*
Camping Valldaro, Carrer del Camí Vell 63, 17250
Playa de Aro (Gerona) [972-81 75 15; fax 972-81 66 62;
info@valldaro.com; www.valldaro.com]
Exit A7 junc 7 onto C65 dir Sant Feliu. Turn L onto C31 for Playa
de Aro thro Castillo de Aro & site on R, 1km fr Playa at km 4.2.
V lge, pt shd; htd wc; chem disp; mv service pnt; baby facs;
shwrs inc; EHU (5A) inc; gas; lndry (inc dryer); shop; rest, snacks;
bar; playgrnd; 2 pools; paddling pool; waterslides; beach 1km;
watersports; tennis; horseriding 2km; golf 3km; games area; bike
hire; wifi; entmnt; 50% statics; dogs €2.90; phone; extra for lger
pitch; adv bkg; red long stay. "Excel family site; some lge pitches;
many facs." ♦ 1 Apr-25 Sep. € 48.00 (CChq acc)   2010*

PLAYA DE ARO *3B3* (2km S Coastal) *41.8098, 3.0466*
Camping Riembau, Calle Santiago Rusiñol s/n, 17250
Playa de Aro (Gerona) [972-81 71 23; fax 972-82 52 10;
camping@riembau.com; www.riembau.com]
Fr Gerona take C250 thro Llagostera, turn for Playa de Aro.
Fr Playa de Aro take C253 twd Sant Feliu. Site access rd 2km
on R. V lge, pt shd; wc; chem disp; baby facs; shwrs inc; EHU
(5A) inc; gas; lndry; rest, snacks; bar; shop; beach 800m;
2 pools (1 indoor); playgrnd; tennis; fitness cent; games area;
games rm; entmnt; internet; 40% statics; phone; adv bkg;
some rd noise. ♦ Easter-30 Sep. € 36.00   2011*

PLAYA DE OLIVA see Oliva *4E2*

PLAYA DE PALS see Pals *3B3*

PLAYA DE PINEDO see Valencia *4E2*

PLAYA DE VIDIAGO see Llanes *1A4*

PLAYA TAMARIT see Tarragona *3C3*

POBLA DE SEGUR, LA *3B2* (3km NE Rural) *42.2602, 0.9862*
Camping Collegats, Ctra N260, Km 306, 25500 La Pobla de
Segur (Lleida) [973-68 07 14; fax 973-68 14 02; camping@
collegats.com; www.collegats.com] Fr Tremp N to La Pobla
on N260. Site sp in town at traff lts, turn R onto N260 dir Sort.
Ent by hairpin bend. Last section of rd narr & rough. Med, mkd
pitch, shd; wc; chem disp; shwrs; EHU €5; gas; lndry; shop
& 4km; snacks; bar; BBQ; playgrnd; pool; games area; some
statics (sep area); dogs; poss cr; Eng spkn; quiet; CKE/CCI.
"Clean facs; site not suitable lge o'fits; twin-axle vans not acc;
conv NH." ♦ 1 Apr-31 Oct. € 20.00   2011*

⊞ **POBOLEDA** *3C2* (300m SW Rural) *41.23298, 0.84305*
Camping Poboleda, Plaça Les Casetes s/n, 43376
Poboleda (Tarragona) [tel/fax 977-82 71 97; poboleda@
campingsonline.com; www.campingpoboleda.com]
By-pass Reus W of Tarragona on T11/N420 then turn N
onto C242 sp Les Borges del Camp. Go thro Alforja over Col
d'Alforja & turn L onto T207 to Poboleda & foll camping sp
in vill. Alt rd 50m W called Calle Major though steep on exit
fr site. Med, mkd pitch, terr, pt shd; htd wc; chem disp; baby
facs; fam bthrm; EHU (4A) inc; lndry rm; shop, rest, snacks, bar
in vill; pool; lake sw 8km; tennis; wifi; TV; dogs; phone; Eng
spkn; quiet; ccard acc; CKE/CCI. "In heart of welcoming vill in
mountain setting; friendly, helpful owner; not suitable lge o'fits
as access thro vill." ♦ € 32.60   2011*

POLA DE SOMIEDO *1A3* (250m E Rural) *43.09222, -6.25222*
Camping La Pomerada de Somiedo, 33840 Pola de Somiedo (Asturias) [985-76 34 04; csomiedo@infonegocio.com] W fr Oviedo on A63, turn S onto AS15/AS227 to Augasmestas & Pola de Somiedo. Site adj Hotel Alba, sp fr vill. Route on steep, winding, mountain rd - suitable sm, powerful o'fits only. Sm, mkd pitch, pt shd; wc; chem disp; mv service pnt; shwrs inc; EHU €4.20; shop, rest bar in vill; quiet. "Mountain views; nr national park." 1 Apr-31 Dec. € 19.00   2009*

⊞ **PONFERRADA** *1B3* (10km W Rural) *42.56160, 6.74590*
Camping El Bierzo, 24550 Villamartín de la Abadia (León) [tel/fax 987-56 25 15; info@campingbierzo.com; www.campingbierzo.com] Exit A6 junc 399 dir Carracedelo; after rndabt turn onto NV1 & foll sp Villamartín. Bef ent Villamartín turn L & foll site sp. Med, pt shd; wc; chem disp; mv service pnt (ltd); shwrs inc; EHU (3A) €3.78; shops 2km; rest; bar; playgrnd; 90% statics; phone; bus 1km; adv bkg; quiet; ccard not acc; CKE/CCI. "Attractive, rvside site in pleasant area; gd facs; friendly, helpful owner takes pride in his site; Roman & medieval attractions nr." ◆ ltd. € 25.50   2015*

PONT D'ARROS see Vielha *3B2*

⊞ **PONT DE BAR, EL** *3B3* (2.6km E Rural) *42.37458, 1.63687*
Camping Pont d'Ardaix, N260, Km 210, 25723 El Pont de Bar (Lleida) [973-38 40 98; fax 973-38 41 15; pontdardaix@clior.es; www.pontdardaix.com] On Seo de Urgel-Puigcerdà rd, N260, at rear of bar/rest Pont d'Ardaix. Med, terr, pt shd; wc; mv service pnt; shwrs inc; EHU (3-5A) €5.10-7.10; gas; lndry; shop & 4km; rest; bar; playgrnd; pool; 80% statics; dogs €5.30; phone; Eng spkn; quiet; CKE/CCI. "In pleasant valley on bank of Rv Segre; touring pitches on rv bank; site poss scruffy & unkempt LS; gd NH; vill 2.5km away." ◆ € 20.60   2011*

PONT DE SUERT *3B2* (3km N Rural) *42.43083, 0.73861*
Camping Can Roig, Ctra Boí, Km 0.5, 25520 El Pont de Suert (Lleida) [973-69 05 02; fax 973-69 12 06; info@campingcanroig.com; www.campingcanroig.com] N of Pont de Suert on N230 turn NE onto L500 dir Caldes de Boí. Site in 1km. Med, mkd pitch, hdstg, pt sl, pt shd; wc; chem disp; shwrs inc; EHU (5A) €5.15; gas; lndry; shop & 3km; snacks; bar; playgrnd; paddling pool; 5% statics; dogs €3.60; adv bkg; quiet; ccard acc. "NH en rte S; beautiful valley; informal, friendly, quirky site (free range poultry); v relaxed atmosphere; helpful owner; fabulous valley & national park with thermal springs; poss scruffy (2015)." 1 Mar-31 Oct. € 27.00   2015*

⊞ **PONT DE SUERT** *3B2* (5.5km N Rural) *42.44833, 0.71027*
Camping Alta Ribagorça, Ctra Les Bordes s/n, Km 131, 25520 Pont de Suert (Lleida) [973-69 05 21; fax 973-69 06 97; ana.uma@hotmail.com] Fr N on N230 site sp S of Vilaller on L. Sm, mkd pitch, terr, pt shd; htd wc; chem disp; shwrs inc; EHU (5A) inc; lndry; rest; bar; playgrnd; pool; 10% statics; dogs; Eng spkn; rd noise. "Fair NH." € 19.50   2009*

⊞ **PONT DE SUERT** *3B2* (16km NE Rural) *42.51900, 8.84600*
Camping Taüll, Ctra Taüll s/n, 25528 Taüll (Lleida) [973 69 61 74; www.campingtaull.com] Fr Pont de Suert 3km N on N230 then NE on L500 dir Caldes de Boí. In 13km turn R into Taüll. Site sp on R. Sm, pt sl, terr, pt shd; htd wc; chem disp; baby facs; shwrs inc; EHU €6; lndry rm; shop, rest, bar 300m; 30% statics; dogs €3; clsd 15 Oct-15 Nov; poss cr; quiet; CKE/CCI. "Excel facs; taxis into National Park avail; ltd touring pitches; suitable sm m'vans only; many bars & rest in pretty vill." € 28.50   2014*

⊞ **PONT DE SUERT** *3B2* (5km NW Rural) *42.43944, 0.69860*
Camping Baliera, Ctra N260, Km 355.5, Castejón de Sos, 22523 Bonansa (Huesca) [974-55 40 16; fax 974-55 40 99; info@baliera.com; www.baliera.com] N fr Pont de Suert on N230 turn L opp petrol stn onto N260 sp Castejón de Sos. In 1km turn L onto A1605 sp Bonansa, site on L immed over rv bdge. Site sp fr N230. Lge, mkd pitch, pt sl, terr, shd; htd wc; chem disp; mv service pnt; baby facs; shwrs inc; EHU (5-10A) €5; gas; lndry (inc dryer); shop; rest in ssn; snacks; bar; BBQ; playgrnd; pool; paddling pool; rv fishing; lake sw 10km; bike hire; horseriding 4km; golf 4km; weights rm; wifi; sat TV; 50% statics; dogs €3.80; phone; site clsd Nov & Xmas; poss cr; Eng spkn; quiet; ccard acc; red LS; CKE/CCI. "Excel, well-run, peaceful site in parkland setting; walking in summer, skiing in winter; excel cent for touring; conv Vielha tunnel; all facs up steps; pt of site v sl; helpful owner proud of his site; clean facs, some rvside pitches." ◆ € 32.40 (CChq acc)   2014*

PORT DE LA SELVA, EL *3B3* (2km N Coastal) *42.34222, 3.18333* **Camping Port de la Vall, Ctra Port de Llançà, 17489 El Port de la Selva (Gerona) [972-38 71 86; fax 972-12 63 08; portdelavall@terra.es]** On coast rd fr French border at Llançà take GI612 twd El Port de la Selva. Site on L, easily seen. Lge, pt shd; wc; shwrs; EHU (3-5A) €5.65; gas; lndry; shop; rest, snacks; bar; playgrnd; shgl beach adj; internet; some statics; dogs €2.95; phone; poss cr; adv bkg; poss noisy; ccard acc; red LS. "Easy 1/2 hr walk to harbour; gd site; sm pitches & low branches poss diff - check bef siting." 1 Mar-15 Oct. € 43.00 (4 persons) 2011*

PORT DE LA SELVA, EL *3B3* (1km S Coastal) *42.32641, 3.20480* **Camping Port de la Selva, Ctra Cadaqués s/n, Km 1, 17489 El Port de la Selva (Gerona) [972-38 72 87 or 972-38 73 86; info@campingselva.com; www.campingselva.com]** Exit A7 junc 3 or 4 onto N260 to Llança, then take GI 612 to El Port de la Selva. On ent town turn R twd Cadaqués, site in R in 1km. Med, mkd pitch, pt shd; wc; chem disp (wc); shwrs inc; EHU (4A) inc (poss no earth); lndry; shop & 1km; rest, snacks, bar 1km; playgrnd; pool; sand/shgl beach 1km; games area; TV; 25% statics; dogs €2.50; poss cr; adv bkg; quiet; ccard not acc; red LS; CKE/CCI. "Excel for coastal & hill walking; well-run site; gd, clean facs; gd beach; pleasant, attractive vill; poss diff for lge m'vans due low branches." 1 Jun-15 Sep. € 37.00 2010*

PORT DE LA SELVA, EL *3B3* (1km SW Coastal) *42.33462, 3.19683* **Camping L'Arola, Ctra. Llança-El Port de la Selva, 17489 El Port de la Selva (Gerona) [972-38 70 05; fax 972-12 60 81]** Off N11 at Figueras, sp to Llançà on N260. In 20km turn R to El Port de la Selva. Site on L (N side of coast rd) bef town. Sm, hdstg, unshd; wc; chem disp; shwrs; EHU (10A) €5; lndry rm; shops 1km; rest, snacks; bar; shgl beach adj; 5% statics; dogs €3.21; bus; poss cr; adv bkg; ccard acc; CKE/CCI. "Nr sm, pleasant town with gd shops, rests, harbour, amusements for all ages; scenic beauty; v friendly owner." ♦ ltd. 1 Jun-30 Sep. € 21.50 2010*

POTES *1A4* (1km W Rural) *43.15527, -4.63694* **Camping La Viorna, Ctra Santo Toribio, Km 1, Mieses, 39570 Potes (Cantabria) [942-73 20 21; fax 942-73 21 01; info@campinglaviorna.com; www.campinglaviorna.com]** Exit N634 at junc 272 onto N621 dir Panes & Potes - narr, winding rd (passable for c'vans). Fr Potes take rd to Fuente Dé sp Espinama, in 1km turn L sp Toribio. Site on R in 1km, sp fr Potes. Med, mkd pitch, terr, pt shd; htd wc; chem disp; mv service pnt; baby facs; shwrs inc; EHU (6A) €3.40 (poss rev pol); lndry (inc dryer); shop & 2km; rest, snacks; bar; BBQ; playgrnd; pool high ssn; paddling pool; bike hire; wifi; bus 1km; poss cr; Eng spkn; adv bkg; quiet; ccard acc; CKE/CCI. "Lovely views; gd walks; friendly, family-run, clean, tidy site; gd pool; ideal Picos de Europa; conv cable car, 4x4 tours, trekking; mkt on Mon; festival mid-Sep v noisy; some pitches diff in wet & diff lge o'fits; excel." ♦ 1 Apr-31 Oct. € 24.00 2014*

POTES *1A4* (3km W Rural) *43.15742, -4.65617* **Camping La Isla-Picos de Europa, Ctra Potes-Fuente Dé, 39586 Turieno (Cantabria) [tel/fax 942-73 08 96; campicoseuropa@terra.es; www.liebanaypicosdeeuropa.com]** Take N521 W fr Potes twd Espinama, site on R in 3km thro vil of Turieno (app Potes fr N). Med, mkd pitch, pt sl, shd; wc; chem disp; mv service pnt; shwrs inc; EHU (6A) €3.60 (poss rev pol); gas; lndry; shop; rest; bar; BBQ; playgrnd; pool (caps req); walking; horseriding; cycling; 4x4 touring; hang-gliding; mountain treks in area; wifi; some statics; phone; poss cr; Eng spkn; adv bkg; poss noisy high ssn; ccard acc; red long stay; CKE/CCI. "Delightful, family-run site; friendly, helpful owners; gd san facs; conv cable car & mountain walks (map fr recep); many trees & low branches; rec early am dep to avoid coaches on gorge rd; highly rec; lovely loc, gd facs." Easter-31 Oct. € 20.50 2012*

POTES *1A4* (5km W Rural) *43.15527, -4.68333* **Camping San Pelayo, Ruta Potes-Fuente Dé, Km 5, 39587 San Pelayo (Cantabria) [tel/fax 942-73 30 87; info@campingsanpelayo.com; www.campingsanpelayo.com]** Take CA185 W fr Potes twd Espinama, site on R in 5km, 2km past Camping La Isla. Med, mkd pitch, pt sl, pt shd; wc; chem disp; shwrs inc; EHU (6A) inc; lndry (inc dryer); shop; rest, snacks; bar; playgrnd; pool; paddling pool; bike hire; games rm; wifi; TV; bus; poss cr; adv bkg; quiet, but noise fr bar; ccard acc high ssn; red long stay; CKE/CCI. "Friendly, helpful owner; some sm pitches; conv mountain walking; excel pool." Easter-15 Oct. € 17.00 2010*

PRADES see Vilanova de Prades *3C2*

⊞ **PRADES** *3C2* (1km W Rural) *41.31129, 0.98020* **Camping Prades, Ctra T701, Km 6.850, 43364 Prades (Tarragona) [977-86 82 70; camping@campingprades.com; www.campingprades.com]** Fr S take N420 W fr Reus, C242 N to Albarca, T701 E to Prades. Fr N exit AP2/E90 junc 9 Montblanc; N240 to Vimbodi; TV7004 to Vilanova de Prades; L at rndabt to Prades; go thro town, site on R in 500m. Narr rds & hairpins fr both dirs. Lge, mkd pitch, pt shd; wc; chem disp; mv service pnt; baby facs; shwrs; EHU (3A) €5.50; gas; lndry; shop; rest, snacks; bar; playgrnd; pool; paddling pool; bike hire; wifi; entmnt; TV rm; 60% statics; phone; bus 200m; poss cr; adv bkg; ccard acc; CKE/CCI. "Beautiful area; in walking dist of lovely, tranquil old town; excel, helpful staff." ♦ € 31.00 2011*

PUEBLA DE CASTRO, LA see Graus *3B2*

PUEBLA DE SANABRIA *1B3* (10km NW Rural) *42.13111, -6.70111* **Camping El Folgoso, Ctra Puebla de Sanabria-San Martin de Castañeda, Km 13, 49361 Vigo de Sanabria (Zamora) [980-62 67 74; fax 980-62 68 00; info@campingelfolgoso.com; www.campingelfolgoso.com]** Exit A52 sp Puebla de Sanabria & foll sp for Lago/Vigo de Sanabria thro Puente de Sanabria & Galende; site 2km beyond vill of Galende; sp. Med, pt sl, terr, shd; wc; chem disp; shwrs €1; EHU (5A) €2.50; gas; lndry; shop high ssn; rest high ssn; snacks; bar; playgrnd; bike hire; statics; phone; ccard acc. "Lovely setting beside lake, and woods, v cold in winter." ♦ ltd. 1 Apr-31 Oct. € 18.00 2012*

PUEBLA DE SANABRIA *1B3* (10km NW Rural) *42.11778, -6.69116* **Camping Peña Gullón, Ctra Puebla de Santabria-Ribadelago, Km 11.5, Lago de Sanabria, 49360 Galende (Zamora) [980-62 67 72]** Fr Puebla de Sanabria foll sp for Lago de Sanabria. Site 3km beyond vill of Galende clearly sp. Lge, pt shd; wc; shwrs inc; EHU (15A) €2.51; gas; lndry; shop in ssn; rest; playgrnd; lake adj; poss cr; quiet; red long stay; CKE/CCI. "Site in nature park 35km fr Portugal's Montesinho Park; rec arr by 1200; beautiful area; excel site." 28 Jun-31 Aug.
€ 17.00   2011*

⊞ **PUERTO DE MAZARRON** *4G1* (3km NE Rural/Coastal) *37.58981, -1.22881* **Camping Las Torres, Ctra N332, Cartagena-Mazarrón, Km 29, 30860 Puerto de Mazarrón (Murcia) [968-59 52 25; fax 968 59 55 16; info@campinglastorres.com; www.campinglastorres.com]** Fr N on A7/E15 exit junc 627 onto MU602, then MU603 to Mazarrón. At junc with N322 turn L to Puerto de Mazarrón & foll Cartagena sp until site sps. Lge, hdg/mkd pitch, terr, hdstg, pt shd; wc; chem disp; mv service pnt; 40% serviced pitch; baby facs; shwrs inc; EHU (6A) inc; gas; lndry; rest (w/end only); snacks; bar; sm shop & 3km; playgrnd; 2 pools (1 htd, covrd); sand/shgl beach 2km; tennis; bike hire; wifi; entmnt; sat TV; 60% statics; dogs; phone; bus 1km; Eng spkn; adv bkg rec in winter; poss noisy; ccard acc; red LS/long stay; CKE/CCI. "Unspoilt coastline; busy at w/end; well-managed, family site; poss full in winter; excel pool; sm pitches." ◆ € 24.50   2010*

⊞ **PUERTO DE MAZARRON** *4G1* (5km NE Coastal) *37.5800, -1.1950* **Camping Los Madriles, Ctra a la Azohía 60, Km 4.5, 30868 Isla Plana (Murcia) [968-15 21 51; fax 968-15 20 92; info@campinglosmadriles.com; www.campinglosmadriles.com]** Fr Cartegena on N332 dir Puerto de Mazarrón. Turn L at rd junc sp La Azohía (32km). Site in 4km sp. Fr Murcia on E15/N340 dir Lorca exit junc 627 onto MU603 to Mazarrón, then foll sp. (Do not use rd fr Cartegena unless powerful tow vehicle/gd weight differential - use rte fr m'way thro Mazarrón). Lge, hdg/mkd pitch, hdstg, pt sl, pt shd; wc; chem disp; mv service pnt; serviced pitches; shwrs inc; EHU (10A) €5; gas; lndry; shop; rest high ssn; bar; playgrnd; 2 htd pools; jacuzzi; shgl beach 500m; games area; wifi; no dogs; bus; poss cr; Eng spkn; adv bkg (fr Oct for min 2 months only); quiet; ccard acc high ssn; red long stay/LS/CKE/CCI. "Clean, well-run, v popular winter site; adv bkg ess fr Oct; some sm pitches, some with sea views; sl bet terrs; 3 days min stay high ssn; v helpful staff; excel." ◆ € 48.50   2014*

⊞ **PUERTO DE MAZARRON** *4G1* (2km E Rural/Coastal) *37.56777, -1.2300* **Camping Los Delfines, Ctra Isla Plana-Playa El Mojon, 30860 Puerto de Mazarrón (Murcia) [tel/fax 968-59 45 27; www.campinglosdelfines.com]** Fr N332 turn S sp La Azohía & Isla Plana. Site on L in 3km. Med, mkd pitch, hdstg, pt sl, pt shd; htd wc; chem disp; mv service pnt; serviced pitches; baby facs; private san facs avail; shwrs inc; EHU (5A) €3; gas; lndry; snacks & bar high ssn; BBQ; playgrnd; shgl beach adj; TV; 5% statics; dogs €3; quiet; poss cr; Eng spkn; phone; red long stay; CKE/CCI. "Gd sized pitches; popular LS." ◆ € 41.00   2009*

⊞ **PUERTO DE MAZARRON** *4G1* (5km SW Coastal) *37.56388, -1.30388* **Camping Playa de Mazarrón, Ctra Mazarrón-Bolnuevo, Bolnuevo, 30877 Mazarrón (Murcia) [968-15 06 60; fax 968-15 08 37; camping@playamazarron.com; www.playamazarron.com]** Take Bolnuevo rd fr Mazarrón, at rndabt go strt, site immed on L. Lge, mkd pitch, hdstg, pt shd; wc; 90% serviced pitches; chem disp; mv service pnt; shwrs inc; EHU (5A) €4; gas; lndry; shop, rest (high ssn); snacks, bar; playgrnd; sand beach adj; tennis; games area; internet; TV; dogs free; bus; phone; poss v cr; adv bkg; red long stay/LS; ccard acc. "Some lge pitches but tight turning for lge o'fits; friendly staff; metal-framed sunshades in ssn on most pitches but low for m'vans; poss poor daytime security; gd for wheelchair users; popular & v cr in winter - many long stay visitors." ◆ € 37.00   2011*

⊞ **PUERTO DE SANTA MARIA, EL** *2H3* (2km SW Coastal) *36.58768, -6.24092* **Camping Playa Las Dunas de San Antón, Paseo Maritimo La Puntilla s/n, 11500 El Puerto de Santa María (Cádiz) [956-87 22 10; fax 956-86 01 17; info@lasdunascamping.com; www.lasdunascamping.com]** Fr N or S exit A4 at El Puerto de Sta María. Foll site sp carefully to avoid narr rds of town cent. Site 2-3km S of marina & leisure complex of Puerto Sherry. Alt, fr A4 take Rota rd & look for sp to site & Hotel Playa Las Dunas. Site better sp fr this dir & avoids town. Lge, pt sl, pt shd; wc; chem disp; mv service pnt; shwrs inc; EHU (5-10A) €3.10-5.89; gas; lndry; shop (high ssn); snacks; bar; playgrnd; pool adj; sand beach 50m; sports facs; wifi; internet; 30% statics; phone; guarded; poss cr; adv bkg rec; poss noisy disco w/end; red facs LS; ccard acc; CKE/CCI. "Friendly staff; conv Cádiz & Jerez sherry region, birdwatching areas & beaches; conv ferry or catamaran to Cádiz; facs poss stretched high ssn; there is hot water in bthrms and washing up area but only the basins on one side of each rm; pitches quiet away fr rd; take care caterpillars in spring - poss dangerous to dogs; dusty site but staff water rds." ◆ € 10.00   2013*

PUIGCERDA *3B3* (2km NE Rural) *42.44156, 1.94174* **Camping Stel, Ctra de Llívia s/n, 17520 Puigcerdà (Gerona) [972-88 23 61; fax 972-14 04 19; puigcerda@stel.es; www.stel.es]** Fr France head for Bourg-Madame on N820 (N20) or N116. Cross border dir Llívia on N154, site is 1km after rndabt on L. Lge, mkd pitch, terr, pt shd; htd wc; chem disp; mv service pnt; baby facs; shwrs; EHU (7A) €4.50; lndry (inc dryer); shop; rest, snacks; bar; BBQ; playgrnd; htd pool; paddling pool; canoeing; watersports; archery; bike hire; games area; golf 4km; wifi; entmnt; TV rm; 10% statics; dogs; site open w/ends only in winter; Eng spkn; adv bkg; some rd noise; ccard acc. "Pitches on upper terr quieter; superb scenery; sep area for campers with pets; gd walking, cycling." ◆ 3 Jun-11 Sep. € 36.40 (CChq acc)   2011*

PUYARRUEGO see Ainsa *3B2*

QUEVEDA see Santillana del Mar *1A4*

RIANO *1A3* (7km E Rural) *42.97361, -4.92000* **Camping Alto Esla, Ctra León-Santander, 24911 Boca de Huérgano (León) [987-74 01 39; camping@altoesla.eu; www.altoesla.eu]** SW on N621 fr Potes just past junc with LE241 at Boca de Huérgano. Site on L. (See Picos de Europa in Mountain Passes & Tunnels in the section Planning & Travelling at front of guide). Sm, pt sl, pt shd; wc; chem disp; mv service pnt; EHU (5A) €2.68 (poss rev pol); lndry; shops 500m; bus 300m; bar; phone; quiet; ccard acc; CKE/CCI. "Lovely setting; superb views; attractive site; ltd EHU; excel san facs." ♦ 26 Jun-8 Sep. € 18.00   2011*

⊞ **RIAZA** *1C4* (1.5km W Rural) *41.26995, -3.49750* **Camping Riaza, Ctra de la Estación s/n, 40500 Riaza (Segovia) [tel/fax 921-55 05 80; info@camping-riaza.com; www.camping-riaza.com]** Fr N exit A1/E5 junc 104, fr S exit 103 onto N110 N. In 12km turn R at rndabt on ent to town, site on L. Lge, hdg pitch, unshd; htd wc; chem disp; mv service pnt; baby facs; shwrs inc; EHU (15A) €4.70; lndry (inc dryer); shop; rest, snacks; bar; BBQ; playgrnd; pool; paddling pool; games area; games rm; internet; some statics; dogs free; phone; bus 900m; Eng spkn; adv bkg; quiet. "Vg site; various pitch sizes - some lge; excel san facs; easy access to/fr Santander or Bilbao; beautiful little town." ♦ € 40.30   2014*

RIBADEO *1A2* (4km E Coastal) *43.55097, -6.99699* **Camping Playa Peñarronda, Playa de Peñarronda-Barres, 33794 Castropol (Asturias) [tel/fax 985-62 30 22; camping penarrondacb@hotmail.com; www.campingplaya penarronda.com]** Exit A8 at km 498 onto N640 dir Lugo/Barres; turn R approx 500m and then foll site sp for 2km. Med, mkd pitch, pt shd; wc; chem disp; mv service pnt; shwrs inc; EHU (6A) €4 (poss rev pol); gas; lndry; shop; rest, snacks; bar; BBQ; playgrnd; sand beach adj; games area; bike hire; some statics; phone; Eng spkn; quiet; red long stay; CKE/CCI. "Beautifully-kept, delightful, clean, friendly, family-run site on 'Blue Flag' beach; rec arr early to get pitch; facs clean; gd cycling along coastal paths & to Ribadeo; ltd facs LS, sm pitches; gd sized pitches, little shd." Holy Week-25 Sep. € 23.60   2012*

RIBADEO *1A2* (3km W Rural) *43.53722, -7.08472* **Camping Ribadeo, Ctra Ribadeo-La Coruña, Km 2, 27700 Ribadeo (Lugo) [982-13 11 68; fax 982-13 11 67; www.camping ribadeo.com]** W fr Ribadeo on N634/E70 twd La Coruña, in 2km pass sp Camping Ribadeo. Ignore 1st camping sp, take next L in 1.4km. Lge, mkd pitch, pt shd; wc; chem disp; mv service pnt; shwrs inc; EHU (3A) €3.20 (rev pol); gas 4km; lndry; shop; rest, snacks; bar; BBQ; playgrnd; pool; sand beach 2km; no dogs; bus 500m; quiet; red for 10+ days; CKE/CCI. "Gd NH; friendly, family owners; gd san facs, request hot water for shwrs; everything immac; highly rec; many interesting local features." Holy Week & 1 Jun-30 Sep. € 19.00   2010*

RIBADEO *1A2* (18km W Coastal) *43.56237, -7.20762* **Camping Gaivota, Playa de Barreiros, 27792 Barreiros [982 12 44 51; campinggaivota@gmail.com; www.campingpobladogaivota. com]** Fr Berreiros take N634, turn L at KM 567, betRibadeo & Foz. Foll camping sp. Med, hdg pitch, pt shd; wc; chem disp; mv service pnt; shwrs inc; EHU (6A); gas; lndry (inc dryer); shop; rest; snacks; bar; BBQ; beach adj; wifi; TV rm; 5% statics; dogs; phone; public transport 2km; twin axles; quiet. "V well cared for; superb beaches; family run; pleasant bar & rest; excel." ♦ 28 Mar-15 Oct. € 30.00   2015*

RIBADESELLA *1A3* (3km W Rural) *43.46258, -5.08725* **Camping Ribadesella, Sebreño s/n, 33560 Ribadesella (Asturias) [tel/fax 985 858293 or 985 857721; info@camping-ribadesella.com; www.camping-ribadesella. com]** W fr Ribadesella take N632. After 2km fork L up hill. Site on L after 2km. Poss diff for lge o'fits & alt rte fr Ribadesella vill to site to avoid steep uphill turn can be used. Lge, mkd pitch, pt sl, terr, pt shd; wc; chem disp; baby facs; shwrs inc; EHU (5A) €4.80; gas; lndry; shop, rest, snacks, bar; BBQ; playgrnd; htd, covrd pool; sand beach 4km; tennis; games area; games rm; dog €2.50; poss cr; adv bkg; quiet; ccard acc; red LS/long stay; CKE/CCI. "Clean san facs; some sm pitches; attractive fishing vill; prehistoric cave paintings nrby." ♦ 27 Mar-20 Sep. € 33.00   2015*

RIBADESELLA *1A3* (8km W Coastal/Rural) *43.47472, -5.13416* **Camping Playa de Vega, Vega, 33345 Ribadesella (Asturias) [tel/fax 985-86 04 06; info@campingplayadevega.com; www.campingplayadevega.com]** Fr A8 exit junc 333 sp Ribadesella W, thro Bones. At rndabt cont W dir Caravia, turn R opp quarry sp Playa de Vega. Fr cent of Ribadesella (poss congestion) W on N632. Cont for 5km past turning to autovia. Turn R at sp Vega & site. Med, hdg pitch, pt terr, pt shd; wc; chem disp; serviced pitch; shwrs inc; EHU €3.50; lndry; shop; beach rest, snacks; bar; BBQ; sand beach 400m; TV; dogs; bus 700m; phone; quiet; ccard acc; CKE/CCI. "Sh walk to vg beach thro orchards; sm pitches not suitable lge o'fits; poss overgrown LS; immac san facs; a gem of a site; beware very narr bdge on ent rd." 15 Jun-15 Sep. € 21.00   2015*

⊞ **RIBEIRA** *1B2* (10km N Rural) *42.62100, -8.98600* **Camping Ría de Arosa II, Oleiros, 15993 Santa Eugenia (Uxía) de Ribeira (La Coruña) [981- 86 59 11; fax 981-86 55 55; rural@campingriadearosa.com; www.campingriadearosa. com]** Exit AP9 junc 93 Padrón & take N550 then AC305/VG11 to Ribeira. Then take AC550 to Oleiros to site, well sp. V lge, hdg/mkd pitch, shd; htd wc; chem disp; mv service pnt; baby facs; shwrs inc; EHU (6A) inc; gas; lndry; supmkt; rest, snacks; bar; BBQ; playgrnd; pool; sand beach 7km; fishing; tennis; games area; games rm; wifi; TV; some statics; dogs €2.50; phone; Eng spkn; adv bkg; quiet; ccard acc; red LS; CKE/CCI. "Beautiful area; helpful, friendly staff; excel; lots to do; excel pool; great facs." ♦ € 28.50   2015*

RIBEIRA *1B2* (8km NE Coastal) *42.58852, -8.92465* **Camping Ría de Arosa I, Playa de Cabio s/n, 15940 Puebla (Pobra) do Caramiñal (La Coruña) [981-83 22 22; fax 981-83 32 93; playa@campingriadearosa.com; www.campingriadearosa. com]** Exit AP9/E1 junc 93 or N550 at Padrón onto VG11 along N side of Ría de Arosa into Puebla do Caramiñal. Site is 1.5km S of Pobra, sp fr town. Lge, pt shd; wc; chem disp; mv service pnt; shwrs; EHU (6A) €4.60; gas; lndry; shop; rest, snacks; bar; playgrnd; sand beach adj; watersports; bike hire; internet; TV; some statics; dogs €2.50; phone; poss cr; adv bkg; quiet; ccard acc. 13 Mar-15 Oct. € 24.00   2010*

RIBERA DE CARDOS see Llavorsí *3B2*

⊞ **RIBES DE FRESER** *3B3* (500m NE Rural) *42.31260, 2.17570* **Camping Vall de Ribes, Ctra de Pardines, Km 0.5, 17534 Ribes de Freser (Girona) [tel/fax 972-72 88 20 or 620-78 39 20; info@campingvallderibes.com; www.camping vallderibes.com]** N fr Ripoll on N152; turn E at Ribes de Freser; site beyond town dir Pardines. Site nr town but 1km by rd. App rd narr. Med, mkd pitch, terr, pt shd; htd wc; chem disp; shwrs inc; EHU (6A) €4.30; lndry rm; shop 500m; rest; bar; playgrnd; pool; 50% statics; dog €4.60; train 500m; quiet; CKE/CCI. "Gd, basic site; steep footpath fr site to town; 10-20 min walk to stn; cog rlwy train to Núria a 'must' - spectacular gorge, gd walking & interesting exhibitions; sm/med o'fits only; poss unkempt statics LS; spectacular walk down fr the Vall de Nuria to Queralbs." € 23.00   2013*

RIOPAR *4F1* (7.6km E Rural) *38.48960, -2.34588* **Campsite Rio Mundo, Ctra Comarcal 412, km 205, 02449 Mesones (Albacete) [967-43 32 30; fax 967-43 32 87; riomundo@ campingriomundo.com; www.campingriomundo.com]** On N322 Albacete-Bailén, turn off at Reolid dir Riópar. Camp site 7km past Riópar on side rd on L (km-marker 205) (Mesones). Med, mkd pitch, hdstg, shd; wc; chem disp; mv service pnt; shwrs inc; lndry rm; gas; shop; rest, snacks; bar; BBQ; playgrnd; pool; bike hire; fishing; games area; wifi; dogs €3.40; Eng spkn; adv bkg; quiet; ccard acc; red LS; CKE/CCI. "Well run site in mountainous nature reserve by Rv Mundo; gd dogs walks; spotless san facs." ♦ ltd. 20 Mar-13 Oct. € 35.50   2011*

⊞ **RIPOLL** *3B3* (2km N Rural) *42.21995, 2.17505* **Camping Ripollés, Ctra Barcelona/Puigcerdà, Km 109.3, 17500 Ripoll (Gerona) [972-70 37 70; fax 972-70 35 54]** At km 109.3 up hill N fr town; well sp. Steep access rd. Med, mkd pitch, pt sl, pt shd; htd wc; chem disp; mv service pnt; baby facs; shwrs inc; EHU (4A); lndry; shop 2km; rest, snacks; bar; BBQ; playgrnd; pool; tennis; 20% statics; dogs €2.80; phone; adv bkg; quiet; ccard acc; CKE/CCI. "V pleasant; gd bar/rest; not suitable med/lge o'fits." ♦ € 19.00   2011*

RIPOLL *3B3* (1km S Rural) *42.18218, 2.19552* **Camping Solana del Ter, Ctra Barcelona-Puigcerdà, C17, Km 92.5, 17500 Ripoll (Gerona) [972-70 10 62; fax 972-71 43 43; camping@solanadelter.com; www.solanadelter.com]** Site sp S of Ripoll on N152 behind hotel & rest. Med, mkd pitch, hdstg, pt shd; htd wc; chem disp; baby facs; shwrs inc; EHU (4A) €5.90; lndry; shop; rest, snacks; bar; playgrnd; pool high ssn only; paddling pool; tennis; TV; Eng spkn; phone; some rd & rlwy noise; ccard acc; CKE/CCI. "Historic monastery in town; scenic drives nr." Holy Week-15 Oct. € 27.00   2010*

⊞ **RIPOLL** *3B3* (6km NW Rural) *42.23522, 2.11797* **Camping Molí Serradell -, 17530 Campdevànol (Gerona) [tel/fax 972-73 09 27; calrei@teleline.es]** Fr Ripoll N on N152; L onto Gl401 dir Gombrèn; site on L in 4km. NB 2nd site. Sm, pt shd; htd wc; chem disp; mv service pnt; shwrs inc; EHU €4.50; lndry (in dryer); shop; rest; 75% statics; poss cr; quiet; red LS; CKE/CCI. € 25.40   2009*

⊞ **ROCIO, EL** *2G3* (1km N Rural) *37.14194, -6.49250* **Camping La Aldea, Ctra del Rocío, Km 25, 21750 El Rocío,Almonte (Huelva) [959-44 26 77; fax 959-44 25 82; info@campinglaaldea.com; www.campinglaaldea.com]** Fr A49 turn S at junc 48 onto A483 by-passing Almonte, site sp just bef El Rócio rndabt. Fr W (Portugal) turn off at junc 60 to A484 to Almonte, then A483. Lge, hdg/mkd pitch, hdstg, pt shd; htd wc; chem disp; mv service pnt; baby facs; shwrs inc; EHU (10A) €6.50; gas; lndry (inc dryer); shop; rest, snacks; bar; BBQ; playgrnd; htd pool high ssn; sand beach 16km; horseriding nrby; van washing facs; wifi; 30% statics; dogs €3; phone; bus 500m; poss cr; Eng spkn; adv bkg; rd/ motocross noise; red long stay/LS; ccard acc; CKE/CCI. "Well-appointed & maintained site; winter rallies; excel san facs; friendly, helpful staff; tight turns on site; most pitches have kerb or gully; pitches soft after rain; gd birdwatching (lagoon 1km); interesting town; avoid festival (in May-7 weeks after Easter.) when town cr & site charges higher; poss windy; excel birdwatching nrby." ♦ ltd. € 42.50   2014*

RODA DE BARA *3C3* (2km E Coastal) *41.17003, 1.46427* **Campsite Stel Cat 1., Ctra N340, Km 1182, 43883 Roda de Barà (Tarragona) [977-80 20 02; fax 977-80 05 25; rodadebara@stel.es; www.stel.es]** Exit AP7 junc 31, foll sps for Tarragona on N340. Site on L immed after Arco de Barà. Lge, mkd pitch, pt shd; wc; chem disp; mv service pnt; baby facs; htd private bthrms avail; shwrs inc; EHU (5A) inc; gas; lndry (inc dryer); shop; rest, snacks; bar; BBQ; playgrnd; htd pool; waterslides; sand beach adj; watersports; tennis; sports & entmnt; bike hire; games area; golf 20km; wifi; TV; 10% statics; no dogs; phone; poss cr; adv bkg; some rd/rlwy noise; red long stay/LS; CKE/CCI. "Some sm pitches; excel, well maintained site;1st class san facs; 2 mins walk fr sandy beach; more expensive than some but worth the money." ♦ 7 Apr-25 Sep. € 57.40   2011*

⊞ **RODA DE BARA** *3C3* (3km E Coastal/Rural) *41.17034, 1.46708* **Camping Arc de Barà, N340, Km 1182, 43883 Roda de Barà (Tarragona) [977-80 09 02; camping@ campingarcdebara.com; www.campingarcdebara.com]** Exit AP7 junc 31 or 32, foll sp Arc de Barà on N340 dir Tarragona. Site on L after 5km shortly after Camping Park Playa Barà. NB When app fr N ess to use 'Cambia de Sentido' just after Arc de Barà (old arch). Lge, shd; htd wc; chem disp; baby facs; shwrs inc; EHU (5A) €3.50; gas; lndry (inc dryer); shop high ssn; supmkt 200m; rest, snacks; bar; BBQ; pool; paddling pool; sand beach adj; games area; 75% statics in sep area; dogs €2.80; phone; bus adj; site clsd Nov; poss cr; Eng spkn; rlwy noise; ccard acc; CKE/CCI. "Ltd number sm touring pitches; gd, clean NH en rte Alicante; phone ahead winter/LS to check open, minimum price in high ssn 01/07 - 31/08." ♦ € 28.00 (3 persons)   2011*

RONDA *2H3* (4km NE Rural) *36.76600, -5.11900* **Camping El Cortijo, Ctra Campillos, Km 4.5, 29400 Ronda (Málaga) [952-87 07 46; fax 952-87 30 82; elcortijo@hermanosmacias. com; www.hermanosmacias.com]** Fr Ronda by-pass take A367 twd Campillos. Site on L after 4.5km opp new development 'Hacienda Los Pinos'. Med, mkd pitch, pt shd; wc; chem disp; mv service pnt; serviced pitches; baby facs; shwrs inc; EHU inc; lndry; shop; rest; bar; playgrnd; pool; tennis; games area; bike hire; 5% statics; dogs; phone; Eng spkn; some rd noise; CKE/CCI. "Friendly, helpful owner; conv NH." ♦ 1 Apr-15 Oct. € 16.00   2011*

⊞ **RONDA** *2H3* (1km S Rural) *36.72111, -5.17166*
Camping El Sur, Ctra Ronda-Algeciras Km 1.5, 29400
Ronda (Málaga) [952-87 59 39; fax 952-87 70 54;
info@campingelsur.com; www.campingelsur.com]
Site on W side of A369 dir Algeciras. Do not tow thro Ronda.
Med, mkd pitch, hdstg, terr, sl, pt shd; htd wc; chem disp;
mv service pnt; baby facs; shwrs inc; EHU (5-10A) €4.30-5.35
(poss rev pol &/or no earth); lndry; shop; rest adj; snacks; bar;
playgrnd; pool high ssn; wifi; dogs €1.70; phone; poss cr; Eng
spkn; adv bkg; quiet; red long stay/LS; CKE/CCI. "Gd rd fr coast
with spectacular views; long haul for lge o'fits; busy family-run
site in lovely setting; conv National Parks & Pileta Caves; poss
diff access some pitches due trees & high kerbs; hard, rocky
grnd; san facs poss stretched high ssn; easy walk to town;
friendly staff; vg rest; excel." ♦ € 24.40   2014*

ROQUETAS DE MAR see Almería *4G1*

ROSES *3B3* (200m SW Coastal) *42.26888, 3.1525* **Camping
Rodas, Calle Punta Falconera 62,17480 Roses (Gerona)
[972-25 76 17; fax 972-15 24 66; info@campingrodas.com;
www.campingrodas.com]** On Figueras-Roses rd, at o'skts
of Roses sp on R after supmkt. Lge, hdg/mkd pitch, pt shd;
wc; chem disp; serviced pitches; shwrs inc; EHU (6A) inc; gas;
lndry; shop adj; rest, snacks; bar; lndry; sm playgrnd; htd
pool; paddling pool; sand beach 600m; bus 1km; poss cr;
Eng spkn; adv bkg; quiet; ccard acc; CKE/CCI. "Well-run site;
site rds all tarmac; Roses gd cent for region." 1 Jun-30 Sep.
€ 31.50   2009*

⊞ **ROSES** *3B3* (1km W Urban/Coastal) *42.26638, 3.16305*
Camping Joncar Mar, Ctra Figueres s/n, 17480 Roses
(Gerona) [tel/fax 972-25 67 02; info@campingjoncarmar.
com; www.campingjoncarmar.com] At Figueres take C260
W for Roses. On ent Roses turn sharp R at last rndabt at end
of dual c'way. Site on both sides or rd - go to R (better) side,
park & report to recep on L. Lge, pt sl, pt shd; htd wc; chem
disp; baby facs; shwrs; EHU (6-10A) poss no earth; gas; lndry;
shop; rest; bar; playgrnd; pool; sand beach 150m; golf 15km;
entmnt; games rm; internet; 15% statics; dogs €2.40; phone;
bus 500m; poss cr; Eng spkn; adv bkg; rd noise; ccard acc; red
LS/long stay. "Conv walk into Roses; hotels & apartment blocks
bet site & beach; poss cramped/tight pitches; narr rds; vg value
LS; new san facs 2015." € 32.00   2015*

ROSES *3B3* (2km W Coastal) *42.26638, 3.15611* Camping Salatà,
Port Reig s/n, 17480 Roses (Gerona) [972-25 60 86; fax 972-
15 02 33; info@campingsalata.com; www.campingsalata.com]
App Roses on rd C260. On ent Roses take 1st R after Roses
sp & Caprabo supmkt. Lge, mkd pitch, hdstg, pt shd; htd wc;
chem disp; baby facs; shwrs inc; EHU (6-10A) inc; gas; lndry
(inc dryer); shop; rest, snacks; bar; playgrnd; htd pool high
ssn; sand beach 200m; wifi; 10% statics; dogs €2.80 (not
acc Jul/Aug); phone; poss cr; Eng spkn; adv bkg; red long
stay/LS; ccard acc; CKE/CCI. "Vg area for sub-aqua sports;
vg clean facs; red facs LS; pleasant walk/cycle to town." ♦
19 Feb-13 Nov. € 45.00   2011*

ROTA see Puerto de Santa María, El *2H3*

RUILOBA see Comillas *1A4*

⊞ **SABINANIGO** *3B2* (6km N Rural) *42.55694, -0.33722*
Camping Valle de Tena, Ctra N260, Km 512.6, 22600
Senegüe (Huesca). [974-48 09 77 or 974-48 03 02; correo@
campingvalledetena.com; www.campingvalledetena.com]
Fr Jaca take N330, in 12km turn L onto N260 dir Biescas. In
5km ignore site sp Sorripas, cont for 500m to site on L - new
ent at far end. Lge, mkd pitch, terr, unshd; htd wc; chem disp;
mv service pnt; serviced pitches; baby facs; shwrs inc; EHU (6A)
€6; lndry; shop; rest, snacks; bar; playgrnd; pool; paddling
pool; sports facs; hiking & rv rafting nr; entmnt; internet; TV
rm; 60% statics; dogs €2.70; phone; Eng spkn; adv bkg; rd
noise during day but quiet at night; "Helpful staff; steep, narr
site rd; sm pitches; excel, busy NH to/fr France; beautiful area;
in reach of ski runs; v busy." € 21.00   2013*

⊞ **SACEDON** *3D1* (500m E Rural) *40.48148, -2.72700* **Camp
Municipal Ecomillans, Camino Sacedón 15, 19120 Sacedón
(Guadalajara) [949-35 10 18, 949 35 17 80; fax 949-35 10 73;
ecomillans63@hotmail.com; www.campingsacedon.com]**
Fr E on N320 exit km220, foll Sacedón & site sp; site on L.
Fr W exit km 222. Med, mkd pitch, hdstg, pt sl, shd; wc (cont);
shwrs; EHU €5; lndry rm; shop 500m; lake sw 1km; quiet. "NH
only in area of few sites; sm pitches; san facs v poor; LS phone
to check open." ♦ € 15.50   2013*

⊞ **SAGUNTO** *4E2* (7km NE Coastal) *39.72027, -0.19166*
Camping Malvarrosa de Corinto, Playa Malvarrosa de
Corinto, 46500 Sagunto (València) [962-60 89 06; fax 962-
60 89 43; camalva@live.com; www.malvacorinto.com]
Exit 49 fr A7 onto N340, foll dir Almenara-Casa Blanca. Turn
E twd Port de Sagunto & Canet d'en Berenguer on CV320.
Site poorly sp. Lge, pt shd; wc; chem disp; sauna; shwrs inc;
EHU (5-10A) €4.40; gas; lndry; shop & 5km; rest, snacks; bar;
BBQ; playgrnd; sand & shgl beach adj; tennis; horseriding;
gym; 85% statics; dogs €2.70; phone; poss cr; Eng spkn; quiet;
red ow ssn/long stay; CKE/CCI. "Lovely site under palm trees;
friendly, helpful owners; gd facs; many feral cats & owners'
dogs on site; excel pitches adj beach; ltd touring pitches but
access to some poss diff; ltd facs & poss neglected LS; no local
transport." € 19.00   2010*

SAHAGUN *1B3* (1km W Rural) *42.37188, -5.04280*
Camping Pedro Ponce, Avda Tineo, s/n 24326 Sahagun
[987 78 04 15; fax 987 78 00 84; campingsahagun@
hotmail.com; www.villadesahagun.es] Leave A231 at junc
46 onto N120. Foll sp Shagun. Site on in 1km. Lge, unshd; wv;
chem disp; shwrs inc; EHU (6A); lndry; shop 2km; rest; bar;
playgrnd; pool; entmnt; wifi; 60% statics; dogs; phone; public
transpost adj; twin axles; Eng spkn; noisy; ccard acc. "Excel
municipal site; modern facs; sep area for tourers; interesting
town; vg." ♦ 1 Mar-31 Oct. € 17.00   2015*

⊞ **SALAMANCA** *1C3* (15km NE Rural) *41.05805, -5.54611*
Camping Olimpia, Ctra de Gomecello, Km 3.150, 37427
Pedrosillo el Ralo (Salamanca) [923-08 08 54 or 620-
46 12 07; fax 923-35 44 26; info@campingolimpia.com;
www.campingolimpia.com] Exit A62 junc 225 dir Pedrosillo
el Ralo & La Vellés, strt over rndabt, site sp. Sm, hdg pitch, pt
shd; htd wc; chem disp; shwrs inc; EHU €3; lndry (inc dryer); rest,
snacks; bar; playgrnd; pool; entmnt; bus 300m; site clsed 8-16 Sep;
Eng spkn; adv bkg; some rd nois; CKE/CCI. "Helpful, friendly &
pleasant owner; really gd 2 course meal for €10 (2014); handy
fr rd with little noise & easy to park; poss open w/ends only LS;
excel; grass pitches; clean facs." € 20.00   2015*

SALAMANCA *1C3* (5km E Rural) *40.97611, -5.60472*
Camping Don Quijote, Ctra Aldealengua, Km 1930, 37193 Cabrerizos (Salamanca) [tel/fax 923-20 90 52; info@ campingdonquijote.com; www.campingdonquijote.com] Fr Madrid or fr S cross Rv Tormes by most easterly bdge to join inner ring rd. Foll Paseo de Canalejas for 800m to Plaza España. Turn R onto SA804 Avda de los Comuneros & strt on for 5km. Site ent 2km after town boundary sp. Fr other dirs, head into city & foll inner ring rd to Plaza España. Site well sp fr rv & ring rd. Med, hdg/mkd pitch, hdstg, pt shd; wc; chem disp; mv service pnt; baby facs; shwrs inc; EHU (10A) €4.50 (poss earth fault, 2010); lndry; shop; supmkt 3km; rest, snacks; bar; playgrnd; pool; paddling pool; beach 200m; rv fishing; wifi; 10% statics; dogs; phone; bus; poss cr w/end; adv bkg; quiet; red CKE/CCI. "Gd rv walks; conv city cent; basic, clean facs; 45 mins easy cycle ride to town along rv; rv Tormes flows alongside site with pleasant walks; friendly owner; highly rec." ♦ 1 Mar-31 Oct. € 23.00 (CChq acc)   2015*

"That's changed – Should I let The Club know?"

If you find something on site that's different from the site entry, fill in a report and let us know. See www.caravanclub.co.uk/europereport.

SALAMANCA *1C3* (7km E Urban) *40.94722, -5.6150*
Camping Regio, Ctra Ávila-Madrid, Km 4, 37900 Santa Marta de Tormes (Salamanca) [923-13 88 88; fax 923-13 80 44; recepcion@campingregio.com; www.campingregio.com] Fr E on SA20/N501 outer ring rd, pass hotel/camping sp visible on L & exit Sta Marta de Tormes, site directly behind Hotel Regio. Foll sp to hotel. Lge, mkd pitch, pt sl, pt shd; wc; chem disp; mv service pnt; baby facs; shwrs inc; EHU (10A) €3.95 (no earth); gas; lndry; shop & 1km; hypmkt 3km; rest, snacks in hotel; bar; playgrnd; hotel pool high ssn; bike hire; wifi; TV; 5% statics; dogs; phone; bus to Salamanca; car wash; poss cr; Eng spkn; quiet; ccard acc; CKE/CCI. "In LS stop at 24hr hotel recep; poss no hdstg in wet conditions; conv en rte Portugal; refurbished facs to excel standard; site poss untidy, & ltd security in LS; spacious pitches but some poss tight for lge o'fits; take care lge brick markers when reversing; hourly bus in and out of city; excel pool; vg; facs up to gd standard." ♦ € 23.00   2015*

SALAMANCA *1C3* (3km NW Rural) *40.99945, -5.67916*
Camping Ruta de la Plata, Ctra de Villamayor, 37184 Villares de la Reina (Salamanca) [tel/fax 923-28 95 74; recepcion@campingrutadelaplata.com; www.camping rutadelaplata.com] Fr N on A62/E80 Salamanca by-pass, exit junc 238 & foll sp Villamayor. Site on R about 800m after rndabt at stadium 'Helmántico'. Avoid SA300 - speed bumps. Fr S exit junc 240. Med, some hdg/mkd pitch, terr, pt sl, pt shd; htd wc; chem disp; mv service pnt; shwrs inc; EHU (6A) €2.90; gas; lndry; shop & 1km; snacks; bar; playgrnd; pool high ssn; golf 3km; TV rm; dogs €1.50; bus to city at gate; poss cr; rd noise; red snr citizen/CKE/CCI. "Family-owned site; some gd, san facs tired (poss unhtd in winter); ltd facs LS; less site care LS & probs with EHU; conv NH; helpful owners; bus stop at camp gate, every hr." ♦ ltd. € 27.00   2014*

SALDES *3B3* (3km E Rural) *42.2280, 1.7594* Camping Repos del Pedraforca, Ctra B400, Km 13.5, 08697 Saldes (Barcelona) [938-25 80 44; fax 938-25 80 61; pedra@campingpedraforca.com; www.campingpedraforca. com] S fr Puigcerdà on C1411 for 35km, turn R at B400, site on L in 13.5km. Lge, mkd pitch, pt sl, shd; htd wc; chem disp; mv service pnt; baby facs; sauna; shwrs inc; EHU (3-10A) €4.50-6.95; lndry (inc dryer); shop; rest, snacks high ssn; bar; playgrnd; 2 htd pools (1 covrd); paddling pool; bike hire; gym; wifi; entmnt; TV rm; 50% statics; dogs €2.50; phone; Eng spkn; some rd noise; adv bkg; red long stay; ccard acc; CKE/ CCI. "Tow to pitches avail; vg walking; in heart of nature reserve; poss diff ent long o'fits; lger, sunnier pitches on R of site; excel." ♦ € 29.00   2010*

SALOU *3C2* (2km NE Coastal) *41.08840, 1.18270*
Camping La Pineda de Salou, Ctra Tarragona-Salou, Km 5, 43481 La Pineda-Vilaseca (Tarragona) [977-37 30 80; fax 977-37 30 81; info@campinglapineda.com; www.campinglapineda.com] Exit A7 junc 35 dir Salou, Vilaseca & Port Aventura. Foll sp Port Aventura then La Pineda/ Platjes on rd TV 3148. Med, mkd pitch, pt shd; wc; baby facs; chem disp; sauna; shwrs; EHU (5A) €4.80; gas; lndry; shop; rest, snacks; bar; playgrnd; pool & paddling pool; spa cent; beach 400m; watersports; fishing; tennis; horseriding; bike hire; mini club; tourist info; entmnt; TV; some statics; dogs €4 (not acc mid-Jul to mid-Aug); phone; ccard acc; red LS. "Conv Port Aventura & Tarragona." € 45.00   2009*

SALOU *3C2* (1km S Urban/Coastal) *41.0752, 1.1176*
Camping Sangulí, Paseo Miramar-Plaza Venus, 43840 Salou (Tarragona) [977-38 16 41; fax 977-38 46 16; mail@sanguli.es; www.sanguli.es] Exit AP7/E15 junc 35. At 1st rndbt take dir to Salou (Plaça Europa), at 2nd rndabt foll site sp. V lge, mkd pitch, hdstg, pt sl, shd; htd wc; chem disp; mv service pnt; some serviced pitches; baby facs; shwrs inc; EHU (10A) inc; gas; lndry; shop; 2 supmkts; rest, snacks; bar; BBQ; playgrnd; 3 pools & 3 paddling pools; waterslide; jacuzzi; sand beach 50m; games area; tennis; games rm; fitness rm; entmnt; excursions; cinema; youth club; mini-club; amphitheatre; wifi; TV; dogs; 35% statics; phone; bus; car wash; Eng spkn; adv bkg rec Jul-Aug; some rlwy noise; red LS/long stay/snr citizens; ccard acc; CKE/CCI. "Quiet end of Salou nr Cambrils & 3km Port Aventura; site facs recently updated/upgraded; excel, well-maintained site." ♦ 4 Apr-2 Nov. € 70.00   2014*

See advertisement on previous page

SAN FULGENCIO *4F2* (7km ENE Coastal) *38.12094, -0.65982* Camper Park San Fulgencio, Calle Mar Cantábrico 7 Centro Comercial las Dunas (Alicante) [966-72 53 17 or 679-62 26 93; infosol@camperparksanfulgencio.com; www.camperparksanfulgencio.com] Fr N on AP7, take exit 740 twd Guardamar; At rndabt exit onto CV-91. 2nd exit at next rndabt then 3rd exit at another rndabt and stay on CV91. Take 1st exit at rndabt onto N-332, merge onto N332 and go thro 1 rndabt. At next rndabt take 3rd exit onto Calle Mar Cantábrico, go thro next rndabt and site is on the L. Sm, unshd, hdstg; wc; chem disp; mv service pnt; shwrs; EHU (5A) inc; lndry; 1.75km to wooden area nr beach & sea; wifi; bus to Alicante 150m; Eng spkn. "Sm m'van only site; gd facs; friendly helpful owner; gd atmosphere; Sat mkt; vg." € 14.00   2013*

SAN MIGUEL DE SALINAS see Torrevieja *4F2*

⊞ **SAN SEBASTIAN/DONOSTIA** *3A1* (5km NW Rural) *43.30458, -2.04588* **Camping Igueldo, Paseo Padre Orkolaga 69, 20008 San Sebastián (Guipúzkoa) [943-21 45 02; fax 943-28 04 11; info@campingigueldo.com; www.campingigueldo.com]** Fr W on A8, leave m'way at junc 9 twd city cent, take 1st R & R at rndabt onto Avda de Tolosa sp Ondarreta. At sea front turn hard L at rndabt sp to site (Avda Satrústegui) & foll sp up steep hill 4km to site. Fr E exit junc 8 then as above. Site sp as Garoa Camping Bungalows. Steep app poss diff for lge o'fits. Lge, hdg/mkd pitch, terr, pt shd, 40% serviced pitches; wc; chem disp; baby facs; shwrs inc; EHU (10A) inc; gas; lndry; shop; rest, bar high ssn; playgrnd; pool 5km; sand beach 5km; TV; phone; bus to city adj; poss cr/noisy; Eng spkn; red long stay/LS; CKE/CCI. "Gd, clean facs; sm pitches poss diff; spectacular views; pitches muddy when wet; excel rest 1km (open in winter)." ♦ € 33.50   2012*

SAN TIRSO DE ABRES *1A2* (450m N Rural) *43.41352, -7.14141* **Amaido, El Llano, 33774 San Tirso de Abres [tel/fax 985-47 63 94; amaido@amaido.com; www.amaido.com]** Head N on A6 twds Lugo & exit 497 for N-640 twds Oviedo/Lugo Centro cidade. At rndabt take 4th exit onto N-640, turn R at LU-P-6104, turn R onto Vegas, then take 2nd L. Site at end of rd. Med, hdg pitch, terr, pt shd, wc; chem disp; mv service pnt; baby facs; fam bthrm; shwrs; EHU (6A); lndry; shop; BBQ; playgrnd; games area; bike hire; wifi; TV rm; dogs; twin axles; adv bkg; red LS. "Lovely wooded site set in a circle around facs; farm animals; vg site." ♦ ltd. 10 Apr-15 Sep. € 28.00   2014*

SAN VICENTE DE LA BARQUERA *1A4* (1km E Coastal) *43.38901, -4.3853* **Camping El Rosal, Ctra de la Playa s/n, 39540 San Vicente de la Barquera (Cantabria) [942-71 01 65; fax 942-71 00 11; info@campingelrosal.com; www.campingelrosal.com]** Fr A8 km 264, foll sp San Vicente. Turn R over bdge then 1st L (site sp) immed at end of bdge; keep L & foll sp to site. Barier height 3.1m. Med, mkd pitch, pt sl, terr, pt shd; wc; chem disp; shwrs; EHU (6A) €4.80; gas; lndry; shop; rest, snacks; bar; sand beach adj; wifi; phone; poss cr; Eng spkn; adv bkg; quiet; ccard acc; red LS/long stay; CKE/CCI. "Lovely site in pine wood o'looking bay; surfing beach; some modern, clean facs; helpful staff; vg rest; easy walk or cycle ride to interesting town; Sat mkt; no hot water at sinks." ♦ 1 Apr-30 Sep. € 27.00   2014*

SAN VICENTE DE LA BARQUERA *1A4* (6km E Coastal) *43.38529, -4.33831* **Camping Playa de Oyambre, Finca Peña Gerra, 39540 San Vicente de la Barquera (Cantabria) [942-71 14 61; fax 942-71 15 30; camping@oyambre.com; www.oyambre.com]** E70/A8 Santander-Oviedo, exit sp 264 S. Vicente de la Barquera, then N634 for 3 km to Comillas exit on the Ctra La Revilla-Comillas (CA 131) bet km posts 27 and 28. Lge, mkd pitch, terr, pt sl, pt shd; wc; chem disp; mv service pnt; shwrs inc; EHU (10A) €4.55; gas; lndry; shop & 5km; rest, snacks; bar; pool; beach 800m; playgrnd; wifi; 40% statics; bus 200m; Eng spkn; adv bkg; ccard acc; CKE/CCI. "V well-kept site; clean, helpful owner; quiet week days LS; gd base for N coast & Picos de Europa; 4x4 avail to tow to pitch if wet; some sm pitches & rd noise some pitches; conv Santander ferry; immac san facs." 6 Mar-30 Sep. € 27.50   2015*

SANT ANTONI DE CALONGE see Palamós *3B3*

SANT FELIU DE GUIXOLS *3B3* (1km N Urban/Coastal) *41.78611, 3.04111* **Camping Sant Pol, Ctra Dr Fleming 1, 17220 Sant Feliu de Guixols (Gerona) [972-32 72 69 or 972-20 86 67; fax 972-32 72 11 or 972-22 24 09; info@campingsantpol.cat; www.campingsantpol.cat]** Exit AP7 junc 7 onto C31 dir Sant Feliu. At km 312 take dir S'Agaro; at rndabt foll sp to site. Med, hdg/mkd pitch, terr, shd, htd wc; chem disp; mv service pnt; some serviced pitches; baby facs; shwrs inc; EHU (10A) €4; lndry; shop; rest; bar; BBQ; playgrnd; 2 htd pools; sand beach 350m; games rm; bike hire; wifi; 30% statics; dogs €2; sep car park; Eng spkn; adv bkg; quiet - some rd noise; ccard acc; red long stay/snr citizens/CKE/CCI. "Vg, well-run site; excel facs; lovely pool; cycle track to Gerona." ♦ 26 Mar-12 Dec. € 53.00   2009*

See advertisement above

SANT JOAN DE LES ABADESSES see Sant Pau de Segúries *3B3*

⊞ **SANT JORDI** *3D2* (2km SW Rural) *40.49318, 0.31806* Camping Maestrat Park, 12320 Sant Jordi (Castellón) **[964-86 08 89 or 679-29 87 95 (mob); info@maestratpark.es; www.maestratpark.es]** Exit AP7 junc 42 onto CV11 to Sant Rafel del Riu. At rndabt with fuel stn take CV11 to Traiguera; then at rndabt take 1st exit onto N232 dir Vinarós & at next rndabt take 2nd exit sp Calig. Site 2km on L. Sm, hdg/mkd pitch, hdstg, pt sl, pt shd; wc; chem disp; mv service pnt; baby facs; shwrs inc; EHU (10-16A) €4.50; lndry (inc dryer); shop; rest; snacks; bar; BBQ; playgrnd; pool; paddling pool; beach 10km; games rm; bike hire; internet; wifi; TV; 25% statics; dogs; phone; bus; twin axles; Eng spkn; adv bkg; quiet; red long stay/LS; CKE/CCI. "Excel; club memb owner; excel for v lge o'fits." ♦ € 25.00   2015*

SANT LLORENC DE LA MUGA see Figueres *3B3*

⊞ **SANT PAU DE SEGURIES** *3B3* (500m S Rural) *42.26292, 2.36913* Camping Els Roures, Avda del Mariner 34, 17864 Sant Pau de Segúries (Gerona) **[972-74 70 00; fax 972-74 71 09; info@elsroures.com; www.elsroures.com]** On C38/C26 Camprodón S twd Ripoll for 6km. In Sant Pau turn L 50m after traff lts. Site on R after 400m. Lge, mkd pitch, terr, shd; wc; mv service pnt; baby facs; shwrs inc; EHU (4-8A) €3.20-6.50; gas; lndry; shop; rest; bar; playgrnd; 2 pools; tennis; cinema; games rm; gym; internet; 80% statics; dogs €3.50; phone; bus 200m; poss cr; some noise; CKE/CCI. "Gd." ♦ € 26.00   2011*

⊞ **SANT PAU DE SEGURIES** *3B3* (4km SW Rural) *42.25549, 2.35081* Camping Abadesses, Ctra Camprodón, Km 14.6, 17860 Sant Joan de les Abadesses (Gerona) **[630-14 36 06; fax 972-70 20 69; info@campingabadesses.com; www.campingabadesses.com]** Fr Ripoll take C26 in dir Sant Joan, site approx 4km on R after vill. Steep access. Sm, mkd pitch, terr, unshd; htd wc; baby facs; shwrs; EHU (6A) €2.88; gas; lndry; shop; snacks; bar; playgrnd; pool; games area; wifi; 70% statics; dogs €3.21; bus 150m; quiet; ccard acc. "Vg facs; gd views fr most pitches; steep access to recep; poss diff access around terraces." ♦ € 22.00   2011*

SANT PERE PESCADOR *3B3* (1km E Coastal) *42.18908, 3.1080* Camping La Gaviota, Ctra de la Playa s/n, 17470 Sant Pere Pescador (Gerona) **[972-52 05 69; fax 972-55 03 48; info@lagaviota.com; www.lagaviota.com]** Exit 5 fr A7 dir Sant Martí d'Empúries, site at end of beach rd. Med, hdg/mkd pitch, pt shd; wc; chem disp; baby facs; shwrs inc; EHU (5A) €3.70; gas; lndry; shop; rest; bar; playgrnd; direct access sand beach 50m; games rm; internet; 20% statics; phone; dogs €4; poss cr; Eng spkn; adv bkg; quiet; ccard acc; red long stay; CKE/CCI. "V friendly owners; gd, clean site; excel facs & constant hot water; some sm pitches & narr site rds; poss ltd access for lge o'fits; take care o'hanging trees; poss mosquito problem." ♦ 19 Mar-24 Oct. € 38.00   2009*

SANT PERE PESCADOR *3B3* (200m E Rural) *42.18747, 3.08891* **Camping Riu,** Ctra de la Playa s/n, 17470 Sant Pere Pescador (Gerona) [972-52 02 16; fax 972-55 04 69; info@campingriu.com; www.campingriu.com] Fr N exit AP7 junc 4 dir L'Escala & foll sp Sant Pere Pescador, then turn L twds coast, site on L. Fr S exit AP7 junc 5 dir L'Escala, then as above & turn R to beaches & site. Lge, mkd pitch, shd; wc; chem disp; baby facs; shwrs inc; EHU (5A) €3.90; gas; lndry; shop & 300m; rest, snacks; bar; BBQ; playgrnd; pool; sand beach 2km; rv fishing adj; kayak hire; games area; entmnt; internet; 5% statics; dogs €3.40; Eng spkn; adv bkg; quiet; ccard acc; red long stay; CKE/CCI. "Excel boating facs & fishing on site; gd situation; site rec." ♦ 4 Apr-19 Sep. € 38.00   2009*

SANT PERE PESCADOR *3B3* (1km SE Coastal) *42.18180, 3.10403* **Camping L'Àmfora,** Avda Josep Tarradellas 2, 17470 Sant Pere Pescador (Gerona) [972-52 05 40; fax 972-52 05 39; info@campingamfora.com; www.campingamfora.com] Fr N exit junc 3 fr AP7 onto N11 fro Figueres/Roses. At junc with C260 foll sp Castelló d'Empúries & Roses. At Castelló turn R at rndabt sp Sant Pere Pescador then foll sp to L'Amfora. Fr S exit junc 5 fr AP7 onto GI 623/GI 624 to Sant Pere Pescador. V lge, hdg/mkd pitch, pt shd; htd wc; chem disp; mv service pnt; serviced pitches; baby facs; private san facs avail; shwrs inc; EHU (10A) inc; gas; lndry (inc dryer); ice; supmkt; rest, snacks; bar; BBQ (charcoal/elec); playgrnd; 4 pools; waterslide; paddling pool; sand beach adj; windsurf school; fishing; tennis; horseriding 5km; bike hire; entmnt; wifi; games/TV rm; 15% statics; dogs €4.95; no o'fits over 10m Apr-Sep; phone; adv bkg; Eng spkn; quiet; ccard not acc; red long stay/LS/snr citizens/ CKE/CCI. "Excel, well-run, clean site; helpful staff; immac san facs; gd rest; poss flooding on some pitches when wet; Parque Acuatico 18km." ♦ 14 Apr-27 Sep. € 60.40 (CChq acc) SBS - E22   2014*

See advertisement opposite

SANT PERE PESCADOR *3B3* (2km SE Coastal) *42.16194, 3.10888* **Camping Las Dunas,** 17470 Sant Pere Pescador (Gerona) (Postal Address: Aptdo Correos 23, 17130 L'Escala) [972-52 17 17 or 01205 366856 (UK); fax 972-55 00 46; info@campinglasdunas.com; www.campinglasdunas.com] Exit AP7 junc 5 dir Viladamat & L'Escala; 2km bef L'Escala turn L for Sant Martí d'Empúries, turn L bef ent vill for 2km, camp sp. V lge, mkd pitch, pt sl, pt shd; wc; chem disp; mv service pnt; baby facs; serviced pitches; shwrs inc; EHU (6A) inc; gas; lndry (inc dryer); kiosk; supmkt; souvenir shop; rest, snacks; bar; BBQ; playgrnd; pool; paddling pool; sand beach adj; watersports; tennis; games area; games rm; money exchange; cash machines; doctor; wifi; entmnt; TV; 5% statics; dogs €4.50; phone; quiet; adv bkg (ess high ssn); Eng spkn; red LS; CKE/CCI. "Greco-Roman ruins in Empúries; gd sized pitches - extra for serviced; busy, popular site; excel, clean facs; vg site." ♦ 17 May-19 Sep. € 56.50   2014*

See advertisement inside the back cover

SANT PERE PESCADOR *3B3* (3km SE Coastal) *42.17701, 3.10833* **Camping Aquarius,** Camí Sant Martí d'Empúries, 17470 Sant Pere Pescador (Gerona) [972-52 00 03; fax 972-55 02 16; camping@aquarius.es; www.aquarius.es] Fr AP7 m'way exit 3 on N11, foll sp to Figueres. Join C260, after 7km at rndabt at Castello d'Empúries turn R to Sant Pere Pescador. Cross rv bdge in vill, L at 1st rndabt & foll camp sp. Turn R at next rndabt, then 2nd L to site. Lge, pt shd; wc; chem disp; mv service pnt; serviced pitches; baby facs; fam bthrm; shwrs; EHU (6-15A) €4-8; gas; lndry; supmkt; rest, snacks; bar; 2 playgrnds; sand beach adj; nursery in ssn; games rm; games area; car wash; internet; some statics; dogs €4.10; phone; cash point; poss cr; Eng spkn; adv bkg (ess Jul/Aug); quiet; ccard not acc; red LS/long stay/snr citizens (except Jul/Aug)/CKE/CCI. "Immac, well-run site; helpful staff; vg rest; windsurfing; vast beach; recycling facs; excel site, highly rec; gd value ACSI site; wind gets v high." ♦ ltd. 15 Mar-2 Nov. € 56.70   2013*

SANT PERE PESCADOR *3B3* (1.3km S Coastal) *42.18816, 3.10265* Camping Las Palmeras, Ctra de la Platja 9, 17470 Sant Pere Pescador (Gerona) [972-52 05 06; fax 972-55 02 85; info@campinglaspalmeras.com; www.campinglaspalmeras.com] Exit AP7 junc 3 or 4 at Figueras onto C260 dir Roses/Cadaqués rd. After 8km at Castelló d'Empúries turn S for Sant Pere Pescador & cont twd beach. Site on R of rd. Lge, mkd pitch, shd; wc; chem disp; mv service pnt; some serviced pitches; baby facs; shwrs inc; EHU (5-16A) €3.90; gas; lndry (inc dryer); shop; rest, snacks; bar; playgrnd; htd pool; paddling pool; sand beach 200m; tennis; bike hire; games area; games rm; wifi; entmnt; TV; dogs €4.50; phone; cash point; poss cr; Eng spkn; adv bkg; quiet; red LS/CKE/CCI. "Pleasant site; helpful, friendly staff; superb, clean san facs; gd cycle tracks; nature reserve nrby; excel." ♦ 15 Apr-5 Nov. € 47.70   2010*

See advertisement on previous page

SANT PERE PESCADOR *3B3* (4km S Rural/Coastal) *42.15222, 3.11166* Camping La Ballena Alegre, Ctra Sant Martí d'Empúries, 17470 Sant Pere Pescador (Gerona) [902-51 05 20; fax 902 51 05 21; info2@ballena-alegre.com; www.ballena-alegre.com] Fr A7 exit 5, dir L'Escala to rd GI 623, km 18.5. At 1st rndabt turn L dir Sant Martí d'Empúries, site on R in 1km. V lge, mkd pitch, hdstg, terr, unshd; htd wc; chem disp; mv service pnt; some serviced pitches; baby facs; shwrs inc; EHU (10A) inc; gas; lndry (inc dryer); supmkt; rest, snacks; bar; BBQ; playgrnd; 3 pools; sand beach adj; watersports; tennis; games area; games rm; fitness rm; bike hire; money exchange; surf shop; doctor; wifi; entmnt; TV rm; 10% statics; dogs €4.75; poss cr; Eng spkn; adv bkg; quiet; ccard not acc; red LS/snr citizens/long stay; CKE/CCI. "Excel site; superb facs." ♦ 14 May-26 Sep. € 56.00   2010*

⊞ SANT QUIRZE SAFAJA *3C3* (2km E Rural) *41.72297, 2.16888* Camping L'Illa, Ctra Sant Feliu de Codina-Centelles, Km 3.9, 08189 Sant Quirze Safaja (Barcelona) [938-66 25 26; fax 935-72 96 21; info@campinglilla.com; www.campinglilla.com] N fr Sabadell on C1413 to Caldes de Montbui; then twds Moià on C59. Turn R at vill sp, cont thro vill to T-junc, site ent opp junc. Lge, mkd pitch, hdstg, terr, pt shd; htd wc; chem disp; shwrs inc; EHU (6A) €5.50; gas; lndry; rest, snacks; bar; sm shop; playgrnd; pool; paddling pool; games area; games rm; TV; 50% statics; dogs €5; phone; bus 100m; site clsd mid-Dec to mid-Jan; Eng spkn; adv bkg; CKE/CCI. "Easy drive to Barcelona; poss open w/end only LS." € 28.00   2010*

⊞ SANTA CILIA DE JACA *3B2* (3km W Rural) *42.55556, -0.75616* Camping Los Pirineos, Ctra Pamplona N240, Km 300.5, 22791 Santa Cilia de Jaca (Huesca) [tel/fax 974-37 73 51; info@campingpirineos.es; www.campingpirineos.es] Fr Jaca on N240 twd Pamplona. Site on R after Santa Cilia de Jaca, clearly sp. Lge, hdg/mkd pitch, hdstg, terr, shd; wc; chem disp; mv service pnt; baby facs; shwrs inc; EHU (10A) €6 (check for earth); gas; lndry; shop; rest, snacks; bar; playgrnd; pool in ssn; paddling pool; tennis; games area; 30% statics; dogs; phone; site clsd Nov & open w/ends only LS; Eng spkn; adv bkg; some rd noise; ccard acc; red LS; CKE/CCI. "Excel site in lovely area; ltd access for tourers & some pitches diff lge o'fits; gd bar/rest on site; on Caminho de Santiago pilgrim rte; conv NH." ♦ € 26.00   2009*

SANTA CRISTINA DE ARO see Playa de Aro *3B3*

SANTA CRUZ see Coruña, La *1A2*

⊞ SANTA ELENA *2F4* (350m E Rural) *38.34305, -3.53611* Camping Despeñaperros, Calle Infanta Elena s/n, Junto a Autovia de Andalucia, Km 257, 23213 Santa Elena (Jaén) [tel/fax 953-66 41 92; info@campingdespenaperros.com; www.campingdespenaperros.com] Leave A4/E5 at junc 257 or 259, site well sp to N side of vill nr municipal leisure complex. Med, mkd pitch, hdstg, pt shd; wc; chem disp; mv service pnt; all serviced pitches; shwrs inc; EHU (10A) €4.25 (poss rev pol); gas; lndry; sm shop; rest high ssn; snacks; bar; playgrnd; pool; internet; wifi; TV & tel points all pitches; dogs free; many statics; phone; bus 500m; adv bkg; poss noisy w/end high ssn; ccard acc; red long stay/CKE/CCI. "Gd winter NH in wooded location; gd size pitches but muddy if wet; gd walking area, perfect for dogs; friendly, helpful staff; clean san facs; disabled facs wc only; conv national park & m'way; gd rest; sh walk to vill & shops; site v rural; beautiful area." ♦ ltd. € 32.00   2014*

SANTA MARINA DE VALDEON *1A3* (500m N Rural) *43.13638, -4.89472* Camping El Cardo, El Cardo, 24915 Santa Marina de Valdeón (León) [tel/fax 987-74 26 76; campingelcares@hotmail.com] Fr S take N621 to Portilla de la Reina. Turn L onto LE243 to Santa Marina. Turn L thro vill, just beyond vill turn L at camping sp. Vill st is narr & narr bdge 2.55m on app to site. Do not attempt to app fr N if towing - 4km of single track rd fr Posada. Med, terr, pt shd; wc; chem disp; shwrs; EHU (5A) €3.20; lndry (inc dryer); shop; rest; bar; 10% statics; dogs €2.10; phone; bus 1km; quiet; ccard acc; CKE/CCI. "Lovely, scenic site high in mountains; gd base for Cares Gorge; friendly, helpful staff; gd views; tight access - not rec if towing or lge m'van." ♦ Holy Week & 15 Jun-16 Sep. € 19.00   2010*

"We must tell The Club about that great site we found"

Get your site reports in by mid-August and we'll do our best to get your updates into the next edition.

SANTA MARTA DE TORMES see Salamanca *1C3*

⊞ SANTA PAU *3B3* (2km E Rural) *42.15204, 2.54713* Camping Ecològic Lava, Ctra Olot-Santa Pau, Km 7, 17811 Santa Pau (Gerona) [972-68 03 58; fax 972-68 03 15; vacances@i-santapau.com; www.i-santapau.com] Take rd GI 524 fr Olot, site at top of hill, well sp & visible fr rd. Lge, mkd pitch, pt shd; wc; chem disp (wc); shwrs inc; baby facs; EHU €4.20; gas; lndry; shop 2km; rest, snacks; bar; playgrnd; pool; horseriding adj; dogs; phone; Eng spkn; adv bkg; quiet; ccard acc. "V helpful staff; gd facs; v interesting, unspoilt area & town; in Garrotxa Parc Naturel volcanic region; v busy with tourists all ssn; walks sp fr site; Pyrenees museum in Olot; tourist train fr site to volcano; excel rests in medieval town." € 24.50   2011*

⊞ **SANTA POLA** *4F2* (1km NW Urban/Coastal) *38.20105, -0.56983* **Camping Bahía de Santa Pola, Ctra de Elche s/n, Km. 11, 03130 Santa Pola (Alicante) [965-41 10 12; fax 965-41 67 90; campingbahia@gmail.com; www.campingbahia.com]** Exit A7 junc 72 dir airport, cont to N332 & turn R dir Cartagena. At rndabt take exit sp Elx/Elche onto CV865, site 100m on R. Lge, mkd pitch, hdstg, pt shd; htd wc; chem disp; mv service pnt; baby facs; shwrs inc; EHU (10A) €3; gas; lndry (inc dryer); shop; supmkt; rest; playgrnd; pool; sand beach 1km; sat TV; 50% statics; dogs; phone; bus adj; Eng spkn; adv bkg; rd noise; ccard acc; red long stay/LS/ CKE/CCI. "Helpful, friendly manager; well-organised site; sm pitches; recep in red building facing ent; excel san facs; site rds steep; attractive coastal cycle path." ♦ € 25.00   2014*

⊞ **SANTAELLA** *2G3* (5km N Rural) *37.62263, -4.85950* **Camping La Campiña, La Guijarrosa-Santaella, 14547 Santaella (Córdoba) [957-31 53 03; fax 957-31 51 58; info@campinglacampina.com; www.campinglacampina.com]** Fr A4/E5 leave at km 441 onto A386 rd dir La Rambla to Santaella for 11km, turn L onto A379 for 5km & foll sp. Sm, mkd pitch, hdstg, pt sl, pt shd; wc; chem disp; baby facs; shwrs inc; EHU (10A) €4; gas; lndry; shop & 6km; rest, snacks; bar; BBQ; playgrnd; pool; TV; dogs €2; bus at gate to Córdoba; Eng spkn; adv bkg; rd noise; ccard acc; red long stay/LS; CKE/CCI. "Fine views; friendly, warm welcome; popular, family-run site; many pitches sm for lge o'fits; guided walks; poss clsd winter – phone to check." ♦ € 20.50   2009*

SANTANDER *1A4* (5km NE Coastal) *43.48916, -3.79361* **Camping Cabo Mayor, Avda. del Faro s/n, 39012 Santander (Cantabria) [tel/fax 942-39 15 42; info@cabomayor.com; www.cabomayor.com]** Sp thro town but not v clearly. On waterfront (turn R if arr by ferry). At lge junc do not foll quayside, take uphill rd (resort type prom) & foll sp for Faro de Cabo Mayor. 200m bef lighthouse on L. Lge, mkd pitch, terr, unshd; wc; chem disp (wc); baby facs; shwrs inc; EHU (10A) inc; gas; lndry; shop; rest, snacks; bar; playgrnd; pool high ssn; many beaches adj; TV; 10% statics; no dogs; phone; wifi; poss cr; Eng spkn; no ccards; CKE/CCI. "Med to lge pitches; site popular with lge youth groups high ssn; shwrs clsd 2230-0800; conv ferry; pitches priced by size, pleasant coastal walk to Sardinero beachs; gd NH; well organised & clean; gd facs; no hot water for washing up." ♦ 27 Mar-12 Oct. € 31.00   2015*

⊞ **SANTANDER** *1A4* (12km E Rural) *43.44777, -3.72861* **Camping Somo Parque, Ctra Somo-Suesa s/n, 39150 Suesa-Ribamontán al Mar (Cantabria) [tel/fax 942-51 03 09; somoparque@somoparque.com; www.somoparque.com]** Fr car ferry foll sp Bilbao. After approx 8km turn L over bdge sp Pontejos & Somo. After Pedreña climb hill at Somo Playa & take 1st R sp Suesa. Foll site sp. Med, pt shd; wc; chem disp; shwrs & bath; EHU (6A) €3 (poss rev pol); gas; shop; snacks; bar; playgrnd; beach 1.5km; 99% statics; site clsd 16 Dec-31 Jan; some Eng spkn; quiet; CKE/CCI. "Friendly owners; peaceful rural setting; sm ferry bet Somo & Santander; poss unkempt LS & poss clsd; NH only." € 23.00   2012*

SANTANDER *1A4* (6km W Coastal) *43.47678, -3.87303* **Camping Virgen del Mar, Ctra Santander-Liencres, San Román-Corbán s/n, 39000 Santander (Cantabria) [942-34 24 25; fax 942-32 24 90; cvirdmar@ceoecant.es; www.campingvirgendelmar.com]** Fr ferry turn R, then L up to football stadium, L again leads strt into San Román. If app fr W, take A67 (El Sardinero) then S20, leave at junc 2 dir Liencres, strt on. Site well sp. Lge, mkd pitch, pt shd; wc; chem disp; mv service pnt; shwrs; EHU (4-10A) €4; lndry; shop; supmkt 2km; rest, snacks; bar; playgrnd; pool; sand beach 300m; no dogs; bus 500m; adv bkg; quiet; red long stay; CKE/ CCI. "Basic facs; poss ltd hot water; some sm pitches not suitable lge o'fits; site adj cemetary; phone in LS to check site open; expensive LS." ♦ ltd. 1 Mar-10 Dec. € 28.00   2014*

⊞ **SANTANDER** *1A4* (2km NW Coastal) *43.46762, -3.89925* **Camping Costa San Juan, Avda San Juan de la Canal s/n, 39110 Soto de la Marina (Cantabria) [tel/fax 942-57 95 80 or 629-30 36 86; info@hotelcostasanjuan.com; www.hotelcostasanjuan.com]** Fr A67 take S20 twds Bilbao, exit junc 2 & foll sp Liencres. In 2km at Irish pub turn 1st R to Playa San Juan de la Canal, site behind hotel on L. Sm, pt shd; wc; shwrs inc; EHU (3-6A) €3.20 (poss rev pol); rest; bar; sand beach 400m; wifi; TV rm; 90% statics; no dogs; bus 600m; poss cr; quiet. "NH for ferry; muddy in wet; poss diff lge o'fits; gd coastal walks; 2 pin adaptor needed for elec conn." € 28.70   2014*

⊞ **SANTIAGO DE COMPOSTELA** *1A2* (3km NE Urban) *42.88972, -8.52444* **Camping As Cancelas, Rua do Xullo 25, 35, 15704 Santiago de Compostela (La Coruña) [981-58 02 66 or 981-58 04 76; fax 981-57 55 53; info@ campingascancelas.com; www.campingascancelas.com]** Exit AP9 junc 67 & foll sp Santiago. At rndabt with lge service stn turn L sp 'camping' & foll sp to site turning L at McDonalds. Site adj Guardia Civil barracks - poorly sp. Lge, mkd pitch, pt sl, shd; wc; chem disp; baby facs; shwrs inc; EHU (6A) €4.60; gas; lndry; shop, rest, snacks & bar in ssn; BBQ; playgrnd; pool & paddling pool high ssn; wifi; entmnt; TV; dogs; phone; bus 100m; poss v cr; Eng spkn; quiet; red LS; CKE/CCI. "Busy site-conv for pilgrims; rec arr early high ssn; some sm pitches poss diff c'vans & steep ascent; gd clean san facs but stretched when site busy; gd rest; bus 100m fr gate avoids steep 15 min walk back fr town (LS adequate car parks in town); poss interference with car/c'van electrics fr local transmitter - if problems report to site recep; LS recep in bar; arr in sq by Cathedral at 1100 for Thanksgiving service at 1200; helpful owner." ♦ € 34.00   2015*

SANTILLANA DEL MAR *1A4* (3km E Rural) *43.38222, -4.08305* **Camping Altamira, Barrio Las Quintas s/n, 39330 Queveda (Cantabria) [942-84 01 81; fax 942-26 01 55; altamiracamping@yahoo.es]** Clear sp to Santillana fr A67; site on R 3km bef vill. Med, mkd pitch, pt sl, terr, unshd; wc; shwrs; EHU (3A)- (5A) €2 (poss rev pol); gas; lndry; sm shop; rest; bar; pool; sand beach 8km; horseriding; TV rm; 30% statics; bus 100m; poss cr; Eng spkn; adv bkg ess high ssn; ccard acc in ssn; CKE/CCI. "Pleasant site; ltd facs LS; nr Altimira cave paintings; easy access Santander ferry on m'way; gd coastal walks; open w/end only Nov-Mar - rec phone ahead; excel." 10 Mar-7 Dec. € 21.40   2013*

⊞ **SANTILLANA DEL MAR** 1A4 (1km NW Rural) 43.39333, -4.11222 **Camping Santillana del Mar, Ctra de Comillas s/n, 39330 Santillana del Mar (Cantabria) [942-81 82 50; fax 942-84 01 83; www.campingsantillana.com]** Fr W exit A8 junc 230 Santillana-Comillas, then [oll sp Santillana & site on rd CA131. Fr E exit A67 junc 187 & foll sp Santillana. Turn R onto CA131, site on R up hill after vill. Lge, sl, terr, pt shd; wc; chem disp (wc); mv service pnt; baby facs; shwrs inc; EHU (6A) inc (poss rev pol); gas; lndry (inc dryer); shop; rest, snacks; bar; playgrnd; pool; paddling pool; beach 5km; tennis; bike hire; horseriding; golf 15km; entmnt; internet; car wash; cash machine; 20% statics; dogs; bus 300m; phone; poss cr; Eng spkn; some rd noise; CKE/CCI. "Useful site in beautiful historic vill; hot water only in shwrs; diff access to fresh water & to mv disposal point; narr, winding access rds, projecting trees & kerbs to some pitches - not rec lge o'fits or twin-axles; poss muddy LS & pitches rutted; poss travellers; gd views; lovely walk to town; poor facs (2014); NH." ♦ ltd. € 20.00 (CChq acc) 2014*

SANXENXO 1B2 (2km E Coastal) 42.39638, -8.77777 **Camping Airiños do Mar, Playa de Areas, O Grove, 36960 Sanxenxo (Pontevedra) [tel/fax 986-72 31 54]** Fr Pontevedra take P0308 W twd Sanxenxo & O Grove. Turn L at km post 65; site sp on S side of rd. Access rd needs care in negotiation. Sm, mkd pitch, pt shd; wc; shwrs inc; EHU (16A) €4.81; gas; lndry; shop; rest; bar; beach adj; bus adj; poss cr; Eng spkn; adv bkg; quiet. "Not suitable for m'vans over 2.5m high; c'vans over 6m may need help of staff at ent; bar & rest o'look beach; lovely views." 1 Jun-30 Sep. € 24.60 2011*

SANXENXO 1B2 (4km W Rural/Coastal) 42.39944, -8.85472 **Camping Suavila, Playa de Montalvo 76-77, 36970 Portonovo (Pontevedra) [tel/fax 986-72 37 60; suavila@terra.es; www.campingzodiac.com]** Fr Sanxenxo take P0308 W; at km 57.5 site sp on L. Med, mkd pitch, shd; wc; serviced pitches; baby facs; shwrs inc; EHU (6A) €3.75; gas; lndry; shop; rest, snacks; bar; BBQ; playgrnd; sand beach; TV rm; phone; adv bkg; ccard acc; red long stay; quiet; CKE/CCI. "Warm welcome; friendly owner; sm pitches in 1 pt of site." ♦ ltd. Holy Week-30 Sep. € 19.00 2011*

⊞ **SANXENXO** 1B2 (3km NW Coastal) 42.41777, -8.87555 **Camping Monte Cabo, Soutullo 174, 36990 Noalla (Pontevedra) [tel/fax 986-74 41 41; info@montecabo.com; www.montecabo.com]** Fr AP9 exit junc 119 onto upgraded VRG4.1 dir Sanxenxo. Ignore sp for Sanxenxo until rndabt sp A Toxa/La Toja, where turn L onto P308. Cont to Fontenla supmkt on R - minor rd to site just bef supmkt. Rd P308 fr AP9 junc 129 best avoided. Sm, mkd pitch, terr, pt shd; wc; chem disp; mv service pnt; shwrs inc; EHU €3.90; lndry (inc dryer); shop & 500m; rest, snacks; bar; playgrnd; sand beach 250m; TV; 10% statics; phone; bus 600m; poss cr; Eng spkn; adv bkg; quiet; ccard acc; red long stay/LS; CKE/CCI. "Peaceful, friendly site set above sm beach (access via steep path) with views; sm pitches; beautiful coastline & interesting historical sites; vg." € 23.00 2011*

SANXENXO 1B2 (3km NW Coastal) 42.39254, -8.84517 **Camping Playa Paxariñas, Ctra C550, Km 2.3 Lanzada-Portonovo, 36960 Sanxenxo (Pontevedra) [986-72 30 55; fax 986-72 13 56; info@campingpaxarinas.com; www.campingpaxarinas.com]** Fr Pontevedra W on P0308 coast rd; 3km after Sanxenxo. Site thro hotel on L at bend. Site poorly sp. Fr AP9 fr N exit junc 119 onto VRG41 & exit for Sanxenxo. Turn R at 3rd rndabt for Portonovo to site in dir O Grove. Do not turn L to port area on ent Portonovo. Lge, mkd pitch, pt sl, terr, shd; wc; chem disp; baby facs; shwrs inc; EHU (5A) €4.75; gas; lndry (inc dryer); shop; snacks; bar; BBQ; playgrnd; sand beach adj; wifi; TV; 25% statics; dogs; phone; bus adj; Eng spkn; adv bkg; quiet; ccard acc; red long stay/CKE/CCI. "Site in gd position; secluded beaches; views over estuary; take care high kerbs on pitches; excel san facs - ltd facs LS & poss clsd; lovely unspoilt site; plenty of shd." ♦ 17 Mar-15 Oct. € 41.60 2014*

SARRIA 1B2 (2km E Rural) 42.77625, -7.39552 **Camping Vila de Sarria, Ctra. De Pintín, Km 1 Sarria 27600 [982 53 54 67; info@campingviladesarria.com; www.campingviladesarria.com]** Leave Sarria on LU5602 twds Pintin. Site on L in 1km. Med, pt sl, pt shd; wc; chem disp; shwrs inc; EHU; lndry; shop 2km; rest; snacks; bar; wifi; dogs; bus/train 2km; twin axles; poss cr; Eng spkn; adv bkg; boisy, busy w/ends; ccard acc. "Quiet site on Camino de Santiago Rte; excel rest; v pleasant, welcoming staff; vg." ♦ Easter-30 Sep. € 22.50 2015*

SAVINAN see Calatayud 3C1

SAX 4F2 (5km NW Rural) **Camping Gwen & Michael, Colonia de Santa Eulalia 1, 03630 Sax (Alicante) [965-47 44 19 or 01202 291587 (UK)]** Exit A31 at junc 48 & foll sp for Santa Eulalia, site on R just bef vill sq. Rec phone prior to arr. Sm, hdg pitch, hdstg, unshd; wc; chem disp; fam bthrm; shwrs inc; EHU (3A) €1; lndry; shops 6km; bar 100m; no statics; dogs; quiet. "Vg CL-type site; friendly British owners; beautiful area; gd NH & touring base." 15 Mar-30 Nov. € 14.00 2009*

SEGOVIA 1C4 (3km SE Urban) 40.93138, -4.09250 **Camping El Acueducto, Ctra de la Granja, 40004 Segovia [tel/fax 921-42 50 00; informacion@campingacueducto.com; www.campingacueducto.com]** Turn off Segovia by-pass N110/SG20 at La Granja exit, but head twd Segovia on DL601. Site in approx 500m off dual c'way just bef Restaurante Lago. Lge, mkd pitch, pt sl, pt shd; wc; chem disp; mv service pnt; shwrs inc; EHU (6-10A) €5; gas; lndry; sm shop; mkt 1km; rest adj; bar; BBQ; playgrnd; pool & paddling pool high ssn; bike hire; wifi; some statics; dogs; phone; bus 150m; poss cr; m'way noise; CKE/CCI. "Excel; helpful staff; lovely views; clean facs; gates locked 0000-0800; gd bus service; some pitches sm & diff for lge o'fits; city a 'must' to visit." ♦ ltd. 1 Apr-30 Sep. € 29.60 2014*

SENA DE LUNA 1A3 (1km S Rural) 42.92181, -5.96153 **Camping Río Luna, Ctra de Abelgas s/n, 24145 Sena de Luna (León) [987-59 77 14; lunacamp@telefonica.net; www.campingrioluna.com]** S fr Oviedo on AP66, at junc 93 turn W onto CL626 to Sena de Luna in approx 5km. Site on L, sp. Med, pt shd; htd wc; chem disp; mv service pnt; shwrs inc; EHU (5A) €3.50; lndry; snacks; bar; BBQ; rv sw adj; internet; TV; dogs; phone; adv bkg; quiet; ccard acc. "Vg, scenic site; walking, climbing; cent for wild boar & wolves." ♦ Easter & 1 May-30 Sep. € 15.00 2010*

You can now fill in site reports online

SENEGUE see Sabiñánigo *3B2*

⊞ **SEO DE URGEL** *3B3* (8km N Rural) *42.42777, 1.46333*
**Camping Frontera, Ctra de Andorra, Km 8, 25799 La F
arga de Moles (Lleida) [973-35 14 27; fax 973-35 33 40;
info@fronterapark.com; www.fronterapark.com]**
Sp on N145 about 300m fr Spanish Customs sheds. Access
poss diff. Suggest app fr N - turn in front Customs sheds if
coming fr S. Lge, mkd pitch, hdstg, pt sl, pt shd; htd wc; chem
disp; mv service pnt; baby facs; shwrs inc; EHU (10A) €5.40;
gas; lndry (inc dryer); hypmkt 2km; rest, snacks; bar; playgrnd;
pool; paddling pool; internet; TV rm; 90% statics; dogs €3.60;
phone; car wash; poss cr; adv bkg; noisy; CKE/CCI. "Ideal
for shopping in Andorra; winter skiing; beautiful situation
but poss dusty; sm pitches; helpful owners." ♦ € 23.00
(CChq acc)   2011*

⊞ **SEO DE URGEL** *3B3* (3km SW Urban) *42.34777,
1.43055* **Camping Gran Sol, Ctra N260, Km 230, 25711
Montferrer (Lleida) [973-35 13 32; fax 973-35 55 40;
info@campinggransol.com; www.campinggransol.com]**
S fr Seo de Urgel on N260/C1313 twds Lerida/Lleida. Site
approx 3km on L fr town. Med, pt shd; wc; chem disp (wc);
shwrs inc; EHU (6A) €5.85; gas; lndry; shop; rest; playgrnd;
pool; some statics; dogs free; bus 100m; some Eng spkn; adv
bkg; some rd noise; CKE/CCI. "Gd site & facs (poss stretched if
full); conv for Andorra; beautiful vills & mountain scenery; in LS
phone to check site open; gd NH." ♦ € 21.60   2010*

SEO DE URGEL *3B3* (8.5km NW Rural) *42.37388, 1.35777*
**Camping Castellbò- Buchaca, Ctra Lerida-Puigcerdà 127,
25712 Castellbò (Lleida) [973-35 21 55]** Leave Seo de Urgel
on N260/1313 twd Lerida. In approx 3km turn N sp Castellbò.
Thro vill & site on L, well sp. Steep, narr, winding rd, partly
unfenced - not suitable car+c'van o'fits or lge m'vans. Sm, mkd
pitch, pt sl, pt shd; wc; chem disp (wc); shwrs inc; EHU (5A)
€5.85; lndry; shop; snacks; playgrnd; pool; dogs €3.60; phone;
poss cr; adv bkg; quiet; "CL-type site in beautiful surroundings;
friendly recep; basic fac's." 1 May-30 Sep. € 30.00   2013*

SEVILLA see Dos Hermanas *2G3*

SITGES *3C3* (2km SW Urban/Coastal) *41.23351, 1.78111*
**Camping Bungalow Park El Garrofer, Ctra C246A, Km 39,
08870 Sitges (Barcelona) [93 894 17 80; fax 93 811 06 23;
info@garroferpark.com; www.garroferpark.com]**
Exit 26 on the C-32 dir St. Pere de Ribes, at 1st rndabt take
1st exit, at 2nd rndabt take 2nd exit, foll rd C-31 to campsite.
V lge, hdg/mkd pitch, hdstg, pt shd; htd wc; chem disp; mv
service pnt; baby facs; shwrs inc; serviced pitches; EHU (5-
10A) €4.10 (poss rev pol); gas; lndry; shop; rest, snacks; bar;
playgrnd; pool; shgl beach 900m; windsurfing; tennis 800m;
horseriding; bike hire; games area; games rm; car wash; wifi;
entmnt; TV; 80% statics; dogs €2.65; phone; bus adj (to
Barcelona); recep open 0800-2100; site clsd 19 Dec-27 Jan to
tourers; poss cr; Eng spkn; adv bkg; ccard acc; red snr citizen/
LS; CKE/CCI. "Great location, conv Barcelona, bus adj; sep area
for m'vans; pleasant staff; gd level site; quiet; gd old & new
facs." ♦ 28 Feb-14 Dec. € 49.60   2014*

SITGES *3C3* (1.5km W Urban/Coastal) *41.2328, 1.78511*
**Camping Sitges, Ctra Comarcal 246, Km 38, 08870
Sitges (Barcelona) [938-94 10 80; fax 938-94 98 52;
info@campingsitges.com; www.campingsitges.com]**
Fr AP7/E15 exit junc 28 or 29 dir Sitges. Site on R after El
Garrofer, sp. If app fr Sitges go round rndabt 1 more exit
than sp, & immed take slip rd - avoids a L turn. Lge, mkd
pitch, hdstg, pt shd; htd wc; chem disp; baby facs; shwrs
inc; EHU (4A) €4.80; gas; lndry; shop; rest, snacks; bar; BBQ;
playgrnd; pool high ssn; paddling pool; sand beach 800m; wifi;
30% statics; dogs; phone; bus 300m; train 1.5km; poss cr;
Eng spkn; quiet but some rlwy noise; ccard acc; red long stay/
LS. "Well-maintained, clean site; friendly staff; excel, clean san
facs; some pitches v sm; m'vans with trailers not acc; gd pool,
rest & shop; rec arr early as v popular & busy, espec w/ends; gd
security." ♦ 1 Mar-20 Oct. € 26.50   2010*

SOPELANA see Bilbao *1A4*

> ## "I need an on-site restaurant"
> We do our best to make sure site
> information is correct, but it is always best
> to check any must-have facilities are still
> available or will be open during your visit.

SORIA *3C1* (2km SW Rural) *41.74588, -2.48456* **Camping
Fuente de la Teja, Ctra Madrid-Soria, Km 223, 42004 Soria
[tel/fax 975-22 29 67; camping@fuentedelateja.com;
www.fuentedelateja.com]** Fr N on N111 (Soria by-pass)
2km S of junc with N122 (500m S of Km 223) take exit for
Quintana Redondo, site sp. Fr Soria on NIII dir Madrid sp just
past km 223. Turn R into site app rd. Fr S on N111 stake exit
for Quintana Redondo & foll site sp. Med, mkd pitch, pt sl, pt
shd; wc; chem disp; baby facs; shwrs inc; EHU (6A) €3 (poss
no earth); gas; lndry; hypmkt 3km; rest, snacks; bar; playgrnd;
pool high ssn; TV rm; wifi; few statics; dogs; phone; poss cr;
adv bkg; some rd noise; ccard acc; CKE/CCI. "Vg site; excel, gd
for NH; vg san facs; interesting town; phone ahead to check
site poss open bet Oct & Easter; easy access to site; pitches
around 100sqm, suits o'fits upto 10m; quiet; friendly staff."
♦ ltd. 1 Mar-31 Oct. € 30.00   2014*

SOTO DEL REAL see Manzanares el Real *1D4*

⊞ **TABERNAS** *4G1* (8km E Rural) **Camping Oro Verde,
Piezas de Algarra s/n, 04200 Tabernas (Almería) [687-
62 99 96]** Fr N340A turn S onto ALP112 sp Turrillas. Turn R in
100m into narr tarmac lane bet villas, site on L in 600m, not
well sp. Sm, pt shd, wc; chem disp; shwrs inc; EHU (6-10A)
inc (poss long lead req); gas; lndry; shop 1km; rest, bar nrby in
hotel; BBQ; pool; sand beach 40km; dogs; adv bkg; quiet; red
long stay; CKE/CCI. "In sm olive grove; beautiful views; pitches
muddy in wet; basic san facs; friendly British owners; 'Mini-
Hollywood' 7km where many Westerns filmed; conv Sorbas &
Guadix caves; excel." ♦ € 16.00   2011*

TALARN see Tremp *3B2*

TAMARIT see Tarragona *3C3*

TAPIA DE CASARIEGO *1A3* (2km SW Coastal) *43.56394, -6.95247* **Camping Playa de Tapia, La Reburdia, 33740 Tapia de Casariego (Asturias) [tel/fax 985-47 27 21]** Fr Ribadeo pass thro vill of Serentes on N634 past 1st camping sp. Site on L at 546km post, foll sp to site. Med, hdg/mkd pitch, pt sl, pt shd; wc; chem disp; mv service pnt; child/baby facs; shwrs inc; EHU (16A) €4.06; gas; lndry (inc dryer); shop; rest; bar; high ssn only; sand beach 1m; wifi; dogs; bus 800m; phone; Eng spkn; adv bkg; quiet; CKE/CCI. "Gd access; busy, well-maintained, friendly site; o'looking coast & harbour; poss ltd hot water; walking dist to delightful town."
♦ Holy Week & 1 Jun-15 Sep. € 23.00   2015*

⊞ **TAPIA DE CASARIEGO** *1A3* (2km W Rural) *43.54870, -6.97436* **Camping El Carbayin, La Penela, 33740 [tel/fax 985-62 37 09; www.campingelcarbayin.com]** Take N634/E70 (old coast rd parallel to A8-E70) to Serantes, foll sp to site bet N634 and sea. Sm, mkd pitch, pt sl, pt shd; wc; chem disp; baby facs; shwrs inc; EHU (3A) €3; lndry; shop; rest; bar; playgrnd; sand beach 1km; fishing; watersports; some statics; bus 400m; phone; adv bkg; quiet; ccard acc; CKE/CCI. "Gd for coastal walks & trips to mountains; gd; new san facs."
♦ € 19.50   2013*

⊞ **TARIFA** *2H3* (11km W Coastal) *36.07027, -5.69305* **Camping El Jardín de las Dunas, Ctra N340, Km 74, 11380 Punta Paloma (Cádiz) [956-68 91 01; fax 956-69 91 06; info@lasdunascamping.com; www.campingjdunas.com]** W on N340 fr Tarifa, L at sp Punta Paloma. Turn L 300m after Camping Paloma, site in 500m. Lge, hdg pitch, pt shd; wc; chem disp; serviced pitches; baby facs; shwrs inc; EHU (6A) €5.16; lndry; shop; rest, snacks; bar; playgrnd; beach 50m; entmnt; TV rm; no dogs; phone; noisy; ccard acc; red LS. "Poss strong winds; unsuitable lge o'fits due tight turns & trees; modern facs; poss muddy when wet." ♦ € 35.00   2014*

⊞ **TARIFA** *2H3* (3km NW Coastal) *36.04277, -5.62972* **Camping Rió Jara, Ctra N340, km 81, 11380 Tarifa (Andalucia) [tel/fax 956-68 05 70; campingriojara@terra.com]** Site on S of N340 Cádiz-Algeciras rd at km post 81.2; 3km after Tarifa; clearly visible & sp. Med, mkd pitch, pt shd; wc (some cont); chem disp; mv service pnt; shwrs inc; EHU (10A) €4; gas; lndry (inc dryer); shop; rest, snacks; bar; playgrnd; sand beach 200m; fishing; wifi; dogs €3.50; poss cr; adv bkg; rd noise; ccard acc; red LS; CKE/CCI. "Gd, clean, well-kept site; friendly recep; long, narr pitches diff for awnings; daily trips to N Africa; gd windsurfing nrby; poss strong winds; mosquitoes in summer." ♦ € 45.00   2014*

TARIFA *2H3* (6km NW Coastal) *36.05468, -5.64977* **Camping Tarifa, N340, Km 78.87, Los Lances, 11380 Tarifa (Cádiz) [tel/fax 956-68 47 78; info@campingtarifa.es; www.campingtarifa.es]** Site on R of Cádiz-Málaga rd N340. Med, mkd pitch, hdstg, shd; wc; chem disp; mv service pnt; serviced pitches; baby facs; shwrs inc; EHU (5A) €3.50; gas; lndry; shop; rest, snacks; bar; playgrnd; pool; sand beach adj; wifi; no dogs; phone; car wash; Eng spkn; adv bkg; quiet; red long stay & LS; ccard acc. "Vg; ideal for windsurfing; immed access to beach; lovely site with beautiful pool; v secure - fenced & locked at night; some pitches sm & poss diff access due bends, trees & kerbs; conv ferry to Morocco; poss strong winds." ♦ 1 Mar-31 Oct. € 33.00 (CChq acc)   2009*

⊞ **TARIFA** *2H3* (10km NW Coastal) *36.06908, 5.68036* **Camping Valdevaqueros, Ctra N340 km 75,5 11380 Tarifa [34 956 684 174; fax 34 956 681 898; info@campingvaldevaqueros.com; www.campingvaldevaqueros.com]** Campsite is sp 9km fr Tarifa on the N340 twds Cadiz. Lge, pt sl, pt shd; wc; chem disp; mv service pnt; shwrs; EHU (6A); shop; rest; bar; playgrnd; pool; paddling pool; sandy beach 1km; games area; bike hire; entmnt; wifi; TV; 50% statics; dogs; phone; Eng spkn; adv bkg. "Excel site; watersports nrby." € 43.00   2014*

⊞ **TARIFA** *2H3* (11km NW Coastal) *36.07621, -5.69336* **Camping Paloma, Ctra Cádiz-Málaga, Km 74, Punta Paloma, 11380 Tarifa (Cádiz) [956-68 42 03; fax 956-68 18 80; campingpaloma@yahoo.es; www.campingpaloma.com]** Fr Tarifa on N340, site on L at 74km stone sp Punta Paloma, site on R. Lge, mkd pitch, hdstg, pt sl, terr, pt shd; wc (some cont); chem disp; mv service pnt; shwrs inc; EHU (6A) €4.28; gas; lndry; shop; rest, snacks; bar; playgrnd; pool high ssn; sand beach 1km; waterspsorts; windsurfing; horseriding; bike hire; 20% statics; bus 200m; poss cr; Eng spkn; no adv bkg; quiet; ccard acc; red long stay/LS; CKE/CCI. "Well-run site; vg facs; peaceful away fr busy rds; lge o'fits poss diff due low trees; trips to N Africa & whale-watching; mountain views." ♦ ltd. € 21.50   2009*

TARRAGONA *3C3* (4km NE Coastal) *41.13082, 1.30345* **Camping Las Salinas, Ctra N340, Km 1168, Playa Larga, 43007 Tarragona [977-20 76 28]** Access via N340 bet km 1167 & 1168. Med, shd; wc; shwrs; EHU €3.74; gas; lndry; shop; snacks; bar; beach adj; some statics; bus 200m; poss cr; rlwy noise. Holy Week & 15 May-30 Sep. € 29.00   2011*

TARRAGONA *3C3* (5km NE Coastal) *41.13019, 1.31170* **Camping Las Palmeras, N340, Km 1168, 43080 Tarragona [977-20 80 81; fax 977-20 78 17; laspalmeras@laspalmeras.com; www.laspalmeras.com]** Exit AP7 at junc 32 (sp Altafulla). After about 5km on N340 twd Tarragona take sp L turn at crest of hill. Site sp. V lge, mkd pitch, pt shd; wc; chem disp; baby facs; shwrs inc; EHU (6A) inc; gas; lndry (inc dryer); shop; rest, snacks; bar; playgrnd; pool; paddling pool; sand beach adj; naturist beach 1km; tennis; games area; games rm; wifi; entmnt; some statics; dogs €5; phone; poss cr; rlwy noise; ccard acc; red long stay/snr citizens/LS; CKE/CCI. "Gd beach; ideal for families; poss mosquito prob; many sporting facs; gd, clean san facs; friendly, helpful staff; supmkt 5km; excel site." ♦ 2 Apr-12 Oct. € 45.00 (CChq acc)   2012*

TARRAGONA *3C3* (7km NE Coastal) *41.12887, 1.34415* **Camping Torre de la Mora, Ctra N340, Km 1171, 43008 Tarragona-Tamarit [977-65 02 77; fax 977-65 28 58; info@torredelamora.com; www.torredelamora.com]** Fr AP7 exit junc 32 (sp Altafulla), at rndabt take La Mora rd. Then foll site sp. After approx 1km turn R, L at T-junc, site on R. Lge, hdstg, terr, pt shd; wc; chem disp; mv service pnt; baby facs; shwrs inc; EHU (6A) €5.20; gas; lndry; shop & 1km; rest, snacks; bar; playgrnd; pool; sand beach adj; tennis; sports club adj; golf 2km; entmnt; internet; 50% statics; dogs €3.65; bus 200m; Eng spkn; adv bkg; quiet away fr rd & rlwy; ccard acc; red long stay; CKE/CCI. "Improved, clean site set in attractive bay with fine beach; excel pool; conv Tarragona & Port Aventura; sports club adj; various pitch sizes, some v sm." ♦ 18 Mar-31 Oct.   2013*

SPAIN

TARRAGONA *3C3* (600m NE Urban Coastal) *40.88707, 0.80630*
Camping Nautic, Calle Libertat s/n, 43860 L'Ametlla de Mar Tarragona [34 977 493 031; fax 34 977 456 110; info@campingnautic.com; www.campingnautic.com]
Fr N340 exit at km 1113 sp L'Amettla de Mar (or A7 exit 39). Over rlwy bdge, foll rd to L. Turn R after park and TO on R, foll signs to campsite. Lge, hdstg, terr, pt shd; wc; chem disp; mv service pnt; baby facs; shwrs; EHU; lndry (inc dryer); shop; rest; snacks; bar; playgrnd; pool; paddling pool; beach; games area; wifi; TV; 25% statics; dogs; phone; bus 500m; train 700m; Eng spkn; adv bkg; no ccard acc; CCI. "Vg site; tennis court; 5 mins to attractive town with rest & sm supermkts; lge Mercadona outsite town; site on different levels." ♦ 15 Mar-15 Oct. € 50.00   2014*

TAULL see Pont de Suert *3B2*

TIEMBLO, EL *1D4* (8km W Rural) *40.40700, -4.57400* **Camping Valle de Iruelas, Las Cruceras, 05110 Barraco (Ávila) [918-62 50 59; fax 918-62 53 95; iruelas@valledeiruelas.com; www.valledeiruelas.com]** Fr N403 turn off at sp Reserva Natural Valle de Iruelas. After x-ing dam foll sp Las Cruceras & camping. In 5km foll sp La Rinconada, site in 1km. Med, hdg/mkd pitch, terr, shd; wc; chem disp; baby facs; shwrs inc; EHU €5; lndry; supmkt; rest; bar; playgrnd; pool; paddling pool; canoeing; horseriding; bird hide; quiet; CKE/CCI. "Pleasant, woodland site with wildlife." ♦ Easter-31 Aug. € 26.00   2009*

⊞ **TOLEDO** *1D4* (2km W Rural) *39.86530, -4.04714*
Camping El Greco, Ctra Pueblo Montalban, Km.0.7, 45004 Toledo [tel/fax 925-22 00 90; campingelgreco@telefonica.net; www.campingelgreco.es] Site on CM4000 fr Toledo dir La Puebla de Montalbán & Talavera. When app, avoid town cent, keep to N outside of old town & watch for camping sp. Or use outer ring rd. Diff to find. Med, hdg/mkd pitch, hdstg, pt sl, pt shd; htd wc; chem disp; mv service pnt; shwrs inc; EHU (6A) €4.30 (poss rev pol); gas; lndry; shop; bar; BBQ; playgrnd; pool; paddling pool; games area; dogs; bus to town; train to Madrid fr town; phone; wifi; Eng spkn; ccard acc; CKE/CCI. "Clean, tidy, well-maintained; all pitches on gravel; easy parking on o'skts - adj Puerta de San Martín rec - or bus; some pitches poss tight; san facs clean; lovely, scenic situation; excel rest; friendly, helpful owners; vg; dusty." € 42.00   2014*

TORDESILLAS *1C3* (2.2km SSW Urban) *41.49584, -5.00494*
Kawan Village El Astral, Camino de Pollos 8, 47100 Tordesillas (Valladolid) [tel/fax 983-77 09 53; info@campingelastral.es; www.campingelastral.es]
Fr NE on A62/E80 thro town turn L at rndabt over rv & immed after bdge turn R dir Salamanca & almost immed R again into narr gravel track (bef Parador) & foll rd to site; foll camping sp & Parador. Poorly sp. Fr A6 exit sp Tordesillas & take A62. Cross bdge out of town & foll site sp. Med, hdg/mkd pitch, hdstg, pt shd; htd wc; chem disp; mv service pnt; baby facs; shwrs inc; EHU (5A-10A) €3.60-5 (rev pol); gas; lndry (inc dryer); shop; supmkt in town; rest, snacks; bar; playgrnd; pool in ssn; rv fishing; tennis; bike hire; wifi; TV rm; 10% statics; dogs €2.35; phone; site open w/end Mar & Oct; Eng spkn; quiet, but some traff noise; ccard acc; CKE/CCI. "V helpful owners & staff; easy walk to interesting town; pleasant site by rv; vg, modern, clean san facs & excel facs; vg rest; popular NH; excel site in every way, facs superb; various size pitches; worth a visit." ♦ 1 Mar-31 Oct. € 31.00 (CChq acc) SBS - E03   2014*

TORLA *3B2* (2km N Rural) *42.63948, -0.10948* **Camping Ordesa, Ctra de Ordesa s/n, 22376 Torla (Huesca) [974-11 77 21; fax 974-48 63 47; infocamping@campingordesa.es; www.campingordesa.es]** Fr Ainsa on N260 twd Torla. Pass Torla turn R onto A135 (Valle de Ordesa twd National Park). Site 2km N of Torla, adj Hotel Ordesa. Med, pt shd; wc; chem disp; serviced pitch; baby facs; shwrs; EHU (6A) €5.50; gas 2km; lndry; shop 2km; rest high ssn; bar; playgrnd; pool; tennis; wifi (in adj hotel); some statics (sep area); dogs €3; phone; bus 1km; poss cr; Eng spkn; adv bkg (ess Jul/Aug); quiet; red LS; ccard acc; CKE/CCI. "V scenic; recep in adj Hotel Ordesa; excel rest; helpful staff; facs poss stretched w/ end; long, narr pitches & lge trees on access rd poss diff lge o'fits; ltd facs LS; no access to National Park by car Jul/Aug, shuttlebus fr Torla." 28 Mar-30 Sep. € 31.70   2013*

TORLA *3B2* (8km N Rural) *42.67721, -0.12337* **Camping Valle de Bujaruelo, 22376 Torla (Huesca) [974-48 63 48; info@camping valledebujaruelo.com; www.campingvalledebujaruelo.com]** N fr Torla on A135, turn L at El Puente de los Navarros onto unmade rd for 3.8km. Unsuitable lge m'vans & c'vans. Med, mkd pitch, terr, pt shd; htd wc; chem disp; mv service pnt; shwrs inc; EHU (6A) €4.50; gas; lndry; shop (high ssn) & 8km; rest, snacks; bar; BBQ; some statics; dogs €2; poss cr; Eng spkn; adv bkg; quiet. "In beautiful, peaceful valley in Ordesa National Park; superb views & walking." ♦ Easter-15 Oct. € 19.00   2010*

TORLA *3B2* (1km NE Rural) *42.63181, -0.10685* **Camping Rió Ara, Ctra Ordesa s/n, 22376 Torla (Huesca) [tel/fax 974-48 62 48; campingrioara@ordesa.net; www.campingrioara.com]** Leave N260/A135 on bend approx 2km N of Broto sp Torla & Ordesa National Park. Drive thro Torla; as leaving vill turn R sp Rió Ara. Steep, narr rd down to & across narr bdge (worth it). Sm, pt sl, pt shd; wc; chem disp; mv service pnt; baby facs; shwrs inc; EHU (6A) €4.25; lndry; shop; café; rest 500m; bar; BBQ; wifi; TV; dogs; bus 500m; adv bkg; CKE/CCI. "Attractive, well-kept, family-run site; mainly tents; conv for Torla; bus to Ordesa National Park (high ssn); not rec for lge o'fits due to steep app; gd walking & birdwatching; excel; fantastic views; wonderful area." ♦ 1 Apr-30 Sep. € 24.00   2015*

⊞ **TORRE DEL MAR** *2H4* (1km SW Coastal) *36.7342, -4.1003*
Camping Torre del Mar, Paseo Maritimo s/n, 29740 Torre del Mar (Málaga) [952-54 02 24; fax 952-54 04 31; info@campingtorredelmar.com or campingtorredelmar@hotmail.com; www.campingtorredelmar.com]
Fr N340 coast rd, at rndabt at W end of town with 'correos' on corner turn twds sea sp Faro, Torre del Mar. At rndabt with lighthouse adj turn R, then 2nd R, site adj big hotel, ent bet lge stone pillars (no name sp). Lge, hdg/mkd pitch, hdstg, shd; wc; chem disp; mv service pnt; serviced pitches; shwrs inc; EHU (15A) €4.40 (long lead req); gas; lndry; shop on site & 500m; rest, snacks, bar nrby in ssn; playgrnd; pool & paddling pool; sandy/shgl beach 50m; tennis; sat TV; 39% statics; phone; poss cr all year; quiet but noise fr adj football pitch; red LS/long stay; CKE/CCI. "Tidy, clean, friendly, well-run site; some sm pitches; site rds tight; gd, clean san facs; popular LS; constant hot water." ♦ € 43.60   2014*

SPAIN

⊞ **TORRE DEL MAR** *2H4* (1km W Coastal) *36.72976, -4.10285*
Camping Laguna Playa, Prolongación Paseo Maritimo
s/n, 29740 Torre del Mar (Málaga) [952-54 06 31; fax 952-
54 04 84; info@lagunaplaya.com; www.lagunaplaya.com]
Fr N340 coast rd, at rndabt at W end of town with 'correos'
on corner turn twds sea sp Faro, Torre del Mar. At rndabt with
lighthouse adj turn R, then 2nd R, site sp in 400m. Med, pt
shd; wc; chem disp; mv service pnt; shwrs inc; EHU (5-10A)
€3.70; gas; lndry; shop; rest, snacks; bar; playgrnd; pool; sand
beach 1km; 80% statics; dogs; poss cr; Eng spkn; adv bkg;
quiet; red LS. "Popular LS; sm pitches; excel, clean san facs; gd
location, easy walk to town; NH only." € 29.00   2013*

⊞ **TORRE DEL MAR** *2H4* (2km W Coastal) *36.72660, -4.11330*
Camping Naturista Almanat (Naturist), Ctra de la Torre Alta,
Km 269, 29749 Almayate (Málaga) [952-55 64 62; fax 952-
55 62 71; info@almanat.de; www.almanat.de]
Exit E15/N340 junc 274 sp Vélez Málaga for Torre del Mar.
Exit Torre del Mar on coast rd sp Málaga. In 2km bef lge black
bull on R on hill & bef water tower turn L at sp. If rd not clear
cont to next turning point & return in dir Torre del Mar & turn
R to site at km 269. Site well sp. Lge, hdg/mkd pitch, hdstg
(gravel), pt shd; htd wc; chem disp; mv service pnt (on request);
sauna; shwrs inc; EHU (10-16A) €3.90; gas; lndry; shop; rest;
bar; BBQ; playgrnd; pool; jacuzzi; sand/shgl beach adj; tennis;
wifi; entmnt; cinema; games area; gym; golf 10km; some
statics; dogs €2.70; phone; bus 500m; poss cr; Eng spkn; adv
bkg; quiet but poss noise fr birdscarer; ccard acc; red long stay/
LS/snr citizens up to 50%; INF card. "Superb facs; popular &
highly rec; reasonable dist Seville, Granada, Córdoba; easy
walk/cycle to town; emergency exit poss kept locked; sm
pitches & narr site rds diff for lge o'fits." ♦ € 21.00   2009*

TORRE DEL MAR *2H4* (3km W Coastal) *36.72526, -4.13532*
Camping Almayate Costa, Ctra N340, Km 267, 29749
Almayate Bajo (Málaga) [952-55 62 89; fax 952-55 63 10;
almayatecosta@campings.net; www.campings.net/
almayatecosta] E fr Málaga on N340/E15 coast rd. Exit junc
258 dir Almería, site on R 3km bef Torre del Mar. Easy access.
Lge, mkd pitch, hdstg, shd; wc; chem disp; mv service pnt;
shwrs inc; EHU (10A) €5.10; gas; lndry; supmkt; bar; BBQ;
playgrnd; pool; sand beach 50m; games rm; golf 7km; no
dogs; car wash; phone; Eng spkn; adv bkg; quiet but some rd
noise; ccard acc; red long stay/LS; CKE/CCI. "Helpful manager;
pitches nr beach tight for lge o'fits & access rds poss diff; vg
resort; excel." ♦ 15 Mar-30 Sep. € 43.50   2013*

⊞ **TORREVIEJA** *4F2* (7km SW Rural) *37.97500, -0.75111*
Camping Florantilles, Ctra San Miguel de Salinas-
Torrevieja, 03193 San Miguel de Salinas (Alicante) [965-
72 04 56; fax 966-72 32 50; camping@campingflorantilles.
com; www.campingflorantilles.com] Exit AP7 junc 758
onto CV95, sp Orihuela, Torrevieja Sud. Turn R at rndabt &
after 300m turn R again, site immed on L. Or if travelling on
N332 S past Alicante airport twd Torrevieja. Leave Torrevieja
by-pass sp Torrevieja, San Miguel. Turn R onto CV95 & foll for
3km thro urbanisation 'Los Balcones', then cont for 500m,
under by-pass, round rndabt & up hill, site sp on R. Lge, hdg/
mkd, hdstg, terr, pt shd; wc; chem disp; mv service pnt; shwrs
inc; EHU (10A) inc; gas; lndry; supmkt; snacks; bar; BBQ;
playgrnd; pool & paddling pool (high ssn); 3 golf courses nrby;
sand beach 5km; horseriding 10km; fitness studio/keep fit
classes; workshops: calligraphy, card making, drawing/painting,
reiki, sound therapy etc; basic Spanish classes; walking club;
games/TV rm; 20% statics; no dogs; no o'fits over 10m; recep
clsd 1330-1630; adv bkg; rd noise; ccard acc; red LS; CKE/
CCI. "Popular, British owned site; friendly staff; many long-
stay visitors & all year c'vans; suitable mature couples; own
transport ess; gd cyling, both flat & hilly; conv hot spa baths at
Fortuna & salt lakes." ♦ € 30.00 SBS - E11   2011*

TORROELLA DE MONTGRI *3B3* (6km SE Coastal) *42.01111,
3.18833* Camping El Delfin Verde, Ctra Torroella de
Montgrí-Palafrugell, Km 4, 17257 Torroella de Montgrí
(Gerona) [972-75 84 54; fax 972-76 00 70;
info@eldelfinverde.com; www.eldelfinverde.com]
Fr N leave A7 at junc 5 dir L'Escala. At Viladamat turn R onto
C31 sp La Bisbal. After a few km turn L twd Torroella de
Montgrí. At rndabt foll sp for Pals (also sp El Delfin Verde). At
the flags turn L sp Els Mas Pinell. Foll site sp for 5km. V lge,
mkd pitch, pt sl, pt shd; wc; chem disp; mv service pnt; baby
facs; shwrs inc; EHU (6A) inc; lndry (inc dryer); supmkt; rests;
snacks; 3 bars; BBQ; playgrnd; pool; sand beach adj; fishing;
tennis; horseriding 4km; bike hire; windsurfing; sportsgrnd;
hairdresser; money exchange; games rm; entmnt; disco; wifi;
TV; 40% statics (sep area); winter storage; no dogs 18/7-21/8,
at LS €4; no o'fits over 8m high ssn; poss cr; quiet; ccard acc;
red LS; CKE/CCI. "Superb, gd value site; excel pool; wide
range of facs; clean, modern san facs; all water de-salinated fr
fresh water production plant; bottled water rec for drinking &
cooking; mkt Mon." ♦ 17 May-20 Sep. € 58.00   2011*

See advertisement above

SPAIN

⊞ **TORROX COSTA** *2H4* (2km NNW Urban) *36.73944, -3.94972* **Camping El Pino, Urbanización Torrox Park s/n, 29793 Torrox Costa (Málaga) [952-53 00 06; fax 952-53 25 78; info@campingelpino.com; www.campingelpino. com]** Exit A7 at km 285, turn S at 1st rndabt, turn L at 2nd rndabt & foll sp Torrox Costa N340; in 1.5km at rndabt turn R to Torrox Costa, then L onto rndabt sp Nerja, site well sp in 4km. App rd steep with S bends. Fr N340 fr Torrox Costa foll sp Torrox Park, site sp. Lge, mkd pitch, terr, shd; wc; chem disp; shwrs inc; EHU €3.80 (long lead req); gas; lndry (inc dryer); shop; rest, snacks adj; bar; BBQ; playgrnd; 2 pools; sand beach 800m; games area; golf 8km; wifi; 35% statics; dogs €2.50; phone; car wash; Eng spkn; red LS/long sta/CKE/ CCI. "Gd size pitches but high kerbs; narr ent/exit; gd hill walks; conv Malaga; Nerja caves, Ronda; gd touring base; noise fr rd and bar; san facs adequate." ♦ € 18.00   2013*

See advertisement below

TOSSA DE MAR *3B3* (500m N Coastal) *41.72885, 2.92584* **Camping Can Martí, Avda Pau Casals s/n, 17320 Tossa de Mar (Gerona) [972-34 08 51; fax 972-34 24 61; campingcanmarti@terra.es; www.campingcanmarti.net]** Exit AP7 junc 9 dir Vidreras & take C35 dir Llagostera. Turn R at rndabt onto GI681 to coast, then GI682 to site. Mountain rd fr Sant Feliu not rec. V lge, mkd pitch, pt shd; wc; chem disp; baby facs; shwrs inc; EHU (10A) €3; gas; lndry; shop; rest, snacks; bar; playgrnd; pool & paddling pool; shgl beach 500m; fishing; tennis; horseriding; 10% statics; dogs free; phone; car wash; sep car park; Eng spkn; no adv bkg; quiet; red long stay/LS/CKE/CCI. "Helpful, friendly staff; facs clean." ♦ 15 May-15 Sep. € 32.00   2009*

TOSSA DE MAR *3B3* (4km NE Coastal) *41.73627, 2.94683* **Camping Pola, Ctra Tossa-Sant Feliu, Km 4, 17320 Tossa de Mar (Gerona) [972-34 10 50; campingpola@giverola.es; www.camping-pola.es]** Exit AP7 junc 9 onto C35 dir Sant Feliu de Guíxols. In approx 9km turn R onto GI681 dir Tossa de Mar. In Tossa take GI GE682 dir Sant Feliu. Narr, winding rd but gd. Site sp. Lge, pt sl, pt shd; wc; shwrs inc; EHU (15A) inc; gas; lndry (inc dryer); shop; rest; bar; playgrnd; pool; paddling pool; sand beach adj; tennis; games area; entmnt; some statics; dogs €3.50; bus 500m; sep car park high ssn; adv bkg; ccard acc. "Site deep in narr coastal inlet with excel beach; few British visitors; san facs old but clean; gd." 1 Jun-30 Sep. € 45.00   2009*

⊞ **TOTANA** *4G1* (2km SW Rural) *37.74645, -1.51933* **Camping Totana, Ctra N340, Km 614, 30850 Totana (Murcia) [tel/fax 968-42 48 64; info@campingtotana.es; www.campingtotana.es]** Fr N340/E15 exit at km 612 fr N. Fr S exit km 609. Foll Totana rd, site 2km on R. Sl ent. Sm, hdg/ mkd pitch, hdstg, terr, pt shd; wc; chem disp; shwrs inc; EHU (6A) €3; shop on site & 4km; rest, bar high ssn; BBQ; playgrnd; pool high ssn; games rm; entmnt; 90% statics; dogs €2; Eng spkn; red long stay; CKE/CCI. "Access to sm pitches tight due trees; helpful owners; tidy site; ltd privacy in shwrs; vg NH." € 16.00   2011*

"Satellite navigation makes touring much easier"

Remember most sat navs don't know if you're towing or in a larger vehicle – always use yours alongside maps and site directions.

TREMP *3B2* (4km N Rural) *42.18872, 0.92152* **Camping Gaset, Ctra C13, Km 91, 25630 Talarn (Lleida) [973-65 07 37; fax 973-65 01 02; campingaset@pallarsjussa.net; www.pallarsjussa.net/gaset]** Fr Tremp, take C13/N260 N sp Talarn. Site clearly visible on R on lakeside. Lge, pt sl, terr, pt shd; wc; chem disp; shwrs; EHU (4A) €5.30; lndry; shop; rest 4km; snacks; bar; BBQ; playgrnd; pool; paddling pool; sand beach & lake sw; fishing; tennis; games area; wifi; 15% statics; dogs €3.60; phone; poss cr; quiet; ccard acc. "Picturesque setting; some sm pitches." 1 Apr-15 Oct. € 24.50   2010*

⊞ **TREVELEZ** *2G4* (1km E Rural) *36.99195, -3.27026* **Camping Trevélez, Ctra Órgiva-Trevélez, Km 1, 18417 Trevélez (Granada) [tel/fax 958-85 87 35 or 625-50-27-69 (mob); info@campingtrevelez.net; www.campingtrevelez.net]** Fr Granada on A44/E902 exit junc 164 onto A348 dir Lanjarón, Pampaneira. Cont for approx 50km to on A4132 to Trevélez, site sp. Med, mkd pitch, terr, pt shd; htd wc; chem disp; mv service pnt; shwrs inc; EHU (9A) €3.50; gas; lndry; shop; rest, snacks; bar; playgrnd; pool; rv 1km; entmnt; wifi; few statics; dogs; phone; bus adj; poss cr; Eng spkn; adv bkg; quiet; red long stay. "Excel site; helpful, welcoming owners; access to Mulhacén (highest mountain mainland Spain); lots of hiking." ♦ € 27.00   2011*

SPAIN

UNQUERA

TURIENO see Potes *1A4*

UNQUERA *1A4* (3km N Coastal) *43.39127, -4.50986* **Camping Las Arenas, Ctra Unquera-Pechón, Km. 2, 39594 Pechón (Cantabria) [tel/fax 942-71 71 88; info@campinglasarenas. com; www.campinglasarenas.com]** Exit A8/E70 at km 272 sp Unquera. At rndabt foll CA380 sp Pechón, climb narr winding rd to site ent at top on L. Lge, pt sl, terr, pt shd; wc; chem disp; shwrs inc; EHU (5A) €3.95 (poss rev pol); gas; lndry (inc dryer); rest; shop on site & 3km; bar; playgrnd; pool; shgl beach adj; fishing; bike hire; internet; dogs; poss cr & noisy; Eng spkn; quiet; ccard acc; CKE/CCI. "Magnificent position on terr cliffs; peaceful, well-kept & clean; immac, modern san facs; helpful staff." 1 Jun-30 Sep. € 30.40   2010*

⊞ **VALDEAVELLANO DE TERA** *3B1* (1km NW Rural) *41.94523, -2.58837* **Camping Entrerrobles, Ctra de Molinos de Razón s/n, 42165 Valdeavellano de Tera (Soria) [975-18 08 00; fax 975-18 08 76; entrerobbles@hotmail.com; www.entrerrobles.freeservers.com]** S fr Logroño on N111, after Almarza turn R onto S0-820 to Valdeavellano. In 10km turn R at site sp, site on R in 1km. Med, mkd pitch, pt sl, pt shd; htd wc; chem disp; baby facs; shwrs inc; EHU (6A) €5; lndry (inc dryer); rest, snacks; bar; playgrnd; pool; games area; bike hire; TV rm; 8% statics; dogs; phone; Eng spkn; adv bkg; quiet; ccard acc; red CKE/CCI. "Excel touring base; attractive area but isolated (come prepared); friendly staff; new san facs." ♦ € 19.00   2009*

VALDOVINO *1A2* (700m W Coastal) *43.61222, -8.14916* **Camping Valdoviño, Ctra Ferrol-Cedeira, Km 13, 15552 Valdoviño (La Coruña) [981-48 70 76; fax 981-48 61 31]** Fr Ortigueira on C642; turn W onto C646 sp Cadeira then Ferrol; turn R at camping sp, down hill R again, site on R almost on beach. Med, terr, pt shd; wc; chem disp; baby facs; shwrs inc; EHU (15A) inc; gas; lndry; shop; rest; bar; snacks; playgrnd; sand beach adj; playgrnd; wifi; TV; some statics; no dogs; bus adj; poss cr; quiet; Eng spkn; CKE/CCI. "Pleasant, busy site nr lge beach with lagoon & cliffs but poss windy; locality run down; vg rest." ♦ 10 Apr-30 Sep. € 28.50   2009*

VALENCIA *4E2* (9km S Coastal) *39.39638, -0.33250* **Camping Coll Vert, Ctra Nazaret-Oliva, Km 7.5, 46012 Playa de Pinedo (València) [961-83 00 36; fax 961-83 00 40; info@collvertcamping.com; www.collvertcamping.com]** Fr S on V31 turn R onto V30 sp Pinedo. After approx 1km turn R onto V15/CV500 sp El Salar to exit El Salar Platjes. Turn L at rndabt, site on L in 1km. Fr N bypass València on A7/E15 & after junc 524 turn N twd València onto V31, then as above. Turn L at rndabt, site in 1km on L. Med, hdg/mkd pitch, shd; wc; shwrs inc; EHU €4.81 6A; gas; lndry; shop; bar; BBQ; playgrnd; pool; paddling pool; sand beach 500m; games area; entmnt; 20% statics; dogs €4.28; phone; bus to city & marine park; car wash; poss cr; Eng spkn; adv bkg; quiet; some rd noise; ccard acc; red long stay. "Hourly bus service fr outside site to cent of València & marine park; helpful, friendly staff; san facs need update sm pitches; conv for F1." ♦ 16 Feb-14 Dec. € 22.00   2014*

⊞ **VALENCIA** *4E2* (9.5km S Urban/Coastal) **Camping Park El Saler, Ctra del Riu 548, 46012 El Saler (València) [tel/fax 961-83 02 44; info@campingparkelsaler.com; www.campingparkelsaler.com]** Fr València foll coast rd or V15 to El Saler. Site adj rndabt just N of El Saler. Med, hdg/mkd pitch, hdstg, pt shd; wc; chem disp; shwrs inc; EHU (6A) inc; End spkn; lndry; shop; rest; bar; pool; sand beach 300m; 50% statics; dogs; phone; bus at gate; poss cr; rd noise; CKE/CCI. "Very conv València - hourly bus; tow pin adaptor needed for conn cable; narr pitches & ent." € 25.00   2014*

> ## "There aren't many sites open at this time of year"
>
> If you're travelling outside peak season remember to call ahead to check site opening dates – even if the entry says 'open all year'.

⊞ **VALENCIA** *4E2* (16km S Rural) *39.32302, -0.30940* **Camping Devesa Gardens, Ctra El Saler, Km 13, 46012 València [961-61 11 36; fax 961-61 11 05; alojamiento@ devesagardens.com; www.devesagardens.com]** S fr València on CV500, site well sp on R 4km S of El Saler. Med, mkd pitch, hdstg, pt shd; htd wc; chem disp; mv service pnt; baby facs; EHU (7-15A) €5; gas; lndry; supmkt (high ssn) & 4km; rest; bar; BBQ; playgrnd; pool; beach 700m; tennis; lake canoeing; horseriding; 70% statics; no dogs; phone; bus to València; quiet; adv bkg; ccard acc. "Friendly staff; warden needed to connect to EHU; site has own zoo (clsd LS); excel." ♦ € 22.70   2011*

VALENCIA DE DON JUAN see Villamañán *1B3*

VALL LLOBREGA see Palamós *3B3*

⊞ **VALLE DE CABUERNIGA** *1A4* (1km NE Rural) *43.22800, 4.28900* **Camping El Molino de Cabuérniga, Sopeña, 39510 Cabuérniga (Cantabria) [942-70 62 59; fax 942-70 62 78; cmcabuerniga@campingcabuerniga.com; www.campingcabuerniga.com]** Sopeña is 55 km. SW of Santander. Fr A8 (Santander - Oviedo) take 249 exit and join N634 to Cabezón de la Sal. Turn SW on CA180 twds Reinosa for 11 km. to Sopeña (site sp to L). Turn into vill (car req - low bldgs), cont bearing R foll sp to site. Med, shd; wc; shwrs inc; EHU (3A) €2.67 (check earth); gas; lndry; sm shop; snacks; bar; playgrnd; rv 200m; fishing; tennis; dogs €1.50; phone; bus 500m; adv bkg; quiet; ccard acc; CKE/CCI. "Excel site & facs on edge of vill; no shops in vicinity, but gd location, rds to site narr in places." ♦ € 23.00   2013*

VECILLA, LA *1B3* (1km N Rural) *42.85806, -5.41155* **Camping La Cota, Ctra Valdelugueros, LE321, Km 19, 24840 La Vecilla (León) [987-74 10 91; lacota@campinglacota.com; www.campinglacota.com]** Fr N630 turn E onto CL626 at La Robla, 17km to La Vecilla. Site sp in vill. Med, mkd pitch, shd; wc; chem disp; baby facs; shwrs inc; EHU €3.50; lndry rm; snacks; bar; games area; wifi; 50% statics; open w/ends out of ssn; train nr; quiet; ccard acc. "Pleasant site under poplar trees - poss diff to manoeuvre lge o'fits; gd walking, climbing nr; interesting mountain area; NH only." 23 Mar-30 Sep. € 21.00   2013*

⊞ **VEJER DE LA FRONTERA** *2H3* (10km S Coastal) *36.20084, -6.03506* **Camping Pinar San José, Ctra de Vejer-Caños de Meca, Km 10.2, Zahora 17, 11159 Barbate (Cadiz) [956-43 70 30; fax 956-43 71 74; info@campingpinarsanjose.com; www.campingpinarsanjose.com]** Fr A48/N340 exit junc 36 onto A314 to Barbate, then foll dir Los Caños de Meca. Turn R at seashore rd dir Zahora. Site on L, 2km beyond town. Med, mkd pitch, shd; wc; chem disp; mv service pnt; fam bthrm; shwrs; EHU inc; lndry; shop; rest; playgrnd; pool; paddling pool; sand beach 700m; tennis; games area; wifi; satellite TV; some statics; dogs €2 (LS only); adv bkg; quiet. "Excel, modern facs." ♦ € 64.00   2013*

VELEZ MALAGA *2G4* (16.2km NNW Rural) *36.87383, -4.18527* **Camping Rural Presa la Vinuela, Carretera A-356, Km 30, 29712 La Viñuela Málaga [952-55 45 62; fax 952-55 45 70; campingpresalavinuela@hotmail.com; www.campinglavinuela.es]** Site is on A356 N of Velez Malaga adjoining the W shore of la Vinuela lake. Fr junc with A402, foll sp to Colmenar/Los Romanes. Stay on A356(don't turn off into Los Romanes). Site is on R approx 2.5km after turn for Los Romanes, next to rest El Pantano. Sm, hed/mkd pitch, hdstg, terr, pt shd; wc; chem disp; shwr; EHU (5A); lndry; shop; rest; café; snacks; bar; pool; games area; games rm; wifi; TV; 20% statics; dogs €1.10; Eng spkn; adv bkg; red LS. "Excel site." 1 Jan-30 Sep. € 21.00   2014*

VENDRELL, EL *3C3* (2km S Coastal) *41.18312, 1.53593* **Camping Sant Salvador, Avda Palfuriana 68, 43880 Sant Salvador (Tarragona) [tel/fax 977-68 08 04; campingsantsalvador@troc.es; www.campingsantsalvador.com]** Exit A7 junc 31 onto N340, after 1km turn L. Site bet Calafell & Coma-Ruga. Lge, pt shd; wc; chem disp; baby facs; shwrs inc; EHU (4A) €5; gas; lndry; shop; rest; bar; playgrnd; beach; 75% statics; dogs €2.50; bus adj; poss cr; ccard acc; red long stay/LS; CKE/CCI. "Secure site; not suitable lge o'fits; conv Safari Park & Port Aventura." ♦ 26 Mar-3 Oct. € 29.00   2010*

VENDRELL, EL *3C3* (7km SW Coastal) *41.17752, 1.50132* **Camping Francàs, Ctra N340, Km 1185.5, 43880 Coma-Ruga (Tarragona) [977-68 07 25; fax 977-68 47 73; info@campingfrancas.net; www.campingfrancas.net]** Exit N340 at km stone 303 to Comarruga. Lge, mkd pitch, shd; wc; chem disp; baby facs; shwrs; EHU €3.65; lndry; shop; rest, snacks; bar; BBQ; playgrnd; sand beach adj; watersports; fishing; games area; car wash; wifi; entmnt; some statics; dogs; bus 100m; car wash; adv bkg; quiet. "Pleasant site." ♦ Easter-1 Sep. € 24.50   2010*

VIELHA *3B2* (6km N Rural) *42.73638, 0.76083* **Camping Artiganè, Ctra N230, Km 171, Val d'Arán, 25537 Pont d'Arròs (Lleida) [tel/fax 973-64 03 38; info@campingartigane.com; www.campingartigane.com]** Fr French border head S on N230 for 15km. Fr Vielha head N to France & turn L at Pont d'Arròs. Site on main rd by rv. Lge, pt sl, pt shd; wc; chem disp; baby facs; shwrs inc; EHU (10A) €4.50; gas; lndry rm; shop; rest, snacks, bar in high ssn; BBQ; playgrnd; htd pool; games area; golf; 5% statics; dogs €3.25; bus adj; phone; poss cr; quiet; CKE/CCI. "Scenic area - wild flowers, butterflies; friendly warden; LS site yourself - warden calls; simple/v basic facs, poss stretched when site full." ♦ Holy Week-15 Oct. € 25.00   2011*

⊞ **VIELHA** *3B2* (7km N Rural) *42.73649, 0.74640* **Camping Verneda, Ctra Francia N230, Km 171, 25537 Pont d'Arròs (Lleida) [973-64 10 24; fax 973-64 32 18; info@camping verneda.com; www.campingverneda.com]** Fr Lerida N on N230 twd Spain/France border, site on R adj N230, 2km W of Pont d'Arròs on rvside, 1km after Camping Artigane. Med, pt shd; wc; chem disp; baby facs; shwrs inc; EHU (4A) €3.90; gas; lndry; rest, snacks; bar; playgrnd; pool; horseriding; games rm; bike hire; entmnt; TV; 10% statics; dogs €2.50; adv bkg; Eng spkn; ccard acc; CKE/CCI. "Gd area for walking; site open w/ end rest of year; well-run site; gd facs." € 25.00   2011*

VIELHA *3B2* (6km SE Rural) *42.70005, 0.87060* **Camping Era Yerla D'Arties, Ctra C142, Vielha-Baquiera s/n, 25599 Arties (Lleida) [973-64 16 02; fax 973-64 30 53; yerla@coac.net; www.aranvielha.com/yerla]** Fr Vielha take C28 dir Baquiera, site sp. Turn R at rndabt into Arties, site in 30m on R. Med, shd; htd wc; chem disp; baby facs; shwrs inc; EHU (4-10A) €4.25-5.15; gas; lndry; shop & rest nrby; snacks; bar; pool; skiing nr; some statics; bus 200m; phone; quiet; ccard acc; CKE/CCI. "Pleasant site & vill; ideal for ski resort; san facs gd; gd walking; OK for sh stay." 1 Dec-14 Sep. € 23.70   2012*

⊞ **VIELHA** *3B2* (40.8km SE Rural) *42.50337, 08.0103* **Camping Boneta, 25527 Barruera (nr Pont de Suert) Lleida [973-69 40 86; info@campingboneta.com; www.camping boneta.com]** Head S on N-230, turn L onto Carretera de Barruera/L-500, turn L onto Carrer major, site visible. Sm, pt shd; htd wc; shwrs inc; gas; shop adj; EHU (4A); lndry; rest; bar; pool; bike hire nrby; wifi; horseriding; playgrnd; quiet; dogs; bus; red LS; poss cr. "Friendly; conv Argues Tortes National Park; pleasant mountain vill; gd walking/climbing; lge collection of Romanesque churches in area; unsuitable for larger c'vans; simple facs clean and adequate." Apr-Sep. € 19.00   2011*

VILAGARCIA DE AROUSA *1B2* (4km NE Coastal) *42.63527, -8.75555* **Camping Río Ulla, Bamio, 36612 Vilagarcía de Arousa (Pontevedra) [tel/fax 986-50 54 30; 986505430@ telefonica.net; www.campingrioulla.com]** Fr N exit A9 at km 93 dir Pontecesures & take PO548 twd Vilagarcía de Arousa. Thro Catoira & in 5km turn R at traff lts at top of hill, site in 500m. Med, hdg/mkd pitch, pt shd; wc; chem disp; mv service pnt; baby facs; shwrs inc; EHU (10A) €4; lndry; shop; rest, snacks; bar; BBQ; playgrnd; pool; paddling pool; sand beach adj; games area; TV; 10% statics; bus 200m; Eng spkn; adv bkg; rd & rlwy noise; ccard acc; CKE/CCI. "Helpful owners; excel, clean facs." ♦ Holy Week & 1 Jun-15 Sep. € 20.00   2009*

⊞ **VILALLONGA DE TER** *3B3* (500m NW Rural) *42.33406, 2.30705* **Camping Conca de Ter, Ctra Setcases s/n, Km 5.4, 17869 Vilallonga de Ter (Gerona) [972-74 06 29; fax 972-13 01 71; concater@concater.com; www.concater.com]** Exit C38 at Camprodón; at Vilallonga de Ter do NOT turn off into vill but stay on main rd; site on L. Lge, mkd pitch, hdstg, pt shd; htd wc; chem disp; shwrs inc; EHU (5-15A) €3.50-6.54; lndry (inc dryer); shop; rest; bar; pool; paddling pool; games area; games rm; ski lift 15km; entmnt; 95% statics; dogs €4.30; poss cr; Eng spkn; ccard acc; CKE/CCI. "Pitches sm & cr together; gd." ♦ € 31.00   2010*

⊞ **VILANOVA DE PRADES** 3C2 (500m NE Rural) 41.34890, 0.95860 **Camping Parc de Vacances Serra de Prades, Calle Sant Antoni s/n, 43439 Vilanova de Prades (Tarragona)** [tel/fax 977-86 90 50; info@serradeprades.com; www.serradeprades.com] Fr AP2 take exit 8 (L'Albi) or 9 (Montblanc), foll C240 to Vimbodi. At km 47.5 take TV7004 for 10km to Vilanova de Prades. Site ent on R immed after rndabt at ent to vill. Lge, some hdg/mkd pitch, terr, pt shd; wc; chem disp; mv service pnt; baby facs; shwrs inc; EHU (6A) €5.80 (poss long lead req) gas; lndry (inc dryer); basic shop on site & 8km; rest, snacks; bar; BBQ; playgrnd; htd pool; lake sw 20km; tennis; games area; games rm; wifi; TV rm; many statics; dogs; phone; Eng spkn; adv bkg high ssn; quiet; red long stay/CKE/CCI. "Well-maintained, well-run, scenic, friendly site; clean facs; sm pitches; access some pitches diff due steep, gravel site rds & storm gullies; conv Barcelona; vg touring base/NH." ♦ € 27.00 (CChq acc)   2009*

"That's changed – Should I let The Club know?"
If you find something on site that's different from the site entry, fill in a report and let us know. See www.caravanclub.co.uk/europereport.

VILANOVA I LA GELTRU 3C3 (5km SW Coastal) 41.19988, 1.64339 **Camping La Rueda, Ctra C31, Km 146.2, 08880 Cubelles (Barcelona)** [938-95 02 07; fax 938-95 03 47; larueda@la-rueda.com; www.la-rueda.com] Exit A7 junc 29 then take C15 dir Vilanova onto autopista C32 & take exit 13 dir Cunit. Site is 2.5km S of Cubelles on C31 at km stone 146.2. Lge, mkd pitch, shd; htd wc; chem disp; mv service pnt; shwrs inc; EHU (4A) €6.90; gas; lndry; shop; rest, snacks; bar; sand beach 100m; playgrnd; pool; tennis; horseriding; watersports; fishing; entmnt; car wash; 12% statics; dogs €3.70; phone; bus; train; Eng spkn; adv bkg; quiet; red long stay/LS; ccard acc; red CKE/CCI. "Conv Port Aventura & Barcelona; vg family site." 16 Apr-11 Sep. € 34.50   2010*

⊞ **VILANOVA I LA GELTRU** 3C3 (3km NW Urban) 41.23190, 1.69075 **Camping Vilanova Park, Ctra Arboç, Km 2.5, 08800 Vilanova i la Geltru (Barcelona)** [938-93 34 02; fax 938-93 55 28; info@vilanovapark.com or reservas@vilanovapark.com; www.vilanovapark.com] Fr N on AP7 exit junc 29 onto C15 dir Vilanova; then take C31 dir Cubelles. Leave at 153km exit dir Vilanova Oeste/L'Arboç to site. Fr W on C32/A16 take Vilanova-Sant Pere de Ribes exit. Take C31 & at 153km exit take BV2115 dir L'Arboc to site. Fr AP7 W leave at exit 31 onto the C32 (A16); take exit 16 (Vilanova-L'Arboc exit) onto BV2115 to site. Parked cars may block loop & obscure site sp. V lge, hdg/mkd pitch, hdstg, terr, pt shd; htd wc; chem disp; mv service pnt; some serviced pitches; baby facs; fam bthrm; sauna; shwrs inc; EHU (10A) inc (poss rev pol); gas; lndry (inc dryer); supmkt; rest, snacks; bar; BBQ (gas/elec); playgrnd; 2 pools (1 htd covrd) & fountains; paddling pool; jacuzzi & spa; fitness cent; sand beach 3km; lake sw 2km; fishing; tennis; bike hire; mini golf and jumping pillow for children due to open in 2012; horseriding 500m; golf 1km; games rm; wifi; entmnt; TV rm; 50% statics; dogs €12.50; phone; bus directly fr campsite to Barcelona; poss cr; Eng spkn; adv bkg ess high ssn; ccard acc; red snr citizens/LS/long stay; CKE/CCI. "Gd for children; excel san facs; gd rest & bar; gd winter facs; helpful staff; gd security; some sm pitches with diff access due trees or ramps; conv bus/train Barcelona, Tarragona, Port Aventura & coast; mkt Sat; excel site; superb." ♦ € 61.00 SBS - E08   2013*

See advertisement

VILLADANGOS DEL PARAMO see León 1B3

⊞ **VILLAFRANCA** 3B1 (1.5km S Rural) 42.26333, -1.73861 **Camping Bardenas, Ctra NA-660 PK 13.4, 31330 Villafranca** [34 94 88 46 191; info@campingbardenas.com; www.campingbardenas.com] Fr N leave AP15 at Junc 29 onto NA660 sp Villafranca. Site on R 1.5km S of town. Med, hdstg, unshd; htd wc; chem disp; baby facs; shwr; lndry (inc dryer); shop; rest; bar; BBQ; pool; games rm; 30% statics; ccard acc; CCI. "Gd site for winter stopover en rte to S. Spain; some rd noise; facs ltd in severe weather; excel rest." € 36.50   2014*

⊞ **VILLAFRANCA DE CORDOBA** *2F4* (1km W Rural) *37.95333, -4.54710* **Camping La Albolafia, Camino de la Vega s/n, 14420 Villafranca de Córdoba (Córdoba) [tel/fax 957-19 08 35; informacion@campingalbolafia.com; www.campingalbolafia.com]** Exit A4/E5 junc 377, cross rv & at rndabt turn L & foll sp to site in 2km. Beware humps in app rd. Med, hdg/mkd pitch, hdstg, pt shd; wc; chem disp; mv service pnt; shwrs inc; EHU (10A) €4.20 (long lead poss req); lndry (inc dryer); shop, rest, snacks; bar; BBQ; playgrnd; pool; wifi; TV; some statics; dogs €2.80; bus to Córdoba 500m; phone; Eng spkn; quiet; CKE/CCI. "V pleasant, well-run, friendly, clean site; watersports park nrby; bar and rest clsd end May." ♦ € 24.00   2013*

⊞ **VILLAMANAN** *1B3* (1km SE Rural) *42.31403, -5.57290* **Camping Palazuelo, 24680 Villamañán (León) [tel/fax 987-76 82 10]** Fr N630 Salamanca-León turn SE at Villamañán onto C621 dir Valencia de Don Juan. Site on R in 1km behind hotel. Med, pt shd; wc; shwrs inc; EHU (10A) €2.50; lndry; shop 1km; rest, snacks; pool; quiet but some rd noise; ccard acc. "NH only; neglected & run down LS; poss unclean; ltd privacy in shwrs; Valencia de Don Juan worth visit." € 19.00   2009*

"I like to fill in the reports as I travel from site to site"

You'll find report forms at the back of this guide, or you can fill them in online at www.caravanclub.co.uk/europereport.

VILLAMANAN *1B3* (6km SE Rural) *42.29527, -5.53777* **Camping Pico Verde, Ctra Mayorga-Astorga, Km 27.6, 24200 Valencia de Don Juan (León) [tel/fax 987-75 05 25; campingpicoverd@terra.es]** Fr N630 S, turn E at km 32.2 onto C621 sp Valencia de Don Juan. Site in 4km on R. Med, mkd pitch, wc; shwrs inc; EHU (6A) inc; lndry; shop on site & 1km; rest; snacks 1km; playgrnd; covrd pool; paddling pool; tennis; 25% statics; dogs free; quiet; red CKE/CCI. "Friendly, helpful staff; conv León; picturesque vill; sw caps to be worn in pool; phone ahead to check site open if travelling close to opening/closing dates." ♦ 15 Jun-8 Sep. € 20.00   2014*

VILLAMARTIN DE LA ABADIA see Ponferrada *1B3*

VILLANANE *1B4* (800m N Rural) *42.84221, -3.06867* **Camping Angosto, Ctra Villanañe-Angosto 2, 01425 Villanañe (Gipuzkoa) [945-35 32 71; fax 945-35 30 41; info@camping-angosto.com; www.camping-angosto.com]** S fr Bilbao on AP68 exit at vill of Pobes & take rd to W sp Espejo. Turn L 2.4km N of Espejo dir Villanañe, lane to site 400m on R. Med, some mkd pitch, pt shd; htd wc; chem disp; baby facs; shwrs inc; EHU €4.15 (long cable poss req - supplied by site); lndry; shop; rest, snacks; bar; BBQ; playgrnd; htd, covrd pool; entmnt; TV; 50% statics; dogs; phone; poss cr w/ends; Eng spkn; quiet. "Beautiful area; friendly, helpful staff; open site - mkd pitches rec if poss; gd rest; conv NH fr Bilbao; wonderful site; in LS site seems close but call nbr on gate; site long way fr main rd; poss narr vill app rds." ♦ 15 Feb-30 Nov. € 27.00   2014*

⊞ **VILLARGORDO DEL CABRIEL** *4E1* (3km NW Rural) *39.5525, -1.47444* **Kiko Park Rural, Ctra Embalse de Contreras, Km 3, 46317 Villargordo del Cabriel (València) [962-13 90 82; fax 962-13 93 37; kikoparkrural@kikopark. com; www.kikopark.com/rural]** A3/E901 València-Madrid, exit junc 255 to Villorgordo del Cabriel, foll sp to site. Med, mkd pitch, hdstg, terr, pt shd; wc; chem disp; mv service pnt; some serviced pitches; shwrs inc; EHU (6A) €3.70; gas; lndry (inc dryer); shop, rest, snacks; bar; pool; lake sw 1km; canoeing; watersports; fishing; horseriding; white water rafting; bike hire; TV; some statics; dogs €0.80; some rlwy noise; Eng spkn; adv bkg rec high ssn; ccard acc; red long stay/LS/snr citizens; red CKE/CCI. "Beautiful location; superb, well-run, peaceful site; lge pitches; gd walking; vg rest; many activities; helpful, v friendly family run site;; gd hdstg; excel." ♦ € 33.00   2015*

VILLAVICIOSA *1A3* (8km NE Rural) *43.50900, -5.33600* **Camping La Rasa, Ctra La Busta-Selorio, 33316 Villaviciosa (Asturias) [985-89 15 29; info@campinglarase.com; www.campinglarase.com]** Fr A8 exit km 353 sp Lastres/Venta del Pobre. In approx 500m foll site sp, cross bdge over m'way to site. Lge, hdg/mkd pitch, sl, unshd; wc; chem disp; mv service pnt; serviced pitches; shwrs inc; EHU (6A) €3.10; lndry; sm shop; snacks; bar; playgrnd; pool; sand beach 7km; 60% statics; dogs €2.80; phone; site open w/end LS/winter; Eng spkn; red LS; CKE/CCI. "Pleasant, friendly site; beautiful countryside; conv m'way & coast; tight access rds to sm pitches." ♦ 15 Jun-15 Sep. € 23.00   2009*

VILLAVICIOSA *1A3* (15km NW Rural) *43.5400, -5.52638* **Camping Playa España, Playa de España, Quintes, 33300 Villaviciosa (Asturias) [tel/fax 985-89 42 73; camping@ campingplayaespana.es; www.campingplayaespana.es]** Exit A8 onto N632/AS256 dir Quintes then Villaverde. Site approx 12km fr Villaviciosa & 10km fr Gijón. Last 3km of app rd narr & steep with sharp bends. Med, pt shd; wc; chem disp; shwrs; EHU €4.25 (poss rev pol); gas; lndry; shop; snacks; bar; beach 200m; dogs €3; phone; quiet; ccard acc. "Gd site; lovely coast & scenery with mountains behind; clean; vg san facs." Holy Week & 16 May-19 Sep. € 24.60   2010*

⊞ **VINAROS** *3D2* (5km N Coastal) *40.49363, 0.48504* **Camping Vinarós, Ctra N340, Km 1054, 12500 Vinarós (Castellón) [tel/fax 964-40 24 24; info@campingvinaros. com; www.campingvinaros.com]** Fr N exit AP7 junc 42 onto N238 dir Vinarós. At junc with N340 turn L dir Tarragona, site on R at km 1054. Fr S exit AP7 junc 43. Lge, hdg/mkd pitch, hdstg, pt shd; htd wc; chem disp; mv service pnt; 85% serviced pitches; baby facs; shwrs inc; EHU (6A) €6; gas; lndry; shop 500m; rest adj; snacks; bar; playgrnd; pool; sand/shgl beach 1km; wifi; 15% statics; dogs €3; phone; bus adj; currency exchange; poss cr; Eng spkn; adv bkg - rec high ssn; quiet but some rd noise; ccard acc; red long stay/LS; CKE/CCI. "Excel gd value, busy, well-run site; many long-stay winter residents; spacious pitches; vg clean, modern san facs; elec volts poss v low in evening; gd rest; friendly, helpful staff; rec use bottled water; Peñíscola Castle & Morello worth a visit; easy cycle to town." ♦ ltd. € 50.00   2013*

VINUELA *2G4* (7.5km NW Rural) *36.87383, -4.18527*
Camping Presa La Viñuela, Ctra A356, km 30 29712 Viñuela
[952-55 45 62; fax 952-55 45 70; campingpresalavinuela@
hotmail.com; www.campinglavinuela.es] Site on A356 N of
Velez Malaga adjoining the W shore of la Vinuela lake. Fr junc
with A402, foll sp to Colmenar & Los Romanes. Stay on A356
(don't turn off into Los Romanes). Site is on R approx 2.5km
after the turn for Los Romanes, next to El Pantano rest. Sm,
mkd pitch, hdstg, terr, pt shd; wc; chem disp; shwrs; EHU (5A);
lndry; shop; rest; café; bar; pool; games area; games rm; wifi;
TV in bar; 20% statics; dogs €1.10; End spkn; adv bkg; red LS.
"Excel site." 1 Jan-30 Sep. € 21.00   2014*

VINUESA *3B1* (2km N Rural) *41.9272, -2.7650* **Camping
Cobijo, Ctra Laguna Negra, Km 2, 42150 Vinuesa (Soria)
[tel/fax 975-37 83 31; recepcion@campingcobijo.com;
www.campingcobijo.com]** Travelling W fr Soria to Burgos,
at Abejar R on SO840. by-pass Abejar cont to Vinuesa. Well sp
fr there. Lge, pt sl, pt shd; wc; chem disp; baby facs; shwrs inc;
EHU (3-6A) €4-5.70 (long lead poss req); gas; lndry; shop; rest,
snacks, bar high ssn; BBQ; playgrnd; pool; bike hire; internet;
10% statics; dogs; phone; poss cr w/end; Eng spkn; phone;
quiet; ccard acc; CKE/CCI. "Friendly staff; clean, attractive site;
some pitches in wooded area poss diff lge o'fits; special elec
connector supplied (deposit); ltd bar & rest LS, excel rests in
town; gd walks." ♦ Holy Week-2 Nov. € 17.00   2009*

⊞ **VITORIA/GASTEIZ** *3B1* (3km W Rural) *42.8314, -2.7225*
**Camping Ibaya, Nacional 102, Km 346.5, Zuazo de Vitoria
01195 Vitoria/Gasteiz (Alava) [945-14 76 20; fax 627-
07 43 99; info@campingibaia.com; www.campingibaia.com]**
Fr A1 take exit 343 sp N102/A3302. At rndabt foll sp N102
Vitoria/Gasteiz. At next rndabt take 3rd exit & immed turn L
twd filling stn. Site ent on R in 100m, sp. Sm, mkd pitch, hdstg,
pt sl, pt shd; wc; chem disp; shwrs; EHU (5A) €5.40; gas; lndry
rm; sm shop; supmkt 2km; rest adj; snacks; bar; BBQ; playgrnd;
wifi; 5-10% statics; dogs; phone; poss cr; Eng spkn; rd noise;
CKE/CCI. "NH only; gd, modern san facs; phone ahead to
check open LS; fair site." € 29.50   2014*

VIU DE LINAS see Broto *3B2*

VIVEIRO *1A2* (500m NW Coastal) *43.66812, -7.59998*
Camping Vivero, Cantarrana s/n, Covas, 27850 Viveiro
(Lugo) [982-56 00 04; fax 982-56 00 84; campingvivero@
gmail.com] Fr E twd El Ferrol on rd LU862, turn R in town
over rv bdge & bear R & foll yellow camping sp. Site in 500m
adj football stadium in Covas, sp. Fr W go into town on 1-way
system & re-cross rv on parallel bdge to access rd to site.
Site not well sp - foll stadium sp. Med, shd; wc; chem disp;
shwrs inc; EHU (10A) €4.30; lndry; shop & 1.5km; snacks; bar;
beach 500m; wifi; phone; bus adj; o'night area for m'vans;
ccard acc. "Sh walk to interesting old town, outstanding
craft pottery at sharp RH bend on Lugo rd; vg clean site."
Easter & 1 Jun-30 Sep. € 17.00   2011*

VIVER *3D2* (3.5km W Rural) *39.90944, -0.61833* **Camping Villa
de Viver, Camino Benaval s/n, 12460 Viver (Castellón) [964-
14 13 34; info@campingviver.com; www.campingviver.com]**
Fr Sagunto on A23 dir Terual, approx 10km fr Segorbe turn L
sp Jérica, Viver. Thro vill dir Teresa, site sp W of Viver at end
of single track lane in approx 2.8km (yellow sp) - poss diff for
car+c'van, OK m'vans. Med, hdg pitch, terr, pt shd; htd wc;
chem disp; mv service pnt; some serviced pitches; shwrs inc;
EHU (6A) €3.80; lndry; shop 3.5km; rest, snacks; bar; playgrnd;
pool; TV; 10% statics; dogs €3.10; phone; Eng spkn; adv bkg;
quiet; red long stay; ccard acc; CKE/CCI. "Improved site; lovely
situation - worth the effort." ♦ 1Mar - 1 Nov. € 19.00   2013*

⊞ **ZARAGOZA** *3C1* (6km W Urban) *41.63766, -0.94227*
**Camping Ciudad de Zaragoza, Calle San Juan Bautista de la
Salle s/n, 50012 Zaragoza [876-24 14 95; fax 876-24 12 86;
info@campingzaragoza.com; www.campingzaragoza.com]**
Fr S on A23 foll Adva Gómez Laguna, turn L at 2nd rndabt, in
500m bear R in order to turn L at rndabt, site on R in 750m, sp.
Fr all other dirs take Z40 ring rd dir Terual, then Adva Gómez
Laguna twd city, then as above. Site well sp. Med, mkd pitch,
hdstg, pt sl, unshd; htd wc; chem disp; mv service pnt; baby facs;
shwrs inc; EHU (10A) €4.85; lndry (inc dryer); shop; rest, snacks;
bar; BBQ; playgrnd; pool; tennis; games area; wifi; 50% statics;
dogs €3.04; poss cr; Eng spkn; adv bkg; poss noisy (campers &
daytime aircraft). "Modern san facs but poss unclean LS & pt
htd; poss travellers; unattractive, but conv site in suburbs; gd
stay; gd food at bar; helpful staff; site scruffy." € 28.00 2015*

⊞ **ZARAUTZ** *3A1* (3km NE Coastal) *43.28958, -2.14603* **Gran
Camping Zarautz, Monte Talaimendi s/n, 20800 Zarautz
(Guipúzkoa) [943-83 12 38; fax 943-13 24 86; info@gran
campingzarautz.com; www.grancampingzarautz.com]**
Exit A8 junc 11 Zarautz, strt on at 1st & 2nd rndabt after toll &
foll site sp. On N634 fr San Sebastián to Zarautz, R at rndabt.
On N634 fr Bilbao to Zarautz L at rndabt. Lge, hdg/mkd pitch,
hdstg, pt sl, terr, pt shd; htd wc; chem disp; mv service pnt;
shwrs inc; EHU (6A) inc; gas; lndry (inc dryer); shop; rest; bar;
BBQ; playgrnd; beach 1km (steep walk); games rm; golf 1km;
wifi; TV rm; 50% statics; phone; train/bus to Bilbao & San
Sebastian; poss cr; Eng spkn; no adv bkg; ccard acc; CKE/CCI.
"Site on cliff o'looking bay; excel beach, gd base for coast &
mountains; helpful, friendly staff; some pitches sm with steep
access & o'looked fr terr above; sans facs upgraded but poor
standard and insufficient when cr; excel rest; pitches poss
muddy; NH for Bilbao ferry; rec arr early to secure pitch; v steep
walk to beach; gd for NH; excel train service to San Sebastian;
gd shop on site." ♦ € 29.00   2015*

ZARAUTZ *3A1* (8km E Coastal) *43.27777, -2.12305* **Camping
Playa de Orio, 20810 Orio (Guipúzkoa) [943-83 48 01; fax
943-13 34 33; info@oriokanpina.com; www.oriokanpina.
com]** Fr E on A8 exit junc 33 & at rndabt foll sp Orio, Kanpin &
Playa. Site on R. Or to avoid town cent cross bdge & foll N634
for 1km, turn L at sp Orio & camping, turn R at rndabt to site.
Lge, mkd pitch, pt sl, pt shd; wc; chem disp; mv service pnt; baby
facs; shwrs inc; EHU (5A) inc; gas; lndry (inc dryer); shop high
ssn; rest adj; snacks; bar; playgrnd; pool high ssn; paddling pool;
sand beach adj; tennis; 50% statics (sep area); no dogs; phone;
car wash; poss cr at w/end; Eng spkn; adv bkg; quiet; red LS;
ccard acc; CKE/CCI. "Busy, well maintained site; flats now built
bet site & beach & new marina adj - now no sea views; walks;
gd facs; friendly staff; useful NH bef leaving Spain; interesting sm
town." ♦ 1 Mar-1 Nov. € 33.50   2015*

ZEANURI *3A1* (3km SE Rural) *43.08444, -2.72333* **Camping Zubizabala, Otxandio, 48144 Zeanuri [944-47 92 06 or 660-42 30 17 (mob); zubizabala@gmail.com; www.zubizabala.com]** E fr Bilbao on A8, exit at Galdakao junc 19 onto N240 dir Vitoria/Gasteiz. 2.5km S of Barazar Pass, turn L on minor rd B3542 to Otxandio. Site 300m on R, sp. Sm, mkd pitch, unshd; wc; chem disp; mv service pnt; baby facs; shwrs inc; EHU €3.55; lndry; shop; bar; playgrnd; pool 4km; lake sw 20km; games area; phone; bus at site ent; Eng spkn; adv bkg; quiet; CKE/CCI. "V pleasant, tranquil site in woods; superb countryside; conv Bilbao & Vitoria/Gasteiz." ♦ ltd. 15 Jun-15 Sep. € 25.00   2012*

ZUBIA, LA see Granada *2G4*

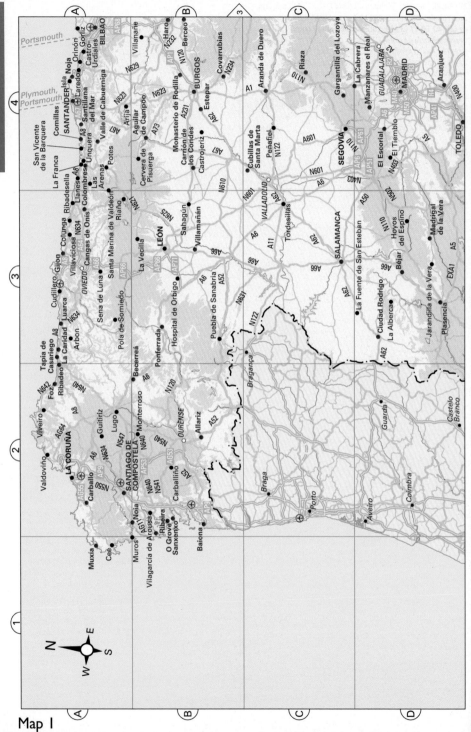

Map 1

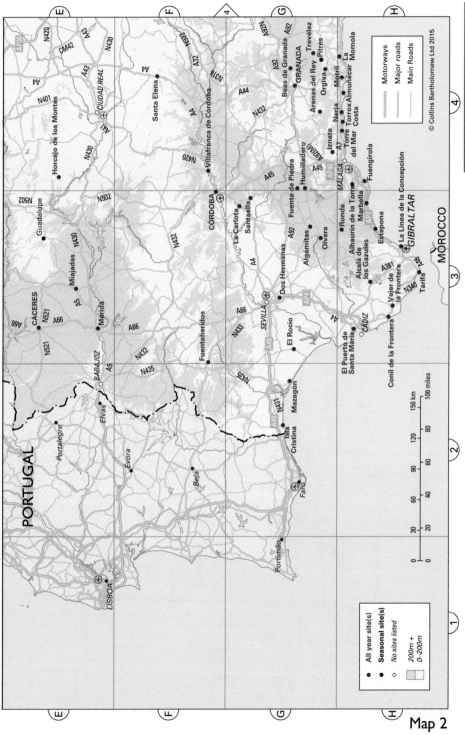

© Collins Bartholomew Ltd 2015

Motorways
Major roads
Main Roads

All year site(s)
Seasonal site(s)
No sites listed
200m +
0–200m

Map 2

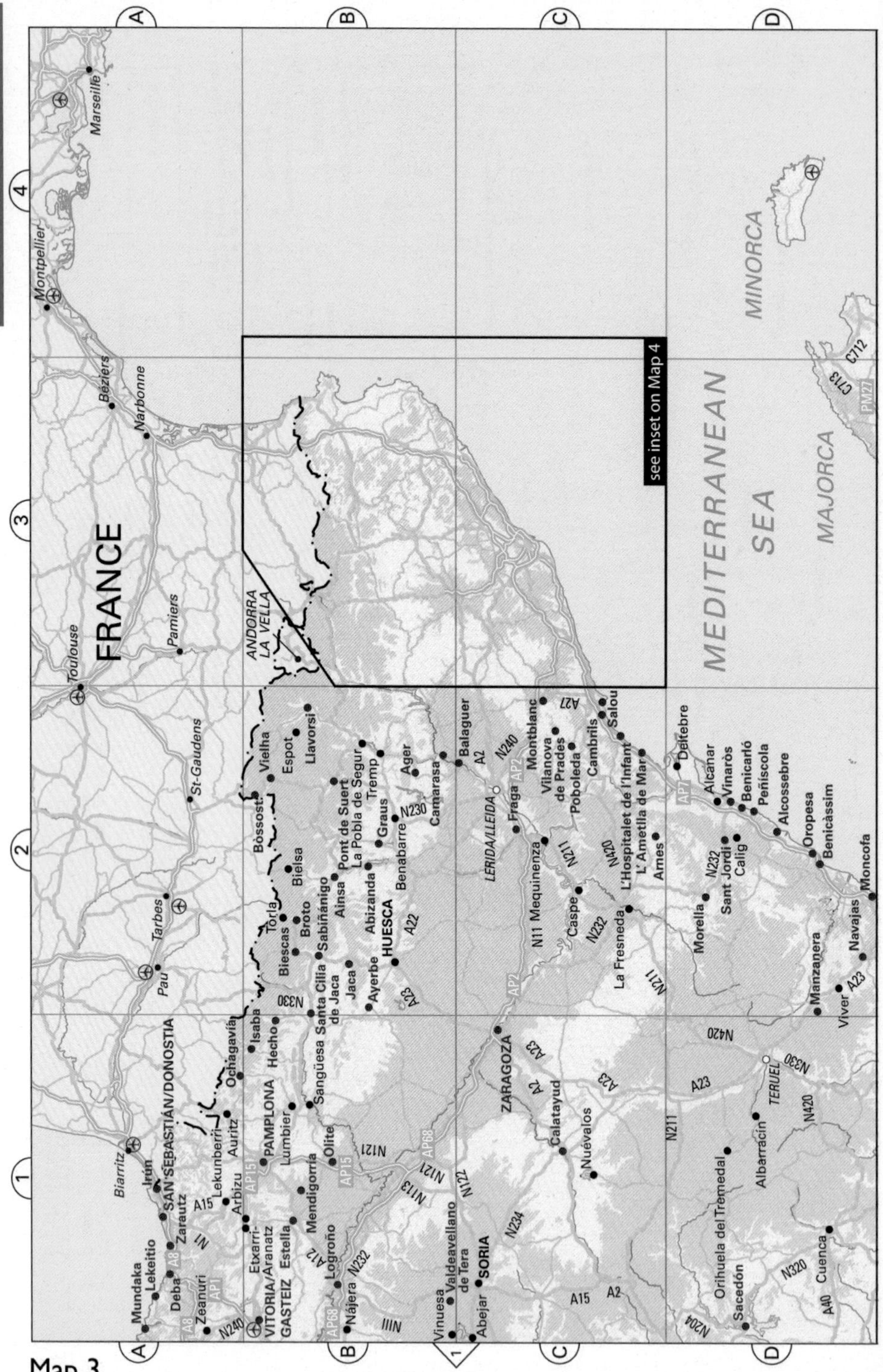

FRANCE

Marseille

Montpellier

Béziers

Narbonne

Toulouse

Pamiers

St-Gaudens

Tarbes

Pau

Biarritz

Irun
Mundaka
Lekeitio
Deba
Zarautz
Zeanuri
SAN SEBASTIAN/DONOSTIA
Arbizu
Lekunberri
Auritz
Etxarri/Aranatz
VITORIA/
GASTEIZ
Estella
Mendigorria
Logroño
Nájera
PAMPLONA
Lumbier
Olite

Ochagavía
Isaba
Hecho
Sangüesa
Santa Cilia
de Jaca
Jaca
Ayerbe

Bóssost
Vielha
Espot
Llavorsí
Bielsa
Broto
Torla
Biescas
Sabiñánigo
Abizanda
HUESCA
Ainsa
Pont de Suert
La Pobla de Segur
Tremp
Graus
Benabarre

Ager
Camarasa
Balaguer
LERIDA/LLEIDA
Fraga
Mequinenza
Caspe
La Fresneda

Montblanc
Vilanova
de Prades
Poboleda
Cambrils
L'Hospitalet de l'Infant
L'Ametlla de Mar
Ames
Salou
Deltebre
Alcanar
Vinaròs
Benicarló
Peñíscola
Alcossebre
Oropesa
Benicàssim
Moncofa
Morella
Sant Jordi
Calig
Manzanera
Navajas
Viver
Albarracín
Orihuela del Tremedal
Sacedón
Cuenca
TERUEL

ZARAGOZA
Calatayud
Nuévalos
SORIA
Vinuesa
Valdeavellano
de Tera
Abejar

ANDORRA
LA VELLA

MEDITERRANEAN
SEA

MINORCA

MAJORCA

see inset on Map 4

N240
A8
AP1
A15
AP15
AP68
A12
N232
AP15
N121
N113
N121
N122
N122
N111
N234
N330
A23
A23
AP2
N230
A22
A22
A2
N240
N230
N211
N420
N232
N420
N211
A23
A2
A15
A2
N330
N320
N320
N420
A40
N420
N211
AP7
N420
A27
A2
AP2
A23
N232

Map 3

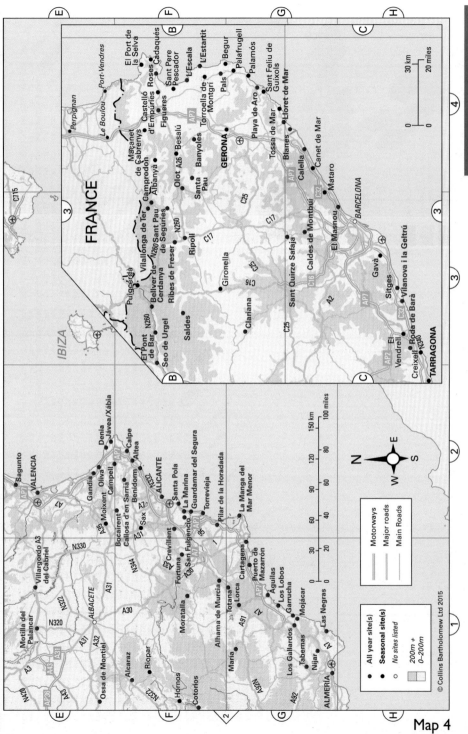

SPAIN

Map 4

189

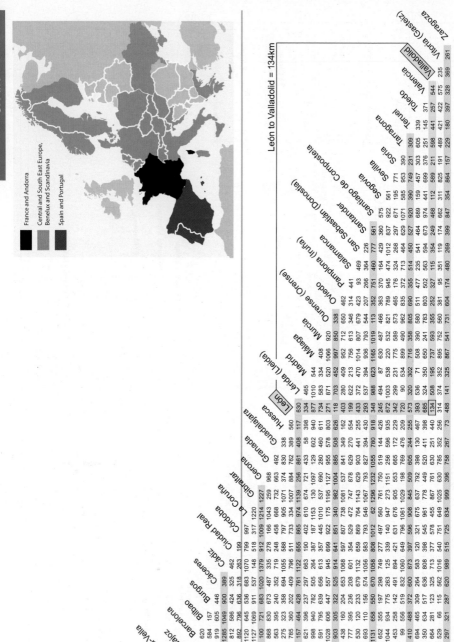

León to Valladolid = 134km

Site Report Form

If campsite is already listed, complete only those sections of the form where changes apply or alternatively use the Abbreviated Site Report form on the following pages.

Sites not reported on for 5 years may be deleted from the guide

Year of guide used	20..........	Is site listed?	Listed on page no.	Unlisted	Date of visit	......./........./.........

A – CAMPSITE NAME AND LOCATION

Country		Name of town/village site listed under *(see Sites Location Maps)*	

Distance & direction from centre of town site is listed under *(in a straight line)*	....................km	eg N, NE, S, SW	Urban	Rural	Coastal

Site open all year?	Y / N	Period site is open *(if not all year)*	................./................. to ..../.................

Site name		Naturist site	Y / N

Site address	

Telephone		Fax	
E-mail		Website	

B – CAMPSITE CHARGES

Charge for outfit + 2 adults in local currency	PRICE	EL PNTS inc in this price?	Y / N	Amps ....

C – DIRECTIONS

Brief, specific directions to site (in km) *To convert miles to kilometres multiply by 8 and divide by 5 or use Conversion Table in guide*	
GPS	Latitude.................................... *(eg 12.34567)* Longitude.................................... *(eg 1.23456 or -1.23456)*

D – CAMPSITE DESCRIPTION

SITE size ie number of pitches	Small Max 50	SM	Medium 51-150	MED	Large 151-500	LGE	Very large 500+	V LGE	Unchanged

PITCH size	*eg small, medium, large, very large, various*		Unchanged

Pitch features if **NOT** open-plan/grassy	Hedged	HDG PITCH	Marked or numbered	MKD PITCH	Hardstanding or gravel	HDSTG	Unchanged

If site is **NOT** level, is it	Part sloping	PT SL	Sloping	SL	Terraced	TERR	Unchanged

Is site shaded?	Shaded	SHD	Part shaded	PT SHD	Unshaded	UNSHD	Unchanged

E – CAMPSITE FACILITIES

WC	Heated	HTD WC	Continental	CONT	Own San recommended		OWN SAN REC	
Chemical disposal point		CHEM DISP		Dedicated point		WC only	
Motorhome waste discharge and water refill point			MV SERVICE PNT			
Child / baby facilities (bathroom)	CHILD / BABY FACS		Family bathroom		FAM BTHRM	
Hot shower(s)	SHWR(S)		Inc in site fee?	Y / N	Price....................*(if not inc)*
ELECTRIC HOOK UP *if not included in price above*	EL PNTS		Price...........................		Amps...........................
Supplies of bottled gas	GAS		On site	Y / N	Or in .... Kms
Launderette / Washing Machine	LNDTTE	Inc dryer Y / N	LNDRY RM *(if no washing machine)*	

You can also complete forms online: www.caravanclub.co.uk/europereport

CUT ALONG DOTTED LINE

F – FOOD & DRINK

Shop(s) / supermarket	SHOP(S) / SUPMKT	On site		or		.... kms	
Bread / milk delivered	TRADSMN						
Restaurant / cafeteria	REST	On site		or		.... kms	
Snack bar / take-away	SNACKS	On site		or		.... kms	
Bar	BAR	On site		or		.... kms	
Barbecue allowed	BBQ	Charcoal		Gas		Elec	Sep area
Cooking facilities	COOKING FACS						

G – LEISURE FACILITIES

Playground	PLAYGRND			
Swimming pool	POOL	On site	or ....km	Heated	Covered
Beach	BEACH	Adj	or ....km	Sand	Shingle
Alternative swimming (lake)	SW	Adj	or ....km	Sand	Shingle
Games /sports area / Games room	GAMES AREA	GAMES ROOM		
Entertainment in high season	ENTMNT			
Internet use by visitors	INTERNET	Wifi Internet	WIFI	
Television room	TV RM	Satellite / Cable to pitches	TV CAB / SAT	

H – OTHER INFORMATION

% Static caravans / mobile homes / chalets / cottages / fixed tents on site				.... % STATICS	
Dogs allowed	DOGS	Y / N	Price per night .... (if allowed)		
Phone	PHONE	On site	Adj		
Bus / tram / train	BUS / TRAM / TRAIN	Adj	or .... km		
Twin axles caravans allowed?	TWIN AXLES Y / N	Possibly crowded in high season		POSS CR	
English spoken	ENG SPKN				
Advance bookings accepted	ADV BKG	Y / N			
Noise levels on site in season	NOISY	QUIET	If noisy, why?		
Credit card accepted	CCARD ACC	Reduction low season		RED LOW SSN	
Camping Key Europe or Camping Card International accepted in lieu of passport	CKE/CCI	INF card required (If naturist site)		Y / N	
Facilities for disabled	Full wheelchair facilities	♦	Limited disabled facilities	♦ ltd	

I – ADDITIONAL REMARKS AND/OR ITEMS OF INTEREST

Tourist attractions, unusual features or other facilities, eg waterslide, tennis, cycle hire, watersports, horseriding, separate car park, walking distance to shops etc	YOUR OPINION OF THE SITE:	
	EXCEL	
	VERY GOOD	
	GOOD	
	FAIR	POOR
	NIGHT HALT ONLY	

Your comments & opinions may be used in future editions of the guide, if you do not wish them to be used please tick ....

J – MEMBER DETAILS

ARE YOU A:	Caravanner		Motorhomer		Trailer-tenter?	
NAME:			MEMBERSHIP NO:			
			POST CODE:			
DO YOU NEED MORE BLANK SITE REPORT FORMS?		YES			NO	

Please use a separate form for each campsite and do not send receipts. Owing to the large number of site reports received, it is not possible to enter into correspondence. Please return completed form to:

The Editor, Overseas Touring Guides, East Grinstead House
East Grinstead, West Sussex RH19 1UA

Please note that due to changes in the rules regarding freepost we are no longer able to provide a freepost address for the return of Site Report Forms. You can still supply your site reports free online by visiting www.caravanclub.co.uk/europereport. We apologise for any inconvenience this may cause.

Site Report Form

If campsite is already listed, complete only those sections of the form where changes apply or alternatively use the Abbreviated Site Report form on the following pages.

Sites not reported on for 5 years may be deleted from the guide

Year of guide used	20.........	Is site listed?	Listed on page no.	Unlisted	Date of visit	......./......./.........

A – CAMPSITE NAME AND LOCATION

Country		Name of town/village site listed under *(see Sites Location Maps)*				
Distance & direction from centre of town site is listed under *(in a straight line)*		...................km	eg N, NE, S, SW	Urban	Rural	Coastal
Site open all year?	Y / N	Period site is open *(if not all year)*	.............../............... to ..../...............			

Site name					Naturist site	Y / N
Site address						
Telephone			Fax			
E-mail			Website			

B – CAMPSITE CHARGES

Charge for outfit + 2 adults in local currency	PRICE		EL PNTS inc in this price?	Y / N	Amps ....

C – DIRECTIONS

Brief, specific directions to site (in km) *To convert miles to kilometres multiply by 8 and divide by 5 or use Conversion Table in guide*	
GPS	Latitude...(eg 12.34567) Longitude...(eg 1.23456 or -1.23456)

D – CAMPSITE DESCRIPTION

SITE size ie number of pitches	Small Max 50	SM	Medium 51-150	MED	Large 151-500	LGE	Very large 500+	V LGE	Unchanged
PITCH size	*eg small, medium, large, very large, various*								Unchanged
Pitch features if **NOT** open-plan/grassy	Hedged	HDG PITCH	Marked or numbered	MKD PITCH	Hardstanding or gravel	HDSTG			Unchanged
If site is **NOT** level, is it	Part sloping	PT SL	Sloping	SL	Terraced	TERR			Unchanged
Is site shaded?	Shaded	SHD	Part shaded	PT SHD	Unshaded	UNSHD			Unchanged

E – CAMPSITE FACILITIES

WC	Heated	HTD WC	Continental	CONT	Own San recommended	OWN SAN REC	
Chemical disposal point		CHEM DISP		Dedicated point		WC only	
Motorhome waste discharge and water refill point				MV SERVICE PNT			
Child / baby facilities (bathroom)		CHILD / BABY FACS		Family bathroom		FAM BTHRM	
Hot shower(s)		SHWR(S)		Inc in site fee?	Y / N	Price...................*(if not inc)*	
ELECTRIC HOOK UP *if not included in price above*		EL PNTS		Price..		Amps..	
Supplies of bottled gas		GAS		On site	Y / N	Or in .... Kms	
Launderette / Washing Machine		LNDTTE		Inc dryer Y / N		LNDRY RM *(if no washing machine)*	

You can also complete forms online: www.caravanclub.co.uk/europereport

CUT ALONG DOTTED LINE

F – FOOD & DRINK

Shop(s) / supermarket	SHOP(S) / SUPMKT	On site		or		.... kms	
Bread / milk delivered	TRADSMN						
Restaurant / cafeteria	REST	On site		or		.... kms	
Snack bar / take-away	SNACKS	On site		or		.... kms	
Bar	BAR	On site		or		.... kms	
Barbecue allowed	BBQ	Charcoal		Gas		Elec	Sep area
Cooking facilities	COOKING FACS						

G – LEISURE FACILITIES

Playground	PLAYGRND						
Swimming pool	POOL	On site		or ....km		Heated	Covered
Beach	BEACH	Adj		or ....km		Sand	Shingle
Alternative swimming (lake)	SW	Adj		or ....km		Sand	Shingle
Games /sports area / Games room	GAMES AREA	GAMES ROOM					
Entertainment in high season	ENTMNT						
Internet use by visitors	INTERNET	Wifi Internet		WIFI			
Television room	TV RM	Satellite / Cable to pitches		TV CAB / SAT			

H – OTHER INFORMATION

% Static caravans / mobile homes / chalets / cottages / fixed tents on site					................% STATICS	
Dogs allowed	DOGS		Y / N	Price per night .... (if allowed)		
Phone	PHONE	On site		Adj		
Bus / tram / train	BUS / TRAM / TRAIN	Adj		or .... km		
Twin axles caravans allowed?	TWIN AXLES Y / N	Possibly crowded in high season			POSS CR	
English spoken	ENG SPKN					
Advance bookings accepted	ADV BKG	Y / N				
Noise levels on site in season	NOISY	QUIET	If noisy, why?			
Credit card accepted	CCARD ACC	Reduction low season		RED LOW SSN		
Camping Key Europe or Camping Card International accepted in lieu of passport	CKE/CCI	INF card required (If naturist site)		Y / N		
Facilities for disabled	Full wheelchair facilities	♦	Limited disabled facilities	♦ ltd		

I – ADDITIONAL REMARKS AND/OR ITEMS OF INTEREST

Tourist attractions, unusual features or other facilities, eg waterslide, tennis, cycle hire, watersports, horseriding, separate car park, walking distance to shops etc	YOUR OPINION OF THE SITE:	
	EXCEL	
	VERY GOOD	
	GOOD	
	FAIR	POOR
	NIGHT HALT ONLY	
Your comments & opinions may be used in future editions of the guide, if you do not wish them to be used please tick		

J – MEMBER DETAILS

ARE YOU A:	Caravanner		Motorhomer		Trailer-tenter?	
NAME:			MEMBERSHIP NO:			
			POST CODE:			
DO YOU NEED MORE BLANK SITE REPORT FORMS?		YES			NO	

Please use a separate form for each campsite and do not send receipts. Owing to the large number of site reports received, it is not possible to enter into correspondence. Please return completed form to:

The Editor, Overseas Touring Guides, East Grinstead House
East Grinstead, West Sussex RH19 1UA

Please note that due to changes in the rules regarding freepost we are no longer able to provide a freepost address for the return of Site Report Forms. You can still supply your site reports free online by visiting www.caravanclub.co.uk/europereport. We apologise for any inconvenience this may cause.

Site Report Form

**If campsite is already listed, complete only those sections of the form where changes apply
or alternatively use the Abbreviated Site Report form on the following pages.**

Sites not reported on for 5 years may be deleted from the guide

Year of guide used	20..........	Is site listed?	Listed on page no.	Unlisted	Date of visit	......../......../........

A – CAMPSITE NAME AND LOCATION

Country		Name of town/village site listed under *(see Sites Location Maps)*		

Distance & direction from centre of town site is listed under *(in a straight line)*		...................km	eg N, NE, S, SW	Urban	Rural	Coastal

Site open all year?	Y / N	Period site is open *(if not all year)*	................./................. to ..../.................			

Site name		Naturist site	Y / N

Site address	

Telephone		Fax	
E-mail		Website	

B – CAMPSITE CHARGES

Charge for outfit + 2 adults in local currency	PRICE		EL PNTS inc in this price?	Y / N	Amps ....

C – DIRECTIONS

Brief, specific directions to site (in km) *To convert miles to kilometres multiply by 8 and divide by 5 or use Conversion Table in guide*	
GPS	Latitude.. *(eg 12.34567)* Longitude.. *(eg 1.23456 or -1.23456)*

D – CAMPSITE DESCRIPTION

SITE size ie number of pitches	Small Max 50	SM	Medium 51-150	MED	Large 151-500	LGE	Very large 500+	V LGE	Unchanged

PITCH size	*eg small, medium, large, very large, various*	Unchanged

Pitch features if **NOT** open-plan/grassy	Hedged	HDG PITCH	Marked or numbered	MKD PITCH	Hardstanding or gravel	HDSTG	Unchanged
If site is **NOT** level, is it	Part sloping	PT SL	Sloping	SL	Terraced	TERR	Unchanged
Is site shaded?	Shaded	SHD	Part shaded	PT SHD	Unshaded	UNSHD	Unchanged

E – CAMPSITE FACILITIES

WC	Heated	HTD WC	Continental	CONT	Own San recommended		OWN SAN REC	
Chemical disposal point		CHEM DISP		Dedicated point		WC only		
Motorhome waste discharge and water refill point				MV SERVICE PNT				
Child / baby facilities (bathroom)		CHILD / BABY FACS		Family bathroom		FAM BTHRM		
Hot shower(s)		SHWR(S)		Inc in site fee?	Y / N	Price....................*(if not inc)*		
ELECTRIC HOOK UP *if not included in price above*		EL PNTS		Price...		Amps...		
Supplies of bottled gas		GAS		On site	Y / N	Or in .... Kms		
Launderette / Washing Machine	LNDTTE		Inc dryer Y / N		LNDRY RM *(if no washing machine)*			

You can also complete forms online: www.caravanclub.co.uk/europereport

CUT ALONG DOTTED LINE

F – FOOD & DRINK

Shop(s) / supermarket	SHOP(S) / SUPMKT	On site		or		.... kms
Bread / milk delivered	TRADSMN					
Restaurant / cafeteria	REST	On site		or		.... kms
Snack bar / take-away	SNACKS	On site		or		.... kms
Bar	BAR	On site		or		.... kms
Barbecue allowed	BBQ	Charcoal		Gas	Elec	Sep area
Cooking facilities	COOKING FACS					

G – LEISURE FACILITIES

Playground	PLAYGRND					
Swimming pool	POOL	On site		or ....km	Heated	Covered
Beach	BEACH	Adj		or ....km	Sand	Shingle
Alternative swimming *(lake)*	SW	Adj		or ....km	Sand	Shingle
Games /sports area / Games room	GAMES AREA	GAMES ROOM				
Entertainment in high season	ENTMNT					
Internet use by visitors	INTERNET	Wifi Internet		WIFI		
Television room	TV RM	Satellite / Cable to pitches		TV CAB / SAT		

H – OTHER INFORMATION

% Static caravans / mobile homes / chalets / cottages / fixed tents on site					................% STATICS
Dogs allowed	DOGS	Y / N	Price per night .... *(if allowed)*		
Phone	PHONE	On site	Adj		
Bus / tram / train	BUS / TRAM / TRAIN	Adj	or .... km		
Twin axles caravans allowed?	TWIN AXLES Y / N	Possibly crowded in high season		POSS CR	
English spoken	ENG SPKN				
Advance bookings accepted	ADV BKG	Y / N			
Noise levels on site in season	NOISY	QUIET	If noisy, why?		
Credit card accepted	CCARD ACC	Reduction low season		RED LOW SSN	
Camping Key Europe or Camping Card International accepted in lieu of passport	CKE/CCI	INF card required *(If naturist site)*		Y / N	
Facilities for disabled	Full wheelchair facilities	♦	Limited disabled facilities	♦ ltd	

I – ADDITIONAL REMARKS AND/OR ITEMS OF INTEREST

Tourist attractions, unusual features or other facilities, eg waterslide, tennis, cycle hire, watersports, horseriding, separate car park, walking distance to shops etc	YOUR OPINION OF THE SITE:	
	EXCEL	
	VERY GOOD	
	GOOD	
	FAIR	POOR
	NIGHT HALT ONLY	

Your comments & opinions may be used in future editions of the guide, if you do not wish them to be used please tick ....

J – MEMBER DETAILS

ARE YOU A:	Caravanner		Motorhomer		Trailer-tenter?	
NAME:			MEMBERSHIP NO:			
			POST CODE:			
DO YOU NEED MORE BLANK SITE REPORT FORMS?		YES			NO	

Please use a separate form for each campsite and do not send receipts. Owing to the large number of site reports received, it is not possible to enter into correspondence. Please return completed form to:

The Editor, Overseas Touring Guides, East Grinstead House
East Grinstead, West Sussex RH19 1UA

Please note that due to changes in the rules regarding freepost we are no longer able to provide a freepost address for the return of Site Report Forms. You can still supply your site reports free online by visiting www.caravanclub.co.uk/europereport. We apologise for any inconvenience this may cause.

Site Report Form

**If campsite is already listed, complete only those sections of the form where changes apply
or alternatively use the Abbreviated Site Report form on the following pages.**

Sites not reported on for 5 years may be deleted from the guide

Year of guide used	20..........	Is site listed?	Listed on page no.	Unlisted	Date of visit	........./........./.........

A – CAMPSITE NAME AND LOCATION

Country		Name of town/village site listed under *(see Sites Location Maps)*	

Distance & direction from centre of town site is listed under *(in a straight line)*		...................km	eg N, NE, S, SW	Urban	Rural	Coastal

Site open all year?	Y / N	Period site is open *(if not all year)*	.................../................... to ..../...................

Site name			Naturist site	Y / N

Site address				

Telephone		Fax	
E-mail		Website	

B – CAMPSITE CHARGES

Charge for outfit + 2 adults in local currency	PRICE		EL PNTS inc in this price?	Y / N	Amps ....

C – DIRECTIONS

Brief, specific directions to site (in km) *To convert miles to kilometres multiply by 8 and divide by 5 or use Conversion Table in guide*	
GPS	Latitude...(eg 12.34567) Longitude...(eg 1.23456 or -1.23456)

D – CAMPSITE DESCRIPTION

SITE size ie number of pitches	Small Max 50	SM	Medium 51-150	MED	Large 151-500	LGE	Very large 500+	V LGE	Unchanged

PITCH size	*eg small, medium, large, very large, various*								Unchanged

Pitch features if **NOT** open-plan/grassy	Hedged	HDG PITCH	Marked or numbered	MKD PITCH	Hardstanding or gravel	HDSTG	Unchanged

If site is **NOT** level, is it	Part sloping	PT SL	Sloping	SL	Terraced	TERR	Unchanged

Is site shaded?	Shaded	SHD	Part shaded	PT SHD	Unshaded	UNSHD	Unchanged

E – CAMPSITE FACILITIES

WC	Heated	HTD WC	Continental	CONT	Own San recommended		OWN SAN REC	
Chemical disposal point		CHEM DISP		Dedicated point		WC only		
Motorhome waste discharge and water refill point			MV SERVICE PNT					
Child / baby facilities (bathroom)		CHILD / BABY FACS		Family bathroom		FAM BTHRM		
Hot shower(s)		SHWR(S)		Inc in site fee?	Y / N	Price...................(if not inc)		
ELECTRIC HOOK UP *if not included in price above*		EL PNTS		Price..		Amps..		
Supplies of bottled gas		GAS		On site	Y / N	Or in .... Kms		
Launderette / Washing Machine	LNDTTE		Inc dryer Y / N		LNDRY RM *(if no washing machine)*			

You can also complete forms online: www.caravanclub.co.uk/europereport

F – FOOD & DRINK

Shop(s) / supermarket	SHOP(S) / SUPMKT	On site		or		.... kms	
Bread / milk delivered	TRADSMN						
Restaurant / cafeteria	REST	On site		or		.... kms	
Snack bar / take-away	SNACKS	On site		or		.... kms	
Bar	BAR	On site		or		.... kms	
Barbecue allowed	BBQ	Charcoal		Gas		Elec	Sep area
Cooking facilities	COOKING FACS						

G – LEISURE FACILITIES

Playground	PLAYGRND						
Swimming pool	POOL	On site		or ....km		Heated	Covered
Beach	BEACH	Adj		or ....km		Sand	Shingle
Alternative swimming *(lake)*	SW	Adj		or ....km		Sand	Shingle
Games /sports area / Games room	GAMES AREA	GAMES ROOM					
Entertainment in high season	ENTMNT						
Internet use by visitors	INTERNET	Wifi Internet			WIFI		
Television room	TV RM	Satellite / Cable to pitches			TV CAB / SAT		

H – OTHER INFORMATION

% Static caravans / mobile homes / chalets / cottages / fixed tents on site						.............% STATICS	
Dogs allowed	DOGS	Y / N	Price per night .... *(if allowed)*				
Phone	PHONE	On site		Adj			
Bus / tram / train	BUS / TRAM / TRAIN	Adj		or .... km			
Twin axles caravans allowed?	TWIN AXLES Y / N	Possibly crowded in high season				POSS CR	
English spoken	ENG SPKN						
Advance bookings accepted	ADV BKG	Y / N					
Noise levels on site in season	NOISY	QUIET	If noisy, why?				
Credit card accepted	CCARD ACC	Reduction low season			RED LOW SSN		
Camping Key Europe or Camping Card International accepted in lieu of passport	CKE/CCI	INF card required *(If naturist site)*			Y / N		
Facilities for disabled	Full wheelchair facilities	♦	Limited disabled facilities		♦ ltd		

I – ADDITIONAL REMARKS AND/OR ITEMS OF INTEREST

Tourist attractions, unusual features or other facilities, eg waterslide, tennis, cycle hire, watersports, horseriding, separate car park, walking distance to shops etc	YOUR OPINION OF THE SITE:	
	EXCEL	
	VERY GOOD	
	GOOD	
	FAIR	POOR
	NIGHT HALT ONLY	

Your comments & opinions may be used in future editions of the guide, if you do not wish them to be used please tick ....

J – MEMBER DETAILS

ARE YOU A:	Caravanner		Motorhomer		Trailer-tenter?	
NAME:			MEMBERSHIP NO:			
			POST CODE:			
DO YOU NEED MORE BLANK SITE REPORT FORMS?		YES			NO	

Please use a separate form for each campsite and do not send receipts. Owing to the large number of site reports received, it is not possible to enter into correspondence. Please return completed form to:

The Editor, Overseas Touring Guides, East Grinstead House
East Grinstead, West Sussex RH19 1UA

Please note that due to changes in the rules regarding freepost we are no longer able to provide a freepost address for the return of Site Report Forms. You can still supply your site reports free online by visiting www.caravanclub.co.uk/europereport. We apologise for any inconvenience this may cause.

Abbreviated Site Report Form

Use this abbreviated Site Report Form if you have visited a number of sites and there are no changes (or only small changes) to their entries in the guide. If reporting on a new site, or reporting several changes, please use the full version of the report form. **If advising prices,** these should be for an outfit, and 2 adults for one night's stay. **Please indicate high or low season prices and whether electricity is included.**

Remember, if you don't tell us about sites you have visited, they may eventually be deleted from the guide.

Year of guide used	20..........	Page No.	....	Name of town/village site listed under	
Site Name				Date of visit	.... /....... /........
GPS	Latitude..(eg 12.34567) Longitude..(eg 1.23456 or -1.23456)				
Site is in: Andorra / Austria / Belgium / Croatia / Czech Republic / Denmark / Finland / France / Germany / Greece / Hungary / Italy / Luxembourg / Netherlands / Norway / Poland / Portugal / Slovakia / Slovenia / Spain / Sweden / Switzerland					
Comments:					

Charge for outfit + 2 adults in local currency	High Season	Low Season	Elec inc in price?	Y / N	............amps
			Price of elec (if not inc)		............amps

Year of guide used	20..........	Page No.	....	Name of town/village site listed under	
Site Name				Date of visit	.... /....... /........
GPS	Latitude..(eg 12.34567) Longitude..(eg 1.23456 or -1.23456)				
Site is in: Andorra / Austria / Belgium / Croatia / Czech Republic / Denmark / Finland / France / Germany / Greece / Hungary / Italy / Luxembourg / Netherlands / Norway / Poland / Portugal / Slovakia / Slovenia / Spain / Sweden / Switzerland					
Comments:					

Charge for outfit + 2 adults in local currency	High Season	Low Season	Elec inc in price?	Y / N	............amps
			Price of elec (if not inc)		............amps

Year of guide used	20..........	Page No.	....	Name of town/village site listed under	
Site Name				Date of visit	.... /....... /........
GPS	Latitude..(eg 12.34567) Longitude..(eg 1.23456 or -1.23456)				
Site is in: Andorra / Austria / Belgium / Croatia / Czech Republic / Denmark / Finland / France / Germany / Greece / Hungary / Italy / Luxembourg / Netherlands / Norway / Poland / Portugal / Slovakia / Slovenia / Spain / Sweden / Switzerland					
Comments:					

Charge for car, caravan & 2 adults in local currency	High Season	Low Season	Elec inc in price?	Y / N	............amps
			Price of elec (if not inc)		............amps

Please fill in your details and send to the address on the reverse of this form.
You can also complete forms online: www.caravanclub.co.uk/europereport

CUT ALONG DOTTED LINE

Year of guide used	20..........	Page No.	....	Name of town/village site listed under	
Site Name					Date of visit .... /....... /........
GPS	Latitude..(eg 12.34567) Longitude..(eg 1.23456 or -1.23456)				

Site is in: Andorra / Austria / Belgium / Croatia / Czech Republic / Denmark / Finland / France / Germany / Greece / Hungary / Italy / Luxembourg / Netherlands / Norway / Poland / Portugal / Slovakia / Slovenia / Spain / Sweden / Switzerland

Comments:

Charge for outfit + 2 adults in local currency	High Season	Low Season	Elec inc in price?	Y / N	............amps
			Price of elec (if not inc)		............amps

Year of guide used	20..........	Page No.	....	Name of town/village site listed under	
Site Name					Date of visit .... /....... /........
GPS	Latitude..(eg 12.34567) Longitude..(eg 1.23456 or -1.23456)				

Site is in: Andorra / Austria / Belgium / Croatia / Czech Republic / Denmark / Finland / France / Germany / Greece / Hungary / Italy / Luxembourg / Netherlands / Norway / Poland / Portugal / Slovakia / Slovenia / Spain / Sweden / Switzerland

Comments:

Charge for outfit + 2 adults in local currency	High Season	Low Season	Elec inc in price?	Y / N	............amps
			Price of elec (if not inc)		............amps

Year of guide used	20..........	Page No.	....	Name of town/village site listed under	
Site Name					Date of visit .... /....... /........
GPS	Latitude..(eg 12.34567) Longitude..(eg 1.23456 or -1.23456)				

Site is in: Andorra / Austria / Belgium / Croatia / Czech Republic / Denmark / Finland / France / Germany / Greece / Hungary / Italy / Luxembourg / Netherlands / Norway / Poland / Portugal / Slovakia / Slovenia / Spain / Sweden / Switzerland

Comments:

Charge for outfit + 2 adults in local currency	High Season	Low Season	Elec inc in price?	Y / N	............amps
			Price of elec (if not inc)		............amps

Your comments & opinions may be used in future editions of the guide, if you do not wish them to be used please tick ....

Name ....

Membership No. ....

Post Code ....

Are you a Caravanner / Motorhomer / Trailer-Tenter?

Do you need more blank Site Report forms?   YES / NO

Please return completed forms to:
The Editor – Overseas Touring Guides
East Grinstead House
East Grinstead
West Sussex
RH19 1FH
Please note that due to changes in the rules regarding freepost we are no longer able to provide a freepost address for the return of Site Report Forms. You can still supply your site reports free online by visiting www.caravanclub.co.uk/europereport.
We apologise for any inconvenience this may cause.

You can also complete forms online: www.caravanclub.co.uk/europereport

Abbreviated Site Report Form

Use this abbreviated Site Report Form if you have visited a number of sites and there are no changes (or only small changes) to their entries in the guide. If reporting on a new site, or reporting several changes, please use the full version of the report form. **If advising prices**, these should be for an outfit, and 2 adults for one night's stay. **Please indicate high or low season prices and whether electricity is included.**

Remember, if you don't tell us about sites you have visited, they may eventually be deleted from the guide.

Year of guide used	20..........	Page No.	....	Name of town/village site listed under			
Site Name					Date of visit		.... /....... /........
GPS	Latitude...(eg 12.34567) Longitude..(eg 1.23456 or -1.23456)						

Site is in: Andorra / Austria / Belgium / Croatia / Czech Republic / Denmark / Finland / France / Germany / Greece / Hungary / Italy / Luxembourg / Netherlands / Norway / Poland / Portugal / Slovakia / Slovenia / Spain / Sweden / Switzerland

Comments:

Charge for outfit + 2 adults in local currency	High Season	Low Season	Elec inc in price?	Y / N	............amps
			Price of elec (if not inc)		............amps

Year of guide used	20..........	Page No.	....	Name of town/village site listed under			
Site Name					Date of visit		.... /....... /........
GPS	Latitude...(eg 12.34567) Longitude..(eg 1.23456 or -1.23456)						

Site is in: Andorra / Austria / Belgium / Croatia / Czech Republic / Denmark / Finland / France / Germany / Greece / Hungary / Italy / Luxembourg / Netherlands / Norway / Poland / Portugal / Slovakia / Slovenia / Spain / Sweden / Switzerland

Comments:

Charge for outfit + 2 adults in local currency	High Season	Low Season	Elec inc in price?	Y / N	............amps
			Price of elec (if not inc)		............amps

Year of guide used	20..........	Page No.	....	Name of town/village site listed under			
Site Name					Date of visit		.... /....... /........
GPS	Latitude...(eg 12.34567) Longitude..(eg 1.23456 or -1.23456)						

Site is in: Andorra / Austria / Belgium / Croatia / Czech Republic / Denmark / Finland / France / Germany / Greece / Hungary / Italy / Luxembourg / Netherlands / Norway / Poland / Portugal / Slovakia / Slovenia / Spain / Sweden / Switzerland

Comments:

Charge for car, caravan & 2 adults in local currency	High Season	Low Season	Elec inc in price?	Y / N	............amps
			Price of elec (if not inc)		............amps

Please fill in your details and send to the address on the reverse of this form.
You can also complete forms online: www.caravanclub.co.uk/europereport

CUT ALONG DOTTED LINE

Year of guide used	20..........	Page No.	....	Name of town/village site listed under	
Site Name					Date of visit .... /....... /........
GPS	Latitude...(eg 12.34567) Longitude...(eg 1.23456 or -1.23456)				

Site is in: Andorra / Austria / Belgium / Croatia / Czech Republic / Denmark / Finland / France / Germany / Greece / Hungary / Italy / Luxembourg / Netherlands / Norway / Poland / Portugal / Slovakia / Slovenia / Spain / Sweden / Switzerland

Comments:

Charge for outfit + 2 adults in local currency	High Season	Low Season	Elec inc in price?	Y / N	............amps
			Price of elec (if not inc)		............amps

Year of guide used	20..........	Page No.	....	Name of town/village site listed under	
Site Name					Date of visit .... /....... /........
GPS	Latitude...(eg 12.34567) Longitude...(eg 1.23456 or -1.23456)				

Site is in: Andorra / Austria / Belgium / Croatia / Czech Republic / Denmark / Finland / France / Germany / Greece / Hungary / Italy / Luxembourg / Netherlands / Norway / Poland / Portugal / Slovakia / Slovenia / Spain / Sweden / Switzerland

Comments:

Charge for outfit + 2 adults in local currency	High Season	Low Season	Elec inc in price?	Y / N	............amps
			Price of elec (if not inc)		............amps

Year of guide used	20..........	Page No.	....	Name of town/village site listed under	
Site Name					Date of visit .... /....... /........
GPS	Latitude...(eg 12.34567) Longitude...(eg 1.23456 or -1.23456)				

Site is in: Andorra / Austria / Belgium / Croatia / Czech Republic / Denmark / Finland / France / Germany / Greece / Hungary / Italy / Luxembourg / Netherlands / Norway / Poland / Portugal / Slovakia / Slovenia / Spain / Sweden / Switzerland

Comments:

Charge for outfit + 2 adults in local currency	High Season	Low Season	Elec inc in price?	Y / N	............amps
			Price of elec (if not inc)		............amps

Your comments & opinions may be used in future editions of the guide, if you do not wish them to be used please tick ....

Name ....

Membership No. ....

Post Code ....

Are you a Caravanner / Motorhomer / Trailer-Tenter?

Do you need more blank Site Report forms?   YES / NO

Please return completed forms to:
The Editor – Overseas Touring Guides
East Grinstead House
East Grinstead
West Sussex
RH19 1FH
Please note that due to changes in the rules regarding freepost we are no longer able to provide a freepost address for the return of Site Report Forms. You can still supply your site reports free online by visiting www.caravanclub.co.uk/europereport.
We apologise for any inconvenience this may cause.

You can also complete forms online: www.caravanclub.co.uk/europereport

Abbreviated Site Report Form

Use this abbreviated Site Report Form if you have visited a number of sites and there are no changes (or only small changes) to their entries in the guide. If reporting on a new site, or reporting several changes, please use the full version of the report form. **If advising prices**, these should be for an outfit, and 2 adults for one night's stay. **Please indicate high or low season prices and whether electricity is included.**

Remember, if you don't tell us about sites you have visited, they may eventually be deleted from the guide.

Year of guide used	20..........	Page No.	....	Name of town/village site listed under	
Site Name				Date of visit	.... /....... /........
GPS	Latitude...(eg 12.34567) Longitude...(eg 1.23456 or -1.23456)				

Site is in: Andorra / Austria / Belgium / Croatia / Czech Republic / Denmark / Finland / France / Germany / Greece / Hungary / Italy / Luxembourg / Netherlands / Norway / Poland / Portugal / Slovakia / Slovenia / Spain / Sweden / Switzerland

Comments:

Charge for outfit + 2 adults in local currency	High Season	Low Season	Elec inc in price?	Y / N	.............amps
			Price of elec (if not inc)		.............amps

Year of guide used	20..........	Page No.	....	Name of town/village site listed under	
Site Name				Date of visit	.... /....... /........
GPS	Latitude...(eg 12.34567) Longitude...(eg 1.23456 or -1.23456)				

Site is in: Andorra / Austria / Belgium / Croatia / Czech Republic / Denmark / Finland / France / Germany / Greece / Hungary / Italy / Luxembourg / Netherlands / Norway / Poland / Portugal / Slovakia / Slovenia / Spain / Sweden / Switzerland

Comments:

Charge for outfit + 2 adults in local currency	High Season	Low Season	Elec inc in price?	Y / N	.............amps
			Price of elec (if not inc)		.............amps

Year of guide used	20..........	Page No.	....	Name of town/village site listed under	
Site Name				Date of visit	.... /....... /........
GPS	Latitude...(eg 12.34567) Longitude...(eg 1.23456 or -1.23456)				

Site is in: Andorra / Austria / Belgium / Croatia / Czech Republic / Denmark / Finland / France / Germany / Greece / Hungary / Italy / Luxembourg / Netherlands / Norway / Poland / Portugal / Slovakia / Slovenia / Spain / Sweden / Switzerland

Comments:

Charge for car, caravan & 2 adults in local currency	High Season	Low Season	Elec inc in price?	Y / N	.............amps
			Price of elec (if not inc)		.............amps

Please fill in your details and send to the address on the reverse of this form.
You can also complete forms online: www.caravanclub.co.uk/europereport

CUT ALONG DOTTED LINE

Year of guide used	20..........	Page No.	....	Name of town/village site listed under	
Site Name				Date of visit	.... /....... /........
GPS	Latitude..(eg 12.34567) Longitude...(eg 1.23456 or -1.23456)				

Site is in: Andorra / Austria / Belgium / Croatia / Czech Republic / Denmark / Finland / France / Germany / Greece / Hungary / Italy / Luxembourg / Netherlands / Norway / Poland / Portugal / Slovakia / Slovenia / Spain / Sweden / Switzerland

Comments:

Charge for outfit + 2 adults in local currency	High Season	Low Season	Elec inc in price?	Y / N	.............amps
			Price of elec (if not inc)		.............amps

Year of guide used	20..........	Page No.	....	Name of town/village site listed under	
Site Name				Date of visit	.... /....... /........
GPS	Latitude..(eg 12.34567) Longitude...(eg 1.23456 or -1.23456)				

Site is in: Andorra / Austria / Belgium / Croatia / Czech Republic / Denmark / Finland / France / Germany / Greece / Hungary / Italy / Luxembourg / Netherlands / Norway / Poland / Portugal / Slovakia / Slovenia / Spain / Sweden / Switzerland

Comments:

Charge for outfit + 2 adults in local currency	High Season	Low Season	Elec inc in price?	Y / N	.............amps
			Price of elec (if not inc)		.............amps

Year of guide used	20..........	Page No.	....	Name of town/village site listed under	
Site Name				Date of visit	.... /....... /........
GPS	Latitude..(eg 12.34567) Longitude...(eg 1.23456 or -1.23456)				

Site is in: Andorra / Austria / Belgium / Croatia / Czech Republic / Denmark / Finland / France / Germany / Greece / Hungary / Italy / Luxembourg / Netherlands / Norway / Poland / Portugal / Slovakia / Slovenia / Spain / Sweden / Switzerland

Comments:

Charge for outfit + 2 adults in local currency	High Season	Low Season	Elec inc in price?	Y / N	.............amps
			Price of elec (if not inc)		.............amps

Your comments & opinions may be used in future editions of the guide, if you do not wish them to be used please tick ....

Name ....

Membership No. ....

Post Code ....

Are you a Caravanner / Motorhomer / Trailer-Tenter?

Do you need more blank Site Report forms?   YES / NO

Please return completed forms to:
The Editor – Overseas Touring Guides
East Grinstead House
East Grinstead
West Sussex
RH19 1FH
Please note that due to changes in the rules regarding freepost we are no longer able to provide a freepost address for the return of Site Report Forms. You can still supply your site reports free online by visiting www.caravanclub.co.uk/europereport.
We apologise for any inconvenience this may cause.

You can also complete forms online: www.caravanclub.co.uk/europereport

Abbreviated Site Report Form

Use this abbreviated Site Report Form if you have visited a number of sites and there are no changes (or only small changes) to their entries in the guide. If reporting on a new site, or reporting several changes, please use the full version of the report form. **If advising prices,** these should be for an outfit, and 2 adults for one night's stay. **Please indicate high or low season prices and whether electricity is included.**

Remember, if you don't tell us about sites you have visited, they may eventually be deleted from the guide.

Year of guide used	20.........	Page No.	....	Name of town/village site listed under			
Site Name					Date of visit		.... /....... /........
GPS	Latitude...(eg 12.34567) Longitude...(eg 1.23456 or -1.23456)						

Site is in: Andorra / Austria / Belgium / Croatia / Czech Republic / Denmark / Finland / France / Germany / Greece / Hungary / Italy / Luxembourg / Netherlands / Norway / Poland / Portugal / Slovakia / Slovenia / Spain / Sweden / Switzerland

Comments:

Charge for outfit + 2 adults in local currency	High Season	Low Season	Elec inc in price?	Y / N	............amps
			Price of elec (if not inc)		............amps

Year of guide used	20.........	Page No.	....	Name of town/village site listed under			
Site Name					Date of visit		.... /....... /........
GPS	Latitude...(eg 12.34567) Longitude...(eg 1.23456 or -1.23456)						

Site is in: Andorra / Austria / Belgium / Croatia / Czech Republic / Denmark / Finland / France / Germany / Greece / Hungary / Italy / Luxembourg / Netherlands / Norway / Poland / Portugal / Slovakia / Slovenia / Spain / Sweden / Switzerland

Comments:

Charge for outfit + 2 adults in local currency	High Season	Low Season	Elec inc in price?	Y / N	............amps
			Price of elec (if not inc)		............amps

Year of guide used	20.........	Page No.	....	Name of town/village site listed under			
Site Name					Date of visit		.... /....... /........
GPS	Latitude...(eg 12.34567) Longitude...(eg 1.23456 or -1.23456)						

Site is in: Andorra / Austria / Belgium / Croatia / Czech Republic / Denmark / Finland / France / Germany / Greece / Hungary / Italy / Luxembourg / Netherlands / Norway / Poland / Portugal / Slovakia / Slovenia / Spain / Sweden / Switzerland

Comments:

Charge for car, caravan & 2 adults in local currency	High Season	Low Season	Elec inc in price?	Y / N	............amps
			Price of elec (if not inc)		............amps

CUT ALONG DOTTED LINE

Year of guide used	20..........	Page No.	....	Name of town/village site listed under	

Site Name				Date of visit	.... /....... /........

GPS Latitude...(eg 12.34567) Longitude...(eg 1.23456 or -1.23456)

Site is in: Andorra / Austria / Belgium / Croatia / Czech Republic / Denmark / Finland / France / Germany / Greece / Hungary / Italy / Luxembourg / Netherlands / Norway / Poland / Portugal / Slovakia / Slovenia / Spain / Sweden / Switzerland

Comments:

Charge for outfit + 2 adults in local currency	High Season	Low Season	Elec inc in price?	Y / N	............amps
			Price of elec (if not inc)		............amps

Year of guide used	20..........	Page No.	....	Name of town/village site listed under	

Site Name				Date of visit	.... /....... /........

GPS Latitude...(eg 12.34567) Longitude...(eg 1.23456 or -1.23456)

Site is in: Andorra / Austria / Belgium / Croatia / Czech Republic / Denmark / Finland / France / Germany / Greece / Hungary / Italy / Luxembourg / Netherlands / Norway / Poland / Portugal / Slovakia / Slovenia / Spain / Sweden / Switzerland

Comments:

Charge for outfit + 2 adults in local currency	High Season	Low Season	Elec inc in price?	Y / N	............amps
			Price of elec (if not inc)		............amps

Year of guide used	20..........	Page No.	....	Name of town/village site listed under	

Site Name				Date of visit	.... /....... /........

GPS Latitude...(eg 12.34567) Longitude...(eg 1.23456 or -1.23456)

Site is in: Andorra / Austria / Belgium / Croatia / Czech Republic / Denmark / Finland / France / Germany / Greece / Hungary / Italy / Luxembourg / Netherlands / Norway / Poland / Portugal / Slovakia / Slovenia / Spain / Sweden / Switzerland

Comments:

Charge for outfit + 2 adults in local currency	High Season	Low Season	Elec inc in price?	Y / N	............amps
			Price of elec (if not inc)		............amps

Your comments & opinions may be used in future editions of the guide, if you do not wish them to be used please tick ....

Name ....

Membership No. ....

Post Code ....

Are you a Caravanner / Motorhomer / Trailer-Tenter?

Do you need more blank Site Report forms?   YES / NO

Please return completed forms to:
The Editor – Overseas Touring Guides
East Grinstead House
East Grinstead
West Sussex
RH19 1FH
Please note that due to changes in the rules regarding freepost we are no longer able to provide a freepost address for the return of Site Report Forms. You can still supply your site reports free online by visiting www.caravanclub.co.uk/europereport.
We apologise for any inconvenience this may cause.

You can also complete forms online: www.caravanclub.co.uk/europereport

Index

Index

PEFC Certified

This product is
from sustainably
managed forests and
controlled sources

PEFC/18-33-254   www.pefc.org